Entrepreneurial Orientation and Opportunities for Global Economic Growth

Orlando Lima Rua
Polytechnic of Porto, Portugal

A volume in the Advances in Business Strategy and Competitive Advantage (ABSCA) Book Series

IGI Global
DISSEMINATOR OF KNOWLEDGE

Published in the United States of America by
IGI Global
Business Science Reference (an imprint of IGI Global)
701 E. Chocolate Avenue
Hershey PA, USA 17033
Tel: 717-533-8845
Fax: 717-533-8661
E-mail: cust@igi-global.com
Web site: http://www.igi-global.com

Library of Congress Cataloging-in-Publication Data

Names: Rua, Orlando Lima, 1979- editor.
Title: Entrepreneurial orientation and opportunities for global economic growth / Orlando Lima Rua, editor.
Description: Hershey, PA : Business Science Reference, [2018]
Identifiers: LCCN 2018009295| ISBN 9781522569428 (hardcover) | ISBN 9781522569435 (ebook)
Subjects: LCSH: Entrepreneurship. | Business enterprises--Technological innovations. | Business networks.
Classification: LCC HB615 .E577868 2018 | DDC 338/.04--dc23 LC record available at https://lccn.loc.gov/2018009295

This book is published in the IGI Global book series Advances in Business Strategy and Competitive Advantage (ABSCA) (ISSN: 2327-3429; eISSN: 2327-3437)

British Cataloguing in Publication Data
A Cataloguing in Publication record for this book is available from the British Library.

For electronic access to this publication, please contact: eresources@igi-global.com.

Advances in Business Strategy and Competitive Advantage (ABSCA) Book Series

ISSN:2327-3429
EISSN:2327-3437

Editor-in-Chief: Patricia Ordóñez de Pablos, Universidad de Oviedo, Spain

MISSION

Business entities are constantly seeking new ways through which to gain advantage over their competitors and strengthen their position within the business environment. With competition at an all-time high due to technological advancements allowing for competition on a global scale, firms continue to seek new ways through which to improve and strengthen their business processes, procedures, and profitability.

The **Advances in Business Strategy and Competitive Advantage (ABSCA) Book Series** is a timely series responding to the high demand for state-of-the-art research on how business strategies are created, implemented and re-designed to meet the demands of globalized competitive markets. With a focus on local and global challenges, business opportunities and the needs of society, the **ABSCA** encourages scientific discourse on doing business and managing information technologies for the creation of sustainable competitive advantage.

COVERAGE

- Competitive Strategy
- Balanced Scorecard
- Strategy Performance Management
- Outsourcing
- Innovation Strategy
- Co-operative Strategies
- Economies of Scale
- International Business Strategy
- Resource-Based Competition
- Tacit Knowledge

IGI Global is currently accepting manuscripts for publication within this series. To submit a proposal for a volume in this series, please contact our Acquisition Editors at Acquisitions@igi-global.com or visit: http://www.igi-global.com/publish/.

The Advances in Business Strategy and Competitive Advantage (ABSCA) Book Series (ISSN 2327-3429) is published by IGI Global, 701 E. Chocolate Avenue, Hershey, PA 17033-1240, USA, www.igi-global.com. This series is composed of titles available for purchase individually; each title is edited to be contextually exclusive from any other title within the series. For pricing and ordering information please visit http://www.igi-global.com/book-series/advances-business-strategy-competitive-advantage/73672. Postmaster: Send all address changes to above address.

Titles in this Series

For a list of additional titles in this series, please visit:
https://www.igi-global.com/book-series/advances-business-strategy-competitive-advantage/73672

Creating Business Value and Competitive Advantage With Social Entrepreneurship
N. Oyku Iyigun (Istanbul Commerce University, Turkey)
Business Science Reference • ©2019 • 435pp • H/C (ISBN: 9781522556879) • US $205.00

Applying Business Intelligence Initiatives in Healthcare and Organizational Settings
Shah J. Miah (Victoria University, Australia) and William Yeoh (Deakin University, Australia)
Business Science Reference • ©2019 • 384pp • H/C (ISBN: 9781522557180) • US $215.00

Strategic Optimization of Medium-Sized Enterprises in the Global Market
Milan Vemić (DAI Europe, Serbia)
Business Science Reference • ©2019 • 386pp • H/C (ISBN: 9781522557845) • US $215.00

Effective Open Innovation Strategies in Modern Business Emerging Research and ...
N. Raghavendra Rao (FINAIT Consultancy Services, India)
Business Science Reference • ©2018 • 159pp • H/C (ISBN: 9781522557210) • US $145.00

Examining the Role of Women Entrepreneurs in Emerging Economies
David Chitakunye (London School of Commerce, UK) and Amandeep Takhar (University of Northampton, UK)
Business Science Reference • ©2018 • 375pp • H/C (ISBN: 9781522551126) • US $235.00

Handbook of Research on Strategic Innovation Management for Improved Competitive ...
George Leal Jamil (InesTec, Portugal) João José Pinto Ferreira (InesTec, Portugal) Maria Manuela Pinto (InesTec, Portugal) Cláudio Roberto Magalhães Pessoa (Universidade Fumec, Brazil) and Alexandra Xavier (InesTec, Portugal)
Business Science Reference • ©2018 • 772pp • H/C (ISBN: 9781522530121) • US $465.00

Utilizing Consumer Psychology in Business Strategy
Tevfik Dalgic (University of Texas at Dallas, USA) and Sevtap Unal (Izmir Katip Celebi University, Turkey)
Business Science Reference • ©2018 • 325pp • H/C (ISBN: 9781522534488) • US $215.00

For an entire list of titles in this series, please visit:
https://www.igi-global.com/book-series/advances-business-strategy-competitive-advantage/73672

IGI Global
DISSEMINATOR OF KNOWLEDGE

701 East Chocolate Avenue, Hershey, PA 17033, USA
Tel: 717-533-8845 x100 • Fax: 717-533-8661
E-Mail: cust@igi-global.com • www.igi-global.com

Table of Contents

Detailed Table of Contents

The purpose of this chapter is to examine the status quo and discuss the interfaces and articulations between the two constructs: entrepreneurship and social development. Thus, this chapter aims to analyze the characteristics of publications related to the themes of entrepreneurship and social development from 1996 to 2016. The methodology used was descriptive research bibliometrics. The research was conducted using the web of science (WoS) database of the ISI web of knowledge, with a total of 1893 articles selected. The survey results showed that the year with the highest number of publications was 2016 (446), followed by the year 2015 (330). Further, the fields of social and behavioral sciences and entrepreneurship and regional development had the largest number of publications with a total of 44 and 42, respectively.

Although companies seek to export in order to meet the growing importance of international markets, vis-à-vis domestic markets, this chapter presents a case study of a company founded by two former high school teachers who started a beverage company in 2015 and quickly reached an early internationalization. The company produces alcoholic beverages and has won international awards regarding the quality of its product, which has given it an important status and opened the door to a process of rapid internationalization. This will be used to explore the theory of entrepreneurship and how two potential entrepreneurs, with employment difficulties in teaching, began with a project that gave birth to a born global firm.

Entrepreneurship is an increasingly studied international phenomenon, often being understood as a way of creating jobs and boosting economic growth, development, and innovation. This chapter aims to take on the problem related to gender and entrepreneurship in the Portuguese society. The goal is to explain the concept of entrepreneur, behavioral, and social differences between the masculine and the feminine gender as entrepreneurs and identify Portuguese female entrepreneurs.

A qualitative, multiple case studies methodology is applied to the sample of eight Portuguese female entrepreneurs, the data collection instrument being the semi-structured interview. Regarding the obtained results, it can be stated that the majority of the interviewees has entrepreneurs in the family, the father being the most mentioned figure as booster of entrepreneur activity. The wish for personal realization and independence are the main factors that motivated self-employment. No entrepreneur felt any discrimination or gender inequality as a female entrepreneur.

Because of its importance as a key factor to economic development, the study of entrepreneurship has been considerably developed in the past decades. Entrepreneurship is broadly diversified, which is associated with, for example, studies in the field of business, social, female, and young entrepreneurship. If, on the one hand, it is a fact that entrepreneurship and its study are mainly associated with the private initiative, there is, on the other hand, a question to be asked: Is there entrepreneurship in the public sector? Though still incipient, the study of entrepreneurship applied to the public sector and the acts of the public managers as entrepreneurs have revealed themselves to be themes with increasing interest. To contribute to a better conceptual understanding of this theme, namely its questions, ideas, and current debate, this work presents some theoretical reflexions and a relevant literature review on entrepreneurship in a public sector context.

The unpredictability of business activities means that entrepreneurs should find a way to adapt and embrace chance. The traditional and predefined process logic offers little support for today's complex and dynamic business environment. One tenet that shaped the direction of entrepreneurship research is the view that the entrepreneurial opportunity discovery and development is linear, systematic, and rational, that is, it is assumed that all factors are measurable and knowable. However, unknowable instances of coincidence, randomness, and chance factors can play a significant role in new venture creation. The authors propose that these factors point to the nonlinear and acausal phenomenon of chance. This research proposal intends to address entrepreneurs' alternative mechanisms, other than the classic formal planning model, to harness opportunities or overcome setbacks arising from chance. To achieve our purpose, the authors examine qualitative data drawn from entrepreneurial activity of Spain and Portugal.

The main objective of this chapter is to analyze the relationship between entrepreneurial orientation and competitive advantage on Portuguese exporting textiles small and medium enterprises (SMEs). Therefore, a quantitative methodological approach was used, conducting a descriptive, exploratory, and transversal empirical study, having applied a questionnaire to a sample of Portuguese SMEs, associated of the Portuguese textile association (ATP). The structural equations model was used for this purpose, using the partial least squares (PLS). Based on survey data from 247 firms, the empirical results indicate that 1) innovation have a positive and significant impact on differentiation, 2) proactivity and risk-taking does not have a positive and significant impact on differentiation, and 3) innovation, proactivity, and risk-taking does not have a positive and significant impact on cost leadership. This study shows that Portuguese textile SMEs seek to support and stimulate new ideas, experimentation, and creativity that surely result in new products, services, and processes.

Social entrepreneurial activity is characterized by the innovative search for resource acquisition, combination, and management to pursue opportunities aiming at fulfilling the organization's mission. The network approach to entrepreneurship assumes that entrepreneurs use their personal network to acquire resources and manage the assets of the organization. This chapter intends to analyze whether social entrepreneurs use their personal network to acquire different resources. The investigation uses a quantitative approach, based on an online survey of individuals involved in the management of Portuguese social organizations. The results attained reveal that social entrepreneurs are usually involved in strong and diversified networks. Their personal networks shape the way human, financial, and informational resources are obtained and managed. The major influence is made by social entrepreneurs' indirect contacts (weak ties) and the benefits they perceive these networks are able to provide.

Venture capital (VC) is an alternative means of access to finance for innovative SMEs to sustain their innovation, growth, and survival. Although VC firms are well established in the UK and USA, they are not well-known worldwide and many SMEs are unaware of their potential. This is a review of research literature on VC, its conceptualization, and synthesis over four decades. VC is gaining increased and varied significance worldwide as a way for innovative SMEs to access funds. Globalization has provided entrepreneurs the opportunity to seek VC globally as reputable VC firms are able to fund innovative projects across countries and continents. As the legal and regulatory regime improve, VC finance opportunities increase with impact on the demand and supply of VC. Innovative SMEs are encouraged to take advantage of globalization and competition among VC firms in their search for VC. Recently, VC firms have become more risk averse regardless of their traditional competence in screening and monitoring.

This chapter analyzes startups from the perspective of the theory of entrepreneurship. Based on a literature review, the historical context of entrepreneurship in the metropolitan area of Guadalajara (MAG) is explored, evaluating the variables that are important to successful entrepreneurship. The authors conclude that Mexico from their national policies and the state of Jalisco from its development plan created the conditions to promote the entrepreneurial ecosystem; however, there are key indicators that slow the growth of startups based on technology and innovation.

Preface

Competition in the global economy of 21st century is complex, demanding, and filled with opportunities and threats (Ireland et al., 2001). The intensity of business competition has increased considerably, forcing organizations to seek and adopt new management perspectives and techniques. Developing and maintaining competitive advantage is a dynamic and never-ending activity (Hung et al., 2010).

Currently, entrepreneurial activity is recognized as one of the main thrusters of industrial dynamism and economic development and growth (Carlsson et al., 2013). The environment involving the economy of a particular country affects the dynamics of entrepreneurship. This one is delimited by an interdependence between economic development and institutions, which affects the quality of administration, access to capital and resources and the entrepreneurs' perception (Acs, Desai & Hessels, 2008). On the other hand, the role of innovation in economic development has been raising questions regarding its effects on the competitiveness of organizations and nations themselves (Correia & Rua, 2016).

Contemporary studies in small business and entrepreneurship have often placed firm growth at the centre of their inquiry (Blackburn, Hart, & Wainwright, 2013). The entrepreneurship orientation (EO)–performance literature is extensive. While Wiklund and Shepherd (2011) findings indicate a positive relationship between EO and failure, there is some scholarly tendency to assume that firms with more EO have superior performance (Wiklund & Shepherd, 2005). Several empirical studies indicate a positive correlation between entrepreneurial orientation and organizational growth (e.g. Covin & Slevin, 1991; Davis, Bell, Payne & Kreiser, 2010; Frank, Kessler & Fink, 2010; Lumpkin & Dess, 1996; Miller, 1983). Similarly, other studies also confirm that entrepreneurial orientation has a positive correlation with export's performance, enhancing business growth (e.g. Okpara, 2009; Zahra & Garvis, 2000). Clearly, this link seems to be one of the few "universal" ones in management research. The strength of this positive association, however, varies considerably across national contexts (Semrau, Ambos & Kraus, 2016).

This book looks to discuss and address the trends and challenges of Entrepreneurship and Innovation to the countries' economic and social development. The editor will seek chapters that address different aspects on this research areas and related topics. Additionally, the book will explore the impact on the citizens and on the countries in which Entrepreneurship and Innovation is being implemented. Specifically, are the citizens prepared for the change of paradigm for *Entrepreneurial Orientation and Opportunities for Global Economic Growth*?

OBJECTIVE OF THE BOOK

This comprehensive and timely publication aims to be an essential reference source, building on the available literature in the field of Entrepreneurship and Innovation for the economic and social development of countries while providing for further research opportunities in this dynamic fields. Thus, the book aims to provide the opportunity for a reflection on this important issue, increasing the understanding of Entrepreneurship and Innovation in the context of organizations' performance, providing relevant academic work, empirical research findings, and an overview of this relevant field of study.

It is hoped that this text will provide the resources necessary for policy makers, technology developers and managers to adopt and implement solutions for an *Entrepreneurial Orientation and Opportunities for Global Economic Growth.*

TARGET AUDIENCE

Policy makers, academicians, researchers, advanced-level students, technology developers, and government officials will find this text useful in furthering their research exposure to pertinent topics in Entrepreneurship and Innovation and assisting in furthering their own research efforts in this field.

ORGANIZATION OF THE BOOK

The book is organized into 10 chapters. A brief description of each of the chapters follows:

Chapter 1 identifies that the growth of the internet is giving rise to the overall importance of digital marketing for business management. In fact, digital marketing is widely accepted as an essential component of business management nowadays, and its share on the marketing budgets is getting bigger. Still, digital marketing professionals also deal with some resistance, especially from small and medium companies from more traditional sectors, and from businesses struggling with limited budgets for marketing and communication.

Chapter 2 establishes the status quo and discuss the interfaces and articulations between the two constructs, Entrepreneurship and Social Development. Thus, this article aims to analyse features of publications related to the themes of Entrepreneurship and Social Development from 1996 to 2016.

Chapter 3 consider that although companies seek to export in order to meet the growing importance of international markets vis-à-vis domestic markets, this one presents a case study of a company founded by two former high school teachers who started a beverage company in 2015 and quickly reached an early internationalization.

Chapter 4 reviews the problem related to gender and entrepreneurship in the Portuguese society. The goal is to explain the concept of entrepreneur, behavioural and social differences between the masculine and the feminine gender as entrepreneurs and identify Portuguese female entrepreneurs.

Chapter 5 contributes to a better conceptual understanding of entrepreneurship's application to the public sector, namely its questions, ideas and current debate, this work presents some theoretical reflections and a relevant literature review on entrepreneurship in a public sector context.

Chapter 6 intends to address entrepreneurs' alternative mechanisms, other than the classic formal planning model, to harness opportunities or overcome setbacks arising from chance. The unpredictability of business activities means that entrepreneurs should find a way to adapt and embrace chance. The traditional and predefined process logic, offers little support for today's complex and dynamic business environment.

Chapter 7 addresses to analyze the relationship between entrepreneurial orientation and competitive advantage on Portuguese exporting textiles small and medium enterprises (SMEs). Based on survey data from 247 firms, our empirical results indicate that: 1) innovation have a positive and significant impact on differentiation; 2) proactivity and risk-taking does not have a positive and significant impact on differentiation; 3) innovation, proactivity and risk-taking does not have a positive and significant impact on cost leadership.

Chapter 8 analyses whether social entrepreneurs use their personal network to acquire different resources. Based on an online survey of individuals involved in the management of Portuguese social organisations, the results attained revealed that social entrepreneurs are usually involved in strong and diversified networks. Their personal networks shape the way human, financial and informational resources are obtained and managed. The major influence is made by social entrepreneurs' indirect contacts (weak ties) and the benefits they perceive these networks are able to provide.

Chapter 9 reviews the literature on venture capital (VC), its conceptualization and synthesis over four decades. Innovative SMEs are encouraged to take advantage of globalization and competition among VC firms in their search for this financial resource. Recently, VC firms have become more risk averse regardless of their traditional competence in screening and monitoring.

Chapter 10 analyses, from the perspective of the theory of entrepreneurship, which are the characteristics of a "Start-up" and how is considered a new type of company within the economic context due to its specific characteristics. Based on a literature review, it is identified the historical context of entrepreneurship until reach the specific context of the conditions of Metropolitan Area of Guadalajara (MAG) to generate the creation and development of Startups, concluding that MAG has created the conditions to promote the entrepreneurial ecosystem; however, there are key indicators that slow detonation and growth of start-ups based on technology and innovation.

Orlando Lima Rua
Polytechnic of Porto, Portugal

REFERENCES

Acs, Z. J., Desai, S., & Hessels, J. (2008). Entrepreneurship, economic development and institutions. *Small Business Economics, 31*(3), 219–234. doi:10.100711187-008-9135-9

Blackburn, R. A., Hart, M., & Wainwright, T. (2013). Small business performance: Business, strategy and owner-manager characteristics. *Journal of Small Business and Enterprise Development*, *20*(1), 8–11. doi:10.1108/14626001311298394

Carlsson, B., Braunerhjelm, P., McKelvey, M., Olofsson, C., Persson, L., & Ylinenpää, H. (2013). The evolving domain of entrepreneurship research. *Small Business Economics*, *41*(4), 913–930. doi:10.100711187-013-9503-y

Correia, M. J., & Rua, O. L. (2016). Innovation in the Portuguese health sector organizations: Empirical evidence from the Community Innovation Survey. *Tékhne - Review of Applied Management Studies*, *14*, 2-9.

Covin, J., & Slevin, D. (1991). A conceptual model of entrepreneurship as firm behavior. *Entrepreneurship Theory and Practice*, *16*(1), 7–25. doi:10.1177/104225879101600102

Davis, J. L., Bell, R. G., Payne, G. T., & Kreiser, P. M. (2010). Entrepreneurial Orientation and Firm Performance: The Moderating Role of Managerial Power. *American Journal of Business*, *25*(2), 41–54. doi:10.1108/19355181201000009

Frank, H., Kessler, A., & Fink, M. (2010, April). Entrepreneurial orientation and business performance-a replication study. *Schmalenbach Business Review*, 175–199.

Hung, R., Yang, B., Lien, B., McLean, G. N., & Kuo, Y.-M. (2010). Dynamic capability: Impact of process alignment and organizational learning culture on performance. *Journal of World Business*, *45*(3), 285–294. doi:10.1016/j.jwb.2009.09.003

Ireland, R. D., Hitt, M. A., Camp, S. M., & Sexton, D. L. (2001). Integrating entrepreneurship and strategic management actions to create firm wealth. *The Academy of Management Executive*, *15*(1), 49–63.

Lumpkin, G., & Dess, G. (1996). Clarifying the entrepreneurial orientation construct and linking it to performance. *Academy of Management Review*, *21*(1), 135–172. doi:10.5465/amr.1996.9602161568

Miller, D. (1983). The correlates of entrepreneurship in three types of firms. *Management Science*, *29*(7), 770–791. doi:10.1287/mnsc.29.7.770

Okpara, J. (2009). Entrepreneurial orientation and export performance: Evidence from an emerging economy. *Int. Rev. Bus. Res. Papers*, *5*(6), 195–211.

Semrau, T., Ambos, T., & Kraus, S. (2016). Entrepreneurial orientation and SME performance across societal cultures: An international study. *Journal of Business Research*, *69*(5), 1928–1932. doi:10.1016/j.jbusres.2015.10.082

Wiklund, J., & Shepherd, D. (2005). Entrepreneurial orientation and small business performance: A configurational approach. *Journal of Business Venturing*, *20*(1), 71–91. doi:10.1016/j.jbusvent.2004.01.001

Wiklund, J., & Shepherd, D. A. (2011). Where to from here? EO-as-experimentation, failure, and distribution of outcomes. *Entrepreneurship Theory and Practice*, *35*(5), 925–946. doi:10.1111/j.1540-6520.2011.00454.x

Zahra, S., & Garvis, D. (2000). International corporate entrepreneurship and firm performance: The moderating effect of international environmental hostility. *Journal of Business Venturing*, *15*(5-6), 469–492. doi:10.1016/S0883-9026(99)00036-1

Chapter 1
How Do Entrepreneurs See Digital Marketing?
Evidence From Portugal

Sandrina Francisca Teixeira
Polytechnic of Porto, Portugal

Belem Barbosa
University of Aveiro, Portugal

Helder Pinto
Polytechnic of Porto, Portugal

ABSTRACT

The growth of the internet is giving rise to the overall importance of digital marketing for business management. In fact, digital marketing is widely accepted as an essential component of business management, and its share of the marketing budget is getting bigger. Still, digital marketing professionals deal with some resistance, especially from small and medium companies from more traditional sectors and from businesses struggling with limited budgets for marketing and communication. Entrepreneurs and startup managers are expected to have a clear acknowledgement of digital marketing tools' benefits, which is confirmed in this study. However, budget constraints limit their willingness to spend money on digital marketing and to hire specialized personnel. This chapter provides valuable cues for digital marketing practitioners and companies that intend to approach startups.

DOI: 10.4018/978-1-5225-6942-8.ch001

INTRODUCTION

Studies on marketing and entrepreneurship arose as a result of the difficulty of applying traditional marketing concepts, very focused on large companies, to the reality of the small businesses. The main differences of small and medium-sized enterprises (SMEs) in relation to the large ones is the availability of resources (financial, human resources, facilities) and their strict potential for developing skills (Stokes, 2000; Gilmore, Carson & Grant, 2001). As a consequence, there are currently lines of research in the initial phase of study on the interface between marketing and entrepreneurship. These lines of research consider that combining marketing and entrepreneurship can help explain the performance of an entrepreneurial company, demonstrating that there are many touch points and possible synergies between the two areas of research. Most of the interface research explores how marketing concepts and principles are particularly relevant in entrepreneurial contexts and how they can help explaining business performance. Furthermore, digital marketing is an essential factor to consider when explaining the performance of new companies. This chapter focus on digital marketing for SMEs, because it is no longer a trend, it has become more and more crucial for these companies.

Many entrepreneurs have relegated digital marketing to the background, but it is currently an essential factor in globalized world we live in. In fact, the mastery of communication technologies has become essential in the business world and, in recent years, the Internet clearly offers a set of great opportunities and challenges of extreme importance, especially for SMEs. The Internet allows to enhance the marketing efforts of these companies in areas as different as efficiency improvement, access to new markets, business-to-business collaboration, customization of goods and services, product creation with customers, and developing relationships with customers, just to name a few (Ansari & Mela, 2003; Barnes et al., 2012; Harrigan et al., 2010; Harris & Rae, 2009).

The new forms of communication and relationship with customers in this digital era have completely modified the way companies engage with their stakeholders, especially their customers. A few years ago, the focus of the companies was the website, however now there are more and more evidence demonstrating how important it is for SME to define and adopt an online marketing mix and interactive applications (Durkin et al., 2013; Barnes et al., 2012; Kim et al., 2011; Bulearca & Bulearca, 2010). This transition to a wide variety of technologies, such as applications for mobile devices, application interfaces, social network sites, and data analysis, are complex and difficult for companies to evaluate their costs and benefits. Hence, in this chapter we intend to understand the importance entrepreneurs attribute to digital marketing, in order to provide indications on how digital marketing professionals and agencies ought to approach this market segment. Despite the increase in literature related to digital marketing for SMEs, the magnitude of the internet and the changes in global markets makes it necessary to carry out additional conceptual and empirical studies (Kim et al., 2011) to explain how digital marketing strategies make sense in this turbulent technological environment (Peltier et al., 2012), and evaluating the perceptions, experiences, and intentions of entrepreneurs in regard to hiring digital marketing experts and implementing digital marketing strategies.

Although digital marketing is useful both for big companies and very small businesses alike, as long as their customers are online, successful executions demand specific expertise that is not widely owned, especially in the case of start-ups and small enterprises. Moreover, the popularity of some digital marketing tools, such as social media, and the user-friendliness and freemium price models of many digital marketing tools, such as website builders, is potentially deceptive for entrepreneurs that while realizing the need to own and manage digital media are not willing to make the adequate investment both in terms of money and regarding skilled personnel, in order to accomplish their business goals online. Due to the importance of the Internet for the buying decision process, not having a capable online presence, or having ineffective online communication may dictate the failure of a start-up business, or at least it will damage its profitability and delaying its success. New businesses must get into the market as effectively as possible, getting the attention and preference of prospects, and being able to convert them.

Thus, it is of utmost importance to understand how entrepreneurs deal with digital marketing, and the factors that help explain its implementation in new business ventures. In this chapter we explore the main contributions from the literature regarding digital marketing application to new businesses. We also present results from a survey that comprises the experiences, points of view, and decisions made by 201 Portuguese Entrepreneurs targeting both national and international markets. Results demonstrate the importance of digital marketing for the entrepreneurs that participated in this study. Although entrepreneurs seem aware of the positive impact of digital marketing tools and skills namely to increase sales and ultimately to the success of startups, budgets are limited and do not cover hiring highly skilled digital marketing professionals. Hence, results highlight the importance of digital marketing tools in their marketing strategies, their decisions, and their future intentions. They also provide some interesting cues that are relevant for digital marketing professionals and for entrepreneurs themselves, being relevant for a wide audience, including students, academics, and practitioners.

BACKGROUND

Digital marketing appeared in the last decades in the context of technological development that made online communication essential for individuals and companies. The Digital Marketing Institute refers to digital marketing as "the use of digital technologies to create integrated, targeted and measurable communication that helps to acquire and retain customers and at the same time build deeper relationships with them" (Smith, 2007, cited by Wymbs, 2011, p. 94). Put simply, digital marketing is defined as a subdivision of marketing that uses modern digital channels to place products and, mainly, to communicate with interested parties, for example, customers and investors that are interested on brands and products (2012).

Digital marketing has some advantages for companies and marketing professionals that make it quite appealing compared to traditional marketing. Digital marketing presents much more measurable results, and thus the decisions can be made using real data (quantitative and qualitative) that are easily obtained and cheap (e.g., website analytics, key performance indicators, digital campaigns analytics). Additionally, internet platforms offer the large capacity of analysis of demographic data details, which in turn allow companies to reach their target markets with great precision; think, for instance, on online advertising, which is targeted to very specific profiles, including characteristics related to lifestyle or precise needs of the user based on online searches she is undertaking. The internet also offers additional opportunities to engage and communicate with customers. One clear example are social media, which enable the company to communicate directly with groups and individual consumers. As a matter of fact, the information available consumers' profiles is detailed, and consequently there is the possibility of customization of the production, the distribution can be individualized, and the communication is bidirectional. The data are related to a customer quota instead of a market quota and the focus is on the maintenance of customers rather than conquering them. The widespread adoption of digital marketing techniques, including social media, contributed significantly to this marketing individualization, where providers of goods and services increasingly communicate with individual consumers and users, obtaining feedback on an individual basis and providing customized solutions for customers (Brady, Fellenz, & Brookes, 2008; Simmons, & Simmons, 2008).

In an increasingly significant number of studies, digital marketing is considered to be strategic because the vision and planning must be integrated and aligned with the global marketing strategies of the companies. In this sequence, if integrated and aligned, digital marketing acts directly and differently in the process of global competitiveness of companies and organizations in general. Digital marketing involves the application of digital technologies in marketing activities in order to achieve greater profitability and customer retention. This is done through the recognition of the importance of digital strategies and the development of a planned approach, in order to improve the client's knowledge, the delivery of a specific integrated communication and online services that match their particular needs, the construction of an interactive relationship with these consumers, and the ability to produce measurable results, thus being able to be integrated into a more broad marketing strategy (Smith, 2007). As Mulhern (2009, p. 86) predicted, "the media digitalization represents a phase change in the history of communication". Companies that understand how customers use new media in their purchasing decisions can develop integrated communication strategies that support their customers at every stage of the purchasing process (Chaffey et al., 2015), and consequently get a competitive advantage that is determinant of their profitability, and ultimately, their success in the market.

In fact, each company should define a consistent strategy in terms of positioning, target segments and communication actions, considering the massive opportunities and challenges provided by the internet. The company should also define objectives, such as, for example, increasing online and offline sales, promoting the company and its products, boosting the company's image and notoriety, creating added value for its customers. It should also design the actions to be carried out online, define the form of content updating and have applications where it can visualize its evolution and online performance (Anderson, 2006) since the strategies of the companies are increasingly more broad, that is to say, they work at the level of traditional and digital marketing simultaneously, as the border between online and offline worlds is getting more and more diffuse.

McAfee and Brynjolfsson (2012) highlight some of the difficulties associated with digital marketing, including lack of leadership, lack of appropriate talent management, lack of adoption of new technologies, bad decision making, and a culture that is not integrally open to an information data-based approach.

The marketing education gap is addressed in several studies (Payne et al., 2011), which highlight the importance of addressing the issues of digital marketing skills at the educational level because it is essential for business graduates to be able to manage the social media campaigns. As Granitz and Pitt (2011) observe, new technologies are affecting both the marketing education curriculum and the tools used to teach it. This is an approach that recognizes that the "digital revolution changed marketing in the core" (Wymbs, 2011, p. 95). As a result, the need for specialized graduates in digital marketing is increasing.

Leeflang, Verhoef, Dahlström and Freundt (2014), in their study "Challenges and solutions for marketing in a digital era", carried out on 777 marketing executives worldwide, identified four major marketing challenges in this new era: the use of customer and data insights to compete effectively, the threatening power of the social media for brands and customer relationships, the omnipresence of new digital metrics, and the subsequent assessment of the effectiveness of the digital marketing activities and the growing hiatus of analytical skills in the companies. Interestingly, three of these major challenges (customer view, metrics and skills gaps) involve data and underlying resources to analyze data. The digital marketing professionals should have stronger skills in data analysis and thus provide companies with a deeper and more up-to-date understanding of the digital environment. The study, in conclusion, suggests that marketing needs to adapt to the new digital age, focusing strongly on the development of quantitative skills; on the development of fact-based proposals and on the development of relationship strategies with the brand and customer taking advantage of the growing engagement of brands and customers through the social media.

According to a study developed by Jo Royle and Audrey Laing (2013), the most significant digital marketing skills gap that emerged from the research was the difficulty for companies to hire employees with strategic knowledge of digital marketing, who managed to integrate this strategic knowledge with traditional marketing and communication approaches. The challenge of an integrated approach to marketing is not new (Valos et al., 2010) and rapid developments in technology makes this an ongoing problem (Akar & Topcu, 2011; Brady et al., 2008). One possible solution would be evidence-based guidance on best practice, which would eliminate some risk inherent to an experimental approach. Interestingly, Royle and Laing (2013) identified some evidence of conservatism in the comments of entrepreneurs on new technical developments and costs associated with experimentation and investment in new technologies and digital marketing.

Naturally, the difficulties felt by large companies are even more noticeable in SMEs and there is a growing number of studies in literature related to the adoption of technology for SME marketing (e.g., Durkin, McGowan, & McKeown, 2013; Bulearca & Bulearca, 2010; Kim et al.., 2011; Simmons et al., 2011) and some focus on microenterprises (e.g., Jones et al., 2014; Barnes et al., 2012; Bharati e Chaudhury, 2006). Still, in our opinion it is necessary to further explore digital marketing adoption by small companies, namely to identify their specific needs, perceptions, and problems, in order to enable adequate strategies to help them.

Hence, the contributions in extant literature present some indications regarding the gaps in the training of digital marketing professionals, while the lack of technical skills, the lack of knowledge on how to create global digital strategies and the entrepreneurs' risk aversion are the main conditioning factors of the entrepreneurs, namely of SMEs, which may limit the adoption of digital marketing, or even compromising the outcomes of digital marketing strategies.

How Portuguese Entrepreneurs See Digital Marketing

The Portuguese reality has particularities that imply the recognition of companies on the importance that they attribute to digital marketing. In fact, Portuguese companies are the smallest in Europe, with an average of 3.1 people at their service. The average size of the companies in Portugal is 99.9% made up of SMEs, which are responsible for 57.4% of the turnover, which is fundamental for the growth of the economy (INE, PORDATA, 2018). Although Portuguese companies already have the notion of the necessity of the digital transformation, the truth is that in Portugal 27% of the medium and large-sized companies are still at level 1 (a scale of 1 to 5) in the Maturity model for the DX of the IDC, against 20% in Western Europe and 13% in the USA. These conclusions have as basis an IDC study, carried out in Portugal in 2016, in which 236 organizations were surveyed and the interviewees were asked to characterize their own degree of maturity in terms of transformation. It was verified with this study that, in Portugal, the organizations are less mature in the process of digital transformation, when compared with the results of the companies in Western Europe, which, in turn, is lagging behind the United States.

Furthermore, in the 2016 annual event of IDC Portugal, a panel dedicated to the study of the necessary qualifications and competencies for the digital transformation, which included the participation of representatives from the Catholic University, the Porto Business School, the Nova IMS and the Instituto Superior Técnico, gave very interesting points of view about the Portuguese context. In this panel, the different participants highlighted the increase of uncertainty in the business environment of the organizations, caused by a greater economic volatility and an acceleration of the technological transformation. The majority of the participants also highlighted the importance of technological literacy for the managers of the national organizations as well as the role that information literacy has for the success of the digital transformation. Therefore, there is an urgent need to improve information literacy, and digital marketing strategies are particularly relevant – as long as they are carefully developed and adequate to the target markets, which, in turn, demand specialized skills, as seen in the previous sections.

The startups are also relevant in the analysis of the Portuguese business structure. According to the study “O Empreendedorismo em Portugal” (Informa D&B, 2016), the profile of the startups has changed in recent years. There are more individual and smaller initiatives, which have, however, a more exporting profile. The study alerts that the first few years in business are crucial for the survival of the startups, as the survival rate drops more markedly in the first years of life: around two thirds of the companies survive to the first year of activity, more than half (53%) go beyond the third year and 42% reach the adult age. In the eighth year of activity, only one third of the companies are still active. However, the companies grow more rapidly in the first years. The turnover increases, on average, 139% in the first year, it is three times higher after two years and five times higher in the eight year. The evolution of the number of employees is less accelerated, growing on average 35% in the first year, doubling only after eight years of activity.

Portugal has 67 scaleups (companies that received more than one million dollars in financing), which have received a total of 350 million dollars (310 million euros) in the last six years. Only in the last year, 130 million dollars (115 million euros) were raised in financing, nearly 40% of the total financing raised between 2010 and 2016, which led the Portuguese entrepreneurial ecosystem to grow "the double of the European average". The conclusions are from the Startup Europe Partnership (SEP) study, which is a partnership between Mind the Bridge and Beta-i, at the Lisbon Investment Summit, in Lisbon.

Farfetch, a Portuguese-British platform for luxury electronic commerce, is the only startup endorsed in more than one billion dollars, of Portuguese origin. However, there is a group of scaleups that are growing rapidly.

These facts corroborate the importance of digital marketing for all Portuguese business companies with a focus on SMEs and new companies that are born with ambitions to work for the national or international market. Again, these results demonstrate the importance of digital marketing for startups. Thus, it is of vital importance the studies that provide information on digital marketing and how it can be used by companies and digital marketing professionals in a meaningful way, since it is currently considered a critical factor for companies to become more competitive.

METHODOLOGY

This study adopted an exploratory quantitative approach, in order to understand how entrepreneurs deal with digital marketing, namely the importance of digital marketing tactics, tools, and skills to develop their businesses. Hence, a self-completion questionnaire was used to collect data on the experience and perceptions of entrepreneurs regarding digital marketing.

The questionnaire was organized in three parts. The first one comprised questions about the entrepreneurs' business characteristics: already in business or planned to be launched, number of collaborators, investment, expected sales volume, markets, marketing budget, digital marketing budget, among others. The overall importance of digital marketing to their business was measured using a 10-item Likert scale, ranging from 1 – minimum to 10 maximum.

The second part of the questionnaire included questions about: (i) the importance of a list of offline and online marketing tools were rated using a 7-point Likert scale ranging from 1- not at all important to 7 – essential; (ii) the relevance of a list of communication channels, ranging from 1 – not at all relevant to 7 very relevant; and (iii) the importance of a list of digital marketing skills, ranging from 1- not at all important to 7 – essential.

The lists of items are presented on tables 3, 4, and 5, and were developed by the authors with the help of a group of 8 marketing professionals experienced in startup businesses. The third part of the questionnaire included questions about the respondents' profiles (e.g., age, education, gender). The questionnaires was subject to a pretest with 20 entrepreneurs. Data was collected during an entrepreneurship fair that was held in Porto, Portugal, in November 16-21, 2015. The study sample comprises 201 Portuguese business owners and future entrepreneurs, whose characteristics are presented on Table 1.

Table 1. Participants' profile

	N	%	Valid %
Entrepreneurs			
Business Owner	114	56.72	57.29
Planning to create a Business	85	42.29	42.71
Missing	2	1.00	
Total	201	100.00	100.00
Expected Number of Employees in 12 Months			
1-2	83	41.29	41.92
3-5	73	36.32	36.87
6-10	23	11.44	11.62
> 10	19	9.45	9.60
Missing	3	1.49	
Total	201	100.00	100.00
Business Sector			
Design/Marketing/Communication	23	11.44	17.42
Primary Sector	2	1.00	1.52
Technology Company	11	5.47	8.33
Industry	5	2.49	3.79
Commerce and Services	47	23.38	35.61
Tourism, Hotels and Restaurants	17	8.46	12.88

continued on following page

Table 1. Continued

	N	%	Valid %
Other	27	13.43	20.45
Missing	69	34.33	
Total	201	100.00	100.00
Age			
< 30 years old	39	19.40	29.32
31 - 40 years old	49	24.38	36.84
41 - 50 years old	28	13.93	21.05
> 50	17	8.46	12.78
Missing	68	33.83	
Total	201	100.00	100.00
Education			
Undergraduate	20	9.95	15.27
Graduation	74	36.82	56.49
Post-graduation	37	18.41	28.24
Missing	70	34.83	
Total	201	100.00	100.00
Gender			
Female	46	22.89	34.85
Male	86	42.79	65.15
Missing	69	34.33	
Total	201	100.00	100.00
Investment in Digital Marketing			
Investing or planning to invest	179	89.05	89.05
Not investing or not planning to invest	22	10.95	10.95
Total	201	100.00	100.00

RESULTS

201 Entrepreneurs participated in this study (Table 1), 114 of which were already business owners and 85 were still planning to create their business. Most of their companies were very small, as only 9.60% were expected to have more than 10 employees within the following 12 months. Most of the respondents were graduates (15.27% are undergraduates). 34.85% were women. The majority of the entrepreneurs that participated in this study were investing or planning to invest in digital marketing (89.05%).

As Table 2 shows, the expected budget for communication and marketing activities was often very low, as 37.31% mentioned that they intended to spend up to 1,500 euro in communication and marketing in the next 12 months. Part of this budget was destined to digital marketing. In fact, 39 respondents (19.4%) intended to spend less than 50 euro per month in digital marketing, 46 (22.9%) between 51 and 100 euro, and 43 (21.4%) more than 500 euro per month. In all cases, most of the digital marketing budget is planned to be available for internal collaborators' activities instead of agencies or freelancers'.

In fact, considering the respondents that had already created their business (N = 114), 15 respondents (13.2%) indicated they had hired a digital marketing freelancer and 6 (5.3%) hired a marketing agency, while 40 (35.1%) use internal resources for the digital marketing tasks. Moreover, 24 (21.1%) of the business owners mentioned that they were deciding on the best solution for managing digital marketing in their businesses.

Table 2. Estimated investment in communication and marketing

	N	%	Valid %
Estimated Investment in Communication and Marketing (Next 12 Months)			
up to 1,500 eur	75	37.31	40.11
from 1,501 to 5000 eur	61	30.35	32.62
from 5,001 to 10,000 eur	21	10.45	11.23
more than 10,000 eur	30	14.93	16.04
Missing	14	6.87	
Total	201	100.00	100.00

Table 3. Relevance of communication channels for their business

	N	Minimum	Maximum	Mean	Standard Deviation
Brochures	124	1	7	3.73	1.862
Outdoors	116	1	7	3.07	1.821
e-mail marketing	123	1	7	5.48	1.381
Website	129	1	7	6.47	0.911
Ads in print media	118	1	7	3.38	1.912
TV advertising	107	1	7	2.73	2.072
Social network sites	130	1	7	6.22	1.161
Video	121	1	7	5.17	1.652
Sponsored campaigns	115	1	7	5.08	1.707
Search engine optimization	122	1	7	6.14	1.194

Entrepreneurs that have participated in this study were invited to rate the importance of different communication channels for their business (Table 3). The most prominent where digital media, namely the website, social network sites, and search engine optimization. Additionally, Students' T-test indicated that the differences in responses between business owners and intenders were not statistically significance for all items considered.

The relative importance of digital marketing amongst other marketing tactics was also demonstrated when we asked participants how they would apply 1,000 euro in order to increase sales. 28.74% of the respondents would actually spend the whole amount on digital, marketing, while only 3.39% would spend it all in traditional marketing and 8.33% would rather invest the whole amount on sales force. The other respondents would share the amount with at least two of the provided types of marketing.

Interestingly, if we look at the importance given to different communication and marketing tools (Table 4) amongst the ones considered more important are three related to digital marketing: the website, content marketing, and social media marketing.

Student's t-test enabled the comparison between business owners and entrepreneurs intending to create a business. We found a statistically significant difference in the importance given to three digital marketing tools: online newsletters ($M_{Business\ Owners}$ = 4.86, $M_{Intenders}$ = 4.37; t(173) = -2.029, p = .044), social media marketing ($M_{Business\ Owners}$ = 5.47, $M_{Intenders}$ = 6.09; t(181,594) = -3.072, p = .002), and online store ($M_{Business\ Owners}$ = 4.85, $M_{Intenders}$ = 5.67; t(137.877) = -2.486, p = .014). In all cases these online

Table 4. Importance of marketing tools

	N	Minimum	Maximum	Mean	Standard Deviation
Brochures	181	1	7	4.43	1.690
Website	183	1	7	6.01	1.432
Online newsletter	176	1	7	5.06	1.711
Printed ads	175	1	7	4.07	1.809
Fairs and professional events	178	1	7	5.02	1.717
Social media marketing	186	1	7	5.72	1,455
Store	155	1	7	4.26	2.007
Online store	152	1	7	5.28	2.050
Reputation management	184	1	7	6.13	1.164
Content marketing	185	1	7	5.94	1.305
Public relations	185	1	7	5.69	1.267

tools were considered more important by entrepreneurs still planning to create a business. Also networking in fairs and professional events was considered more important by entrepreneurs intending to create their business, with differences significant with 95% confidence (MBusiness Owners = 4.74, MIntenders = 5.36; t(174.870) = -2.503, p = .013). The importance given to the other tools did not present statistically significant differences between the two groups of respondents, with a confidence level of 95%.

The entrepreneurs had different views on the importance of the years of experience hold by the digital marketing professional applying to work for their company. In fact, 15.8% expected more than 3 years of experience, while 32.5% considered adequate less than 3 years and 14.0% considered the number of years of experience irrelevant. Still, regarding digital marketing skills, they scored them highly (Table 5), particularly search engine optimization, social media management, content creation, and marketing planning. There were no statistically significant differences in the responses of business owners and other entrepreneurs intending to create their business for a 95% confidence level, except for the skills related to managing online stores $M_{\text{Business Owners}} = 4.95$, $M_{\text{Intenders}} = 5.72$; t(87.998) = -2.433, p = .017), being future business owners more demanding regarding these specific skills.

Finally, respondents that were using digital marketing were asked to rate their satisfaction with the results obtained, and 68.4% were satisfied or very satisfied with the results. Not surprisingly, only 2.7% intended to reduce their digital marketing expenditure in the next year. 21.6% intended to maintain their digital marketing budget,

Table 5. Digital marketing skills' importance

	N	Minimum	Maximum	Mean	Standard Deviation
Website development	115	1	7	5.90	1.353
Designing logos and flyers	116	1	7	5.06	1.638
Social media management	113	1	7	6.11	1.072
Sponsored campaign management	111	1	7	5.52	1.327
Video creation	115	1	7	5.10	1.435
Image edition	113	1	7	5.48	1.254
Mobile apps	107	1	7	4.90	1.619
e-mail marketing	114	1	7	5.58	1.261
Online stores	102	1	7	5.29	1.715
Marketing planning	113	1	7	6.02	1.149
Content creation	114	4	7	6.05	0.985
Search engine optimization	111	2	7	6.19	1.040

and 21.6% intended to more than double it. And when evaluating the importance of digital marketing to their business from 1 to 10 all respondents rated 5 or more points, with a mean of 8.53 (Table 6).

DISCUSSION AND CONCLUSION

Despite some evidence that Portuguese managers may have less digital marketing qualifications as compared to other countries in the European Union (Vieira, 2012), this study gives more positive indications, exhibiting a great familiarity with digital marketing by the entrepreneurs that constituted our sample. Results demonstrate that these entrepreneurs recognized the importance of digital marketing, were familiar with its tools and skills, and attributed an important part of their marketing a communication budgets to digital marketing. Entrepreneurs recognized the relevance of digital marketing namely to increase sales. And their level of satisfaction was high. Still, in most cases the budgets attributed to digital marketing are very limited, as well as the marketing budget as a whole. Moreover, despite most of the entrepreneurs that participated in this study chose to have digital marketing tasks performed by internal collaborators, most of them seem not to value more experienced professionals. This is quite contradictory, considering how important they rank very specific digital marketing skills such as social media management, content creation, and marketing planning, which, clearly will benefit from extended professional experience. So, the results comprised empirical evidence regarding the lack of willingness to make adequate investment both in terms of money but especially regarding skilled personnel in order to get the most out of the digital marketing efforts. And the fact that they are satisfied or very satisfied with the results means that their profits and success are according to expectations.

It is necessary that digital marketing become widely accepted as an essential tool for businesses in current days. It enables the implementation of effective strategies to interact with customers and prospects online, providing advantages that include working globally, targeting very specific niches and segments, measuring carefully the return on investment of marketing expenditures, being able and to start with small budgets, just to name a few. These advantages seem particularly relevant for

Table 6. Digital marketing importance to their business

	N	Minimum	Maximum	Mean	Standard Deviation
Importance of digital marketing to your business	80	5	10	8.53	1.263

new businesses and the launch of new ideas, such as innovative new businesses and entrepreneurship in general. Digital marketing can play an important role in complementing and creating synergies with traditional media, in areas such as selling, identifying and converting prospects, developing relationships and building loyalty. It may provide competitive advantages, and above all poor digital marketing can become an insuperable competitive advantage that will condemn entrepreneurial initiatives.

Management Implications

This chapter provides interesting cues to managers in general, and entrepreneurs in particular. For the ones still not using digital marketing tactics, the results provide clear evidence of the satisfaction and value recognition by the entrepreneurs already using it, and clear intention to increase the investment, and recognizing its positive impact in sales. Still, some participants in this study did not recognize the value of more experienced professionals, which should be carefully considered. Digital marketing tactics are quite complex and demanding despite the availability of numerous free usage tools and the user friendliness of many of the more popular online platforms. Digital marketing expertise will provide better results and avoid wasting resources (and customers).

For digital marketing professionals, there is a huge need to demonstrate the real potential and value of digital marketing (and specialized skills) particularly to small businesses managing very small marketing and communication budgets. Being return on investment one of the most important key performance indicators digital marketers are using, it should be clearly defined as marketing objectives and control measures, in order to adequately evaluate the impact of digital marketing efforts – and consequently gain fair recognition from all business managers.

LIMITATIONS AND FUTURE RESEARCH SUGGESTIONS

Two of the main limitations of this study include the reduced number of participants (N = 201) and the volume of missing values in their responses. Consequently, the results should not be generalized. Considering the interest of the findings, we do recommend that similar studies are conducted with different populations and samples in order to validate the results and to help both entrepreneurs and digital professionals to choose the best strategies for accomplishing their business goals. Future research could also adopt alternative methods and approaches such as longitudinal analyses, focus groups, and in-depth interviews with both entrepreneurs and digital marketing professionals. Qualitative approaches will be useful to better understand the reasons and perceptions of entrepreneurs regarding digital marketing. Studying the factors that explain the gap between the importance acknowledge to digital marketing and the willingness to invest in media and skilled professionals is amongst the topics that need further research. Moreover, longitudinal analyses will be particularly interesting in order to see whether both importance and investment vary during the first years of business.

REFERENCES

Akar, E., & Topcu, B. (2011). An Examination of the Factors Influencing Consumers' Attitudes Toward Social Media Marketing. *Journal of Internet Commerce, 10*(1), 35–67. doi:10.1080/15332861.2011.558456

Anderson, C. (2006). *The Long Tail: Why the Future of Business is Selling Less of More*. New York: Hyperion.

Ansari, A., & Mela, C. F. (2003). E-customization. *JMR, Journal of Marketing Research, 40*(2), 131–145. doi:10.1509/jmkr.40.2.131.19224

Barnes, D., Clear, F., Dyerson, R., Harindranath, G., Harris, L., & Rae, A. (2012). Web 2.0 and microbusinesses: An exploratory investigation. *Journal of Small Business and Enterprise Development, 19*(4), 687–711. doi:10.1108/14626001211277479

Brady, M., Fellenz, M. R., & Brookes, R. (2008). Researching the role of information and communications technology (ICT) in contemporary marketing practices. *Journal of Business and Industrial Marketing, 23*(2), 108–114. doi:10.1108/08858620810850227

Bulearca, M., & Bulearca, S. (2010). Twitter: A viable marketing tool for SMEs? *Global Business & Management Research, 2*(4), 296–309.

Chaffey, D. (2015). *Digital business and E-commerce management*. Pearson Education Limited.

Durkin, M., McGowan, P., & McKeown, N. (2013). Exploring social media adoption in small to medium-sized enterprises in Ireland. *Journal of Small Business and Enterprise Development, 20*(4), 716–734. doi:10.1108/JSBED-08-2012-0094

Gilmore, A., Carson, D., & Grant, K. (2001). SME marketing in practice. *Marketing Intelligence & Planning, Bradford, 19*(1), 6–11. doi:10.1108/02634500110363583

Granitz, N., & Pitt, L. (2011). Teaching about Marketing and Teaching Marketing with Innovative Technology: Introduction to the Special Edition. Journal of Marketing Education, 33(2), 127-130.

Harrigan, P., Schroeder, A., Qureshi, I., Yulin, F., Ibbotson, P., Ramsey, E., & Meister, D. (2010). Internet technologies, ECRM capabilities, and performance benefits for SMEs: An exploratory study. *International Journal of Electronic Commerce*, *15*(2), 7–46. doi:10.2753/JEC1086-4415150201

Harris, L., & Rae, A. (2009). Social networks: The future of marketing for small business. *The Journal of Business Strategy*, *30*(5), 24–31. doi:10.1108/02756660910987581

IDC. (2016). Digital Transformation at Scale. Innovation in a changed world. *Diretions 2016*. Retrieved from http://www.idc.pt/research/reshome.jsp

INE. PORDATA. (2018). *Pequenas e médias empresas em % do total de empresas: total e por dimensão*. Retrieved from https://www.pordata.pt/Portugal/Pequenas+e+m%c3%a9dias+empresas+em+percentagem+do+total+de+empresas+total+e+por+dimens%c3%a3o-2859

Informa D&B (2016). *O empreendedorismo em Portugal* (2nd ed.). Retrieved from http://biblioteca.informadb.pt/files/files/Estudos/SE_Retrato-Empreendedorismo-Portugal.pdf

Jones, P., Simmons, G., Packham, G., Beynon-Davies, P., & Pickernell, D. (2014). An exploration of the attitudes and strategic responses of sole proprietor micro-enterprises in adopting information and communication technology. *International Small Business Journal*, *32*(3), 285–306. doi:10.1177/0266242612461802

Kim, H., Lee, I., & Lee, C. (2011). Building Web 2.0 enterprises: A study of small and medium enterprises in the United States. *International Small Business Journal*, *31*(2), 156–174. doi:10.1177/0266242611409785

Laing, A., & Royle, J. (2013). Bookselling online: An examination of consumer behaviour patterns. *Publishing Research Quarterly*, *29*(2), 110–127. doi:10.100712109-013-9318-3

Leeflang, P. S., Verhoef, P. C., Dahlström, P., & Freundt, T. (2014). Challenges and solutions for marketing in a digital era. *European Management Journal*, *32*(1), 1–12. doi:10.1016/j.emj.2013.12.001

McAfee, A., Brynjolfsson, E., Davenport, T. H., Patil, D. J., & Barton, D. (2012). Big data: The management revolution. *Harvard Business Review*, *90*(10), 60–68. PMID:23074865

Mulhern, F. J. (2009). Integrated marketing communications: From media channels to digital connectivity. *Journal of Marketing Communications*, *15*(2/3), 85–101. doi:10.1080/13527260902757506

Payne, N. J., Campbell, C., Bal, A. S., & Piercy, N. (2011). Placing a Hand in the Fire: Assessing the Impact of a YouTube Experiential Learning Project on Viral Marketing Knowledge Acquisition. *Journal of Marketing Education*, *33*(2), 204–216. doi:10.1177/0273475311410853

Peltier, J., Zhao, Y., & Schibrowsky, J. (2012). Technology adoption by small businesses: An exploratory study of the interrelationships of owner and environmental factors. *International Small Business Journal*, *30*(4), 406–431. doi:10.1177/0266242610365512

Royle, J., & Laing, A. (2014). The digital marketing skills gap, International Journal of Information Management. *The Journal for Information Professionals*, *34*(2), 65-73.

Simmons, G., Armstrong, G., & Durkin, M. (2011). An exploration of small business website optimization: Enablers, influencers and an assessment approach. *International Small Business Journal*, *29*(5), 534–561. doi:10.1177/0266242610369945

Simply Digital Marketing. (2012). *What is Digital Marketing?* Retrieved from http://www.simplydigitalmarketing.com/what-is-digital-marketing

Startup Europe Partnership. (2016). Startups: ecossistema português cresce o dobro da média europeia *SEP Monitor Report*. Retrieved from https://startupeuropepartnership.eu/

Stokes, D. (2000). Putting into marketing: the process of entrepreneurial marketing. *Journal of Research in Marketing and Entrepreneurship*, *2*(1), 1-16.

Valos, M., Ewing, M., & Powell, I. (2010). Practitioner prognostications on the future of online marketing. *Journal of Marketing Management*, *26*(3/4), 361–376. doi:10.1080/02672571003594762

Wymbs, C. (2011). Digital marketing: The time for a new "academic major" has arrived. *Journal of Marketing Education*, *33*(1), 93–106. doi:10.1177/0273475310392544

KEY TERMS AND DEFINITIONS

Content Marketing: Creating content (e.g., blog posts, videos, images, text) to publish in the owned media of the company (e.g., website, pages on social network sites) in order to create value and involve customers and prospects.

Customer Conversion: When the customer or prospect (e.g., the visitor of a website or online store) takes an action according to the objective of the digital marketing strategy (e.g., makes a purchase or subscribe a newsletter).

Digital Marketing: The adaptation of marketing to the online media, namely the internet. It includes online advertising, social media marketing, e-marketing planning, among others. Also referred to as online marketing and internet marketing by some authors.

Freemium Price Models: A price strategy common amongst online products and services. Customers can start by trying a free version, and pay only for additional features (premium version).

Key Performance Indicators: A selection of statistics derived from digital marketing activity that enable an accurate control of the digital marketing efforts.

New Media: The internet and other media that are associated to the digital era. Often compared to traditional media such as television.

Search Engine Optimization: Improvements in website pages' content and design in order to increase its relevance to search engines (e.g., Google) and consequently improve the ranking on the organic search engine results.

Chapter 2
Theoretical and Methodological Paths for Studies About Entrepreneurship and Social Development:
A Longitudinal Study of Scientific Production on the Web of Science in the Period 1996-2016

Maria Carolina Rodrigues
Universidade do Algarve, Portugal

Luciana Aparecida Barbieri da Rosa
Federal University of Santa Maria, Brazil

Caroline Rosseto Camargo
Federal University of Santa Maria, Brazil

Larissa Cristina Barbieri
FESL, Brazil

Clandia Maffini Gomes
Federal University of Santa Maria, Brazil

ABSTRACT

The purpose of this chapter is to examine the status quo and discuss the interfaces and articulations between the two constructs: entrepreneurship and social development. Thus, this chapter aims to analyze the characteristics of publications related to the themes of entrepreneurship and social development from 1996 to 2016. The methodology used was descriptive research bibliometrics. The research was

DOI: 10.4018/978-1-5225-6942-8.ch002

conducted using the web of science (WoS) database of the ISI web of knowledge, with a total of 1893 articles selected. The survey results showed that the year with the highest number of publications was 2016 (446), followed by the year 2015 (330). Further, the fields of social and behavioral sciences and entrepreneurship and regional development had the largest number of publications with a total of 44 and 42, respectively.

INTRODUCTION

Global competition is reflected in the experience of companies and in the new stance adopted by business management. Thus, economic development in the competitive business environment is constantly changing. This new business scenario has guided organizations towards a process of transfiguration regarding developing the transaction as well as planning its internal environment.

From this perspective, Ferraz *et al.* (1997, p. 3) add that the conceptualization of the competitiveness is a factor for the company's success, describing it as "the company's ability to formulate and implement competitive strategies, enabling it to expand or retain on a long term basis, a sustainable market position.".

Research in the field of entrepreneurship has made significant contributions to the initial development of Economics and Psychology. Among the economists, Schumpeter (1988) points out the pioneers to verify and emphasize the importance of the entrepreneur in the economy, represented by the agent who implements innovations, assuming the risks of his actions, collecting profit as his objective. Thus, for the author, entrepreneurship is the 'engine of the capitalist economy', in which the creation of new products and the search for new markets is able to promote the medical and social development (Schumpeter, 1988).

In this context, entrepreneurship is one of the significant pillars marking the changes in the economic environment (Baumol, 1968), especially in informal economy (Carree & Thurik, 2010; Williams & Nadin, 2010). Thus, it's the organizations' responsibility to establish junctures to the environment which will encourage the emergence of companies – economic, social and political institutions that lead to social and economic sustainability (Zarpellon, 2010).

This study compiles perspectives on the theme of entrepreneurship, which are associated with the origin of terminology, conceptualization, theories, and their relevance in the business and social environment. Hence, in order to broaden the knowledge of scientific production related to Entrepreneurship and Social Development, the following question has been asked: "How is the international publications scenario concerned to the theme Entrepreneurship and Social Development available in the Web database of Science from ISI WEB of Knowledge?".

Beginning from the premise of investigating articles that jointly contemplate the subjects of Entrepreneurship and Social Development, this article tries to examine international publications connected to the theme of Entrepreneurship and Social Development available in the Web of Science database of ISI WEB of Knowledge in the period of 1996 to 2016, with the following specific goals:

1. Observe the publications related to the theme of Entrepreneurship and Social Development;
2. To characterize the production and methodological aspects of research;
3. In addition to this introductory section, the article discusses the topic of Entrepreneurship, followed by showing the context of Social Development, and then presenting the method of the study, where the procedures adopted for this research development are described.

Analysis and discussion of the obtained results are carried out in that order and then, final considerations of the study are presented.

LITERATURE REVIEW

Entrepreneurship in Different Aspects

The term *entrepreneurship* has been studied for quite some decades and is therefore, aimed by companies with an economic focus. Entrepreneurship is the driver of economic progress. Several studies indicate that companies are driven by economic development and employment creation (Naudé, 2013). Today, entrepreneurship is primarily considered to be a broad definition.

Schumpeter (1988, p. 48) stated that "the entrepreneur promotes innovation, being this radical, because it destroys and replaces current production schemes. Based on this premise, the concept of creative destruction". Drucker (1999, p. 45) added, "Schumpeter postulated that the dynamic imbalance caused by the innovative entrepreneur, instead of balance and optimization is the 'norm' of a healthy economy and the central reality for economy theory and the economic practice". Thus, the preponderant prospect of these concepts is elaborated with theoretical reference based on institutional economy.

Casero *et al.* (2005, p. 2) agree, by stating that "the Institutional Economy Theory highlights the factors and mechanisms created by the companies to conduct relations of human behaviour through the use of the concept of institution, very broadly". Zarpellon (2010, p. 52) also stated "the most diverse societies have shown great interest in the process of job creation and profit, by creating companies and process development economic and social. Given this reality, the Institutional Economy theory, provides us with a theoretical framework for the study of entrepreneurship".

According to Dornelas (2008), an entrepreneur is an individual who identifies an opportunity and makes it a reality, while being aware of the risks and uncertainties. It is known that there are several definitions for the term *entrepreneur*; however, three aspects have been explored in several studies: 1) the initiative to start a new business and the passion for it; 2) using available resources creatively, transforming the social and economic environment around; 3) accepting the calculated risks and the possibility of failure.

In the first half of the twentieth century, companies emerged and expanded without major consideration towards the environmental and social impacts. In the 80's, a new type of entrepreneurship began to emerge – social entrepreneurship. The terms social and sustainable entrepreneurship have been widely explored in academia (Lumpkin *et al.*, 2011).

Following the footsteps of the pioneers in the field, the importance of entrepreneurship to the economy must be communicated, by highlighting its dominance, especially in their development term and its application to other areas without conceptual loss.

In this scenario, entrepreneurship studies being responsible for economic and social transformations are justified for reasons other than financial ones (Dees, 1998). Social issues have been profusely analysed by the studies of Elkington and Hartigan (2008) and Chell (2007). Environmental responsibility has also been explored (Schaper, 2002; Dixon & Clifford, 2007).

Chaves (2011) emphasises that over the decades, the types and ways of activity have evolved, directing non-profit organizations through the use of instruments and business principles. Therefore, it is extremely important to discuss the possibilities of not-for-profit organisations contributing to sustainability.

The concordance of social, environmental, and economic areas resulted in the concept of sustainable entrepreneurship (Cohen & Winn, 2007). The definition therefore includes the recognition, development, and research of new enterprises that acknowledge, during economic development, responses to environmental and social problems.

Boszczowski and Teixeira (2012, p. 143) add that sustainable entrepreneurship involves "the identification, creation and exploration of new business which contribute to economic development" – the solution to environmental and social problems. Interest in social entrepreneurship has increased in recent years, as evidenced by the numbers of conferences, special editions and research articles that appear in a wide range of publications (Lumpkin *et al.*, 2011).

Similarly, Herranz *et al.* (2011) argue that a social enterprise is defined as a non-profit organization providing products or services competing with other companies, applying their strategy to support social missions.

This being considered, new business models with the objective of creating social, environmental, and economic gains are beginning to emerge. These businesses offer products and standards focused on innovation to meet the needs of institutions and people. However, this new theme of social business needs standardization regarding to its nomenclature (Comini *et al.,* 2012).

As described above, among European countries, most social enterprises are implemented by the civil society with the aim of providing services for collective benefit by providing support to the community of the socially excluded. Thus, social European organizations offer products or services that are deeply attached to their mission (Defourny & Nyssens, 2010).

With regard to imputed relevance from Latin America concerning to solving social problems, especially framing poverty through the application of market instruments, the variable of social business was used in developing countries. Thus, the term has begun to gain importance in Brazil and in other Latin American countries (Tiscoski *et al.*, 2013).

Accordingly, Lacerda (2012) mentioned that social entrepreneurship provides a direction for future generations to live in a better environment, satisfying their basic needs more prudently than in the current society.

In view of the relevance and diffusion of new business models as well as the different concepts and terminologies employed in entrepreneurship, it is essential to structure the research in order to strengthen the area.

Social Development

Social development refers to the human and social capital of a society and it's linked to a positive change in the relationships between members (individuals, groups, institutions) who seek social welfare. It can be understood as a process of enhancing the quality of life of a society in achieving peace, justice, freedom, tolerance, equality, equity, and solidarity.

According to Oliveira (2002), the constant and unrestrained search for economic development has led most of the world's countries to direct their efforts towards the growth of the gross domestic product (GDP), relegating the society's quality of life to second place (Vasconcellos & Garcia, 1998).

Currently, along with the development of industries and businesses, new problems have emerged such as the impact of companies on the environment and society. Evaluating the performance of organizations and taking into account their social responsibility is crucial for the company's activities and long-term success (Sika, 2011).

Veiga (2005) states that the development of capitalism has led to the consolidation that nations' goal would be the economic growth at any cost, without considering social welfare. Until 1960, the definitions of development and economic growth were not differentiated, since the countries involved used industrialization to enrich themselves. Only a few years later it was possible to verify that the intense economic growth was not translated into greater access to education and health, leading to an international debate on development.

According to Oliveira (2002), the debate on development began in April 1945 through the Charter of the United Nations (UN), which was released at the San Francisco Conference. In the same year, the United Nations (UN) was officially created, initially comprising of 51 countries, with the objective of seeking improvement in the quality of life levels and contribution to increase development levels in all directions. Since its inception, the UN has sought to promote growth and improve the quality of life within a greater freedom, promote economic and social progress through international institutions, seek for the international cooperation necessary to solve economic, social, cultural, and humanitarian problems, and promote respect for human rights and fundamental freedoms for all people, regardless of race, creed, colour, language, etc.

Carpintéro and Bacic (2001) point out that it is important to understand the difference between growth and economic development. While economic growth can be seen as a process of increasing wealth unrelated to improving the living conditions of the population, merely a quantitative increase in national, regional or local output; development must be seen as a process of improving conditions of the population involved in the process. Further, it is necessary to rethink the concepts of economic, social, and cultural development. In the process of economic development, an increase in the density of relations between agents is observed. Social and cultural relations sustain, while benefiting from the intense economic relationship, in which society and economy evolve together.

According to Azeez (2014), the concept of social development is new and the initial approaches focused on alleviating poverty, disease, and suffering and improvement of quality of life, employment, health, and subsistence. Charity was the most common approach but was not carried out in an organized and integrated way. While the maximum extent of the concept was religious, communal, and regional, a notable effort was made through government involvement, using social policies, legislation, and welfare programs. All these efforts contributed to shape systematic social development.

There is a major ongoing discussion about the link between the social development of countries and their relationship with entrepreneurship. In this analysis, its importance for job creation and the economic and social development of a nation becomes evident. The relationship between the themes focuses on the relationship between the number of new entrepreneurships and jobs created. However, solving the unemployment problem through entrepreneurial action is not an easy task when the current economic system tends to create less job opportunities (Carpintéro & Bacic, 2001).

Mair & Martí (2006) define social entrepreneurship as a practice for academic research, as it offers a unique opportunity to question concepts and premises in different fields of management and business research. According to the authors, social entrepreneurship is a process that catalyses social change and addresses social needs in a manner that does not generate direct financial benefit for entrepreneurs. So being, entrepreneurship becomes fundamental in helping society to overcome social issues.

The entrepreneur is someone who has been created within the society and therefore, is possessed with internal motivations, which are related to self-realization and the will to apply his knowledge in practice. The entrepreneur has the capacity to turn restlessness into an enterprise based on interactions with people, companies, and institutions. During this interaction, the entrepreneur finds and develops skills that will be necessary for entrepreneurial action. Entrepreneurial action is the fruit of social development, and this action contributes to the development of society by introducing innovations, satisfying specific demands, and making the network of inter-company relationships thicker (Carpintéro & Bacic, 2001).

Bilance (1977) mentions that "social development is the promotion of sustainability in a society that is worthy to empower marginalized groups, women and men, to undertake their own development, to improve their social and economic position and to seek their place in society". For Azeez (2014), social development is a concept commonly used to describe the socioeconomic progress of a particular region or community. In conclusion, the concept of social development is complex and related to social and human development and the various aspects of human life.

The method of study will be explained in next section.

METHODOLOGY

A bibliometric study of the descriptive type quantitative, which used articles published between 1996 and 2016 on Entrepreneurship and Social Development, was implemented.

The data was collected directly from the Web of Science (WOS) database of the Institute of Scientific Information (ISI), one of the largest multidisciplinary databases that includes data, abstracts, and scientific literature. In the field of research, we inserted the words "Entrepreneurship and Social Development", thus identifying the main authors and other characteristics in the articles published between 1996 and 2016, with the objective of examining the context in which the theme is referenced. This information was presented in Excel sheet tables for conducting analysis.

Definition of Scope Study

According Corrall *et al.* (2013, p.666), "Bibliometric techniques have been used in information research and library practice over a long period but have gained renewed momentum with the development of national exercises to assess to the quality of university research, the introduction of performance-based allocation of research funding, and the emergence of new techniques and tools for research evaluation, reflecting the migration of scholarship to the web and the influence of social media".

"Bibliometry" (a term created in 1934 by Otlet in his "Traité de Documentation"), formerly called "statistical bibliography" (a term created in 1923 by Hulme), originated in the twentieth century, known by accompany the growth and development of scientific production in the different areas of science (Araújo, 2006, p. 12).

In Russia, various studies on bibliometrics since 1829 were carried out (Faria *et al.*, 2013), and according to Schmidaier (1984), the first bibliometric study was published in 1917 by Cole and Eales, wherein publications were analysed for the period of 1550–1860.

Therefore, according Garousi (2015, p.46) "Bibliometric studies are established means to measure and analyse publications in the research area" and, Zhao (2011, p. 1) argues that bibliometrics research is "quite strong as well among research valued and conducted by librarians in academic and research libraries"

Thus, a bibliometric research is a mean of transmitting scientific production and ensuring that its objective is reached before the application of a technique capable of measuring the influence of the researchers or newspapers, allowing one to draw the profile and trends, apart from highlighting several areas of knowledge (Oliveira et al., 2013).

According to the authors Silva (2004) and Leite Filho (2008), bibliometry is like an evaluation of the scientific or technical activities of a specific area of knowledge through the quantitative study of publications.

Other authors, such as Rousseau (2001) and Camps et al. (2006), define bibliometrics as a discipline that provides a quantitative study of scientific production through an analysis of its own nature and the transfer of a science in a given period of time. Similarly, Araújo (2006, p. 12) defines bibliometry as a "quantitative and statistical technique for measuring the indexes of production and dissemination of knowledge, scientific". According to Moraes (2013), bibliometrics is the analysis of the scientific production, enabling support to the production of new articles.

The research of the publications to perform bibliometrics was conducted using the search engines of the WOS database. This database contains around 13,000 indexed newspapers, only the most cited ones in their respective areas, such as Entrepreneurship and Regional Development, Procedia Social and Behavioural Sciences, Journal of Business Venturing, International Small Business Journal, and Journal of Business Ethics. There is an index of citations in the WOS where the cited documents by each author and the documents quoted by them are mentioned (Figure 1).

In the Web of Science, the terms "Entrepreneurship" and "Social Development" were surveyed in the period between 1996 and 2016, resulting in a total of 2257 publications, with articles predominating in newspapers from 1418, followed by papers published in conferences (778).

In the present study, the following variables were identified: main authors, title of sources, main institutions, year of publications, main countries and languages, areas of knowledge and the relationship between authors with more publications, and those most cited.

Figure 1. Distribution of articles by type of publication
Source: Own.

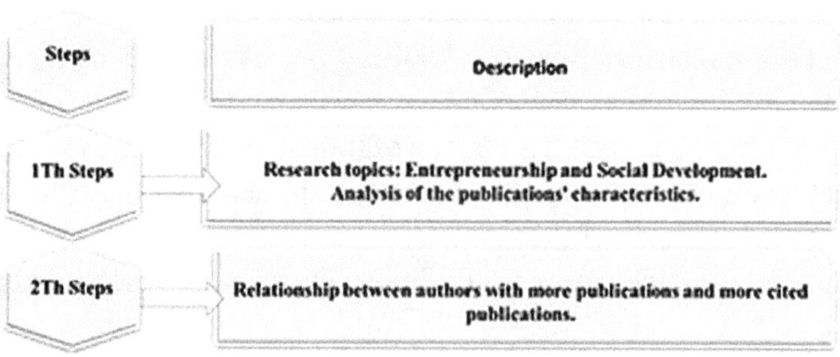

Data Collection Steps

This article was divided into two stages. In the first step, the terms "Entrepreneurship" and "Social Development" were placed in the research field of the WOS database, limited to the period between 1996 and 2016. Then, the overall features of the publications were surveyed.

In the second stage, the most cited publications were considered and compared with the authors who published the most in the same period. The steps of the research are shown in Figure 2.

The bibliometric analysis of this study was performed according to the steps described in Figure 2.

RESULTS

The results of the study presented below identify the main characteristics of scientific production from 1996 to 2016 in the Web of Science database related to the keywords "Entrepreneurship" and "Social Development". After improving the research for the Entrepreneurship and Social Development categories and in order to choose the present results referring to articles and conferences, a total of 2257 articles were obtained. In the following section the general characteristics of the publications are given.

The general characteristics of the publications related to the themes of Entrepreneurship and Social Development in the categories of main authors, title of sources, institutions, year of publications, countries, languages and research areas are presented below.

The top ten authors who published articles related to the chosen topics, Entrepreneurship and Social Development, in the analysed period are presented in Figure 3.

Figure 2. Stages of research
Source: Own.

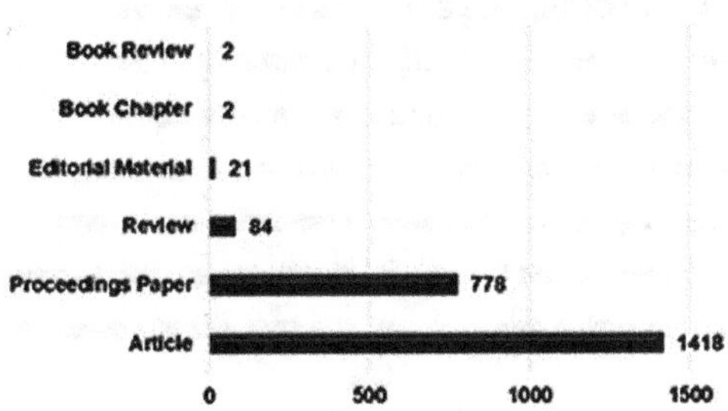

Figure 3. Distribution of articles by authors
Source: Own.

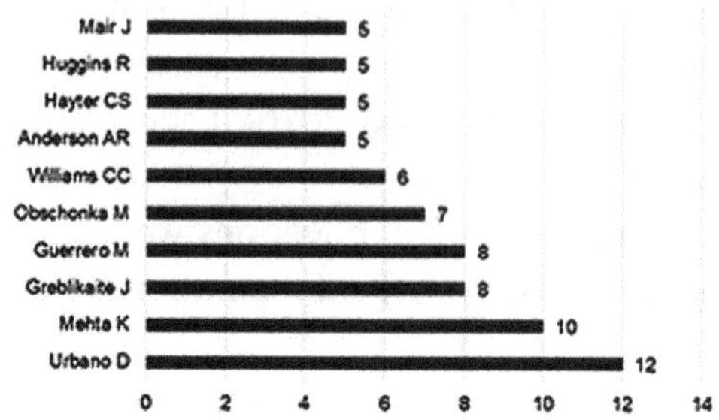

There was multiplicity and diversity regarding the authorship of the work included in the analysis of the themes. It stands out that the author, D. Urban, published a total of 12 articles and K. Mehta a total of 10. No researcher stands out while analysing the themes of Entrepreneurship and Social Development simultaneously.

Figure 4 presents the main sources of publications and number of published articles related to the topic Entrepreneurship and Social Development as well as the Conference Titles in Chart 4.

It was found that there was a predominance of international newspapers, with the largest concentration of publications being "Entrepreneurship and Regional Development" (48), "Procedia Social and Behavioral Sciences" (44), and "Journal of Business Venturing" (33). According to the figure, newspaper articles in the field are references of greater acceptance with respect to the topics under consideration, although there are a significant number of articles in multidisciplinary journals.

Figure 4. Distribution of articles by source
Source: Own.

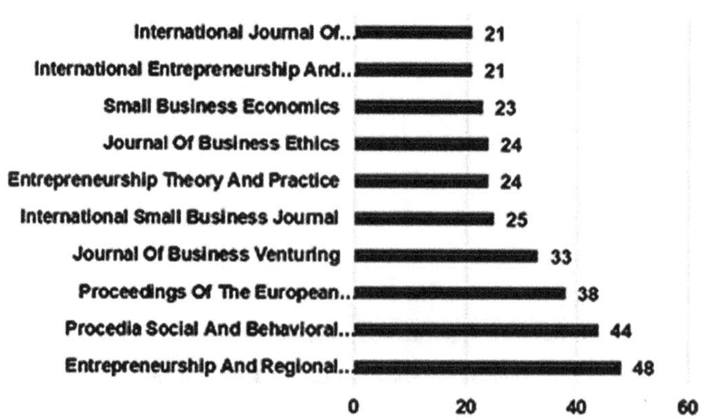

Figure 5. Distribution of articles by title of conferences
Source: Own.

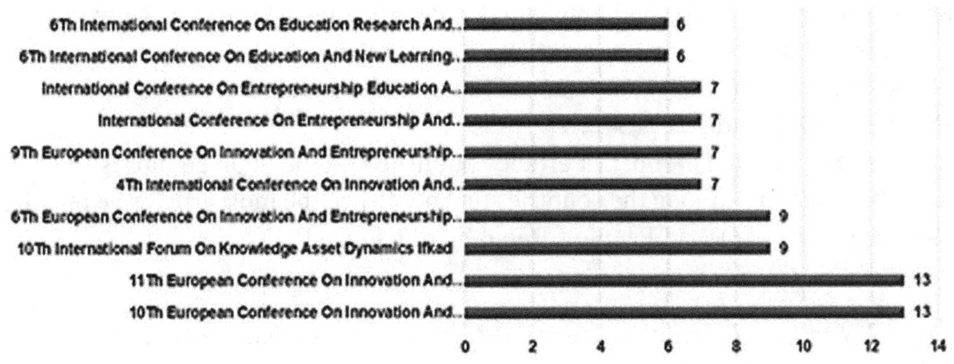

European Conference on Innovation and Entrepreneurship Ecie e International Forum on Knowledge Asset Dynamics Ifkad are two conferences where most articles were published on the subject. This corroborates that the conferences are a reference for acceptance of the articles of these subjects.

Figure 6 shows the ten most prominent institutions and published articles on Entrepreneurship and Social Development.

Figure 6. Distribution of articles by main institutions
Source: Own.

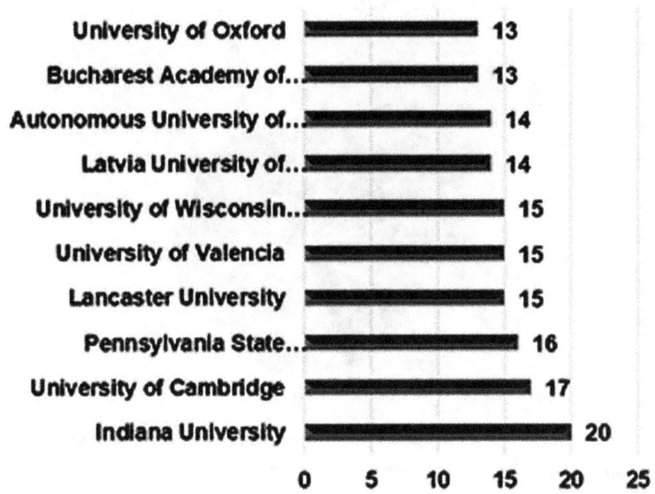

Indiana University (United States) and University of Cambridge (United Kingdom) are among the ten most published on the subject. These results highlight the scope and importance of the theme in higher education institutions around the world.

Figure 7 shows the number of articles that were annually published.

The years with the most publications in the last ten years were as follows: 2016 (45), 2015 (348), and 2017 (342).

Figure 8 shows the number of articles published on the main countries.

It was found that among the countries that published the most articles were USA (399), England (252), and People's Republic of China (191).

Figure 7. Total publications between 1996 and 2016 distributed per year
Source: Own.

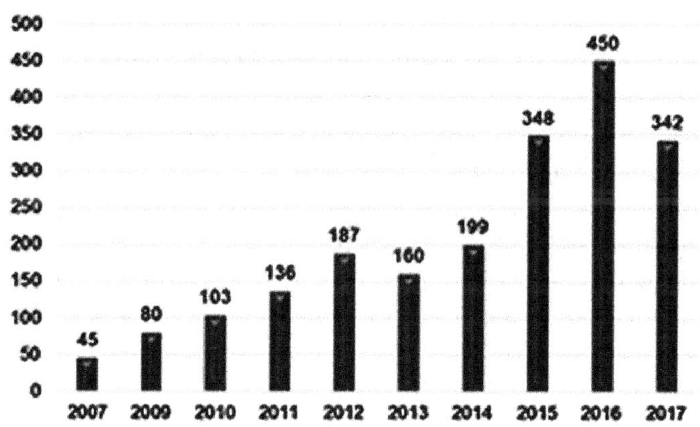

Figure 8. Distribution of articles by country
Source: Own.

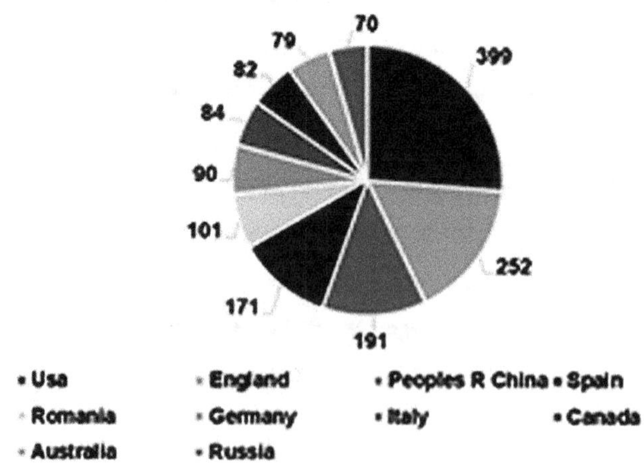

The papers were published mostly in English (2083), as shown in Figure 9.

The research areas with the largest number of publications were Social Sciences (95), Business Economics (56), Environmental Sciences Ecology (45), and Science Technology (36), as shown in Figure 10.

It is observed that the number of publications by area of knowledge (2614) in relation to published articles (1418) reinforces the idea that studies on *Entrepreneurship and Social Development* are interdisciplinary, since research can be related to more than one area of knowledge.

From 1996 to 2016, 2257 citations were identified from the eighty cited articles on Entrepreneurship and Social Development in the Web of Science database, as presented in Table 1. Articles by Kathleen M. Eisenhardt and Claudia Bird Schoonhoven (1996) had 953 citations. Those by Norris F. Krueger, Michael D. Reilly and Alan L. Carsrud (2000) had 917, and Johanna Mair and Ignasi Marti (2006) had 718. It was verified that the most cited articles were in the English language, proving the academic impact of the publications in this language.

Figure 9. Distribution of articles by language
Source: Own.

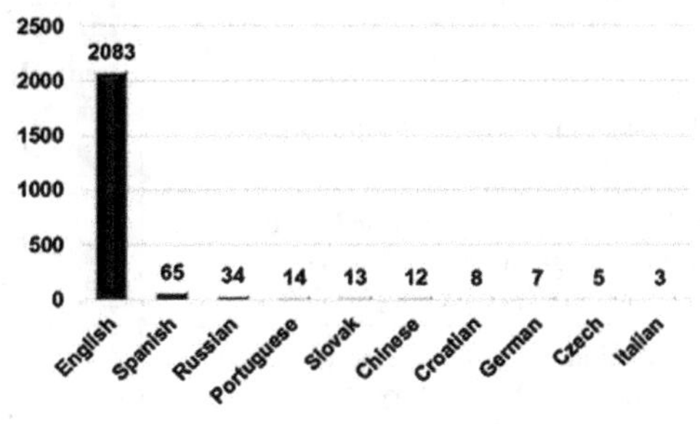

Figure 10. Distribution of articles by research areas
Source: Own.

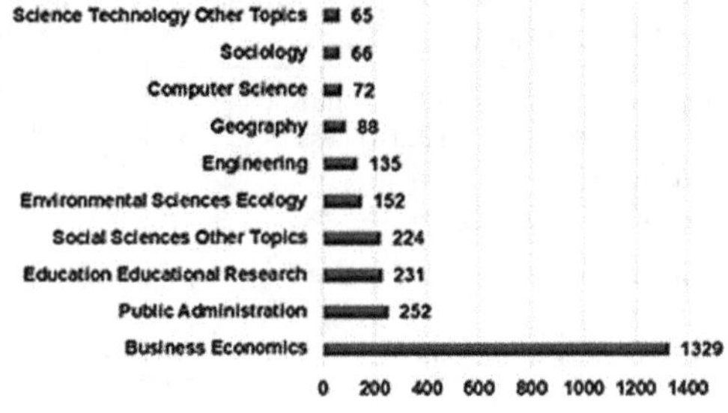

Table 1. List of the eighty most cited publications in the period (1996–2016)

Number of Quotations 1996–2016	Title/Author	Journal/Year
953	**Title:** Resource-based view of strategic alliance formation: Strategic and social effects in entrepreneurial firms **Authors:** Eisenhardt, K.M., & Schoonhoven, CB	**Journal:** Organization Science **Year:** 1996
917	**Title:** Competing models of entrepreneurial intentions **Authors:** Krueger, NF, Reilly, MD, & Carsrud, AL	**Journal:** Journal of Business Venturing **Year:** 2000
718	**Title:** Social entrepreneurship research: A source of explanation, prediction, and delight **Authors:** Mair, J, & Marti, I	**Journal:** Journal of World Business **Year:** 2006
681	**Title:** Network-based research in entrepreneurship - A critical review **Authors:** Hoang, H, & Antoncic, B	**Journal:** Journal of Business Venturing **Year:** 2003
665	**Title:** Internal capabilities, external networks, and performance: A study on technology-based ventures **Authors:** Lee, C, Lee, K, & Pennings, JM	**Journal:** Strategic Management Journal **Year:** 2001
453	**Title:** Reinventing strategies for emerging markets: beyond the transnational model **Authors:** London, T, & Hart, SL	**Journal:** Journal of International Business Studies **Year:** 2004
436	**Title:** University entrepreneurship: a taxonomy of the literature **Authors:** Rothaermel, Frank T., Agung, Shanti D., & Jiang, Lin	**Journal:** Industrial and Corporate Change **Year:** 2007
411	**Title:** Signaling Theory: A Review and Assessment **Authors:** Connelly, Brian L., Certo, S. Trevis; Ireland, R. Duane; Reutzel, Christopher R.	**Journal:** Journal of Management **Year:** 2011
386	**Title:** Personal initiative: An active performance concept for work in the 21st century **Authors:** Frese, M, Fay, D	**Journal:** Research in Organizational Behavior, Vol 23 **Year:** 2001
342	**Title:** Economic development as self-discovery **Authors:** Hausmann, R, Rodrik, D	**Journal:** Journal of Development Economics **Year:** 2003
335	**Title:** Culture and entrepreneurial potential: A nine country study of locus of control and innovativeness **Authors:** Mueller, SL, Thomas, AS	**Journal:** Journal of Business Venturing **Year:** 2001
282	**Title:** Firm networks: external relationships as sources for the growth and competitiveness of entrepreneurial firms **Authors:** Lechner, C, Dowling, M	**Journal:** Entrepreneurship and Regional Development **Year:** 2003
278	**Title:** Toward a theory of community-based enterprise **Authors:** Peredo, AM, Chrisman, JJ	**Journal:** Academy of Management Review **Year:** 2006

continued on following page

Table 1. Continued

Number of Quotations 1996–2016	Title/Author	Journal/Year
266	**Title:** Research in Social Entrepreneurship: Past Contributions and Future Opportunities **Authors:** Short, Jeremy C., Moss, Todd W., Lumpkin, G. T.	**Journal:** Strategic Entrepreneurship Journal **Year:** 2009
261	**Title:** What is protective space? Reconsidering niches in transitions to sustainability **Authors:** Smith, Adrian, Raven, Rob	**Journal:** Research Policy **Year:** 2012
261	**Title:** Creativity and entrepreneurship: A regional analysis of new firm formation **Authors:** Lee, S. Y., Florida, R., & Acs, Z. J.	**Journal:** Regional Studies **Year:** 2004
243	**Title:** Entrepreneurship in and around institutional voids: A case study from Bangladesh **Authors:** Mair, J., & Marti, I.	**Journal:** Journal of Business Venturing **Year:** 2009
238	**Title:** Women Directors on Corporate Boards: A Review and Research Agenda **Authors:** Terjesen, S., Sealy, R., & Singh, V.	**Journal:** Corporate Governance-an International Review **Year:** 2009
234	**Title:** Networks in entrepreneurship: The case of high-technology firms **Authors:** Elfring, T., & Hulsink, W.	**Journal:** Small Business Economics **Year:** 2003
218	**Title:** The distinctiveness of entrepreneurship in transition economies **Authors:** Smallbone, D., & Welter, F.	**Journal:** Small Business Economics **Year:** 2001
190	**Title:** Institutional Work in the Transformation of an Organizational Field: The Interplay of Boundary Work and Practice Work **Authors:** Zietsma, C., & Lawrence, T. B.	**Journal:** Administrative Science Quarterly **Year:** 2010
184	**Title:** The Legitimacy of Social Entrepreneurship: Reflexive Isomorphism in a Pre-Paradigmatic Field **Authors:** Nicholls, A.	**Journal:** Entrepreneurship Theory and Practice **Year:** 2010
175	**Title:** THE ACCIDENTAL ENTREPRENEUR: THE EMERGENT AND COLLECTIVE PROCESS OF USER ENTREPRENEURSHIP **Authors:** Shah, S. K., & Tripsas, M.	**Journal:** Strategic Entrepreneurship Journal **Year:** 2007
173	**Title:** From human capital to social capital: A longitudinal study of technology-based academic entrepreneurs **Authors:** Mosey, S., & Wright, M.	**Journal:** Entrepreneurship Theory and Practice **Year:** 2007
165	**Title:** BUILDING INCLUSIVE MARKETS IN RURAL BANGLADESH: HOW INTERMEDIARIES WORK INSTITUTIONAL VOIDS **Authors:** Mair, J., Marti, I., & Ventresca, M. J.	**Journal:** Academy of Management Journal **Year:** 2012

continued on following page

Table 1. Continued

Number of Quotations 1996–2016	Title/Author	Journal/Year
165	**Title:** Social Entrepreneurship: A Critique and Future Directions **Authors:** Dacin, M., T., Dacin, P. A., & Tracey, P.	**Journal:** Organization Science **Year:** 2011
165	**Title:** Firm networks and firm development: The role of the relational mix **Authors:** Lechner, C., Dowling, M., & Welpe, I.	**Journal:** Journal of Business Venturing **Year:** 2006
162	**Title:** Beyond the single-person, single-insight attribution in understanding entrepreneurial opportunities **Authors:** Dimov, D.	**Journal:** Entrepreneurship Theory and Practice **Year:** 2007
157	**Title:** Sustainable development and entrepreneurship: Past contributions and future directions **Authors:** Hall, J. K., Daneke, G. A., & Lenox, M. J.	**Journal:** Journal of Business Venturing **Year:** 2010
155	**Title:** The social construction of entrepreneurship: Narrative and dramatic processes in the coproduction of organizations and identities **Authors:** Downing, S.	**Journal:** Entrepreneurship Theory And Practice **Year:** 2005
153	**Title:** Social Bricolage: Theorizing Social Value Creation in Social Enterprises **Authors:** Di Domenico, M., Haugh, & H., Tracey, P.	**Journal:** Entrepreneurship Theory And Practice **Year:** 2010
152	**Title:** A lack of insight: Do venture capitalists really understand their own decision process? **Authors:** Zacharakis, A. L., & Meyer, G. D.	**Journal:** Journal of Business Venturing **Year:** 1998
151	**Title:** Renewable energy markets in developing countries **Authors:** Martinot, E., Chaurey, A., Lew, D., Moreira, J. R., & Wamukonya, N.	**Journal:** Annual Review of Energy And The Environment **Year:** 2002
145	**Title:** Entrepreneurship and the evolution of angel financial networks **Authors:** Steier, L., & Greenwood, R.	**Journal:** Organization Studies **Year:** 2000
145	**Title:** Organizing diversity: Evolutionary theory, network analysis and postsocialism **Authors:** Grabher, G., & Stark, D.	**Journal:** Regional Studies **Year:** 1997
144	**Title:** Change and the development of entrepreneurial networks over time: a processual perspective **Authors:** Jack, S., Dodd, S. D., & Anderson, A. R.	**Journal:** Entrepreneurship and Regional Development **Year:** 2008
141	**Title:** Entrepreneurship, innovation and industrial development: Geography and the creative field revisited **Authors:** Scott, A.	**Journal:** Small Business Economics **Year:** 2006

continued on following page

Table 1. Continued

Number of Quotations 1996–2016	Title/Author	Journal/Year
140	**Title:** Institutional Perspectives on Entrepreneurial Behavior in Challenging Environments **Authors:** Welter, F., & Smallbone, D.	**Journal:** Journal of Small Business Management **Year:** 2011
139	**Title:** A Positive Theory of Social Entrepreneurship **Authors:** Santos, F. M.	**Journal:** Journal of Business Ethics **Year:** 2012
128	**Title:** Sustainable innovation, business models and economic performance: an overview **Authors:** Boons, F., Montalvo, C., Quist, J., & Wagner, M.	**Journal:** Journal of Cleaner Production **Year:** 2013
125	**Title:** Risky business? Entrepreneurship in the new independent-power sector **Authors:** Sine, W. D., Haveman, H. A., & Tolbert, P. S.	**Journal:** Administrative Science Quarterly **Year:** 2005
124	**Title:** What determines success? Examining the human, financial, and social capital of Jamaican microentrepreneurs **Authors:** Honig, B.	**Journal:** Journal of Business Venturing **Year:** 1998
123	**Title:** Israeli women entrepreneurs: An examination of factors affecting performance **Authors:** Lerner, M., Brush, C., & Hisrich, R.	**Journal:** Journal of Business Venturing **Year:** 1997
122	**Title:** Why butterflies don't leave: Locational behavior of entrepreneurial firms **Authors:** Stam, E.	**Journal:** Economic Geography **Year:** 2007
122	**Title:** Entrepreneurs' relationships for internationalization: functions, origins and strategies **Authors:** Harris, S., & Wheeler, C.	**Journal:** International Business Review **Year:** 2005
121	**Title:** Ecological entrepreneurship: sustainable development in local communities through quality food production and local branding **Authors:** Marsden, T., & Smith, E.	**Journal:** Geoforum **Year:** 2005
120	**Title:** Academic networks in a trichotomous categorisation of university spinouts **Authors:** Nicolaou, N., & Birley, S.	**Journal:** Journal of Business Venturing **Year:** 2003
119	**Title:** NGDOs as a moment in history: beyond aid to social entrepreneurship or civic innovation? **Authors:** Fowler, A.	**Journal:** Third World Quarterly **Year:** 2000
118	**Title:** Entrepreneurship Research on Network Processes: A Review and Ways Forward **Authors:** Slotte-Kock, S., & Coviello, N.	**Journal:** Entrepreneurship Theory and Practice **Year:** 2010
118	**Title:** Women business owners in traditional and non-traditional industries **Authors:** Anna, A. L., Chandler, G. N., Jansen, E., & Mero, N. P.	**Journal:** Journal of Business Venturing **Year:** 2000

continued on following page

Table 1. Continued

Number of Quotations 1996–2016	Title/Author	Journal/Year
117	**Title:** Socio-cultural factors and entrepreneurial activity: An overview **Authors:** Thornton, P. H., Ribeiro-SoriYear, D., & Urbano, D.	**Journal:** International Small Business Journal **Year:** 2011
114	**Title:** Innovation for Inclusive Growth: Towards a Theoretical Framework and a Research Agenda **Authors:** George, G., McGahan, A. M., & Prabhu, J.	**Journal:** Journal of Management Studies **Year:** 2012
113	**Title:** Risk and trust in the cultural industries **Authors:** Banks, M., Lovatt, A., O'Connor, J., & Raffo, C.	**Journal:** Geoforum **Year:** 2000
110	**Title:** Types' of private family firms: An exploratory conceptual and empirical analysis **Authors:** Westhead, P., & Howorth, C.	**Journal:** Entrepreneurship and Regional Development **Year:** 2007
108	**Title:** Postmaterialism influencing total entrepreneurial activity across nations **Authors:** Uhlaner, L., & Thurik, R.	**Journal:** Journal of Evolutionary Economics **Year:** 2007
107	**Title:** The distinctive challenge of educating social entrepreneurs: A postscript and rejoinder to the special issue on entrepreneurship education **Authors:** Tracey, P., & Phillips, N.	**Journal:** Academy of Management Learning & Education **Year:** 2007
105	**Title:** STRATEGIC NETWORKS AND ENTREPRENEURIAL VENTURES **Authors:** Stuart, T. E., & Sorenson, O.	**Journal:** Strategic Entrepreneurship Journal **Year:** 2007
101	**Title:** Sustainability-oriented innovation of SMEs: a systematic review **Authors:** Klewitz, J., & Hansen, E. G.	**Journal:** Journal of Cleaner Production **Year:** 2014
100	**Title:** Outsiders' business: A critical review of research on immigrant entrepreneurship **Authors:** Rath, J, & Kloosterman, R.	**Journal:** International Migration Review **Year:** 2000
98	**Title:** 'We do good things, don't we?': 'Blended Value Accounting' in social entrepreneurship **Authors:** Nicholls, A.	**Journal:** Accounting Organizations And Society **Year:** 2009
96	**Title:** Research collaboration in universities and academic entrepreneurship: the-state-of-the-art **Authors:** Bozeman, B., Fay, D., & Slade, C. P.	**Journal:** Journal of Technology Transfer **Year:** 2013
95	**Title:** Which institutions encourage entrepreneurial growth aspirations? **Authors:** Estrin, S., Korosteleva, J., & Mickiewicz, T.	**Journal:** Journal of Business Venturing **Year:** 2013
95	**Title:** Entrepreneurial social capital - Conceptualizing social capital in new high-tech firms **Authors:** Anderson, A., Park, J., & Jack, S.	**Journal:** International Small Business Journal **Year:** 2007

continued on following page

Table 1. Continued

Number of Quotations 1996–2016	Title/Author	Journal/Year
94	**Title:** Entrepreneurship education research revisited: The case of higher education **Authors:** Bechard, J. P., & Gregoire, D.	**Journal:** Academy of Management Learning & Education **Year:** 2005
93	**Title:** Social and symbolic capital and responsible entrepreneurship: An empirical investigation of SME narratives **Authors:** Fuller, T., & Tian, Y.	**Journal:** Journal of Business Ethics **Year:** 2006
93	**Title:** Public versus private venture capital: seeding or crowding out? A pan-European analysis **Authors:** Leleux, B., & Surlemont, B.	**Journal:** Journal of Business Venturing **Year:** 2003
93	**Title:** Movers and shakers: chaos makers in tourism development **Authors:** Russell, R., & Faulkner, B.	**Journal:** Tourism Management **Year:** 1999
92	**Title:** Social Enterprises as Hybrid Organizations: A Review and Research Agenda **Authors:** Doherty, B., Haugh, H., & Lyon, F.	**Journal:** International Journal of Management Reviews **Year:** 2014
90	**Title:** Entrepreneurship and development: The role of clusters **Authors:** Rocha, H. O.	**Journal:** Small Business Economics **Year:** 2004
88	**Title:** The New Field of Sustainable Entrepreneurship: Studying Entrepreneurial Action Linking What Is to Be Sustained With What Is to Be Developed **Authors:** Shepherd, D. A., & Patzelt, H.	**Journal:** Entrepreneurship Theory and Practice **Year:** 2011
88	**Title:** Start-ups - Business incubation and social capital **Authors:** Totterman, H., & Sten, J.	**Journal:** International Small Business Journal **Year:** 2005
87	**Title:** The role of networking alliances in information acquisition and its implications for new product performance **Authors:** Soh, P. H.	**Journal:** Journal of Business Venturing **Year:** 2003
86	**Title:** Sustainability-driven entrepreneurship: Principles of organization design **Authors:** Parrish, B. D.	**Journal:** Journal of Business Venturing **Year:** 2010
86	**Title:** Do different institutional frameworks condition the influence of local fear of failure and entrepreneurial examples over entrepreneurial activity? **Authors:** Vaillant, Y., & Lafuente, E.	**Journal:** Entrepreneurship and Regional Development **Year:** 2007
85	**Title:** Sieve, incubator, temple, hub: Empirical and theoretical advances in the sociology of higher education **Authors:** Stevens, M. L., Armstrong, E. A., & Arum, R.	**Journal:** Annual Review of Sociology **Year:** 2008

continued on following page

Table 1. Continued

Number of Quotations 1996–2016	Title/Author	Journal/Year
85	**Title:** Fix or fixation? The contributions and limitations of entrepreneurship and small firms to combating social exclusion **Authors:** Blackburn, R.T., & Ram, M.	**Journal:** Entrepreneurship and Regional Development **Year:** 2006
84	**Title:** The influence of sustainability orientation on entrepreneurial intentions - Investigating the role of business experience **Authors:** Kuckertz, A., & Wagner, M.	**Journal:** Journal of Business Venturing **Year:** 2010
82	**Title:** Architecting gloCal (global-local), real-virtual incubator networks (G-RVINs) as catalysts and accelerators of entrepreneurship in transitioning and developing economies: lessons learned and best practices from current development and business incubation **Authors:** Carayannis, E. G., & von Zedtwitz, M.	**Journal:** Technovation **Year:** 2005
82	**Title:** Depleted communities and community business entrepreneurship: revaluing space through place **Authors:** Johnstone, H., & Lionais, D.	**Journal:** Entrepreneurship and Regional Development **Year:** 2004
81	**Title:** Impact at the 'Bottom of the Pyramid': The Role of Social Capital in Capability Development and Community Empowerment **Authors:** Ansari, S., Munir, K., & Gregg, T.	**Journal:** Journal of Management Studies **Year:** 2012

Source: Own.

Comparing Chart 2 and Table 1 with the analysis carried out in our study, it was possible to verify that the author Urbano, David, one of the ten most published on Entrepreneurship and Social Development between 1996 and 2016, presented one work among the eighty most cited papers as well as 117 citations in the Web of Science.

Table 1 shows the average number of citations (arithmetic mean) from WoS for articles published in 37 different journals, such us: Journal of Business Venturing (16), Entrepreneurship Theory and Practice (7), Entrepreneurship and Regional Development (6), Small Business Economics (4), Strategic Entrepreneurship Journal (3), International Small Business Journal (3) and Organization Science (3). The most cited articles were "Resource-based view of strategic alliance formation: Strategic and social effects in entrepreneurial firms" from Eisenhardt, Kathleen M., & Schoonhoven, Claudia B. (953 citations), published in the journal Organization Science and in Journal of Business Venturing, and "Competing models of entrepreneurial intentions" written by Norris F. Krueger, Michael D. Reilly & Carsrud, Alan L. (917 citations), corroborating that these journals are reference for acceptance of articles about "Entrepreneurship and Social Development" themes.

FINAL CONSIDERATIONS

The results of this bibliometric study, which aimed to verify the characteristics of scientific production related to the themes of *Entrepreneurship* and *Social Development* indicate an increase in publications throughout the analysed period, mainly from the last decade.

The interests and focus of research on the subject are expanding scientific knowledge. Thus, it was possible to map and analyse the scientific production scenario using the Web of Science database, obtaining a sample for analysing 2257 articles.

The articles are related in more than one area of knowledge, and it is considered that the topic is interdisciplinary. It was found that the publication vehicle which presented the largest number of publications (48) was the Entrepreneurship and Regional Development.

United States is the country where most scientific articles are concentrated in, followed by other countries, such as England, the People's Republic of China, and Spain. Multiplicity and diversity were observed regarding the authorship of the works in relation to the authors who published more on the theme.

It was verified that of the ten most published authors on the subject are included in the list of the eighty most cited authors (Urbano, David; Anderson, Alistair and Mair, Johanna), with the most cited being Mair, Johanna with 718 citations. The most prominent institutions in the publications related to Entrepreneurship and Social Development were Indiana University (United States), University of Cambridge (United Kingdom), and Pennsylvania State University (Pennsylvania, USA).

The contribution of this study to Management research stems from the resulting indicators regarding research institutions and journals that stand out most in the production of the knowledge on the theme at an international level.

LIMITATIONS AND FUTURE RESEARCHES

It should be emphasized that the present study had certain limitations regarding to the research carried out. The main limitation is that the research was carried out only with articles from the Web of Science database. Another limitation is in the analysed period.

It is suggested that the research on the topic of *Entrepreneurship and Social Development* should be expanded in future studies, other databases, as well as in other national and international and scientific events, in order to obtain other results on the bibliometric profile of publications related to the theme.

This topic needs to be further studied in Portugal and Brazil, since no Portuguese or Brazilian researcher was included in the list of the most published authors on the subject, reinforcing the idea that this theme needs to be further studied by researchers from these countries.

REFERENCES

Araújo, C. A. (2006). Bibliometria: Evolução histórica e questões atuais. Em Questão, 12(1), 11–32.

Azeez, A. E. (2014). Revisiting the prospects of social entrepreneurship on social development: An analysis. *Quest Journal of Management & Research, 5*(1). Retrieved from https://www.researchgate.net/publication/308803998

Bilance. (1997, September). A world in balance – Bilance stands for Social Development: Policy paper. *Oegstgeest.*

Bose, M., & Godói-de-Sousa, E. (2012). Empreendedorismo social e desenvolvimento social: Desafios e oportunidades. In ENANPEGS, VI. São Paulo: Gestão Social, Políticas Públicas e Território.

Boszczowski, A. K., & Teixeira, R. (2012). O empreendedorismo sustentável e o processo empreendedor: em busca de oportunidades de novos negócios como solução para problemas sociais e ambientais. In *Encontro Nacional da Associação Nacional de Pós-Graduação e Pesquisa em Administração*. São Paulo: Anais.

Camps, D., Recuero, Y., Samar, M. E., & Ávila, R. (2005). Análisis bibliométrico de tesis de doctorado del área de las ciencias de la salud: Primera parte, Odontología. *Revista de la Facultad de Ciencias Medicas de la Universidad Nacional de Cordoba, 62*, 53–56.

Carpintério, J. N. C., & Bacic, M. J. (2001). Empreendedorismo e desenvolvimento. In *World Conference no Business Incubation, outubro*, Rio de Janeiro, Brazil.

Casero, J. C. D., Urbano, D., & Mogollón, R. H. (2005). Teoría económica institucional y creación de empresas. *Revista Investigaciones Europeas de Dirección y Economía de la Empresa, 11*(3), 209–230.

Chell, E. (2007). Social enterprise and entrepreneurship: Towards a convergent theory of the entrepreneurial process. *International Small Business Journal, 25*(1), 3–19. doi:10.1177/0266242607071779

Cohen, B., & Winn, M. I. (2007). Market imperfections, opportunity and sustainable entrepreneurship. *Journal of Business Venturing, 22*(1), 29–49. doi:10.1016/j.jbusvent.2004.12.001

Comini, G., Barki, E., & Aguiar, L. T. (2012). A three-pronged approach to social business: A Brazilian multi-case analysis. *Revista ADM, 47*(3), 385–397. doi:10.5700/rausp1045

Corrall, S., Kennan, M. A., & Afzal, W. (2013). Bibliometrics and Research Data Management Services: Emerging Trends in Library Support for Research. *Library Trends, 61*(3), 636–674. doi:10.1353/lib.2013.0005

Dees, J. G. (1998). *The meaning of social entrepreneurship* (Working paper). Kauffman Center for Entrepreneurial Leadership.

Drucker, P. (1998). *Desafios gerenciais para o século XXI.* São Paulo: Pioneira.

Elkington, J., & Hartigan, P. (2008). *The power of unreasonable people: How social entrepreneurs create markets that change the world.* Boston: Harvard Business School Publishing.

Faria, P. M. O., Leal, E. A., Soares, M. A., & Godoi-de-Sousa, E. (2013). Pesquisa em Contabilidade Gerencial no Brasil: um estudo bibliométrico de 2002 a 2012 nos principais periódicos nacionais. In *Congresso Brasileiro de Custos, 20, Uberlândia. Anais.* São Leopoldo: Associação Brasileira de Custos.

Garousi, V. (2015). A bibliometric analysis of the Turkish software engineering research community. *Scientometrics, 105*(1), 23–49. doi:10.100711192-015-1663-x

Leite Filho, G. A. (2008). Padrões de produtividade de autores em periódicos e congressos na área de contabilidade no Brasil: Um estudo bibliométrico. *Revista de Administração Contemporânea, Curitiba, 12*(2), 533–554. doi:10.1590/S1415-65552008000200011

Mair, J., & Martí, I. (2006). Social entrepreneurship research: A source of explanation, prediction, and delight. *Journal of World Business, 41*(1), 36–44. doi:10.1016/j.jwb.2005.09.002

Moraes, R. O., Igarashi, E. T., Camacho, R. R., & Marques, K. C. M. (2013). Gestão estratégica de custos: Investigação da produção científica no período de 2008 a 2012. In Congresso Brasileiro de Custos, 20, Uberlândia. São Leopoldo: Associação Brasileira de Custos.

Naudé, W. (Ed.). (2013). *Entrepreneurship and economic development: Theory, evidence and policy*. New York: Palgrave Macmillan.

Oliveira, G. B. (2002). Uma discussão sobre o conceito de desenvolvimento. *Revista da FAE, Curitiba*, *5*(2), 37–48.

Oliveira, S. C. M., Barbosa, E. S., Rezende, I. C. C., Silva, R. P. A., & Albuquerque, L. S. (2013). *Bibliometria em artigos de contabilidade aplicada ao setor público. In Congresso Brasileiro de Custos*. São Leopoldo: Associação Brasileira de Custos.

Rousseau, R. (2001). Indicadores bibliométricos y econométricos en la evaluación de instituciones científicas. *Acimed*, *9*, 23–29.

Sá, A. L. (2007). *Ética profissional* (8th ed.). São Paulo: Atlas.

Santos, G. C. D. (2015). Análise bibliométrica dos artigos publicados como estudos bibliométricos na história do congresso Brasileiro de custos. *Pensar Contábil*, *17*(62), 4–13.

Schumpeter, J. A. (1988). *A teoria do desenvolvimento econômico*. São Paulo: Nova Cultural.

Sen, A. K. (2012). *Desenvolvimento como liberdade*. São Paulo: Companhia de Bolso.

Silva, M. R. (2004). *Análise bibliométrica da produção científica docente do programa de pós-graduação em educação especial/UFSCar (Mestrado em Educação Especial)*. São Carlos, Brasil: Universidade Federal de São Carlos.

Vasconcellos, M. A., & Garcia, M. E. (1998). *Fundamentos de economia*. São Paulo: Saraiva.

Veiga, J. E. (2005). *Desenvolvimento Sustentável: O Desafio do Século XXI*. Rio de Janeiro: Garamond.

Zhao, D. (2011). Bibliometrics and LIS education: How do they fit together? *Proceedings of the American Society for Information Science and Technology: ASIST*, *48*(1), 1–4.

KEY TERMS AND DEFINITIONS

Entrepreneur: Is an individual who identifies an opportunity and makes it a reality, while being aware of the risks and uncertainties.

Entrepreneurship: Is the driver of economic progress where companies are driven by economic development and employment creation.

Social Development: Refers to the human and social capital of a society and it's linked to a positive change in the relationships between members (individuals, groups, institutions) who seek social welfare. It can be understood as a process of enhancing the quality of life of a society in achieving peace, justice, freedom, tolerance, equality, equity, and solidarity.

Chapter 3
The Internationalization Process of a Born Global:
A Case Study of a Beverage Firm

António Carrizo Moreira
University of Aveiro, Portugal

Mariana Ramos
University of Aveiro, Portugal

Lisa Freitas Ferraz
University of Aveiro, Portugal

Diogo Martins
University of Aveiro, Portugal

ABSTRACT

Although companies seek to export in order to meet the growing importance of international markets, vis-à-vis domestic markets, this chapter presents a case study of a company founded by two former high school teachers who started a beverage company in 2015 and quickly reached an early internationalization. The company produces alcoholic beverages and has won international awards regarding the quality of its product, which has given it an important status and opened the door to a process of rapid internationalization. This will be used to explore the theory of entrepreneurship and how two potential entrepreneurs, with employment difficulties in teaching, began with a project that gave birth to a born global firm.

DOI: 10.4018/978-1-5225-6942-8.ch003

INTRODUCTION

Internationalization is very important for small and medium-sized firms (SMEs) as it is a consequence of the exploitation of competitive advantages (Stanisauskaite & Kock, 2016).

Internationalization has been traditionally considered an incremental process, in which companies evolved in closed markets and where they gradually increase involvement with international markets through a series of evolutionary stages (Bell, McNaughton, & Young, 2001; Ribau, Moreira, & Raposo, 2015).

The globalization of markets and production has made the international business world a common business arena for all companies whether large, medium or small. Moreover, as international competition is ever present, even for firms competing in their 'local' markets (Ribau et al., 2015), internationalization is ever present in basically all contemporary business activities even among SMEs.

Nowadays, the internationalization of companies has become widespread, thereby stressing the importance of the concept of the internationalization of born globals and the need of researchers and professionals to understand the factors that have an influence on the success of such companies (Tanev, 2012). Research conducted regarding rapid internationalization and Born Globals highlight the way companies start and grow by meeting customers' and international markets' needs (Cavusgil & Knight, 2009). According to the literature, born globals have been playing a key role throughout the years (Danik & Kowalik, 2015). The literature provides clear evidence of rapid and dedicated internationalization of born globals (Bell et al., 2001), by adopting a global approach since their inception or up to their first three years (Madsen & Servais, 1997). However, the literature on Born Global SMEs is still scant (Ribau, Moreira, & Raposo, 2018)

This chapter aims at providing a study on the internationalization process inherent to a company based in Aveiro, Portugal, which produces liqueur and may be considered a born global. For this purpose, the concept shall be explored by taking into account of several authors in the relevant literature, the types of such companies, understanding the main features of this type of companies, the stages inherent thereto in their internationalization process, the success factors and the obstacles they face. The analysis shall be complemented with a review on the challenges that companies engaged in the production and distribution of liqueur face in light of the alcohol trade and consumption policy, considering the situation affecting the company under study.

The analysis of this case study aims at exploring the company's entrepreneurial standpoint in its internationalization process; for such purpose, a qualitative methodology shall be applied, based on an unstructured interview as the method of secondary data collection.

The rest of the paper is structured as followings: The first section covers the literature review of the main types of firms that fall in the international entrepreneurship theory: born globals, international new ventures and innate exporters. The second section depicts the case studies under study. The third section discusses the results and comprises of a summary of thought provoking topics regarding the case analyzed. Section five presents the conclusions of the chapter. Finally, section six covers future research direction.

LITERATURE REVIEW

International entrepreneurship was originally related to the way technological advances and cultural awareness allowed new ventures to access untapped foreign markets (Morrow, 1988; McDougall, & Oviatt, 2000). It comprises novel and innovative activities that cross borders with the aim of creating value and growth in business firms. As such, international entrepreneurship refers to innovative activities pursued by a firm across borders. Innovative encompasses the value-seeking component, as firms leave their home country to seek out new opportunities in unknown or unexplored markets.

International entrepreneurship crosses three different academic disciplines, namely entrepreneurship, international business and strategic management (Wach & Whermann, 2014; Wach, 2015). Although related to IE, international business is quite unique as it focuses on internationalization theory, transaction cost theory, and economic factors leading to internationalization. The contrast between international entrepreneurship and entrepreneurship becomes evident as the latter focuses on the entrepreneur's role as an economic agent, who recognizes and exploits business opportunities. Finally, strategic management covers assets, capabilities, and business strategy employed when doing business abroad, and in this regard, deviates from the scope of international entrepreneurship (Wach, 2015). As such, one can consider that these three disciplines complement each other in the formation of the international entrepreneurship theory.

Based on the concept of international entrepreneurship, one can consider three types of firms that are usually associated to international entrepreneurship: born globals, international new ventures and innate exporters. They are going to be considered in this chapter.

Born Globals

Born globals are greatly emerging around the world. This phenomenon has challenged traditional views on internationalization, where international business has been dominated by large and endowed multinational companies (Madsen & Servais, 1997; Rialp, Rialp, Urbano, & Vaillant, 2005; Ribau et al., 2015; 2018).

Knight and Cavusgil (2004) define born globals as entrepreneurial start-ups that since their establishment seek to derive part of their revenue from product sales in international markets. As mentioned by Ribau et al. (2015), born globals are associated with a proactive and entrepreneurial stance towards internationalization.

Previous research on born globals have emphasized their strong external market orientation, based on a fast internationalization process with a strong competitive position from their very beginning.

The 'born global' label has been adopted as an appealing concept conveying the importance of such companies and the new paradigm they represent in the world economy (Rialp et al., 2005; Baronchelli & Cassia, 2014), where the traditional internationalization process based on Uppsala's model has been abandoned (Ribau et al., 2015). The rise of born globals foresees little or no distinction between markets and opportunities based on national limits. Therefore, it can be argued that the differences between nations have diminished in importance over time, as entrepreneurs are preferably focused on differences in business contexts, usually in terms of culture, political systems and economic conditions. In this sense, it can be said that the concept of international business has been becoming less important and has been replaced by a new concept: *intercontextual business* (Knight & Liesch, 2015).

Many authors have investigated the factors leading new companies to follow the path of a born global. In particular, the following factors have been mentioned: increasing uncertainty and dynamism in the company's environment, which allows the companies to develop international competitive capabilities faster (Oviatt & McDougall, 1999); features of the domestic market (Madsen & Servais, 1997), which allows the companies to satisfy national and international demanding markets; features of the industry, given the fact that the economic situation interferes in the company's success in the internationalization process (Freeman & Cavusgil, 2007); experience of entrepreneurs and managers in foreign markets, being a differentiating factor in international environments (Oviatt & McDougall, 1994); product and company innovation, which allows the companies to adapt their products and services to several international markets (Knight & Cavusgil, 2004) and to gain access to networks, mainly those which might be capable of driving the organization's globalization/ internationalization (Madsen & Servais, 1997).

Smaller companies seem to be more creative, innovative, flexible and fast at meeting the specific needs of customers from both international and domestic markets due to their simple and non-bureaucratic organizational structure (Knight 2001; Oviatt & McDougall, 1994). These companies have been defined in the literature through the use of three concepts: 'Born Globals', 'International new ventures' and 'Innate Exporters'.

The term born global was coined in a research carried out by the Australian Manufacturing Council (Rennie, 1993). This study clearly showed that there are two types of exporters. The first type, including approximately 75% of the companies, is comprised of companies well established in the local market, with good expertise, as well as a solid financial situation and product portfolio. The second group, called born global companies, begins exporting on average within two years following their establishment, totaling 76% of sales from exports (Baronchelli & Cassia, 2014).

According to Oviatt and McDougall (1994), International New Ventures (INVs) are referred to as organizations that, from inception, seek to derive significant competitive advantage from the use of resources and the sale of outputs in multiple countries.

Lastly, 'innate exporters' are defined by Ganitsky (1989) as companies with an innate know-how in international markets thanks to their international outlook in the management, having a high degree of flexibility, but limited range due to their inexperience and lack of resources.

Ganitsky (1989) differentiates innate exporters from adoptive exporters as the former tend to enter markets or fields not explored earlier by other exporters whereas the later tend to create an internal market based on their added-value capabilities to achieve economies of scale and then to develop a global perspective.

International New Ventures

According to Oviatt and McDougall (1994), INVs are organizations that, from inception, seek to derive significant competitive advantage from the sale of their products/services in multiple countries. The distinctive feature of such companies is their international origin, as shown by the significant and observable commitments of resources (e.g., materials, people, financing, time) in more than one nation. Like BGs, INVs benefit from a widely entrepreneurial outlook in order to keep their internationalization process at an early stage (Oviatt & McDougall, 1994). In contrast to the organizations gradually evolving from national to multinational companies, international new ventures start off with a proactive international strategy, but without external assets. However, strategic alliances may be developed for the use of external resources, such as the production or marketing capacity (Coviello, 2015). Although INVs have initially been introduced as very proactive start-ups, nowadays they are considered by other companies to be indistinguishable from BGs (Weerawardena, Mort, Liesch, & Knight, 2007; Zander, McDougall-Covin, & Rose, 2015). According to Oviatt and McDougall (1994), there are several types of INVs: geographically focused start-ups, global start-ups, import/export start-ups and multinational traders.

Geographically focused start-ups primarily serve the specialized needs of a specific region of the world by using external resources. The competitive advantage is in the coordination of the various value chain activities, such as technological development, human resources and production (Oviatt & McDougall, 1994).

The Global Start-up reflects the more radical manifestation of the new international entrepreneurship, since it derives from the significant competitive advantage of the coordination of several organizational activities. Global start-ups not only respond to market globalization, but also act proactively on opportunities to acquire resources (Oviatt & McDougall, 1994).

Import/export start-ups aim at serving certain nations with which the entrepreneur is familiar. Multinational traders serve a range of countries and are constantly seeking trading opportunities where their networks are established or where they can quickly be incorporated (Oviatt & McDougall, 1994).

There is clearly a wide variety of behaviors that INVs might have. Moreover, if we consider that some authors do not make a distinction between INVs and BGs, the combination could include small start-ups firms as well as large trading companies (Cesinger, Danko, & Bouncken, 2012).

Features of Born Globals

Born globals have a number of features, of which the following are worth mentioning:

- International activity right after their establishment (Tanev, 2012). According to Oviatt and McDougall (1994), born globals begin their internationalization from inception or within the first two years. This type of behavior is more prevalent among SMEs that are highly specialized in national and global market 'niches' (Oviatt & McDougall, 1994);
- Limited financial resources (Tanev, 2012). Born globals tend to be relatively small and have less financial, human and tangible resources when compared with large multinational companies dominating global trade (Tanev, 2012);
- They are present in most sectors, however, the large majority operates in the technology sector (Tanev, 2012). Nevertheless, Madsen and Servais (1997) state that start-ups operating in the metal, furniture and food sector have been found in Denmark;
- Managers have a strong international outlook and focus (Tanev, 2012). According to Cavusgil and Knight (2009), born globals' managers do not see foreign markets as a mere addition to their domestic markets. According to the authors, the former have a strong and proactive business mindset arising from technological processes inherent to their creation;

- They follow a differentiated strategy (Tanev, 2012). Born globals tend to adopt differentiated strategies through the development of highly distinctive projects and products aimed at market niches, which may be too small for the preferences of large companies (Tanev, 2012);
- Superior quality products (Tanev, 2012). Born globals explore business opportunities based on the development of new products or services with greater quality and outreach than competitors' offerings (Cavusgil & Knight, 2009);
- Use of advanced Information and Communication Technologies (ICT) (Tanev, 2012). This type of company uses advanced ICT techniques in order to reach customers from global market niches and meet the needs of highly specialized buyers (Cavusgil & Knight, 2009);
- Use of external intermediaries for distribution in international markets (Tanev, 2012). Most BGs tend to expand internationally through exports, international sales involvement or by taking advantage of the resources from independent intermediaries located abroad (Cavusgil & Knight, 2009).

Inherent Stages to the Internationalization Process of Born Globals

According to Gabrielsson et al (2008), born globals are included in a process involving three stages. Stage 1 is the introduction and the early launch stage. Stage 2 is the accumulation of resources and growth, and the last stage is defined as the break-out stage.

In the introduction stage, born globals have limited resources and an underdeveloped organizational structure. Their main resources are the founder(s) and other creative individuals. However, a successful fast-paced internationalization requires a level of international business specialization and financing that such entrepreneurs rarely have. In this stage, growth is highly dependent on the strategy of the chosen channel and the network approach. If BGs intend to collaborate with a multinational company (MNEs), they can achieve a fast growth from the beginning. Conversely, if they decide to work on their own channels and/or networks, it is more likely that the generation of a higher demand takes longer (Gabrielsson et al., 2008).

According to Gabrielsson et al. (2008), in the stage of growth and accumulation of resources, a born global shall often find itself in a global or potentially global industry, i.e. with a large interdependence between markets and a relatively limited number of intervening parties that take advantage of this interdependence.

In order to overcome its resource shortages, the company needs to place itself in relevant channels. However, direct competition is unlikely to be a threat, since BGs offer new products and services not yet in the market. Thus, success in this stage is strongly dependent on the products/services themselves and the organizational capacity to place them on the market.

In this second stage, organizational learning is highly dependent on the ability to learn from early partners and customers with whom the born global cooperates (Gabrielsson et al., 2008).

The third stage, break-out, describes the period in which BGs adopt a strategy based on previously acquired knowledge and experience in order to establish their position in the market and in their network of contacts. The strategic reorientation is influenced by the willingness to be independent from the market and the control of company's own activities. In this stage, born globals continuously develop and grow for future growth (Gabrielsson et al., 2008).

Key Success Factors of Born Globals

Karra, Philips, and Tracey (2004) state that the performance and attitudes of entrepreneurs towards globalization positively affect the increased success of born globals, in particular due to the ability of identifying and creating market opportunities capable of benefitting the business.

Evers (2011) divides the factors for the success of these companies into two groups: attributes of the entrepreneur and attributes of the company. The attributes of the company concern the required focus on product differentiation, the identification of the target audience segments at a global level and the maintenance of close relationships with international customers. Regarding the attributes of the entrepreneur, emphasis is given to objective skills (experience, market knowledge) and subjective skills, such as having a proactive personality and a global mindset (Danik & Kowalik, 2015).

Obstacles to the Development of Born Globals

According to the literature, BGs face several obstacles when preparing to begin their internationalization process. The main obstacles in the export process are associated with market, business and political risks. The main market risks involve the distance between markets, the competition, the differences in the use, specifications and distribution of the product and the complexity in the distribution services. Business risks reflect the problems regarding exchange rate fluctuations, delays in payments, bankruptcies, rejection of the product, delays and damages during export and difficulties in obtaining financing for export. The primary factors included in the political risks are the tariffs and restrictions imposed by foreign governments, the lack of governmental assistance, the high prices in local currency, the regulation of imports, the complexity of the documentation and political turmoil. There are also obstacles determined in the beginning of export, related to insufficient financial resources, insufficient market knowledge and the lack of management commitment (Danik & Kowalik, 2015).

Innate and Adoptive Exporters

Although Ganistsky (1989) puts forward two main types of exporters – innate and adoptive –, he clearly claims that innate exporters can behave as entrepreneurs, when exporters pioneers their way in international markets in order to exploit their resources and capabilities abroad, and imitators, when exporters tend to be more through in order to reduce risks abroad imitating other explorers.

In their quest of foreign markets innate explores tend to be focused on foreign markets in order to properly respond to challenges from abroad. Doing so allows innate exporters to develop competitive strategies to adapt their products to foreign markets. Their growth stem from the clear separation of indigenous and foreign markets. In a different vein, adoptive exporters tend to be much more ethnocentric and committed to the domestic market opportunities and thus perceive export opportunities as marginally important, which may lead them to ignore all the necessary adjustments that need to be introduced product-wise to succeed in international markets.

Innate and adoptive exporters, according to their objectives, strategies, and competitive posture can behave as 'nichers', 'high performers', 'challengers' and 'leaders' (Ganitsky, 1989).

CASE STUDY

The aim of this section is to present the case study of ALPHA[1] explaining its history, as well as its international business history.

The present case study was based on a qualitative methodology, involving the collection of data through an unstructured interview with ALPHA's chief executive officer. The information obtained was complemented with secondary information.

The methodological research is dedicated to researching the instruments, paths or ways of doing science, to the production of techniques of dealing with reality or to the discussion of theoretical-practical approaches (Demo, 1995). Qualitative research is not concerned with the numerical representativity of a study in question, but rather with the deepening of the understanding of a social group, an organization, or a specific situation. Researchers who use qualitative methods seek to explain the reasons for things, expressing what should be done, but do not quantify symbolic values and exchanges, or submit to evidence of fact, since the data analyzed are nonmetric and reflect different approaches (Gerhardt & Silveira, 2009; Villareal, 2017).

The case study is one of several techniques used in social science research. Other techniques include experiments, questionnaires, stories, and archival analysis. The case study is preferable when one intends to examine contemporary events, but only when the relevant behaviors of the case cannot be manipulated. This qualitative technique adds two sources of evidence that are not usually included in the historian's repertoire: observation and systematic interviews (Yin, 2014).

In-depth studies, as the one reported in this chapter, rather that attempting to test hypotheses aims at identifying the main driving forces behind ALPHA's internationalization, its initial export involvement and commitment, its current internationalization process and its future internationalization hurdles, so that one can finally confront ALPHA's evolutionary process with existing theory on entrepreneurship internationalization.

A case study can often be used to answer an explanatory and exploratory (or descriptive) purpose (Maxwell, 1996). Yin (2014) points out that the questions "How?" and "Why?" are directed with a more explanatory sense and therefore more appropriate for research strategies such as case studies, histories and experiences. Yin (2014) mentions that this is due to the fact that such issues deal with operational links that need to be tracked over time. Therefore, following Maxwell's (1996) and Yin's (2014) reasoning, case studies, such as experiments, are replicable to theoretical propositions rather than to populations or universes. In this sense, the case study does not represent a sample and the objective of the researchers is to expand and generalize theories (analytical generalization) and not to enumerate frequencies (statistical generalization).

A considerable range of qualitative approaches use structured and semi-structured interviews (Edwards & Holland, 2013). In this particular case, the use of an unstructured interview provides a greater range of analysis than other interview types, given its qualitative nature, and the purpose of the unstructured interview is the understanding of the situation (Fontana & Frey, 1994).

In unstructured interviews the researcher clearly has research objectives and a topic of study, but the importance of the method is to allow the interviewee to speak through their own perspective, using their own frame of references, ideas and meanings that are familiar to the interviewee (Edwards & Holland, 2013).

Genesis and Evolution of ALPHA

Established early in the second half of 2015, as an urgent response to the employability of one of the company's partners, with higher education in teaching, the company started off by producing homemade pastry, and its name derives from the word

"Tart". At the same time, considering it is a regional product with plenty of tradition amongst the families of the Beira-Mar neighborhood in Aveiro, some bottles of the traditional liqueur of such region have been produced, and this product has evolved from a qualitative standpoint in all experiments performed, thereby becoming the sole product marketed by the company in the first year. This specialization has proved to be an excellent strategy for the entry in the international and domestic market; the company has developed a clear mastery of the production process and product quality, which translated into trust from its customers/consumers. The main characteristics of ALPHA are shown in Table 1.

From Bowl Liqueur ["Licor de Alguidar"] to "Aveiro Liqueur"

The first bottles of 'Licor de Alguidar' were produced in 2015 and marketed under this brand/label with the permanent reference to the product's originating region (traditionally called this way because it was produced in traditional "bowls" from the Aveiro region throughout generations), and the labels showed the symbols of salt fields and *moliceiros* [traditional boats from the Aveiro region]. In the several contacts the company held and interviews it gave to the media, it had the opportunity to mention that the need of giving up the traditional name arose due to it easily being associated with poor hygiene, and so it adopted the brand "Aveiro liqueur" in 2016.

Bryla (2015) mentions that demanding customers with purchasing power are increasingly seeking origin, flavor and other features of the product that are often assigned to the specific origin or production method. Goodman (2003) states that a "qualitative change" can be observed in the economy from the "industrial world", which sets out conventional and highly-standardized quality references in the mass production approach, to the "domestic world" (small scale), in which the quality policy includes concepts such as trust and tradition by giving support to more differentiated, localized and environmentally-friendly products and forms of economic

Table 1. Summary of the characterization of ALPHA

Data of Inception	July of 2015
Economic Activity Code	11013 – Production of liqueurs and other distilled beverages 47112 – Retail sale in non-specialized (food, beverages or tobacco) stores 46341 – Wholesale of alcoholic beverages
Sales Volume	Year 1 $\leq$ 30.000 € Year 2 $\geq$ 300.000 €
Type of Products	Tangerine, mint and strawberry flavored spirits. Liqueur.
Exports (%)	90%
Main Markets	Asia, Africa, and Europe

organization. In fact, the demand for homemade, traditional and local products, whose production processes are well-known, conveys quality and authenticity assurance when the product is purchased. The change of the brand from 'Licor de Alguidar' to 'Aveiro Liqueur' proves the company intended to give the product such attributes, by conveying to the consumer an unequivocal experience of tasting a homemade, traditional, locally-produced product that is firmly established due to its uniqueness and authenticity.

Since the Aveiro region is attractive in terms of different types of tourism, the company clearly aimed at not disaggregating the natural and expectant impact of the "Aveiro" brand associated with a marketable product. Sims (2009) mentions that local food specialities help conveying a sense of authenticity and singularity in the holiday destination and strengthen the external image of the region and of the region's brand (Boyne & Hall 2004). Aldereghi et al. (2016) further argue that, since local food specialities evoke the identity, culture and sustainability of the place of origin, the company aimed to explicitly and implicitly explore such features that are significant upon design of the marketing strategy of the local and regional tourist destinations. Aldereghi et al. (2016) state that local food products have become marketing and branding tools for promoting tourism in recent years due to the key role they play in the local tourist economies. From the different abovementioned authors' views, one can stress the importance of the change of the brand from 'Licor de Alguidar' to 'Aveiro Liqueur', since it contributed positively to the company's marketing strategy, both in terms of entry into local and national market, and the approach towards the international market that shall be analyzed hereinafter. Regarding the existing and inseparable connection of the experience of local product consumption in tourist destinations, Aldereghi et al. (2016) state that the persons who already went on holidays to a tourist destination and had the opportunity to continue consuming the same products where they live in, can not only keep the interest on such destination alive, but also keep consuming the products where they live in.

The Product

As previously mentioned, the product produced and marketed by the company is a spirit drink with three traditional flavors: mint, strawberry and tangerine. It is available in 500ml and 50ml bottles, ensuring leak-proof design and preservation, as well as an easy handling and transportation of the final product. According to the company, the selection process for the larger bottle has been lengthy and thorough, having performed experiments with several references from suppliers and bottle shapes; the chosen reference provides better handling and preservation conditions and is visually more appealing. It was important to have a container accentuating the fact that it is a colorful drink. The company developed a box of chocolates filled with the Aveiro Liqueur on the occasion of Christmas 2016, which was high in demand. The company deems the experience as extremely positive as it tried to diversify the existing product, where the liqueur remained the main element, and by taking advantage of the seasonal opportunity of demand for products with such features. It will certainly be a product to be perfected and invested in the future.

The product is produced artisanally and based on traditional techniques that make it unique. It is positioned in the market, nationally and internationally as colorful, flavor-based spirituous drink bottled in 50 ml bottles. ALPHA originally targeted this liqueur for a niche market, although in 2016 it has extended product line to chocolates containing Aveiro liqueur.

The product principles rest on a strong concentration on product quality, based on ALPHA's production special competences.

Mission and Values

Without false modesty, the company has asserted itself in the market through its website, with the mission of "*Being a reference company in the production of spirit drinks and combining the art of production with the city's history, which creates the Aveiro Liqueur.*" It evokes the principles and values of a family company, in line with the knowledge, production and qualitative mastery of the marketed product. The company intends to establish itself in the market as a reference in the trade of spirit drinks, based on the following values: ethics, honesty, excellence, commitment, innovation and respect.

Promotion in Fairs, Events and Participation in International Competitions

Although this is a young two-year-old company, it has already won four medals (two gold, one silver and one bronze) in the following international competitions: ProdExpo 2016 and the China Wine & Spirits Awards 2016. The company immediately recognized the importance of customers tasting the product so that the customer can come in contact with the product and, since then, it has sought to be represented in several international events in different ways, which allows the company to communicate with stakeholders, foster new relationships and maintain those already established. This company joined the seal "Portugal sou Eu" ["I am Portugal"], having participated in several national fairs, and is looking forward to promoting the company in external markets. It further intends to submit a "Portugal 2020" co-financing project for internationalization measures within the foreseeable future.

Internationalization Strategy

As referred to above, the company has strong dynamics regarding internationalization measures, as well as an approach to the different international markets. When questioned about the export share of each country, the answer is clear and concise: we are experiencing a vast growth stage in several international fronts. Considering the product is highly differentiated, "*we intend to keep investing in the Asian and African market and simultaneously invest in the European market*". With this investment, the company is able to explore specific niches in several markets where differentiation is widespread, such as the Asian market – through refinement – and the African market – countries where sophistication makes the difference. In turn, the European market is difficult due to the high level of competition, and so the differentiated positioning based on uniqueness and refinement may increase the rate of penetration into such markets. The market share of European countries stems from low investment carried out hitherto. The experience of tourists visiting the Aveiro region tasting and purchasing the liqueur is regarded as an extremely positive element in this activity in the European market, despite being insufficient. However, it should be noted that the profits from sales in national territory, particularly in the Aveiro region, represent a positive input for the possibility of entry into the European market, and the company keeps investing in the innovation of presenting the product locally and in the retail channel.

It is clear that ALPHA's success in the international market in a narrow segment was tuned with its search for market share in international markets, as ALPHA was competing in a specific market niche.

In this market entry stage ALPHA had as main objectives survival in the short term, searching a defensive foothold, in international markets.

In the second year ALPHA was flexible enough as to create a new product range, but looking to expand in its domestic market in order not to depend from foreign markets, reducing commercial risks.

DISCUSSION

Being a newly created company, ALPHA reveals some ingenuity in the business approach since it is a family business with a manager with no previous experience in the field – with previous training in the area of education and previous experience was being a high-school teacher. On the other hand, ALPHA was able to identify opportunities in international markets, based on the quality of its products, exploring an unusual market niche: aromatized spirits.

The company bases its production on craft technology, which in the short term could create problems if demand for the product continues to increase at the same pace it has been growing. However, faced with this situation, ALPHA retains its vision and clear strategies. The manager knows that in order to continue conquering market share, he should concentrate all his energies on the quality of his product and on international dissemination through international fairs and liqueur competitions, but he knows that the great challenge of growth may be to opt for less artisanal and more industrialized production methodologies. To this end, the resizing of ALPHA's structure is a priority, seeking to respond to existing and future demand, guaranteeing the quality of the product to the final customer. He also humbly assumes the need to seek / hire specialists in the most diverse organizational areas that make possible ALPHA's sustainable development.

The biggest obstacles to the internationalization of the company are related to the tax on alcohol and alcoholic beverages (as part of special consumption taxes), due to the limitation imposed on the margin of the company. Moreover, taking into account the international policy of controlling alcohol consumption, through the increase of alcoholic beverages taxes, ALPHA is well positioned as a premium drink company and should seek to take advantage of the already achieved markets by seeking to implement strategies to penetrate these international markets to increase its international market share, without abandoning its strategy of diversification of international markets, in order to complement already conquered markets.

Clearly, the company has been in full growth since its inception. The presence in the social networks is very active and dynamic as well as the partnerships with all the tourist agents of the region. The main characteristics of the company are presented in Table 2.

If the theory on international entrepreneurship is relatively vast, one can argue that there are three main typologies that can be put forward to categorize ALPHA as it is characterized by an instant instead of rapid internationalization: BGs, INVs or innate exporters.

If ALPHA is certainly an international as well as a new venture it would be easy to define ALPHA as an INV according to Oviatt and McDougall (2005: 49) "*a business organization that, from inception, seeks to derive significative advantage from the use and the sale of outputs in multiple countries*." However, taking into account that the characteristics of BGs referred above (Tanev, 2012; Cavusgil & Knight, 2009; Madsen & Servais, 1997), one can claim that ALPHA can be considered a Born Global firms as it fulfills the following characteristics:

- International activity right after their establishment;
- Limited financial resources;
- Manager with a strong international outlook and focus;

Table 2. Objective, strategies, key success factors and main competitive guidelines

Objectives	Initially: survival, defensive positioning, short-term profitability
Product Strategy	Product specialization. In the second year diversifies to a non-core product.
Market Strategy	Concentration in a market niche. In the second year ALPHA not only diversifies, but also seeks to expand to the domestic market seeking to reduce commercial risk.
Managerial Skill	Creativity and flexibility.
Competitive Positioning	Secure market niches. Concentrate on product quality, seek market growth and avoid head on strategies. In the second year, it seeks not to ignore low-growth market, but positioning in high-segment markets.
Key Success Factors	New interesting product. Unexploited market niche. Credible international image based on international fairs and liqueur events. Nimble and eager to succeed.
International Profile	Born Global
Mode of Entry in International Markets	International Trade Fairs and Competitions: ProdExpo 2016 (Gold Medal for Tangerine Liqueur and Silver Medal for Mint Liqueur) and China Wine & Spirits Awards 2016 (Gold Medal for Tangerine Liqueur and Bronze Medal for Mint Liqueur)
Characteristics of Entrepreneurial Behavior	Young, innovative, dynamic and enterprising company. Diversification is a deliberate strategy since the beginning of the activity without implying the loss of identity and uniqueness of the brand. Exploitation of authenticity in the Portuguese market. Exploitation of international markets with unique products. Exploitation of prizes won at international fairs leveraging brand awareness in international markets.
Innovation	The company seeks to exploit the authenticity in introducing scents /flavors into the liqueur, giving a different positioning to the product. The artisanal character and the young image of the company and the product are important in order to modify the way the product is seen by the consumers.
Risk Taking Behavior	The entrepreneur took the risk of entering a saturated market, as is the market for alcoholic beverages, assuming a different positioning and creating a unique brand image based on leverage gained in international fairs and exhibitions.
Factors That Strengthen Internationalization Commitment	The values of the company, based on moral values taking into account that it is a family business, as well as the pro-activity of the partners in international promotional programs such as "Portugal sou Eu" of which they have been adhering company since 2016. Above all, the awareness that both business and institutional partnerships strengthen the company and galvanize the approaches to certain markets since the requirements from the legal point of view may sometimes prove to be an obstacle to the negotiation and transaction.
Future Outlook of Internationalization	The continuous exploration of the Asian and African market, as well as investing in the European market which represents a small percentage of the company's exports

- A clear differentiated product and strategy;
- Superior quality products;
- Use of external intermediaries for distribution in international markets.

As ALPHA follows a specialized product market that seeks to explore a defensible international market niche, based on the quality of its products and reputable image gained in international liqueur contests, one can claim that ALPHA can be considered an innate exporter.

Although Ganitsky (1989) explores the concept of innate exporters, which he depicts in four different types of companies (nichers, high performers, challengers and leaders), it is plausible to include innate exporters in the Born global category, as BGs are based on the concept of rapid internationalization. Taking into account ALPHA's behavior, and the international entrepreneurship theory, one can claim that based on its rapidly internationalization process and on its international market orientation, it behaves as a BG / INV. Based on its clear focus on exports and as it is not a technology-based company on can defend that it is a Born Global company rather than an INV, although many authors use the concepts indistinctively.

CONCLUSION

In the literature review section regarding Born Globals, it was referred that one of the characteristics of these companies is that in the future it is expected that entrepreneurs will make no differentiation between the national market and the international market. Although conditioned by individual and market-specific characteristics and consumption profiles, it is expected that market presence ceases to exist on the basis of the national/international business concept as the intercontextual business concept is more stringent, given the prevalence of alcoholic beverages market specificities. It is also mentioned the ease that small companies have in responding to the demands of the international market for their simple organization and bureaucratic absence, as well as innovative capacity. While ALPHA has responded positively at an early stage, there is a pressing need to look to the future growth of the company.

ALPHA can be considered as having a Born Global profile, translated both in its internationalization path and in its sales volumes that point to a clear prominence of the international market. Nevertheless, the national market, especially the local market, has been strongly targeted through the communication, promotion and diversification of its products. For the company it is important to maintain its identity and specificity, presenting a traditional artisanal production that results in a final product that aggregates history and commercial potential. Being a newly created company, it presents a real growth, in the second year, twenty times higher than the first year and 90% of its sales volume corresponds to the foreign market. These data, as part of the interview conducted with the literature review, allow us to consider that ALPHA is in the "introduction and the early launch stage", but is ready to embrace "the accumulation of resources and growth", and its strategy and attitude reveals the success factors of most Born Globals (differentiation of the product, identification of the segments of the target audience at a global level and maintaining close relations with international clients) as well as the attributes of the entrepreneur (proactive personality and a global mentality).

FUTURE RESEARCH DIRECTIONS

Although research on internationalization is quite reach, it would be interesting to analyze pre-internationalization behavior to depict the possible causes that foster and hinder the internationalization process among many small and medium-sized Born Globals.

It was clear that ALPHA wanted to embark in an international, global perspective. However, it is not clear how the manager spotted the opportunity of launching the Aveiro Liqueur following an outward looking perspective. This opens up new opportunities for research as it would be of added value to analyze how managers' behavior might generate proactive internationalization behavior, which might explain why some firms suddenly embrace born global behaviors.

REFERENCES

Alderighi, M., Bianchi, C., & Lorenzini, E. (2016). The impact of local food specialities on the decision to (re)visit a tourist destination: Market-expanding or business-stealing? *Tourism Management, 57*, 323–333. doi:10.1016/j.tourman.2016.06.016

Anderson, P., & Gordon, R. (2011). Science and alcohol policy: A case study of the EU strategy on alcohol. *Addiction (Abingdon, England), 106*(1), 55–66. PMID:21324022

Baronchelli, G., & Cassia, F. (2014). Exploring the antecedents of born-global companies' international development. *The International Entrepreneurship and Management Journal, 10*(1), 67–79. doi:10.100711365-011-0197-9

Bell, J., McNaughton, R., & Young, S. (2001). Born-again global' firms: An extension to the 'born global' phenomenon. *Journal of International Management*, *7*(3), 173–189. doi:10.1016/S1075-4253(01)00043-6

Boyne, S., & Hall, D. (2004). Place promotion through food and tourism: Rural branding and the role of websites. *Place Branding*, *1*(1), 80–92. doi:10.1057/palgrave.pb.5990007

Bryla, P. (2015). The role of appeals to tradition in origin food marketing. A survey among Polish consumers. *Appetite*, *91*(1), 302–310. doi:10.1016/j.appet.2015.04.056 PMID:25916623

Cavusgil, S. T., & Knight, G. (2009). *Born global firms: A new international enterprise*. New York: Business Expert Press. doi:10.4128/9781606490136

Cesinger, B., Danko, A., & Bouncken, R. (2012). Born globals: (almost) 20 years of research and still not 'grown up'? *International Journal of Entrepreneurship and Small Business*, *15*(2), 171–190. doi:10.1504/IJESB.2012.045203

Coviello, N. (2015). Re-thinking research on born globals. *Journal of International Business Studies*, *46*(1), 17–26. doi:10.1057/jibs.2014.59

Danik, L., & Kowalik, I. (2015). Success factors and development barriers perceived by the Polish born global companies. Empirical study results. *Journal for East European Management Studies*, *20*(3), 360–390. doi:10.5771/0949-6181-2015-3-360

Demo, P. (1995). *Metodologia Científica em Ciências Sociais*. São Paulo: Editora Atlas.

Edwards, R., & Holland, J. (2013). *What is Qualitative Interviewing*? New York: Bloombury.

Evers, N. (2011). International new ventures in "low tech" sectors: A dynamic capabilities perspective. *Journal of Small Business and Enterprise Development*, *18*(3), 502–528. doi:10.1108/14626001111155682

Fontana, A., & Frey, J. H. (1994). Interviewing: The art of science. In N. K. Denzin & Y. S. Lincoln (Eds.), *Handbook of Qualitative Research* (pp. 361–376). Thousand Oaks, CA: Sage Publications.

Freeman, S., & Cavusgil, S. T. (2007). Toward a typology of commitment states among managers of born-global firms: A study of accelerated internationalization. *Journal of International Marketing*, *15*(4), 1–40. doi:10.1509/jimk.15.4.1

Gabrielsson, M., Kirpalani, V., Dimitratos, P., Solberg, C., & Zucchella, A. (2008). Born globals: Propositions to help advance the theory. *International Business Review*, *17*(4), 385–401. doi:10.1016/j.ibusrev.2008.02.015

Ganitsky, J. (1989). Strategies for innate and adoptive exporters: Lessons from Israel's case. *International Marketing Review*, *6*(5), 50–65. doi:10.1108/EUM0000000001523

Gerhardt, T., & Silveira, D. (2009). *Métodos de Pesquisa*. Porto Alegre: Editora da UFRGS.

Goodman, D. (2003). The quality 'turn' and alternative food practices: Reflections and agenda. *Journal of Rural Studies*, *19*(1), 1–7. doi:10.1016/S0743-0167(02)00043-8

Karra, N., Philips, N., & Tracey, P. (2008). Building the born global firm developing entrepreneurial capabilities for international new venture success. *Long Range Planning*, *41*(4), 440–459. doi:10.1016/j.lrp.2008.05.002

Knight, G. (2001). Entrepreneurship and strategy in the international SME. *Journal of International Management*, *7*(3), 155–171. doi:10.1016/S1075-4253(01)00042-4

Knight, G. A., & Cavusgil, S. T. (2004). Innovation, organizational capabilities, and the born-global firm. *Journal of International Business Studies*, *35*(2), 124–141. doi:10.1057/palgrave.jibs.8400071

Knight, G. A., & Liesch, P. W. (2015). Internationalization: From incremental to born global. *Journal of World Business*, *51*(1), 93–102. doi:10.1016/j.jwb.2015.08.011

Madsen, T. K., & Servais, P. (1997). The internationalization of born globals: An evolutionary process? *International Business Review*, *6*(6), 561–583. doi:10.1016/S0969-5931(97)00032-2

Maxwell, J. A. (1996). *Qualitative Research Design: An Interactive Approach*. London: Sage.

McDougall, P. P., & Oviatt, B. M. (2000). International entrepreneurship: The intersection of two research paths. *Academy of Management Journal*, *43*, 902–908.

Morrow, J. F. (1988). International entrepreneurship: A new growth opportunity. *Nursing Management*, *3*, 59–61.

Oviatt, B. M., & McDougall, P. P. (1994). Toward a theory of international new ventures. *Journal of International Business Studies*, *25*(1), 45–64. doi:10.1057/palgrave.jibs.8490193

Oviatt, B. M., & McDougall, P. P. (1999). A framework for understanding accelerated international entrepreneurship. In A. M. Rugman & R. W. Wright (Eds.), *Research in global strategic management: International entrepreneurship* (pp. 23–40). Stamford, CT: JAI Press. doi:10.1016/S1064-4857(99)07055-2

Rennie, M. (2016). Born global. *The McKinsey Quarterly*, *4*, 45–52.

Rialp, A., Rialp, J., Urbano, D., & Vaillant, J. (2005). The Born-global phenomenon: A comparative case study research. *Journal of International Entrepreneurship*, *3*(2), 133–171. doi:10.100710843-005-4202-7

Ribau, C. P., Moreira, A. C., & Raposo, M. (2015). Internationalisation of the firm theories: A shematic synthesis. *International Journal of Business and Globalisation*, *15*(4), 528–554. doi:10.1504/IJBG.2015.072535

Ribau, C. P., Moreira, A. C., & Raposo, M. (2018). SME internationalization research: Mapping the state of the art. *Canadian Journal of Administrative Sciences*, *35*(2), 280–303. doi:10.1002/cjas.1419

Sims, R. (2009). Food, place and authenticity: Local food and the sustainable tourism experience. *Journal of Sustainable Tourism*, *17*(3), 321–336. doi:10.1080/09669580802359293

Stanisauskaite, V., & Kock, S. (2016). The dynamic development of international entrepreneurial networks. In H. Etemad, S. Denicolai, B. Hagen, & A. Zucchella (Eds.), *The changing global economy and its impact on international entrepreneurship* (pp. 119–135). Cheltenham, UK: Edward Elgar. doi:10.4337/9781783479849.00012

Tanev, S. (2012). Global from the start: The characteristics of born-global firms in the technology sector. *Technology Innovation Management Review*, *2*(3), 5–8. doi:10.22215/timreview/532

Villareal, O. (2017). Is it desirable, necessary and possible to perform research using case studies? *Cuadernos de Gestión*, *17*(1), 147–172. doi:10.5295/cdg.140516ov

Wach, K. (2015). Entrepreneurial orientation and business internationalisation process: The theoretical foundations of international entrepreneurship. *Entrepreneurial Business and Economics Review*, *3*(2), 9–24. doi:10.15678/EBER.2015.030202

Wach, K., & Wehrmann, C. (2014). Entrepreneurship in international business: International entrepreneurship as the intersection of two fields. In A. S. Gubik & K. Wach (Eds.), *International Entrepreneurship and Corporate Growth in Visegrad Countries* (pp. 9–22). Miskolc: University of Miskolc.

Weerawardena, J., Mort, G. S., Liesch, P. W., & Knight, G. (2007). Conceptualizing accelerated internationalization in the born global firm: A dynamic capabilities perspective. *Journal of World Business*, *42*(3), 294–306. doi:10.1016/j.jwb.2007.04.004

Yin, R. (2014). *Case Study Research. Design and Methods*. London: Sage.

Zander, I., McDougall-Covin, P., & Rose, E. (2015). Born globals and international business: Evolution of a field of research. *Journal of International Business Studies*, *46*(1), 27–35. doi:10.1057/jibs.2014.60

KEY TERMS AND DEFINITIONS

Born Global: It is a type of company that, from its inception, seeks to derive a competitive advantage to compete in many countries. It normally pursues a vision of becoming global and globalizes rapidly without any preceding long term domestic or internationalization period or experience. Usually born globals are small, technology-oriented companies that operate in several international markets.

Case Study: It is a qualitative methodology, normally used in social sciences, that seeks to interpret a reality through a particular perspective. It is normally used to answer questions like "how" and "why." It is commonly used to addresses constructivist research processes.

Globalization: It is a worldwide movement toward economic, financial, trade, and communications integration. It is normally envisaged as a lack of trade barriers between nations, which are removed through free trade agreements throughout the world and between nation states. It implies the opening of local and nationalistic perspectives to a broader outlook of an interconnected and interdependent world with free transfer of capital, goods, and services across national frontiers, in which investment opportunities soar.

International Entrepreneurship: The term international entrepreneurship was originally related to the way technological advances and cultural awareness allowed new ventures to access untapped foreign markets. It comprises novel and innovative activities that crosses borders with the aim of creating value and growth in business firms. As such, it refers to innovative activities pursued by a firm across borders. Innovative encompasses the value-seeking component, as firms leave their home country to seek out new opportunities in unknown or unexplored markets.

Internationalization: It is the process of increasing involvement of enterprises in international markets. It involves a strategy carried out by firms that decide to compete in foreign markets. It involves cross border transactions of goods, services, or resources between two or more firms or organizations that belong to two different countries.

Internationalization Process: It involves the emphasis of a trajectory of a company in its transition from a national market to a particular foreign market. It normally involves several entry modes (exports, FDI, franchising, etc.) that exert a critical influence on the subsequent trajectory, as well as on cost related to the internationalization process. The two most important theories that explain the internationalization process are the Uppsala model and the network-based approach.

ENDNOTE

1 For confidentiality reasons ALPHA's real name cannot be disclosed.

Chapter 4
Female Entrepreneurship in Portugal:
Case Study for Micro-Companies in the Northern of Portugal

Maria Clara Ribeiro
Polytechnic of Porto, Portugal

Liliana Santos
Polytechnic of Porto, Portugal

Diana Martins
Catholic University of Porto, Portugal

ABSTRACT

Entrepreneurship is an increasingly studied international phenomenon, often being understood as a way of creating jobs and boosting economic growth, development, and innovation. This chapter aims to take on the problem related to gender and entrepreneurship in the Portuguese society. The goal is to explain the concept of entrepreneur, behavioral, and social differences between the masculine and the feminine gender as entrepreneurs and identify Portuguese female entrepreneurs. A qualitative, multiple case studies methodology is applied to the sample of eight Portuguese female entrepreneurs, the data collection instrument being the semi-structured interview. Regarding the obtained results, it can be stated that the majority of the interviewees has entrepreneurs in the family, the father being the most mentioned figure as booster of entrepreneur activity. The wish for personal realization and independence are the main factors that motivated self-employment. No entrepreneur felt any discrimination or gender inequality as a female entrepreneur.

DOI: 10.4018/978-1-5225-6942-8.ch004

INTRODUCTION

The tertiarization of the economies, the decentralization of the value chain on a global level and the introduction of new technologies have translated into a reduction of the number of workers and a rise in precarious, temporary and partial employment. Thus, aspects such as labour stability and lifelong employment have become less and less common to many individuals. A category of workers emerges, without labour stability and with a very precarious perspective towards the future, and who look for alternative ways to create employment and family subsistence.

Entrepreneurship is a rising professional category that arose as an alternative way of creating a job position and of social inclusion due to the large social inequalities that one sees in the job market.

In Portugal, there is a growing number of entrepreneurs who look to seize a business opportunity, hand in hand with those who became entrepreneurs because they could not find a better job opportunity (GEM, 2012).

Entrepreneurship has a very differentiated scope of interpretations, although there are some aspects which are common to all authors, connecting it to innovation or creation. According to Robbins (2001), entrepreneurship is a way for individuals to look for opportunities, organising the resources they need and, through innovation, open their own business, without fear of taking on their risks and possible rewards, satisfying their needs and wants.

The different concepts and definitions of entrepreneurship do not distinguish between gender, as entrepreneur features can be found in both men and women, although the first definitions are mainly directed at the masculine gender. However, literature on the gender influence on entrepreneurship supports that men are in bigger number at the beginning of activities (Langowitz & Minniti, 2007; McKay, Phillimore & Teasdale, 2010; Singer, Amoros & Moska, 2015; Themudo, 2009).

Studies demonstrated that there has been a growing increase in entrepreneur women in the last years. However, comparing men and women's participation in the job market is not an easy task. Murani (2003) claims that the growth of female participation in the working world is real, still holding, however, several issues and constraints connected to inequality and precariousness. Delors (1996) mentions that "inequalities are, in fact, at the root of the permanent inferiorities that weigh on women through their lives"; Eagly (1987) ran in accordance, pinpointing how difficult it is for women to have an entrepreneur activity and also be responsible for domestic chores, for raising children and for supporting the elderly.

Even today, women continue to be vulnerable to attitudes and behaviours of discrimination such as inequality in remuneration, difficulty on integrating or reintegrating into the job market, limited access to progression in their career and other resources. Although women have on average higher levels of qualification when compared to men, their condition in a job context is more precarious, often leading to the decision of creating their own job.

There are several studies that evaluate women's insertion on independent work, analysing their characteristics and potential consequences. Regarding psychological and behavioural features, entrepreneur women present a heavy desire for independence and realization. Some studies have demonstrated that women open companies because of their wish to feel fulfilled and independent, because they realise there are market opportunities, because of difficulties in career progression, because of the need of survival and as a way to conciliate work and family (Machado, St.-Cyr, Mione & Alves, 2003).

Entrepreneurship represents a new sector for female economic activity. There are now new markets and work perspectives offered for women to develop their enthusiasm, energy, abilities and competences. The flexibility associated with this type of work is an additional encouraging factor, especially for women that need this work flexibility in order to deal with their family responsibilities (Apergis & Economou, 2010).

It is proposed, in this work, to identify the main differences related to gender in the exercise of an entrepreneur activity in Portugal, and focus on female entrepreneurship in particular.

This work is divided into two parts. In the first, entrepreneurship regarding gender is approached, where we present the differences between genders in the access to entrepreneur activity and during it. Thus, some differentiating features and some inequalities between genders are highlighted, and some difficulties specific to the female gender when exercising entrepreneurial activity are identified. In the second one, the adopted methodological procedures are described: study model, identification of the interviewees, instruments, procedures in the collection and analysis of the data, finishing with the study's conclusions.

BACKGROUND

Entrepreneurship by Gender

For Freire, Corrêa and Ribeiro (2011), "Gender and entrepreneurship are two thematic areas that, contained in the human sciences, can be united into one that is permanent and of reciprocal conjugation, to demonstrate how gender relationships are inserted into the entrepreneurial context. Historically, the ways of undertaking in the job market, of living occupational experiences, challenging the administrative imaginary and articulate life at work are different for men and women".

The interest in knowing the intrinsic matters to an entrepreneur woman was triggered several years ago by a fair few authors. Gosselin and Grisé (1990) made a study called "Are entrepreneur women challenging our definitions of entrepreneurship?". This study counted with the collaboration of 400 female entrepreneurs who answered a questionnaire, exploring their own features as entrepreneurs, their previous experiences and their vision of their companies' future, among other matters. The authors concluded that, to women, the existence of a small and somewhat stable business model is extremely important. They also verified that women with a high degree of education did not recognise the entrepreneurial phase as something transitory in their lives and constantly looked for recognition for their work.

Moore and Buttner (1997) state that women do not measure success only through the financial results of their companies, but also the personal fulfilment accomplished by the employees' satisfaction. Afterwards, O'Meally (2000) looked to research the education, teachings and social values of the entrepreneur woman. He verified that, in the USA, women begin commercial activities twice as fast as their male counterparts.

Machado (1999), in his article "Tendencies of the management behaviour of the entrepreneur woman", studied the main management features adopted by entrepreneur women and concluded that women have a management tendency to: have set goals, keep a simple structure and maintain a strategic innovative behaviour. He also verified that female entrepreneurs have a management style of the cooperative and leadership sort, and that they lend a lot of importance to quality. The author concluded that entrepreneur women try to satisfy all contributors, as if they were taking care of people.

There are some more differences between the genders regarding the initial process of a business (Hisrich & Peters, 2004). Although both genders are interested and have some experience in their own business, men tend to begin a business related to their previous job or complementary to their branch of speciality. On the contrary, women abandon their previous occupation with a possible feeling of frustration and make it into a personal search, not just a professional one.

Regarding support groups, women identify their partner as the main source of support, followed by friends and, finally, those involved in the business. Men, on the other hand, identify as their first option external counsellors such as lawyers or accountants, and only then the partner. This kind of choice reveals that entrepreneur men put less confidence in family counselling than women.

The majority of female entrepreneurs is in the age group of 35 to 40 years old when they begin their entrepreneurial project, a little later than men. This can be linked to family and children.

New studies show that women do not tend to be as obsessive with their careers as men, because they have other equally important priorities. According to a study carried out by Guvenen, Kurusco and Ozkan (2009), among the workers with higher levels of education, women have lower wages because they work less hours and interrupt their careers more often due to their families.

According to data from Sebrae (2008), the reasons that took women to open their own business are: identification of a business opportunity (62.1%), previous experience (30.3%), or because they are unsatisfied with the company they worked in (13%). Thus, we can divide the reasons into three big groups: entrepreneurs by chance, forced or creative.

Jonathan (2005) characterises women entrepreneurs as fearless, self-confident and passionate, and as people who review themselves in their enterprises. The psychological and behavioural features more usually identified in entrepreneur women are the strong desire for independence and accomplishment, being innovative, persuasive, easily adaptable to change and believing that their future is a result of their actions (Peñaloza, Diógenes & Sousa, 2008).

The entrepreneurial character of women can also be influenced by the social context in which they live. Religious and cultural factors are directly related to the social construction of women's role in the societies they are inserted in (Bastian, Sidani & El Amine, 2018). It is therefore vital to understand that contextual inequalities have consequences in women's performances in society (Winkler & Medeiros, 2011).

The GEM (2007) project undertook an analysis of entrepreneurial motivation and revealed that there are sizable differences between the genders. Entrepreneurship means "opportunity that results from the desire to seize, by self-initiative, a possibility of business that exists in the market, through the creation of a company. On the other hand, entrepreneurship induced by need results from the absence of other opportunities of obtaining income (namely, dependent work) that makes individuals create a business, since they consider they have no better alternatives" (GEM, 2012).

Therefore, there is a higher percentage of men who begin a business to seize an opportunity than women. This difference of percentage is equally felt in countries of low, medium and high income where the analysis of the year of 2007 was made. However, regarding entrepreneurship motivated by need, there is not a significant difference between genders.

According to the GEM report (2012), in Portugal, 37.5% of early-stage entrepreneurs create their own company moved by the opportunity to increase their income and 20.8% are moved by the opportunity to reach independence, thus making up 58.3% of the entrepreneurs that begin their activity motivated by opportunity. The need is at the root of 26.2% of early-stage entrepreneurs and the junction of these two motives move 15.6% of entrepreneurs.

The results are similar for the remaining participant countries: the opportunity entrepreneurship prevails in the economies that are innovation-oriented (53.5%), and in the economies that are production factor-oriented, need entrepreneurship prevails (40.5%).

The reasons behind this are still a subject of analysis. There are several possible explanations, from individual characteristics, economic framework or simply as a result of an evolutionary process. Lindo, Cardoso, Rodrigues and Wetzel (2007) defend that "Because they still have big domestic responsibilities, women need to look for strategies to soften the existing conflicts between these two important instances of their lives".

According to Buttner (2001), the women that begin their entrepreneurial activity due to the emergence of an opportunity and not because of a need, do it because they aspire to the schedule flexibility that self-employment provides. Thus, through the creation of their own job place and, consequently, their adjusted work schedule, they try to solve some conflicts that may exist between their family and professional lives (Lima1 & Santos, 2018).

Studies reveal that women's primary motivations are similar to men's, such as the motivation for a higher economic profitability, desire for independence, the need to reach something and the aspiration for work satisfaction (Greene, Brush & Gatewoodln, 2007). However, the several inequalities between men entrepreneurs and women entrepreneurs continue to exist.

Inequalities of Entrepreneurship

Gomes, Santana, Antonialli and Correia (2009) argue that "The debate on inequality between the feminine and masculine features on the work environment is a target for much discussion. As a general rule, those who study the matter believe that women possess differences when compared to men. However, organisations are impregnated with masculine values". On somc aspccts of the entrepreneurship ecosystem (institutional, organizational and individual levels), women are at a disadvantage (Brush, Edelman, Manolova & Welter, 2018). GEM (2018) points towards the need for introducing institutional mechanisms in order to reduce gender differences in access to business.

Regarding the independence of the woman, Raposo and Astoni (2007) underline the importance of women voicing their rights and consequent responsibilities of these rights. They mention that "the independence conditions acquired by women go beyond the Feminist Revolution of 1969, when several women protesters burned intimate clothing on public square".

According to Diáz-Garcia and Jiménez-Moren (2010), women face entrepreneurship in a less beneficial way as men do because, since women have different socialisation processes when compared to men, they will face opportunities in a different way as well. According to these authors, some women may have a negative, pre-conceived idea about entrepreneurship that may affect them when taking the decision to create a business. On the one hand, "a negative perception can install a fear of failure, which was proved to be an important dissuading factor in creating new companies for women. There is also evidence that women who have a pro-active personality are significantly affected by the exposure to the common "male" stereotype on entrepreneurs and, therefore, there is a significant decrease in entrepreneurial intentions." (Diáz-Garcia & Jiménez-Moren, 2010). However, the same authors also refer that "if entrepreneurship is viewed by women as a career option that is strongly correlated with their own features and values, they will be more inclined towards creating their own company". Therefore, and quoting Portela, Hespanha, Nogueira, Teixeira and Batista (2008), "stereotypes persist, the most common being that women are less able to run businesses".

In the last few years, we have seen an increase in women's participation in leading roles and also as entrepreneurs. According to Allen, Langowitz, Elam and Dean (2007), investment in female entrepreneurship represents a way for countries to economically raise the number of new companies created. Taking into account that women represent half of the world population, the number of companies that have been created is also rising, consisting mainly of small and medium companies, being a strong contribute to the creation of new job posts, innovation and development, both at an economic and at a social level.

In this sense, female participation in the job market has significantly risen. Some statistical data indicates that there are women in all business branches and in all segments. However, as mentioned above, there are still inequalities in terms of opportunities in the entrepreneurial world, such as differences in income according to gender and obstacles in career progression.

Currently, the woman has an increasingly active role and of great importance in the national and world economy. She identifies opportunities, studies creative capacities in the productive activity and assumes risks and uncertainties in the enterprises.

According to Minniti and Naude (2010), from the past 30 years of studies on entrepreneurship it is possible to conclude that there are less women than men who own businesses. The authors claim that there are many reasons for the differences between genders, and that these differences lead to repercussions on a socioeconomic level. To these authors, the motivation that entrepreneur women have when they begin a business may be different from men's due to cultural reasons or discrimination. Therefore, "Perhaps men and women have different socioeconomic features and, if we were to correct factors such as education, wealth, family and job status, these differences could disappear" (Minniti & Naude, 2010).

According to Fossen (2011), there are differences in terms of financial and interpersonal abilities between men and women, such as, for example, that women show a stronger tendency to conceive their financial abilities as being inferior to men's, although they believe they possess better interpersonal abilities. Furthermore, this author considers that women have different ways of managing companies than men, since that "when a woman creates a business, she does not simply acquire a separate economic entity, on the contrary, she involves herself in a net of relationships that include family, community and business. The importance of creating personal bonds to the woman entrepreneur contrasts with the need for the man entrepreneur to have autonomy and a structured decision making framework" (Fossen, 2011).

To Greene et al. (2007), "the strategic choice is moulded by the experiences to which the individuals are exposed to, since women and men have socialisation experiences that are fundamentally different and that result from the development of unique capacities". These authors also consider that the companies that are managed by women are based on relationships between employees and clients and are more focused on the creation and development of teams. Therefore, women have a higher tendency to adopt a relational strategy in the way in which they manage their businesses; however, they also have access to less resources on an early stage and are closed at a precocious time when compared to companies run by men.

In fact, Ahl (2006) mentioned that when one evaluates men and women, regardless of the kind of business they possess, women usually receive negative evaluations, since their businesses are generally of smaller in dimension, with a slower growth rate and less lucrative than men's.

Justo (2008) sustain that the problem originated from the foundation of the professional motivations and in the perceptions that entrepreneurs have regarding business success. Therefore, and as previously mentioned, men and women have different reasons for creating companies that may translate into the way in which they will manage said company. Men are, according to some studies, quicker when taking decisions and worry about the repercussions and consequences of their decisions in the short term. On the contrary, women tend to consider more minutely the consequences of their decisions in the long term (Gomes et al., 2009). Women also tend to face risks in a more conservative way, possibly due to the higher difficulty in obtaining capital. Therefore, "contrarily to men, entrepreneur women refer finding difficulties and possible credit discrimination during the phase of capital formation" (Greene et al., 2007, p.183).

Additionally, women also have more difficulties in sustaining entrepreneurial success due to the lack of affective and social support, the difficulty in entering international markets and in obtaining financing, due also to the size of their companies, lack of time for themselves, difficulty in conciliating work and family and the absence of reference models of other female entrepreneurs (Machado, 2002; GEM, 2017).

METHODOLOGY, SAMPLE AND RESULTS

Methodological Aspects of Qualitative Analysis

The undertook research corresponds to a qualitative approach. For this study, qualitative techniques were used, such as the semi-structured interview, field observation and content analysis, through the transcription of the interviews. The three big research questions (RQ) that this study proposes itself to answer are:

RQ1: Which are the influences (family and social) to become a female entrepreneur?
RQ2: What was the reason behind becoming a female entrepreneur (opportunity/need)?
RQ3: Which are the difficulties in becoming a female entrepreneur in Portugal?

Haguette (1997) defines interview as "a process of social interaction between two people in which one of them, the interviewer, aims to obtain information from the other, the interviewee".

The criteria used to choose the interviewees were: women who initiated an entrepreneurial activity, who are responsible for their management and who have their business for at least 6 months at the date of the interview. The collection of the data was made through personal interviews with interview scripts during the second semester of 2014. The interviews were taped and posteriorly transcribed with the authorization of the interviewees.

The semi-structured interviews conciliate open and closed questions, thus allowing the interviewee to develop certain topics with more precision. The interviewer will follow a set of previously defined questions, but in an informal way. Therefore, the interviewer should take into consideration that, when adequate, he or she should direct the conversation to the matter of interest, with additional questions, if necessary. The main advantage of this kind of interview is that it can represent a better sample of the population when compared to structured and rigid interviews. Contrarily to the questionnaires sent by mail, which have a very low rate of response, interviews have a much wider range of response, being more likely that people will accept to talk about certain matters as opposed to writing the answers (Selltiz, Jahoda, Coo & Deutsch, 1987). Besides, this kind of interview, as well as the open interview, has as an advantage its flexibility regarding duration, and the fact that it can go more in depth concerning certain topics without the pressure of counting the time.

Furthermore, the interaction established between the interviewer and the interviewee favours more spontaneous answers, since there is more proximity and openness between the two sides. Therefore, they are interviews that facilitate the investigation of affective and evaluative aspects of the interviewees, attributing personal meanings to their attitudes and behaviours.

To build the interviews, a guide was made based on the three general questions to which this study aims to answer: influences, reasons and difficulties faced by interviewees. Each question is based on the referenced literature (Table 1).

From the research questions, arose the propositions that made up the interview guide (Table 2).

Sample and Results

The collected sample corresponds to eight female entrepreneurs between 32 and 55 years old, working mainly in micro companies, from the service area in the North region of Portugal (Braga, Oliveira de Azeméis, Paços de Ferreira, Porto, Paredes). Out of the eight interviewees, five have a BSc, and as a general rule there are entrepreneurs in the family sphere (Tables 3 and 4).

Table 1. Revision of the literature and matters of research

Which are the influences (family and social) to become a female entrepreneur?	What is the reason (opportunity/need) behind becoming a female entrepreneur?	Which are the difficulties in becoming a female entrepreneur in Portugal?
Apergis & Economou (2010). Buttner (2001). Diáz-Garcia & Jiménez-Moren (2010). Greene, Brush & Gatewoodln, (2007). Justo (2008). Machado (2002). Minniti & Naude (2010). Peñaloza, Diógenes & Sousa (2008). Rubio-Banon & Esteban-Lloret (2016).	APME - Associação Portuguesa de Mulheres Empresárias (Set. 2007). Buttner (2001). GEM (2007, 2012, 2016). Hisrich&Peters (2004). Pérez-Pérez & Avilés-Hernández (2016) Sebrae (2008).	Andreoli & Borges (2007). Bayagan (2000). Célestin (2002). Cloutier, Bernard & Tremblay (2009). Delors (1996). GEM (2012). Greene, Brush & Gatewoodln (2007). Guvenen, Kuruscu & Ozkan (2009). Instituto Nacional de Estatística (2012, 2013). Lindo et al. (2007). Machado (2002). Marlow & Patton (2005). Murani (2003). Portela et al. (2008). Silveira & Gouvêa (2008)

Source: Own

Table 2. Research questions of research and of the interview

What factors influenced you in becoming an entrepreneur?	Was there anything in particular that led you to begin the business? (Firing? Work dissatisfaction? Others?)	Did you do any kind of planning to the opening of the business?
Is someone from your family an entrepreneur?	How did you identify the business opportunity?	Did you begin alone or in a society? If with partners: did they complete their qualifications/competences to begin the business?
Was your education (university/course/private school) important to the opening of the business?	What are your strong suits and aspects to improve as an entrepreneur?	Which were the biggest difficulties you faced in your business and how were they overcome?
Have you had any previous professional experience before becoming an entrepreneur and what was it?		In what way did your career affect your family life?
		What are the positive and the negative sides of being an entrepreneur?
		What advice would you give someone that wishes to open a business?
		How do you face the competitive market in Portugal?
		Do you suffer or have suffered prejudice or difficulty for being a woman as runner of your own business?

Source: Own

Table 3. Interviewees' profile

Entrepreneur	Age	Schooling	First Business	Entrepreneurs in the Family	Business Partners
1	51	4th grade	No	Yes	Yes
2	36	BSc	Yes	Yes	No
3	55	4th grade	Yes	Yes	Yes
4	37	BSc	No	Yes	No
5	33	BSc	Yes	No	No
6	48	Bsc	Yes	Yes	Yes
7	32	Bsc	Yes	Yes	Yes
8	49	High school	Yes	Yes	Yes

Source: Own

Table 4. Companies' profile

Company	Beginning of Activity	Activity	Area	Branch of Activity	No of Employees
1	2000	Services	Restaurants	Restaurants	3
2	2011	Services	Web portals	Event/Product promotion	4
3	1995	Services	Restaurants	Self-service	4
4	2012	Services	Marketing	Development and implementing marketing actions	1
5	2011	Services	Physical well-being activities	Physical well-being activities	0
6	1983	Industry	Furniture	Furniture manufacturing	25
7	2014	Services	Commerce	Honey trade	2
8	1992	Services	Tourism	Travel agency	11

Source: Own

Taking the exposed matter into account, three general research questions were drawn, which are essentially a set of questions to which answers were obtained. From the three questions, the following was possible to conclude:

RQ1: Which were the influences (family and social) to become an entrepreneur?

Regarding the family influences, the vast majority of the interviewees refers that they were influenced and incentivised by the father, also an entrepreneur himself, to have a business of their own. Therefore, there is a pattern in the interviews in identifying the father as the main influencer of the entrepreneurial activity.

Regarding the reasons behind wanting to run a business of their own, they are essentially related to personal fulfilment and independence. Some also point the flexibility of the work schedule as a positive factor, making it easier to conjugate the professional and family life. This confirms the study of Apergis and Economou (2010), who mentioned flexible schedules as a boosting factor of self-employment. Peñaloza, Diógenes & Sousa (2008) had also mentioned these two factors as the more frequently identified by female entrepreneurs.

From the reasons mentioned by the interviewees, the passion for what they do is the common ground between them, revealing that, although the booster for beginning their professional activity is different, the reason to continue to bet increasingly on their own companies is the same. Therefore, and accordingly to Hisrich's theory (2004), as mentioned, women look not only for a new profession, but mainly personal fulfilment.

RQ2: What was the reason to become an entrepreneur (opportunity/need)?

The motivation to open a business for the majority of entrepreneurs is related to the desire for personal fulfilment and independence, allied to the perception of market opportunities —— entrepreneurship by opportunity (GEM, 2018). Therefore, the majority of the interviewed entrepreneurs began their activity by themselves due to the identification of a market opportunity. Only the entrepreneur who develops her activity in the branch of restaurants (self-service) revealed that she had begun her professional activity because of a lack of employment, falling into the category of entrepreneurship by need, taking GEM Portugal's (2012) definition into account. These results do not confirm the internationally verified fact that more women are motivated by need, rather than opportunity (GEM, 2017).

We then confirm the data referred beforehand by the GEM Portugal reports concerning the rise of the percentage of individuals that become entrepreneurs because of the possibility of seizing a business opportunity, instead of lack of better employment opportunities.

The identification of market opportunities was, to some of the interviewees, boosted by a dissatisfaction regarding their previous job, which was not providing them with the desired personal and professional fulfilment.

The majority of the entrepreneurs identified as their main strong suits persistence and polyvalence. They consider that these characteristics may have eased the boosting of entrepreneurship by opportunity.

RQ3: What were the difficulties in becoming an entrepreneur in Portugal?

Regarding the difficulties felt by the interviewees, two of the entrepreneurs revealed that the main obstacle they felt was in conciliating the role of mother with their professional life. They consider they may have overlooked a little of their children's education in favour of their career and that they have lost a part of their children's lives (Eagly, 1987). However, the dedication effort they made ended up strengthening the family bonds throughout the years.

Three of the entrepreneurs identify as main obstacle the limited financial resources at the beginning of the professional activity. The fact that they did not yet have an image or name in the market made it more difficult to access financing, confirming Marlow and Patton's theory (2005) and GEM (2018), that evidenced the difficulty felt by female entrepreneurs in accessing financing. However, this fact is not due to a possible discrimination against women, as Greene et al. (2007) defended; it is mainly due to the current state of the economy.

Finally, two of the entrepreneurs refer that the main difficulty they had to face until date was due to the high number of competitors in the market and the consecutive test to the viability of the project and need for adjustment.

Regarding the advantages of being entrepreneurs, the majority of the interviewees mentioned independence and personal fulfilment as the most positive factors, confirming Greene et al.'s theory (2007), that pointed as the primary motivation the desire for independence and aspiration for satisfaction at the workplace. Machado et al. (2003) also mentioned that female entrepreneurs begin companies for reasons related to the desire of fulfilment and independence.

The least positive side of the entrepreneurial activity pointed by three of the interviewed entrepreneurs was family life, since they ended up having less time to dedicate to their families. This matter was also identified by Eagly (1987) and Machado (2002), who evidenced the difficulty in conciliating work and family by female entrepreneurs.

However, two of the entrepreneurs considered that schedule flexibility helped conciliating their family life and their professional life, confirming the theory advanced by Buttner (2001) that mentions schedule flexibilization as one of the factors that moves some women to become entrepreneurs. Aspergis and Economou (2010) also considered schedule flexibility a booster to entrepreneurs.

Finally, contrarily to what was argued by authors such as Murani (2003), Delors (1996), Silveira and Gouvêa (2008), Marlow and Patton (2005), Geene et al. (2007), López-Zafra, García-Retamero and Eagly (2009), Quevedo, Izar and Romo (2010), none of the interviewed entrepreneurs felt throughout the years of professional activity any kind of prejudice or gender inequality; on the contrary, all of them underline the fact that they have been very supported by their business partners, clients, suppliers or even investors. In the same sense are the conclusions drawn in GEM (2017), in which the trend is the decrease of the gender gap.

SOLUTIONS AND RECOMMENDATIONS

The main difficulties suggested by the entrepreneurs involved in this study were the possibility of attracting financing, due to bank restrictions on financing, on the one hand, and the reconciliation between business and family life, on the other hand.

The authors point out the following solutions and recommendations.

Development of policies facilitating entrepreneurship, namely light taxation schemes for start-ups and micro and small enterprises, and reduction of national and municipal bureaucracy. Encourage the investments of the "angels", coupled with the traditional credit granting system, allowing investment to be sustained at more favourable interest rates. Make available, through public and private programs, the local creation and development of business accelerators, identifying businesses that can serve as a reference for the replication of best practices in an inclusive environment (especially without gender discrimination) and the most appropriate financing lines for the characteristics of the business and accessible in the region. In addition to training, per se, specific and individualized programs should be used to strengthen the skills and resources of management at the household and family level, since they appear as facilitators of the beginning and growth of the business in the "female ". Public and social policies in support of motherhood and the elderly, in particular with the multiplication of the network of kindergartens and elderly homes with local proximity, will allow the realization and development of female entrepreneurship and entrepreneurial ecosystems.

FUTURE RESEARCH DIRECTIONS

Taking into account that this study is a starting point for the study of female entrepreneurship in Portugal, it should be pointed out that there are still several gaps to be completed, which should be the basis for future research topics.

Other methodologies can be used, and it is possible to combine qualitative and quantitative methodologies, reinforcing their complementarity. The use of a convenient sample, with a very limited geographical scope, brings limitations of generalization to the study. The extension of the sample to other regions of the country and to other sectors of activity could enrich the study and allow the use of complementary methodologies of a quantitative nature.

Changes in the traditional financing framework, closely linked to the economic environment, as well as the possibility of using other forms of financing, should be discussed in the future.

Connecting to the public and private network of support for both the children and the parents of the creation and survival of women-led enterprises in regional and local terms should be studied in the future.

The genetic or hereditary influence that entrepreneurial parents may have on potentially entrepreneurial daughters could also be the subject of a more detailed study.

Therefore, different research questions should be reoriented and re-elaborated, taking into account the set of evidence gathered and the analysis carried out in this study.

CONCLUSION

This work aimed to be a contribution to the study of female entrepreneurship in Portugal.

The conclusions drawn from the investigation should be analysed taking into account the context and its specific limitations. Throughout the study, we emphasise the fact that, although it is a multiple case study, the small number of interviews does not allow for the generalisation or theoretical transferability of the results. This is due to, between other reasons, the qualitative study that, as its main instrument is the semi-structured interview, implies a morose and minute data collection. The sample by convenience is another limitation of this study; although it is diversified, it was not random, due to the adhesion difficulties found because of geographical constraints.

Taking these limitations into account, the following conclusions are highlighted:

- Role of the father figure as booster of the entrepreneurial activity
- Personal fulfilment and independence as the first reason for entrepreneurial activity (entrepreneurship by opportunity)
- Most of the entrepreneurs identified persistence and polyvalence as their main strengths. They consider that these characteristics could have facilitated the boost of opportunity entrepreneurship
- Difficulty in conciliating family and entrepreneurial life. However, on the contrary, flexibilization of working hours, thus making it easier to combine work and family life, is pointed out by two of the eight entrepreneurs
- Difficulty in attracting financial resources to the boot of the entrepreneurial activity, due to bank constraints in concession of credit
- High number of competing companies in the market and the consecutive test to the feasibility of the project. implies an adjustment of the business model
- No constraint due to gender

REFERENCES

Ahl, H. (2006). Why research on women entrepreneurs needs new directions. *Entrepreneurship Theory and Practice*, *30*(5), 595–621. doi:10.1111/j.1540-6520.2006.00138.x

Allen, E., Langowitz, N., Elam, A., & Dean, M. (2007). *The Global Entrepreneurship Monitor 2007 Report On Women and Entrepreneurship*. Academic Press.

Andreoli, T. P., & Borges, W. A. (2007). Empreendedorismo Feminino: Uma Análise do Perfil Empreendedor e das Dificuldades Enfrentadas por Mulheres Detentoras de Um Pequeno Negócio. Presented paper at the XI EPEAD – Encontro Paranaense dos Estudantes de Administração, Paraná.

Apergis, N., & Economou, V. P. (2010). Incentives and female entrepreneurial activity: Evidence from panel firm level data. *International Advances in Economic Research*, *16*(4), 371–387. doi:10.100711294-010-9277-9

APME – Associação Portuguesa de Mulheres Empresárias. (2017). *A APME e o empreendedorismo*. Lisboa: Author.

Bastian, B. L., Sidani, Y. M., & El Amine, Y. (2018). Women entrepreneurship in the Middle East and North Africa: A review of knowledge areas and research gaps. *Gender in Management*, *33*(1), 14–29. doi:10.1108/GM-07-2016-0141

Bayagan, G. (2000), Women Entrepreneurs in SMEs: realizing the benefits of globalization and the knowledge – based Economy. *OECD, Workshop 4: Improving knowledge about women's entrepreneurship*.

Brush, C., Edelman, L. F., Manolova, T., & Welter, F. (2018). A gendered look at entrepreneurship ecosystems. *Small Business Economics*, 1–16. doi:10.100711187-018-9992-9

Buttner, E. H. (2001). Examining female entrepreneur management styles: An Analysis Using a Relational Frame. *Journal of Business Ethics*, *29*(3), 253–269. doi:10.1023/A:1026460615436

Célestin, J.-B. (2002). *A Qualidade de Emprego. Direcção-Geral do Emprego e Formação Profissional*. Lisboa: DGEFP.

Cloutier, L., Bernard, P., & Tremblay, D. G. (2009). Job quality and gender inequality: Key changes in Québec over the last decade. *Studies in Social Justice*, *3*(2), 191–212. doi:10.26522sj.v3i2.1015

Delors, J. (1996). *Educação, um tesouro a descobrir: Relatório para a UNESCO da Comissão Internacional sobre Educação para o século XXI*. São Paulo: Cortez.

Diáz-Garcia, M. C., & Jiménez-Moren, J. (2010). Entrepreneurial intention: The role of gender. *The International Entrepreneurship and Management Journal*, *6*(3), 261–283. doi:10.100711365-008-0103-2

Eagly, A. (1987). *Sex differences in behavior: A social-role interpretation*. Hillsdale, NJ: Academic Press.

Fossen, F. M. (2011). Gender differences in entrepreneurial choice and risk aversion – a decomposition based on a microeconometric model. *Applied Economics*, *44*(14), 1795–1812. doi:10.1080/00036846.2011.554377

Freire, D. A., Corrêa, R., & Ribeiro, H. C. (2011). *Género e empreendedorismo: um olhar sobre a pesquisa do G.E.M. – Global Entrepreneurship Monitor*. Empreendedorismo e Inovação.

GEM. (2007). *Avaliação do potencial empreendedor em Portugal*. The Global Entrepreneurship Monitor, Project GEM Portugal.

GEM. (2008). *Global Entrepreneurship Monitor (GEM)*. Executive Report.

GEM. (2012). *Um estudo sobre o Empreendedorismo*. The Global Entrepreneurship Monitor, Project GEM Portugal.

GEM. (2016). *Global Entrepreneurship Monitor (GEM)*. Executive Report.

GEM. (2017). *Global Entrepreneurship Monitor 2016/2017 – Report on Women's Entrepreneurship*.

GEM. (2018). *Global Entrepreneurship Monitor (GEM)*. Global Report 2017/18.

Gomes, A. F., Santana, W. G., Antonialli, L. M., & Correia, E. L. (2009). Trajetórias e estratégias de mulheres: Um estudo conquistense. *Revista de Gestão USP*, *16*(1), 69–87. doi:10.5700/rege359

Gosselin, L. H., & Grisé, J. (1990). Are women owner-managers challenging our definitions of entrepreneurship? An in-depth survey. *Journal of Business Ethics*, *9*(4/5), 423–433. doi:10.1007/BF00380341

Greene, P. G., Brush, C. G., & Gatewood, E. G. (2007). Perspectives on women entrepreneurs: Past findings and new directions. *Praeger Perspectives on Entrepreneurship*, *1*, 181–204.

Guvenen, F., Kuruscu, B., & Ozkan, S. (2009). *Tributação de Capital Humano e Desigualdade Salarial: Uma Análise Cross-Country*. National Bureau of Economic Research Working Paper, 15526.

Haguette, T. M. F. (1997). *Metodologias qualitativas na Sociologia*. Petrópolis: Vozes.

Hisrich, R. D., & Peters, M. P. (2004). *Empreendedorismo*. São Paulo: Bookman.

Instituto Nacional de Estatística - INE. (2013). *Censos 2011*. Lisboa: INE.

Instituto Nacional de Estatística – INE. (2013). *Destaque – Informação à comunicação social. 8 de março: Dia Internacional da Mulher*. Lisboa: INE.

Jonathan, E. G. (2005). Mulheres empreendedoras: Medos, conquistas e qualidade de vida. *Psicologia em Estudo*, *10*(3), 373–382. doi:10.1590/S1413-73722005000300005

Justo, R. (2008). *La influencia del género y entorno familiar en el éxito y fracaso de las iniciativas emprendedoras* (Doctoral dissertation). Universidad Autonoma de Madrid, Spain.

Langowitz, N., & Minniti, M. (2007). The entrepreneurial propensity of women. *Entrepreneurship Theory and Practice*, *31*(3), 341–364. doi:10.1111/j.1540-6520.2007.00177.x

Limal, F. S., & Santos, A. B. C. (2017). The Characteristics and Challenges of Female Entrepreneurship in the Market. *International Journal of Advances in Management and Economics*, *6*(4), 1–4.

Lindo, M. R., Cardoso, P. M., Rodrigues, M. E., & Wetzel, U. (2007). Vida pessoal e vida profissional: Os desafios de equilíbrio para mulheres empreendedoras do Rio de Janeiro. *Revista de Administração Contemporânia*, *1*(1), 1–15.

López-Zafra, E., Garcia-Retamero, R., & Eagly, A. H. (2009). Congruencia del rol de género y aspiraciones de las mujeres a posiciones de liderazgo. *Revista de Psicología Social*, *24*(1), 99–108. doi:10.1174/021347409786923005

Machado, V. H. (1999). *Tendências do comportamento gerencial da mulher empreendedora*. Paper presented at the XXIII Encontro da Associação Nacional de Pós-Graduação em Administração – ENANPAD, Foz do Iguaçu.

Machado, V. H. (2002). *Identidade empreendedora de mulheres no Paraná* (Doctoral dissertation). Universidade Federal de Santa Catarina, Florianópolis.

Machado, V. H., St-Cyr, L., Mione, A., & Alves, M.C. (2003), O Processo de criação de empresas por mulheres. *Revista de Administração Económica – RAE*, *2*(2). Doi:10.1590/S1676-56482003000200007

Marlow, S., & Patton, D. (2005). All credit for men? Entrepreneurship, finance and gender. *Entrepreneurship Theory and Practice*, *29*(6), 717–735. doi:10.1111/j.1540-6520.2005.00105.x

McKay, S., Phillimore, J., & Teasdale, S. (2010). *Exploring the 'Gendered' nature of social entrepreneurship: Women's leadership, employment and participation in the third sector*. Paper presented in the 60th Political Studies association annual conference, Edinburgh, UK.

Minniti, M., & Naude, W. (2010). What do we know about the patterns and determinants of female entrepreneurship across countries? *European Journal of Development Research*, *22*(3), 277–293. doi:10.1057/ejdr.2010.17

Moore, D. P., & Buttner, E. H. (1997). *Women entrepreneurs moving beyond the glass ceiling*. London: Sage.

Murani, M. (2003). *As novas fronteiras da desigualdade: homens e mulheres no mercado de trabalho*. São Paulo: Senac.

O'Meally, N. B. (2000). *Fostering women's entrepreneurship: education, management training and societal values*. Paper presented at the Conference on Women Entrepreneurs in SMEs: Realising the Benefits of Globalization and the Knowledge-based Economy, Paris, France.

Peñaloza, V., Diógenes, C. G., & Sousa, S. J. (2008). Escolha profissional no curso de administração: Tendências empreendedoras e gênero. *Revista de Administração Mackenzie*, *9*(8), 151–167. doi:10.1590/S1678-69712008000800009

Pérez-Pérez, C., & Avilés-Hernández, M. (2016). Explanatory factors of female entrepreneurship and limits elements. *Suma de Negócios*, *7*(15), 25–31. doi:10.1016/j.sumneg.2015.12.004

Portela, J., Hespanha, P., Nogueira, C., Teixeira, M. S., & Batista, A. (2008). *Microempreendedorismo em Portugal: experiências e perspetivas*. Lisboa: Instituto António Sérgio do Sector Cooperativo – INSCOOP.

Quevedo, L. M., Izar, J. M., & Romo, R. L. (2010). Factores endógenos y exógenos de mujeres y hombres empreendedores de España, Estados Unidos y México. *Investigacion y Ciencia*, *18*(46), 57–63.

Raposo, K. C. S., & Astoni, S. A. F. (2007). A mulher em dois tempos: A construção do discurso feminino nas revistas dos anos 50 e na atualidade. *Revista do Centro Universitário São Camilo*, *8*(2), 36–37.

Robbins, S. P. (2001). *Administração: mudanças e perspetivas*. São Paulo: Saraiva.

Rubio-Banón, A., & Esteban-lloret, N. (2016). Cultural factors and gender role in female entrepreneurship. *Suma de Negocios*, *7*(15), 9–17. doi:10.1016/j.sumneg.2015.12.002

Seabre. (2008). *Serviço Brasileiro de Apoio às Micro e Pequenas Empresas*. Relatório do Prêmio Mulher de Negócios 2006-2010. Brasilia.

Selltiz, M., Jahoda, S. W. C., & Deutsch, M. (1987). *Métodos de pesquisa nas relações sociais*. São Paulo: EPU.

Silveira, A., & Gouvêa, A. B. (2008). Empreendedorismo Feminino: Mulheres Gerentes de Empresas. *Faces Revista de Administração, 7*(3), 124–138.

Singer, J. J., Amoros, J. E., & Moska, D. (2015). *Global Entrepreneurship Monitor 2014*. Global Report.

Themudo, N. S. (2009). Gender and the nonprofit sector. *Nonprofit and Voluntary Sector Quarterly, 38*(4), 663–683. doi:10.1177/0899764009333957

Winkler, C. A., & Medeiros, J. (2011). *Mulheres empreendedoras: uma questão de género*. Paper presented at the Simpósio Género e Políticas Públicas, Londrina.

ADDITIONAL READING

Daniels, C., Herrington, M., & Kew, P. (2016). *Global Entrepreneurship Monitor 2015/2016: Special Report on Entrepreneurial Finance*. Global Entrepreneurship Research Association.

Fernandes, E. P., & Mota-Ribeiro, S. (2017). 'Respect' and 'Self-Determination': Women entrepreneurs' identities and entrepreneurial discourses. *Gender in Management, 32*(1), 66–80. doi:10.1108/GM-04-2016-0093

Gomes, A. F., Santana, W. G. P., Araújo, U. P., & Martins, C. M. F. (2014). Empreendedorismo Feminino como Sujeito de Pesquisa. *Revista Brasileira de Gestão de Negócios, 16*(51), 319–342. doi:10.7819/rbgn.v16i51.1508

Pato, L., Breda, Z., & Figueiredo, V. (2015). Women's entrepreneurship and local sustainability: The case study of a Portuguese rural initiative. *Revista Turismo e Desenvolvimento, 23*, 119–128.

Poggesi, S., Mari, M., & De Vita, L. (2015). What's new in female entrepreneurship research? Answers from the literature. *The International Entrepreneurship and Management Journal*. doi:10.100711365-015-0364-5

Raknerud, A., & Rønsen, M. (2014). Why are there so few female entrepreneurs? An examination of gender differences in entrepreneurship using Norwegian registry. *Discussion Papers - Statistics Norway, Research Department*, 790.

Santos, G., Marques, C. S., & Ratten, V. (2018). *Entrepreneurial women's networks: the case of D'Uva – Portugal wine girls. International Journal of Entrepreneurial Behavior & Research.* doi:10.1108/IJEBR-10-2017-041

Santos, G. M. C., Marques, C. S., Ferreira, J. J., Gerry, C., & Ratten, V. (2017). Women's entrepreneurship in Northern Portugal: Psychological factors versus contextual influences in the economic downturn. *World Review of Entrepreneurship, Management and Sustainable Development, 13*(4), 418. doi:10.1504/WREMSD.2017.085027

Terrell, K., & Troilo, M. (2010). Values and female entrepreneurship. *International Journal of Gender and Entrepreneurship, 2*(3), 260–286. doi:10.1108/17566261011079242

Yadav, V., & Unni, J. (2016). Women entrepreneurship: Research review and future directions. *Journal of Global Entrepreneurship Research, 6*(12). doi:10.118640497-016-0055-x

KEY TERMS AND DEFINITIONS

Entrepreneurial Initiative: Individual's ability to turn ideas into action. It includes the ability to plan and manage projects in order to achieve objectives, but also creativity, innovation, and risk taking.

Entrepreneurship by Need: Results from the absence of other opportunities of obtaining income (namely, dependent work) and that makes individuals create a business, since they consider they have no better alternatives. Emerges generally in a strongly countercyclical economy.

Entrepreneurship by Opportunity: Results from the desire to seize, by self-initiative, a possibility of business that exists in the market, through the creation of a company at the nexus of individual aspirations with economic and social conditions perceived as favorable to create a new product or service, either in an existing market or a new one. Emerges generally in a pro-cyclical economy.

Female Entrepreneurship: Female entrepreneurship is an economic activity of the women who think of a business enterprise, initiate it, organize and combine the factors of production, operate the enterprise, and undertake risks and handle economic uncertainty involved in running a business enterprise.

Family Responsibilities: In many cultures, women are more likely to shoulder a greater share of child-caring duties and they support more the elder family members. Children may demand their mothers' undivided attention, which can be a challenge for female entrepreneurs to deal with. Women in this situation must balance their family life with their duties as entrepreneurs.

Gender Discrimination: Historically, studies show that men have an advantage over women when it comes to starting a business. More recent studies indicate that the perceived disparity between male and female entrepreneurs doesn't actually exist and gender is not a determining factor in the success or failure of a new business venture, even though, in practical terms, the different segmentation of family responsibilities includes gender discrimination.

Micro and Small Companies: Micro companies have fewer than 10 employees and an annual turnover (the amount of money taken in a particular period) or balance sheet (a statement of a company's assets and liabilities) below €2 million. Small enterprise: fewer than 50 employees and an annual turnover or balance sheet below €10 million.

Multiple Case Studies Methodology: Qualitative analysis means that the observations are analyzed without the support of numerical methods and coding the observations to quantitative scales. Instead, it is based on the context of the observations, the experiences of the observer and rational argumentation. The strength of conclusions from case studies is not very high, and it is claimed that the use of multiple cases yields more robustness to the conclusions from the study.

Chapter 5
Is There Entrepreneurship Within the Public Sector?
A Literature Review

Raquel Pereira
Polytechnic of Porto, Portugal

Maria Clara Ribeiro
Polytechnic of Porto, Portugal

Orlando Manuel Martins Marques Lima Rua
Polytechnic of Porto, Portugal

Diana Martins
Catholic University of Porto, Portugal

ABSTRACT

Because of its importance as a key factor to economic development, the study of entrepreneurship has been considerably developed in the past decades. Entrepreneurship is broadly diversified, which is associated with, for example, studies in the field of business, social, female, and young entrepreneurship. If, on the one hand, it is a fact that entrepreneurship and its study are mainly associated with the private initiative, there is, on the other hand, a question to be asked: Is there entrepreneurship in the public sector? Though still incipient, the study of entrepreneurship applied to the public sector and the acts of the public managers as entrepreneurs have revealed themselves to be themes with increasing interest. To contribute to a better conceptual understanding of this theme, namely its questions, ideas, and current debate, this work presents some theoretical reflexions and a relevant literature review on entrepreneurship in a public sector context.

DOI: 10.4018/978-1-5225-6942-8.ch005

INTRODUCTION

The theme of entrepreneurship, as a field of research and investigation, has seen, in the last decades, a remarkable growth in its study and application. There has been considerable interest in the contribution of entrepreneurship to economic development (Stought, 2016). Entrepreneurship (and the activity of entrepreneuring) are key factors for economic growth and development insofar as they are considered sources of innovation and thus contribute to increased productivity and efficiency (Acs & Szerb, 2007; Stephens, Partridge & Faggian, 2013; Trettin & Welter, 2013).

While the literature that addresses the theme of entrepreneurship in the context of the private sector is vast, with regard to its application to the public sector, and to the performance of public managers as entrepreneurs, literature is still scarce, although it is a subject of growing interest (Diefenbach, 2011; Klein, Mahoney & McGahan, 2010; Matthews, 2014; Zampetakis & Moustakis, 2007; Zerbinatia & Souitarisb, 2007).

Considering the challenges faced by today's societies, which inevitably require a creative response / approach from national, regional and local governments, several researchers recognize the need for more research on this subject in order to better understand the relevance entrepreneurship (and entrepreneurial activity) in the context of the public sector and its organizations.

Thus, the main goal of this work is to discuss the concept, raise theoretical reflections and review the literature on entrepreneurship (intrapreneurship) in the context of the public sector, in order to contribute to a better conceptual understanding of this theme, namely its issues, ideas and current debate. We begin, in section I, by reviewing the concept of entrepreneurship and its application in the context of the public sector. Next, and in order to have a perception of the "state of the art", we present a literature review, namely, the main contributions of literature specifically applied to local / regional public (political) entrepreneurship. Finally, we present some final considerations.

BACKGROUND

Entrepreneurship: What Does It Mean?

Stought (2016, p. 130), refer that "The interest in entrepreneurship and its contribution to economic development has seen a great development in the last two decades". In fact, the theme of entrepreneurship, as a field of research and investigation, has seen an exponential growth in its study and application. There are several terms to describe and characterize entrepreneurship. The works of Diefenbach (2011) and

Leyden (2016) present a detailed revision of the different terms and application of the entrepreneurship concept. Therefore, it is not our purpose to make a thorough review of the term and its application. We intend, above all, to introduce the determinant aspects underlying the concept and then apply and understand it when applied to the context of the public sector.

The activity of undertaking is seen as a determinant for economic growth and development insofar as it constitutes a source of innovation and therefore contributes to increased productivity and efficiency (Acs & Szerb, 2007; Stephens et al., 2013; Trettin & Welter, 2013). According to the OECD (2003), the adoption of pro-entrepreneurial policies is a way to increase growth and economic diversity, ensure the competitiveness of markets and contribute to the reduction of unemployment and the social problems of poverty and dependence of the Social State. The large and growing interest in entrepreneurship is demonstrated by the tremendous growth of university programs on the subject (Stought, 2016) as well as by the increasing number of studies carried out on the subject (Santos & Teixeira, 2009).

From the perspective of Pinchot and Pellman (2004) as well as Tidd, Bessant and Pavitt (2008), the study of entrepreneurship can be considered under three approaches:

- The individual approach, which seeks to understand the profile and behavior of the entrepreneur, being an object of study, fundamentally, in the area of Psychology;
- The approach to action. It is the object of research on organizational and institutional studies and aims to study entrepreneurship as a process of innovation;
- The context approach, which analyzes the conditions that affect and result from the entrepreneurial action, being object of study of the areas of Economy and Sociology.

Although it is recognized that the origins of the term entrepreneurship / entrepreneur can be attributed to classic economists of the eighteenth century, one of the most important contributions is from Joseph Schumpeter (1883-1950) for whom the process of economic development is associated with innovations and innovative entrepreneur. He is seen as the responsible for the "creative destruction" of the current economic order, by introducing new products and services, or by creating new forms of organization or by exploiting new sources of natural resources. According to Sadler (2000), this economic perspective of entrepreneurship, which considers the entrepreneur as the agent who introduces innovation and takes the risk, generating new businesses and companies, is complemented by the perspective of those who seek to understand the profile and behavior of this agent. The same author also indicates that this behavioral perspective of analyzing the entrepreneurial profile was introduced by Mcclelland (1961) and later developed by Stevenson and Jarillo (1990) and Bygrave (1993). Nowadays, is widely argued that the profile and entrepreneurial skills can be developed and influenced by the context and the surroundings of the entrepreneurial agent – "the entrepreneurial ecosystem". Acording to Isenberg (2013), the entrepreneurial ecosystem incompasses six dimensions: governance and politics measures, quality of human resources, favorable culture, consistent financial system, institutional support and open markets.

In this context, fiscal benefits, public investment funds, bureaucracy reduction, education and higher education, availability of infrastructure, macroeconomic stability, networks of entrepreneurs, access to and availability of financing, and the existence of institutions and / or organizations that promote and adopt facilitative measures may be included in entrepreneurship[1].

How, then, can we define entrepreneurship?

Quoting Lumpkin and Dess (1996, p. 136), the entrepreneurial process refers to "the practices, methods and decision making styles that lead to entrepreneurship". Entrepreneurship is the process by which individuals - individually or within an organization - identify and "pursue" opportunities without looking at the resources they currently control (Mathews, 2014; Stevenson & Jarillo, 1990). This perspective is complemented by Heinonen (2001) who considers that entrepreneurship integrates the capacity for vision and action as it relates to the identification of opportunities, the capacity to assume and manage risk, as well as to the organization and coordination of resources. Stought (2016, p. 131) referes that "entrepreneurship is often defined as the process by which a business starts and grows, and entrepreneurs are those who start and grow businesses".

We can thus mention that the entrepreneur, in general, is seen as the agent who has the initiative and motivation to start their own business or company and seeks to achieve his goals. We can also add that the concept of entrepreneurship has been applied to several different contexts or domains, such as gender entrepreneurship, young / senior, cultural, social, rural, institutional, etc., their importance and their role in growth and economic development being analyzed in the context of private enterprise. In fact, it is true that those scholars who have contributed to the intellectual history of who the entrepreneur is and what he (she) does have focused on the entrepreneur in a private sector market environment" (Leyden & Link, 2015 p. 2). Also Heinonen (2001) and Zerbinatia and Souitarisb (2007) share the perspective that the study, as well as the research on entrepreneurship, are very connected to the sector and private initiative.

However, there is a question that arises. Is entrepreneurship restricted to private enterprise?

As Kearney, Hisrich and Roche (2009) point out, entrepreneurship is not restricted to the private sector. For Slaughter and Leslie (1999), entrepreneurship occurs in companies / institutions / organizations, in markets and in governments. Heinonen (2001) adds that the public and private sector, in the real economy, are not disconnected areas with no impact on each other, but interconnected in many different ways. In the same line of thought, Klein et al. (2010, p. 3) refer that "public objectives are closely linked to private ones, by definition, as they are part and parcel of the objective function of a private individual". Further on, the authors add that "private entrepreneurship occurs in a public context, and public action is undertaken by individual actors. As a result, the modern state contains elements of both private and public entrepreneurial behaviour" (Klein et al., 2010, p. 11).

If it is a fact that entrepreneurship and the study of entrepreneurship are fundamentally associated with private initiative, is it legitimate to question whether we can find the activity of undertaking at the level of governments and public and local administrations and institutions? How important is public entrepreneurship in the economic and social development of a region or territory?

Concept of Public Entrepreneurship

The budgetary constraints faced by most economic systems, whether in a national context or in a regional or local context, highlight the need for efficiency and effectiveness in the performance of public institutions and organizations, which are designed to respond to the demands, problems and needs of citizens. This framework of contraction of financial resources, but that at the same time is more demanding regarding the quality of public services that allow to improve the quality of life of the citizens, constitutes, for several authors, such as Heinonen (2001); Leitão and Alves (2016); Matthews (2014); Secchi (2010); Zerbinatia and Souitarisb (2007), a potentiating factor for the emergence of entrepreneurial strategies in the context of the public sector. However, and quoting Llewellyn and Jones (2003, p. 246) "what is understood by the term public sector entrepreneurship is far from consistent, to which they add while entrepreneurship can be linked to tangible benefits, there are also significant contradictions within the term in its public service context that have profound policy implications" (Llewellyn & Jones, 2003, p. 264).

Indeed, the definition of public entrepreneurship is not a simple task. On the one hand, we have the institutions / organizations per se which, from the perspective of the institutional / organizational entrepreneurship theory, can have an entrepreneurial orientation (action approach). On the other hand, we have the individuals that integrate these institutions / organizations, which can adopt entrepreneurial behaviors (individual approach). There are also authors, such as Schnellenbach (2007), who point out that the concept of public entrepreneurship and political entrepreneurship are often used indiscriminately. However, for Klein et al. (2010) and Schneider and Teske (1992), there is a slight difference between them that may be associated with the unit of analysis. This, in the first case, may refer to the local / regional authority / community, national governments or even to the international community. In turn, political entrepreneurship restricts its unit of analysis to the political agent or authority, such as elected politicians or lobbyists of established or created interest groups. Another feature of the political entrepreneur refers to the personal benefits to the individual being pointed out by Klein et al. (2010, p. 5) "political entrepreneurs are likely to undertake actions that foster economic value if they are also personally benefited from these actions in ways other than the mere private appropriation of value created". According to the organization Center for Public Impact (CPI, 2016), public entrepreneurs are internal agents to governments but whose fundamental action will have to combine two roles - public servant and entrepreneur - that, although different, may require the same competence. This indicates that, in the context of the challenges facing national, regional, local governments and their public services, for the CPI (2016, p. 2) "the future public servant will increasingly need to think and act like an entrepreneur - building new relationships, leveraging resources, working across sectors and acting, and sometimes failing, fast". In line with this perspective, we can also point out the position of Morris and Jones (1999), as well as Bernier and Hafsi (2007), in that they consider that public entrepreneurship is the process by which it is possible to create value for citizens, by combining public and private resources to explore social opportunities. In a similar perspective, Caruana, Ewing, and Ramaseshan (2002, p. 54) refer that "public sector entities can provide a new value to the various stakeholders by adopting an entrepreneurial approach with the resources over which they have control". Roberts (1992) adds that public entrepreneurship is a process of generating, designing and implementing innovative ideas in the public sector. Diefenbach (2011), Leyden and Link (2015), Leyden (2016) argue that public entrepreneurship involves innovative public policy initiatives capable of generating economic prosperity. This indicates that public entrepreneurship is a process that involves an innovative and proactive role of public management, including improving the efficiency of internal processes, raising alternative revenues, and developing other innovative solutions to meet the economic and social needs and promote the improvement of the quality of life of society (Diefenbach, 2011).

Other authors seek to define the profile of the public entrepreneur. Both Roberts (1992) and Ramamurti (1986) point out that the public entrepreneur is a highly confident and motivated person capable of generating, developing, and adopting innovative ideas in the public domain. In the same sense, Zampetakis and Moustakis (2007) consider that the public entrepreneur is a person who works in the public sector, who has the capacity to create and develop an energetic environment and workplace and that, through strategic vision and orientation of change to the organization, develops and offers a set of quality activities and services for the citizen.

In a more inclusive and concrete perspective, Klein et al. (2010) develop and present an analysis proposal of the relations between public entrepreneurship and private entrepreneurial behavior. According to them public (and political) entrepreneurship is manifested in four main activities: a) activities to create and manage new public resources; b) activities aimed at developing and establishing new public organizations; c) activities aimed at changing the institutional context and d) activities aimed at taking advantage of the effects of private activity for the pursuit of the common good.

We present, in table 1, a summary of some of the main dimensions / characteristics associated with entrepreneurship / public entrepreneurs, elaborated from the perspective of Diefenbach (2011) and Kearney et al. (2009).

Considering that the mission of public sector institutions / organizations is to provide a response to citizens' needs and problems, we can say that, from that perspective, local and regional powers / governments play a leading role to reach those ends. In the Portuguese context, although public policies are defined at the national level, it is the regional and local powers that have to frame and apply them locally, with the ultimate aim of promoting the growth and development of their regions. Indeed, the role of local and regional public authorities now goes far beyond regional intervention to ensure basic infrastructures and equipment (Gouveia, 2009). It is necessary to ensure quality social and health services, cultural and leisure

Table 1. Dimensions of public entrepeneurship

Dimension	Public Entrepreneur
Organization	Public sector organization
Person	Public agent
Main goal/function	Create value for citizens through the unique combination of resources
Motivation/reward	Low rewards/financial incentives. Rewards are mainly nonmonetary, namely political rewards and/or social goals
Competencies	Excellent political competencies; able to develop sources of power; uses public relations and social communication means as an advantage
Risks and failures	Assumes calculated risks; able to assume big organizational risks without assuming big personal risks
Innovation	Seek to overcome bureaucratic and political barriers that often restrict innovation
Perspective towards the future	Self-confident, optimistic and bold; high tolerance towards ambiguity

Source: Adapted from Diefenbach (2011) and Kearney et al. (2009).

services, to promote sport and sports activities, to adopt measures of support and access to education, and to combat school drop-out and failure.

In addition, a fundamental activity of regional and local public authorities also involves attracting investment and promoting a favorable environment for the creation of new companies. This is also the view of Nolan (2003, p. 1), who refers that "increasing the rate of enterprise creation is now an almost universal concern for local authorities, as well as central governments wishing to accelerate development in disadvantaged localities. Furthermore, in some localities, especially those that have limited prospects for attracting inward investment, promoting entrepreneurship is the only significant economic development strategy available at the local level".

According to this perspective, Acs and Szerb (2007, p. 111) also point out that "policy makers across all levels of government should not only have a strong interest in promoting entrepreneurship directly, but should also consider the impact their decisions on a range of issues are likely to have on entrepreneurial activity". In this regard, Gnyawali and Fogel (1994) already mentioned that, given the role of entrepreneurship in regional economic growth and development, the formulation of public policies should favor the development of conditions that promote entrepreneurship and opportunities for entrepreneurs.This is also the perspective of Klein et al. (2010), as well as Leyden and Link (2015).

In a recent work, Dhliwayo (2017) proposes a definition of Public Sector Entrepreneurship that is built from a literature review. This concept proposal takes into account a broad vision of the several government functions that the author aggregates in three categories: civil-political service agent, economic facilitation and administration and commercial market participation. These are, according to the author, the typologies that entrepreneurship in the public sector can assume. In the first case, actions and measures defined and carried out by public and political actors are included, aimed at ensuring a set of effective and efficient services (for example, providing digital platforms, securing forms of financing) for the citiziens, in a way that guarantees the conditions favorable to the generation and implementation of new opportunities. The second case encompasses all the necessary conditions to create a favourable environment conducive to the entrepreneurship of citizens and the private sector (for example, regulatory and legal conditions and regimes that favour entrepreneurship, intellectual property protection laws). In the third case, the active participation of the public sector in the markets is considered, namely in the strategic sectors or that require very high infrastructural investments. Therefore, "Public Sector Entrepeneurship emconpasses the state's role is to satisfy the civil-political needs of the citizen, regulating and facilitating the economic arena to ensure the efficient supply of goods and services. The state also find itself playing a strategic role in the commercial supply of goods and services where in, it owns and operates business entities in direct competition with other market forces. It may do so in order to ensure that it maximises on its social, political and economic mandates to its citizens" (Dhliwayo, 2017, p.16).

Considering the review carried out, and the perspectives of the different authors, we can indicate that institutions and favourable political and legal conditions play a decisive role in economic behaviour, since they influence the individual action in terms of decisions, expectations and motivations. However, it also indicates that the theme of entrepreneurship in the public sector is still an area where there are multiple perspectives and definitions, which indicates that it is a theme that remains in debate and evolution.

Recognizing these facts, which is, then, our understanding regarding what public entrepreneurship is?

On the one hand, considering the role assumed by local and regional public authorities, as well as the relevance of the context and surrounding support (*entrepreneurial ecosystem)*, our understanding is that public (political) entrepreneurship is associated with the whole set of measures adopted and developed to support self-employed entrepreneurs, to start their own business, but also to give them support through the developed networks. In this sense, we share the view of Heinonen (2001), Hwang and Powell (2004), Klein et al. (2010), Leyden and Link (2015), (Parracho, 2017) who point out the importance that public processes and actors can play in fostering entrepreneurial behavior. On the other hand, it encompasses all the innovative ways of action and acting of public powers, and their agents, that promote economic growth, collaboration with the market and the citiziens as to encourage sustainable development.

PUBLIC SECTOR ENTREPRENEURSHIP

Considering the concept / profile of the public entrepreneur previously reviewed, and considering that the pursuit of economic profit does not fit into the framework of the public entrepreneurial sector (Zampetakis & Moustakis, 2007), there is an imposing question: is there entrepreneurship in the context of the public sector? What are its determinants?

Although it is recognized that public entrepreneurship is a key concept in the subject, being also in line with the demand for efficiency and effectiveness in government management (Zampetakis & Moustakis, 2007), the literature on public (political) entrepreneurship is still incipient and fundamentally based on qualitative methods (Trettin & Welter, 2011). If it is true that the literature wich deals with entrepreneurship is vast, regarding its application to the public sector and the performance of public managers as entrepreneurs, literature is still scarce, although it is a growing subject of interest (Diefenbach, 2011; Edwards, Jones, Lawton &

Llewellyn, 2002; Klein et al., 2010; Matthews, 2014; Moon, 1999; Zerbinatia & Souitarisb, 2005; Zampetakis & Moustakis, 2007).

More recently, some empirical studies have emerged that seek to identify the determinants of public entrepreneurial behavior as well as their link to the environmental and organizational context. In this context, we will try, in this section, to review literature contributions, especially those applicable to the public entrepreneurship scope.

It is widely recognized that entrepreneurship / entrepreneurial activity, being dependent on characteristics intrinsic to the individual (individual determinants), is also determined, influenced and shaped by its entire context (contextual / environmental determinants). In a recent work, Kearney and Meynhardt (2016) suggest a model, which they call "model of public sector corporate entrepreneurship strategy (CES)", in which they seek to synthesize, integrate and link the key concepts that create public value and develop new economic activities that benefit their multiple stakeholders. As indicated in the model (Figure 1), the external envelope inherent to the public sector influences the strategy which, in turn, is decisive in shaping the internal components and results.

Considering that the priority of the public sector will be to respond to the diverse and different needs of society, not forgetting that it is necessary to guarantee its financial stability, the authors conclude that: "CES in the public sector incorporates (1) the external environmental conditions that generate entrepreneurial activity; (2) entrepreneurial strategic vision, organizational conditions, entrepreneurial orientation and individual behaviors that reflect the overall level of such processes and behaviors; and (3) public value as an outcome of CES within organizational

Figure 1. Model of public sector corporate entrepreneurship strategy (CES)
Source: Kearney and Meynhardt (2016, p. 546).

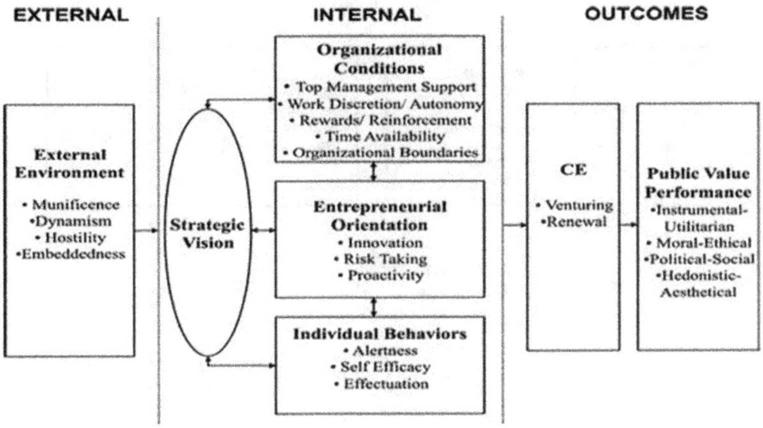

outcomes resulting from entrepreneurial actions, including the development of venturing and renewal, in turn, leads to enhanced levels of performance" (Kearney and Meynhardt, 2016, p. 561).

As such, the authors add that, "by adapting some of the entrepreneurial principles and strategies that have been effective in the private sector, top management of the public sector has a similar opportunity to transform the public sector through CES and thus to contribute to a functioning society" (Kearney & Meynhardt, 2016, p. 564).

This perspective of applying the theory of entrepreneurship to the activities of the public sector had previously been applied by Heinonen (2001) to the case of Finland. In his work, the author, applying the theory of entrepreneurship to public sector activities, seeks to identify the entrepreneurial practices of public sector organizations in Finland. These practices are divided, according to Heinonen (2001), in two different types: (a) in the development of a model of entrepreneurial action in public sector organizations (intrapreneurship); (b) developing a local industrial policy to support small and medium-sized enterprises (SMEs), in particular municipal agencies that provide services to support the promotion and development of an entrepreneurial, competitive and profitable business environment for their region. In this way, the author seeks to identify the determinants of organizational entrepreneurship (intrapreneurship) in the context of the public sector, namely, local / regional bodies.

External pressures for entrepreneurship / change in public institutions or organizations tend to be minor, in the course of their own mission and the fact that they do not face competition. Thus, in these institutions / organizations, the pressures to generate incentive and motivation for change / entrepreneurship come much more from within the public body itself, and also from the manager's own behavior /

Figure 2. The factors influencing intrapreneurship in public sector organizations
Source: Heinonen (2001, p. 5).

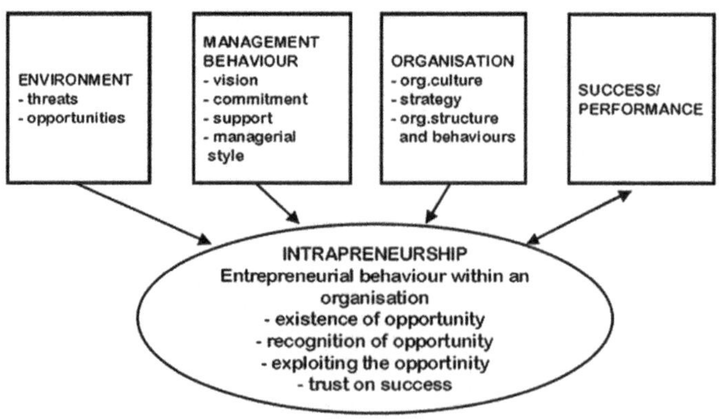

leadership. As such, the author, based on several works, presents a compilation of the determinants of entrepreneurship in the municipal public organization, according to the scheme of Figure 2.

In this context, it can be seen that there are three dimensions that can influence the entrepreneurial behavior of the organization. In addition to interacting with the external environment, and the organization's ability to react to changes arising from this environment, the manager's management and leadership capabilities are also key factors which influence entrepreneurial activity. Another dimension comes from the organization itself, that is, from its strategy, structure / behavior and organizational culture. These three dimensions affect the entrepreneurial behavior, which can influence the success / performance of the organization, which in turn can reinforce and influence this behavior.

Regarding the policy of industrial development and support to SMEs, the author acknowledges that for the agencies studied, although their goals and strategies are well defined, the way in which they are presented makes it very difficult to measure their results. Nevertheless, the author concludes that although two thirds of the municipal agencies studied are developing development projects with SMEs, the overall level of innovation in these activities was relatively low, reflecting poor performance from the point of view of entrepreneurship.

Diefenbach (2017), in his work on the case of Germany's Federal Labor Agency, seeks to study, on the one hand, the antecedents of the entrepreneurial orientation of public organizations (e.g., what makes them innovative, proactive and risk-taking) and, on the other, to know how the entrepreneurial orientation is related to the goal of creating public value. Based on an exhaustive literature review in three domains, "literature on corporate entrepreneurship (i.e., entrepreneurship within existing private sector organizations), public entrepreneurship (i.e., entrepreneurship in the public sector), and public value management is reviewed" (Diefenbach, p. 4), the author defined a model (empirically tested through structural equations) directed to the public sector middle managers. The author directs the model to this category of managers because, according to the literature, they constitute the main group of initiators, they are the most enterprising and the most creative, and the empirical studies in this area are very scarce (Diefenbach, 2017). In this sense, applying to the public context the theory of entrepreneurial behaviour, resulting from the theory of entrepreneurship in the private sector, the results indicate that public entrepreneurship results from an entrepreneurial orientation within the public organization being directly related to management support, motivations of the staff, multiple expectations and the time and the proximity of the managers with the people and the surrounding context. In this way, public entrepreneurship is associated and related to pro-activity and search for effectiveness and efficiency in the creation of public value (Diefenbach, 2017).

In a study applied to the United States of America (USA), Schneider and Teske (1992) tried to analyze the determinants of public entrepreneurship. The authors studied 114 US "suburban communities" to test the relationship between the propensity for the emergence of public entrepreneurship and the existence of local facilitating conditions and the likelihood of factors that increase corporate profits. With regard to individual determinants, the authors have identified "blocking behaviors" (eg, bureaucratic manipulation of services) as the primary individual strategic determinant that entrepreneurs adopt in order to restrict the emergence of competing entrepreneurs. Contextual determinants are demographic factors (such as population growth and racial diversity), as well as the fiscal (applied taxes) and budgetary (allocation, redistribution and development expenditure) conditions identified as the main determinants of local public entrepreneurship. In their perspective, the authors indicate that entrepreneurship, within the public context, compared to entrepreneurship in the private sector (this, especially, related to personal and individual characteristics) is more dependent on collective and institutional strength and will to adopt changes, innovations and risk taking.

The work of Bartlett and Dibben (2002), in a study applied in the United Kingdom (UK) and based on twelve case studies on innovation in the context of local public governments, presents additional arguments for the discussion about the nature of public entrepreneurship and its motivations. Using a sample of twelve representative cases of different types of organizations as well as different policy contexts, the authors' work indicates that it is possible to identify two distinctive types of entrepreneurship / public entrepreneur: a) one that is focused on meeting the public/collective needs and which the authors have designated "public" champion; and (b) the so-called "empowered" champion which is motivated primarily by personal concerns. Quoting Bartlett and Dibben (2002, p. 112) "'empowered' champions where motivated by more personal concerns, which tended to relate to their desire to 'make a mark' and their enjoyment of the change process itself". The authors also suggest that local public governments are not bureaucratic organizations where there is no room for entrepreneurship and innovation. On the contrary, the authors' perspective is that in the context of local public governments, innovation and entrepreneurship are intertwined, so the role and performance of public managers assume their importance in the development, implementation and consolidation of innovation in the public sector (Bartlett & Dibben, 2002).

In their study of ten local governments (five in the UK and five in Italy), Zerbinatia and Souitarisb (2005) sought to identify different types of public (political) entrepreneurs and their determinants in the application / funding of European structural funds. The authors consider that entrepreneurship is determined and influenced by individual but also contextual characteristics. In relation to the former, they emphasize the importance of the individual's strategic and management capacities which can be observed at the level of: a) the commitment to opportunity, that is, the individual's ability to react and adopt changes; (b) commitment to management, including the ability to coordinate and manage uncontrolled resources; (c) the commitment to the resources and control of those resources. Regarding contextual / environmental determinants, the authors recognize that, in the case of the funding of structural funds, changes in national policies and the local economic situation of the regions influence the activities of public (political) entrepreneurs. In addition, contextual / environmental determinants are also closely associated with the "rewards philosophy". Their study leads the authors to conclude that public sector entrepreneurs are motivated primarily by nonmonetary rewards such as promotion and increase of responsibilities, re-election and career advancement, and social recognition.

The work of Zampetakis and Moustakis (2007) seeks to identify the determinants of entrepreneurship in the public sector in Greece. The results of the study indicate that, as for individual determinants, and like for private entrepreneurs, public sector entrepreneurs are self-confident and highly motivated individuals, with educational levels, gender and title-position being the main individual determinants. Similarly to Zerbinatia and Souitarisb (2005), the authors also identify as individual determinants certain management capacities of the public entrepreneur, namely the commitment to the opportunity and the strategic orientation / vision. As for contextual determinants, the results indicate the (non-monetary) compensation system as an important determinant, which is in line with the work of Zerbinatia and Souitarisb (2005).

In a paper applied to Portugal, Teixeira and Silva (2012) look to analyze and interrelate different dimensions of public entrepreneurship at the local level, in order to identify their determinants. In a different perspective from other studies on entrepreneurship, whose approach focuses on the individual, this study adopts a more collective perspective, placing emphasis on the municipality and not the Mayor (Teixeira & Silva, 2012). The authors present an analysis of (local) political entrepreneurship that encompasses three fundamental dimensions: the application / obtaining of European funds (funds) (in line with Zerbinatia and Souitarisb, 2007); the possession and construction of infrastructures to support entrepreneurship; and social activities (infrastructures) and the services and activities necessary for the development of entrepreneurship and those activities. Therefore, the authors' approach encompasses the entrepreneurial nature of the Mayor, the quality and availability of the municipality's resources and the social-economic characteristics of the region (Teixeira & Silva, 2012). The results indicate, as individual determinants, the age, gender, and entrepreneurial management skills and capacities, which is in line with previously reviewed works by Zerbinatia and Souitarisb (2007) and Zampetakis and Moustakis (2007). In what concerns the contextual determinants, i.e., the socioeconomic characteristics of municipalities, those tending to be more entrepreneurial are those that tend to verify the following characteristics: deficits in communication infrastructures, those whose population has a higher level of schooling, those with levels and a business structure dominated by SMEs (Teixeira & Silva, 2012).

The previously presented revision allows to indicate that the studies present different perspectives, methods and analysis units. As to make comparing these main literature contributions when it comes to public entrepreneurship easier, we present, in table 2, a summary of those studies regarding the goals, methods, analysis units and main results.

Table 2. Public Entrepeneurship Literature

Author(s)/Study	Main Purpose	Method	Country / Unit of Analysis	Finfing(s)
Schneider and Teske (1992)	To analyze the determinants of local public entrepreneurship	Quantitative (probit estimation)	USA / 114 US "suburban communities"	Main determinants of local public entrepreneurship are contextual determinants: demographic factors (population growth; racial diversity); fiscal (higher tax rate) and budgetary (more ressources)
Bartlett and Dibben (2002)	To define and distinguish the nature of public entrepeneurship types.	Qualitative (study case)	UK / 12 cases of different types of organizations	Identified two types of public entrepreneur: the *"public" champion* –focused on meeting the public/collective needs; the *"empowered" champion* – primarily motivated by personal concerns
Heinonen (2001)	To identify the entrepreneurial practices of public sector organizations, by applying the theory of entrepreneurship.	Qualitative (study case) and quantitative (structured questionnaire)	Finland / 2 public sector organizations and 71 municipal support agencies (owned, at least partly) by municipalities.	Three dimensions can influence the entrepreneurial behavior of public sector organization: the manager's management and leadership capabilities; external environment; strategy and organizational behavior and culture.
Zerbinatia and Souitarisb (2005)	To analyse and test the applicability of entrepreneurship theory in the public sector	Qualitative (study case)	UK and Italy / 5 local governments in each country	Local public entrepreneurial behaviour is determined and influenced by individual (strategic and management capacities) and contextual conditions (local economic situation, social recognition, nonmonetary rewards such as promotion and increase of responsibilities, re-election and career advancement).
Zampetakis and Moustakis (2007)	To identify the determinants of entrepreneurship in Greek public sector	Quantitative (Bayesian factor analysis, conjoint analysis and cluster analysis.)	Greece / public servants of 15 Greek prefectures	Individual characteristics of public sector entrepeneurs are similar to the private entrepreneurs. Public sector entrepreneurs are self-confident and highly motivated individuals, with educational levels, gender and title-position being the main individual determinants.

continued on following page

Table 2. Continued

Author(s)/Study	Main Purpose	Method	Country / Unit of Analysis	Finfing(s)
Teixeira e Silva (2012)	To interrelate different dimensions of public entrepreneurship, at the local level, in order to identify their determinants	Quantitative (estimation of econometric specifications)	Portugal / 108 Portuguese municipalities	Local political entrepreneurship has a positive and significant, but indirect impact, on the creation of new businesses (high and medium technology).
Diefenbach (2011)	To study what determines middle managers entrepreneurial orientation in public sector organizations.	Quantitative (structural equation modelling)	Germany / 250 middle managers of Germany's Federal Labor Agency	Public value orientation is strongly and positively related with entrepreneurial orientation. Factors influencing entrepreneurial orientation are: management support, multitude of expectations, staff motivation,, the managers' localism, and the managers' tenure in the current position/ department.
Kearney and Meynhardt (2016)	To conceptualize corporate entrepreneurship strategy (CES) in the public sector, by adapting entrepreneurial strategies from the private sector	Conceptual (literature review)	Generic / Organizations	Defination of a CES to the public sector. Public entrepreneurship, and the development of a CES, depends on the individual entrepreneurial orientation, being supported by top management, which will support the allocation of organizational conditions and, in turn, will enhance performance and efficiency in promoting the satisfaction of society needs.

Source: Compiled by the authors

DISCUSSION AND FUTURE RESEARCH DIRECTIONS

The main purpose of this work was to discuss the concept of public entrepeneurship, to raise theoretical reflections and to present a review of the literature on entrepreneurship in the public sector. Our work begins with one question: is there entrepreneurship within the public sector? In our view, the answer to this question is affirmative. Indeed, the analysis carried out in this section indicates that, in fact, entrepreneurship also occurs outside the context of the private sector and, therefore, occurs in the context of the public sector. The literature broadly recognizes that entrepreneurship in the public sector exists, and the innovative and proactive role implicit in it is important in creating value and improving the quality of life of citizens. Nevertheless, this premise is not above criticism. According to Diefenbach (2011, p.40) *public managers, just like private managers, might go too far in their entrepreneurship*. Instead of seeking the public interest, they can act on behalf of their own and private interests, exercise dominance over others, use public funds improperly and may even pose a threat to democratic government. However, as the author points out, these cases might be the exception, rather than the rule.

The review carried out reveals that the literature on public entrepreneurship seems to be a topic of growing interest. The literature review shows that the authors/studies adopt different concepts/perspectives, methods and units of analysis. In our perspective, the literature review indicates that we can point to two groups of studies in the context of public entrepreneurship:

- Those whose unit of analysis is the public institution / organization. Following a conceptual approach, they seek to apply the theory of corporate entrepreneurship of the private sector to the public context, in order to analyze the constraints (internal and external) to the public organization that influence their entrepreneurial orientation and, thus, to define strategies to increase their ability to create value and provide services to citizens.
- Those whose unit of analysis is the individual – the entrepreneurial agent. Following an empirical approach, and as a support of both qualitative and quantitative methodologies, they end up having as focus the analysis of the profile of this agent, their motivations and determinants to adopt an entrepreneurial behaviour. In this context, studies indicate that individual determinants, which include factors such as age, educational level, employment position, management, strategic vision, trust and motivation, tend to positively influence levels of public entrepreneurship.

Another observation that can be drawn is that there is a considerable amplitude of the theme of public entrepreneurship insofar as the studies adopt different conceptualizations applied to different contexts and units of analysis. In fact, as Dhliwayo (2017) points out, while it is recognized that the public sector can be entrepreneurial, like the private sector, the concept of public entrepreneurship is not clearly defined. This happens because, on the one hand, research has not dealt with the discussion of different concepts and ideas. On the other hand, due to the fact that the literature is still incipient, there is still no strong theoretical consolidated body. Therefore, we share the view of some authors who, although they recognize the pertinence and relevance of some theoretical and/or based on qualitative methodologies works, the research and empirical evidence are still scarce.

Thus, we consider that additional research is needed. Firstly, it is needed a strong discussion that confronts the different perspectives of the researchers, in order to reach a consensus regarding the concept of public entrepreneurship and the different levels and scopes that it can integrate.

Considering that the public sector entrepreneurship is a complex process involving different actors (e.g., the public institution/organization - national, local or regional government; individuals - top managers, middle managers, public servants) more studies and research are required, whether at the individual level or multi-level studies, in order to understand how they may, or may not, interrelate in entrepreneurship activities.

Indeed, so that we can understand and even quantify the role of each actor, there is a need to expand the methods used to study the public entrepreneurship process. In this context, there is a need for comparison. It would be interesting to develop research that involves different countries; different levels of government; and multicase comparative studies, when considering the same unit of analysis. According to several authors, most studies on public entrepreneurship are qualitative (Dienfenbach, 2011; Zampetakis & Moutakis, 2007; Zerbinati & Souitaris, 2005) and apply a conceptual and descriptive approach (Meynhardt & Diefenbach, 2012). Thus, the definition of rigorous theoretical models and the use of quantitative methodologies should be developed and adopted, in order to identify the determinants of public entrepreneurship, at different levels, as well as its effects on economic development and growth. The development of a "more refined" analysis would complement the available studies and develop the knowledge regarding the role of public entrepreneurship for the society.

We consider another line concerning public sector entrepreneurship research. It is related with the current challenges faced by societies and governments (e.g., budgetary constraints, demographic challenges sustainable development). How can the public sector be innovative, entrepreneurial and efficient using scarce resources? That is another emerging dimension which requires multidisciplinary research areas, including public sector entrepreneurship.

CONCLUSION

It is widely recognized that entrepreneurship is a determining factor in promoting economic growth and development. More recently, researchers are concerned with analyzing the political and legal conditions of support for entrepreneurial behavior, as well as the extensive ecosystem that may reinforce or restrict such behavior and the willingness to take the risk (Hwang & Powell, 2004). In this context, local and regional authorities can play a decisive role in defining and creating conditions to promote entrepreneurial behavior.

Entrepreneurship in the context of the public sector is an emerging research area that involves a variety of terms, concepts and issues (Klein et al., 2010). Indeed, although it may not yet be fully and explicitly defined, entrepreneurship in the context of the public sector is a key concept for the current political and economic framework, which is governed by criteria of efficiency and effectiveness in public governance. Indeed, the context and constraints around entrepreneurship in the public sector are multiple and diverse. Public entrepreneurs face political interference, reduced and biased reward systems, multiple and sometimes ambiguous objectives, constraints associated with business cycles, limited autonomy, and restrictive human resource policies (Morris & Jones, 1999).Consequently, entrepreneurship in the public sector can be associated with entrepreneurial orientation and management skills. Therefore, it involves, besides the definition of objectives, the entrepreneurial action necessary to carry out the mission of the public organization / institution. At the same time, this entrepreneurial action is also important for achieving individual / personal satisfaction levels (Heinonen, 2001).

The public entrepreneurship subject is assuming increasing importance. "The idea of public entrepreneurship is to increase opportunities to take challengeable ideas and find ways to offer more public choices and benefits, providing high-quality services to citizens" (Kim, 2010, p.781). It is expected to occur a development of research in this context, especially because of the challenges facing societies and governments today. These can occur not only at the level of budgetary constraints, but also at the level of demographic challenges and at the level of increased competition between regions to attract investment. The challenges posed by sustainable development and the need to preserve the environment, availability of energy and natural resources are also major challenges facing society and governments. According to Bekkers and Tummers (2018, p. 210) "Innovation in the public sector is high on the agenda of public managers and politicians, as well as companies, societal organizations and citizens. Innovation is needed to address grand societal challenges (...)". Public entrepreneurship is thus of paramount importance as the response to these challenges. It requires a creative approach that will inevitably involve local, regional and national governments and an increasingly concerted and shared action of public and private action.

REFERENCES

Acs, Z. J., & Szerb, L. (2007). Entrepreneurship Economic Growth and Public Policy. *Small Business Economics*, *28*(2-3), 109–122. doi:10.100711187-006-9012-3

Bartlett, D., & Dibben, P. (2002). Public Sector Innovation and Entrepreneurship: Case Studies from Local Government. *Local Government Studies*, *28*(4), 107–121. doi:10.1080/714004159

Bekkers, V., & Tummers, L. (2018). Innovation in the public sector: Towards an open and collaborative approach. *International Review of Administrative Sciences*, *84*(2), 209–213. doi:10.1177/0020852318761797

Bernier, L., & Hafsi, T. (2007, May). The changing nature of public entrepreneurship. *Public Administration Review*.

Bygrave, W. D. (1993). Theory Building in the Entrepreneurship Paradigm. *Journal of Business Venturing*, *8*(3), 255–280. doi:10.1016/0883-9026(93)90031-Y

Caruana, A., Ewing, M. T., & Ramaseshan, B. (2002). Effects of some environmental challenges and centralization on the entrepreneurial orientation and performance of public sector entities. *The Service Industries Management Journal*, *22*(2), 43–58. doi:10.1080/714005076

CPI. (2016). *Enter the public entrepreneur: Implementing innovation in the public sector*. Briefing Bulletin. Retrieved from: https://www.centreforpublicimpact.org/public-entrepreneurship-briefing-bulletin/

Dhliwayo, S. (2017). *Defining public-sector entrepreneurship. A conceptual operational construct*. University of Johannesbourg. Retrieved from http://hdl.handle.net/10210/241340

Diefenbach, F. E. (2011). *Entrepreneurship in the Public Sector: When Middle Managers Create Public Value* (Dostoral Dissertation). Gabler Research, Gabler Verlag Wiesbaden. Retrieved from: http://www1.unisg.ch/www/edis.nsf/SysLkpByIdentifier/3883/$FILE/dis3883.pdf

Edwards, C., Jones, G., Lawton, A., & Llewellyn, N. (2002). Public entrepreneurship: Rhetoric, reality, and context. *International Journal of Public Administration*, *25*(12), 1539–1554. doi:10.1081/PAD-120014260

Gnyawali, D., & Fogel, D. (1994). Environments for entrepreneurship development: Key dimensions and research implications. *Entrepreneurship Theory and Practice*, *18*(4), 43–62. doi:10.1177/104225879401800403

Gouveia, P. (2009). *Municípios, Economia Solidária e Desenvolvimento Local: caminho possível para um "outro" desenvolvimento*. Departamento de Economia do Instituto Universitário de Lisboa, 2009. Retrieved from: https://repositorio.iscte-iul.pt/handle/10071/3718

Heinonen, J. (2001). *Entrepreneurship in public sector organisations*. Turku School of Economics and Business Administration, Small Business Institute, Finland. 2011. Retrieved from: http://citeseerx.ist.psu.edu/viewdoc/summary?doi=10.1.1.199.5050

Hwang, H., & Powell, W. (2004). Institutions and entrepreneurship. *The Handbook of Entrepreneurship*. Retrieved from: https://web.stanford.edu/group/song/papers/HwangPowell.pdf

Isenberg, D. (2013). *The Entrepreneurship Ecosystem Strategy as a New Paradigm for Economic Policy: Principles for Cultivating Entrepreneurship*. Dublin, Ireland: Institute of International European Affairs.

Kearney, C., Hisrich, R. D., & Roche, F. (2009). Public and private sector entrepreneurship: Similarities, differences or a combination? *Journal of Small Business and Enterprise Development*, *16*(1), 26–46. doi:10.1108/14626000910932863

Kearney, C., & Meynhardt, T. (2016). Directing Corporate Entrepreneurship Strategy in the Public Sector to Public Value: Antecedents, Components, and Outcomes. *International Public Management Journal*, *19*(4), 543–572. doi:10.1080/10967494.2016.1160013

Kim, Y. (2010). Stimulating Entrepreneurial Practices in the Public Sector: The Roles of Organizational Characteristics. *Administration & Society*, *42*(7), 780–814. doi:10.1177/0095399710377432

Klein, P. G., Mahoney, J. T., McGahan, A. M., & Pitelis, C. N. (2010). Toward a theory of public entrepreneurship. *European Management Review*, *7*(1), 1–15. doi:10.1057/emr.2010.1

Leitão, J., & Alves, H. (2016). *Entrepreneurial and innovative practices in Public Institutions. A quality of life approach*. Springer International Publishing. doi:10.1007/978-3-319-32091-5

Leyden, D. P. (2016). Public-sector entrepreneurship and the creation of a sustainable innovative economy. *Small Business Economics*, *46*(4), 553–564. doi:10.100711187-016-9706-0

Leyden, D. P., & Link, A. N. (2015). *Public Sector Entrepreneurship: U.S. Technology and Innovation Policy*. New York: Oxford University Press. doi:10.1093/acprof:oso/9780199313853.001.0001

Llewellyn, N., & Jones, G. (2003). Controversies and conceptual development. Examining public entrepreneurship. *Public Management Review*, *5*(2), 245–266. doi:10.1080/1461667032000066426

Lumpkin, G. T., & Dess, G. G. (1996). Clarifying the Entrepreneurial Orientation Construct and Linking it to Performance. *Academy of Management Review*, *21*(1), 135–172. doi:10.5465/amr.1996.9602161568

Mason, C., & Brown, R. (2013). Creating good public policy to support high-growth firms. *Small Business Economics*, *40*(2), 211–225. doi:10.100711187-011-9369-9

Matthews, J. (2014). Entrepreneurship in the public sector: new possibilities? In P. Davidsson (Ed.), *Australian Centre for Entrepreneurship Research Exchange Conference 2014. Proceedings*. Sydney, NSW: Queensland University of Technology. Retrieved from http://eprints.qut.edu.au/71108/2/Matthews__Entrepreneurship_in_the_public_sector_-_ACERE.pdf

Mcclelland, D. C. (1961). *The Achieving Society*. New York: Irvington Publishers. doi:10.1037/14359-000

Meynhardt, T., & Diefenbach, F. (2012). What Drives Entrepreneurial Orientation in the Public Sector? Evidence from Germany's Federal Labor Agency. *Journal of Public Administration Research and Theory Advance Access*. Retrieved from: https://www.researchgate.net/publication/260100763

Moon, M. J. (1999). The Pursuit of Managerial Entrepreneurship: Does Organization Matter? *Public Administration Review*, *59*(1), 31–46. doi:10.2307/977477

Morris, M., & Jones, F. (1999). Entrepreneurship in established organisations: The case of the public sector. *Entrepreneurship Theory and Practice*, *24*(1), 71–91. doi:10.1177/104225879902400105

Nolan, A. (2003). *Entrepreneurship and Local Economic Development: Policy Innovations in Industrialized Countries*. Retrieved from: http://citeseerx.ist.psu.edu/viewdoc/download?doi=10.1.1.199.4169&rep=rep1&type=pdf

OECD. (2003). *Entrepreneurship and Local Economic Development*. Paris: OECD.

Parracho, A. R. (2017). *The Portuguese Startup Ecosystem: Key Success Factors on the Entrepreneurial Ecosystem*. Universidade Católica Portuguesa. Retrieved from: https://repositorio.ucp.pt/bitstream/10400.14/21833/1/152115100.pdf

Pinchot, G. (1985). *Intrapreneuring: Why you don't have to leave the Corporation to become an entrepreneur*. New York: Harper & Row.

Pinchot, G., & Pellman, R. (2004). *Intra-empreendedorismo na prática: um guia de inovação nos negócios*. Rio de Janeiro: Elsevier.

Ramamurti, R. (1986). Public entrepreneurs: Who they are and how they operate. *California Management Review*, *28*(3), 142–158. doi:10.2307/41165207

Roberts, N. C. (1992). Public entrepreneurship and innovation. *Policy Studies Review*, *11*(1), 55–74. doi:10.1111/j.1541-1338.1992.tb00332.x

Sadler, R. J. (2000). Corporate entrepreneurship in the public sector: The dance of the chameleon. *Australian Journal of Public Administration, 59*(2), 25–43. doi:10.1111/1467-8500.00149

Santos, C., & Teixeira, A. C. C. (2009). The evolution of the literature on entrepreneurship. Uncovering some under researched themes. *FEP Working Papers, 335,* 1–41.

Schneider, M., & Teske, P. (1992). Toward a theory of the political entrepreneur: Evidence from local government. *The American Political Science Review, 86*(3), 737–747. doi:10.2307/1964135

Schnellenbach, J. (2007). Public entrepreneurship and the economics of reform. *Journal of Institutional Economics, 3*(2), 183–202. doi:10.1017/S1744137407000641

Secchi, L. (2010). Entrepreneurship and participation in public management reforms at the local level. *Local Government Studies, 36*(4), 511–527. doi:10.1080/03003930.2010.494103

Slaughter, S., & Leslie, L. (1997). *Academic Capitalism: Politics, Policies and the Entrepreneurial University*. Baltimore, MD: Johns Hopkins University Press.

Stephens, M., Partridge, D., & Faggian, A. (2013). Innovation, entrepreneurship and economic growth in lagging regions. *Journal of Regional Science, 53*(5), 778–812. doi:10.1111/jors.12019

Stevenson, H., & Jarillo, J. C. (1990). A paradigm of entrepreneurship: Entrepreneurial management. *Strategic Management Journal, EUA, 11*, 17–27.

Stought, R. (2016). Entrepreneurship and Regional Economic Development: Some reflections. *Investigaciones Regionales – Journal of Regional Research, 36,* 129-150.

Teixeira, A. C., & Silva, C. (2012). A new perspective on local political entrepreneurship: Evidence from Portugal. *Local Economy, 27*(4), 332–354. doi:10.1177/0269094212439151

Tidd, J., Bessant, J., & Pavitt, K. (2008). Gestão da Inovação. *The Bookman.*

Trettin, L., & Welter, F. (2011). Challenges for spatially oriented entrepreneurship research. *Entrepreneurship and Regional Development, 23*(7/8), 575–602. doi:10.1080/08985621003792988

Zampetakis, L., & Moustakis, V. (2007). Entrepreneurial behaviour in the Greek public sector. *International Journal of Entrepreneurial Behaviour & Research, 13*(1), 19–38. doi:10.1108/13552550710725165

Zerbinatia, S., & Souitarisb, V. (2005). Entrepreneurship in the public sector: A framework of analysis in European local governments. *Entrepreneurship and Regional Development, 17*(1), 43–64. doi:10.1080/0898562042000310723

ADDITIONAL READING

Andrade, C. R., Lopes, D. P. T., & Ckagnazaroff, I. B. (2016). Public Entrepreneurship and Quality of Life: The Perspectives of Public Entrepreneurs from the State of Minas Gerais (Brazil). In J. Leitão & H. Alves (Eds.), *Entrepreneurial and Innovative Practices in Public Institutions. Applying Quality of Life Research (Best Practices).* Cham: Springer. doi:10.1007/978-3-319-32091-5_3

Bernier, L. (2014). Public enterprises as policy instruments: The importance of public entrepreneurship. *Journal of Economic Policy Reform, 17*(3), 253–266. doi:10.1080/17487870.2014.909312

Catney, P., & Henneberry, J. M. (2016). Public entrepreneurship and the politics of regeneration in multi-level governance. *Environment and Planning C. Politics and Space, 34*(7), 1324–1343.

Daniel, H. (2013). Public entrepreneurship: Desiring social change, creating sociality. *Entrepreneurship and Regional Development, 25*(1-2), 34–51. doi:10.1080/08985626.2012.746883

Mitra, J. (2012). Entrepreneurship, Innovation and Regional Development: An Introduction. New York. Routledge, Taylor and Francis Group.

Pugalis, L., Davidson, J., McLeay, F., & Round, A. (2016). Tough Times, Difficult Choices and Public Entrepreneurship: Is Sponsorship a Winning Solution? In J. Liddle (Ed.), *New Perspectives on Research, Policy & Practice in Public Entrepreneurship (Contemporary Issues in Entrepreneurship Research (pp, 37 – 59). Emerald Group Publishing Limited.* doi:10.1108/S2040-724620160000006002

Raposo, M. (2009). Support Policies to Entrepreneurship. In R. Baptista & J. Leitao (Eds.), *Public Policies for Fostering Entrepreneurship. International Studies in Entrepreneurship, 22* (pp. 133–148). New York: Springer. doi:10.1007/978-1-4419-0249-8_7

Scott, J. T. (2016). Creativity for Invention Insights: Corporate Strategies and Opportunities for *Public Entrepreneurship. Economia e Politica Industriale, 43*(4), 409–448. doi:10.100740812-016-0039-4

Smith, E. (2013). Entrepreneurship at the Local Government Level: Stimulating and restraining forces in the Swedish waste management industry. *Public Management Review, 16*(5), 708–732. doi:10.1080/14719037.2012.743580

Weiss, M. (2014). "Government Entrepreneur" is Not an Oxymoron. *Harvard Business Review*. Retrieved from: https://hbr.org/2014/03/government-entrepreneur-is-not-an-oxymoron

KEY TERMS AND DEFINITIONS

Economic Development: Is a dynamic long-term phenomenon that reflects the changes that are taking place in the economic, social, political, and cultural structures in an economic system. The economic development concept integrates the idea of economic growth, the increase of the production, and consumption opportunities, but it goes beyond this, considering that it is a process that implies the improvement in living standards, namely, better jobs, reduction in inequality income distribution, greater and better access to education and health, and improve of environmental protection.

Entrepreneur: Is a person who identifies an opportunity and has the initiative and motivation to start his (or her) own business and, regardless of the risk, seeks to overcome obstacles and challenges in order to achieve its objectives.

Entrepreneurial Ecosystem: Is a system composed of a range of stakeholders, public and private, individual and collective, as well as the full set of policy measures defined and adopted to enhance their action, articulation, and co-development, in order to promote entrepreneurship, value creation, and economic development. Approaches to define entrepreneurial ecosystems usually consider some key dimensions: high human capital qualification, open markets, favourable culture, consistent financial system, governance and policy measures, institutional and business support.

Entrepreneurship: Entrepreneurship is the process by which individuals—individually or within an organization—want to develop, implement, organize, and manage a new business (or changes in existing companies) with all the risks implied, in order to create economic value and make a profit.

Intra-Entrepreneurship: Is the practice of developing a new project within an existing organization, carried out by the employees or managers, to explore a new opportunity and create economic value.

Literature Review: Is the process of analyzing and evaluating previous research and information in a particular subject area. It is the first stage of a research paper or project and its purpose is to describe, summarize, and evaluate the ideas and arguments of other researchers.

Private Sector: Is the part of a country's economy which includes the personal sector (households) and corporate sector (companies). Therefore, it is the part of a country's economy run by economic agents seeking profit. Usually, private sector agents are free from state control. Nevertheless, government and private agents establish public-private partnership, in order to, jointly, deliver services or goods to citizens.

Public Sector: Includes the areas of a country's economy which are controlled by the state. In most of the countries, the public sector comprises the national, regional, and local governmental authorities, including the policy measures defined and adopted by those authorities, in order to provide public services (e.g., public infrastructures, public education, and health care) to citizens without seeking to generate profit. The public ownership firms, which provide services and goods for sale, and usually operate on a commercial basis (seeking profit), are not included in public sector.

Public Sector Entrepreneurship: Encompasses the whole set of measures adopted and developed by local, regional, and national authorities to support self-employed entrepreneurs to start their own businesses but also to give them support through the developed networks. Additionally, it encompasses all the innovative ways of action and acting of public powers and their agents that promote economic growth, collaboration with the market, and the citizens as to encourage sustainable development.

ENDNOTE

1 Two important tools for the evaluation of the entrepreneurial ecosystem of countries are the indexes developed by The Global Entrepreneurship and Development Index (GEDI index – http://thedegi.org) and the Global Entrepreneurship Monitor (GEM – www.gemconsortium.org). These instruments explain the entrepreneurial context/ecosystem, as well as the entrepreneurial activity of each country, allowing their governments to adopt improvement measures.

Chapter 6
Entrepreneurship and Chance:
Evidence of Happy Coincidences, Serendipity, Synchronicity, Black Swan Events, or the "Hand of God"?

Alexandra França
University of Vigo, Spain

Orlando Lima Rua
Polytechnic of Porto, Portugal

ABSTRACT

The unpredictability of business activities means that entrepreneurs should find a way to adapt and embrace chance. The traditional and predefined process logic offers little support for today's complex and dynamic business environment. One tenet that shaped the direction of entrepreneurship research is the view that the entrepreneurial opportunity discovery and development is linear, systematic, and rational, that is, it is assumed that all factors are measurable and knowable. However, unknowable instances of coincidence, randomness, and chance factors can play a significant role in new venture creation. The authors propose that these factors point to the nonlinear and acausal phenomenon of chance. This research proposal intends to address entrepreneurs' alternative mechanisms, other than the classic formal planning model, to harness opportunities or overcome setbacks arising from chance. To achieve our purpose, the authors examine qualitative data drawn from entrepreneurial activity of Spain and Portugal.

DOI: 10.4018/978-1-5225-6942-8.ch006

INTRODUCTION

The role of entrepreneurship has become evident since the end of the last century. In modern open economies it has become an important area for economic growth and development (Toma, Grigore, & Marinescu, 2014).

Entrepreneurship is a creative human process, which implies person's will of taking on responsibilities and the mental ability of identifying opportunities where others find only chaos, contradictions, or confusion (Toma et al., 2014). To be an entrepreneur is therefore to act upon a possibility that one has identified and is worth pursuing (McMullen & Shepherd, 2006).

Entrepreneurship is flourishing as a discipline and many scholars have recognized the richness of the entrepreneurship field and incorporated the concept by rethinking theories, developing conceptual models, introducing new constructs, and performing a variety of empirical studies. This plurality certainly signifies an enrichment of the field (Hoskisson et al., 2011).

Yet, scarce attention has been paid to luck, chance, serendipity or misfortunes are still insufficiently researched areas in organization studies and entrepreneurship (Lennerfors & Rehn, 2014). Indeed, there is a disregard of chance in the scientific inquiry (Bandura, 1998).

The world is unpredictable and uncontrollable; it favours ingenuity, improvisation and imagination rather than faith in traditional and predefined process logic. Of course that in times of change, stress and uncertainty, people seek order and meaning in their lives. The inability to predict and control events that can have harmful consequences is highly upsetting (Bandura, 1998). However, chaos is not only a threat; it also creates opportunities for knowledge and ideas. Chance, as Louis Pasteur well noted, 'favours the prepared mind' and this combination lies at the heart of serendipity, for example. Chance makes fascinating turning points in life (Gabriel, Muhr, & Linstead, 2014).

The creation of new ventures is neither simple nor smooth, as there are a number of context specific factors that entrepreneurs need to account for. Despite their importance, the chance of many events is unrecognized and even denied. Columbus, for instance, discovered America's coasts while searching for India (Dew, 2009). In other words, unknowable instances of coincidence, randomness and chance factors can play a significant role in new venture creation.

Chance events are usually related to unplanned, accidental, unpredictable, or unintentional encounters that have an impact on life. For example, chance events were reported as influencing the career decisions of 69.1% of the studied individuals (Bright, Pryor, & Harpham, 2005).

In this research proposal, we suggest that there are good theoretical reasons for assuming that chance events have a logical place in the opportunity discovery framework. We attempt to answer the primordial question: What leads a person to wake up one morning and decide to start a new business? And how do they go about it?

The outline of this research proposal is as follows: after this brief introduction, a very succinct literature review is made. Next, we identify several research questions and present the research objectives. In the following section we present the methodology and final remarks.

LITERATURE REVIEW

Currently, it is generally acknowledged that entrepreneurial activity is one of the primary drivers of industrial dynamism, economic development, and growth (Carlsson et al., 2013).

Indeed, societies do not grow and prosper without entrepreneurs. For the purpose of this research, entrepreneurship is defined as one's ability and willingness to perceive new economic opportunities, seize and market these opportunities in the face of uncertainty. This may consist in new products, new processes, new modes of organization, and new product-market combinations, but they may also consist in spotting new opportunities (Bjørnskov & Foss, 2008; Wennekers & Thurik, 1999).

Thus, there are two key elements of entrepreneurial behaviour: the ability to recognize an opportunity or even to create an opportunity (Alvarez, Barney, & Young, 2010), and the exploitation or commercialization of the opportunity. That is, entrepreneurial behaviour combines entrepreneurial spotting and creation with exploitation (Audretsch, 2012).

But, what are Entrepreneurial Opportunities?

An entrepreneurial opportunity consists of "a set of ideas, beliefs and actions that enable the creation of future goods and services in the absence of current markets for them" (Sarasvathy et al., 2010), p.142). Sarasvathy et al. (2010) provide a typology of entrepreneurial opportunities: opportunity recognition, opportunity discovery and opportunity creation.

The concept of opportunity has been defined in a wide variety of fields including economics, entrepreneurship, and strategy. Thus, opportunities exist when there are competitive imperfections in factor or product markets (Alvarez, & Barney, 2007). Entrepreneurs exploit these competitive imperfections to generate economic profits (Schumpeter, 1934).

However, the entrepreneur will need others to adopt the emerging opportunity, so opportunities are co-created between the entrepreneur, customers, suppliers, and other stakeholders. Once the opportunity and the market are co-created, the entrepreneur will try to capture as much value as possible. In this sense, the process of shape a co-created opportunity is often a barrier to imitation. For this reason, exploiting co-created opportunities can generate sustained competitive advantages and large economic profits (Alvarez, & Barney, 2014).

The process of generating opportunities involves individuals, firms, universities, and other research institutions, whose research and development activities create new knowledge (Mueller, 2007). Moreover, entrepreneurial opportunities can arise if existing organizations do not capitalize knowledge to the full extent and may serve as "seedbed" for new ventures (Agarwal el al., 2004).

Entrepreneurship can be a mechanism that converts knowledge into growth (Acs, Audretsch, Braunerhjelm, & Carlsson, 2012; Acs, & Sanders, 2013). Therefore, entrepreneurial behaviour is a response to profitable opportunities from knowledge spillover (Acs, Audretsch, & Lehmann, 2013).

The theory identifies new knowledge as one source of entrepreneurial opportunities and considers entrepreneurship as a channel to transmit knowledge. Universities not only produce human capital but also serve as incubators where researchers and professors can teach and conduct research (Qian, Acs, & Stough, 2013).

Nevertheless, knowledge spillover is dependent of a strong regional component, taking advantage of spatial proximity to research facilities, universities, and industry specific agglomerations (Mueller, 2007).

Yet why do some people pursue entrepreneurial opportunities while others do not?

Although we acknowledge that opportunity contexts influence entrepreneurial behaviour, we also recognize that individuals are different. Some of these differences involve the willingness to incur risk or prefer autonomy and self-direction, while others simply have differential access to scarce and expensive resources, such as financial capital, human capital, social capital, information, and other even have cognitive psychological abilities (Audretsch, 2012; Turkina & Thai, 2013).

As Shane (2003) point out, "entrepreneurs are people that make different decisions when confronted with similar opportunities" (p. 261). This means that given the same information individuals will react differently. Findings suggest that country's socio-psychological characteristics significantly affect the probability of a person being an opportunity entrepreneur. Indeed, these socio-psychological characteristics are significant predictors that help to explain some variance in opportunity entrepreneurship. Modern societies that value personal independence, self-reliance, individualism and gender equality are more conducive to opportunity entrepreneurship than traditional ones characterized by collectivism, authoritarianism and hierarchy in social relations and traditional views of gender roles (Turkina & Thai, 2013)

It is well known that entrepreneurship requires motivation and the more confident and optimistic individuals are in their own abilities and skills, the more likely they are to pursue entrepreneurship (Wood, McKelvie, & Haynie, 2014).

Entrepreneurship literature explicitly distinguishes between opportunity entrepreneurship (pursuit of business opportunities) and necessity entrepreneurship (forced self-employment due to a lack of alternative employment options) (Graham, 2005). There is general agreement in the literature that opportunity entrepreneurship is more beneficial because, unlike necessity entrepreneurship, it is growth oriented (Acs, 2006) and therefore enhances economic growth (Carree, & Thurik, 2010), increases productivity (Sirmon, Hitt, Ireland, & Gilbert, 2010) and enhances creativity and innovation (Luke, Verreymme, & Kearins, 2007).

Regardless the opportunity being searched for or being the result of a "aha moment", both need actions. In other words, entrepreneurs must form and exploit opportunities (Alvarez, & Barney, 2007). They need to deploy resources to exploit their opportunities. Pursuing an opportunity is possible only by acting and facing the uncertainty in every stage of the process (Dimov, 2007). Conceptually, the opportunity development is shown in Figure 1.

However, is entrepreneurial opportunity discovery and development that linear, systematic and rational? Are all factors measurable and knowable? Although the model incorporates the key process of new venture creation, there might be several factors that need to be addressed by the literature that are not yet clearly covered by the academia, specially chance events.

Figure 1. Opportunity Development Process
Souce: França et al. (2017).

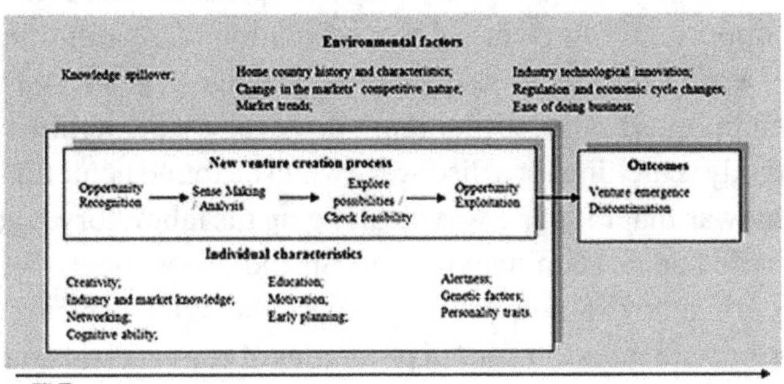

Under certain conditions, chance events set in motion a myriad of effects that alter the course of lives. A happenstance encounters unveilings an all-new life path. Had this encounter not occurred, the persons' lives would have taken quite different courses (Bandura, 1998).

For the purposes of the present discussion we define chance as "any event happening in the absence of any obvious design (randomly or accidentally), one that is irrelevant to any present need, or one of which the cause is unknown" (Rond, 2014, p. 343). These events may have both positive and negative aspects.

A chance event is very difficult to identify because the concept is seldom discussed and rarely defined. Moreover, the exact nature of these events is also difficult to define and specified. Indeed, many encounters that would otherwise qualify as chance events are ignored because they lack special meaning. Chance events are complex mixes of situational and personal features (Shanahan & Porfeli, 2006).

The fact that being unpredictable and unplanned is important, as they may account for unique differences in how people perceive and are prepared for chance events (Rice, 2014). Some people just simply transform chance events into an opportunity for learning whereas others gain nothing.

Serendipity

Serendipity is more than luck and it can lead to surprising opportunities. It is difficult to suggest the classic 'rationality' regarding entrepreneurship. Successful entrepreneurs are responsive to the fragility of opportunities that they identify in uncertain environment and so they use less sophisticated planning. Serendipity addresses uncertainty rather than risk and it is in these contexts that lays the greatest potential for economic profit. For example, the origin of Post-it notes is a good example of serendipitous discovery that came from the development of an imperfect adhesive (Merrilees, Miller, & Tiessen, 1998).

Many entrepreneurship scholars, and many entrepreneurs, instinctively conceive a serendipitous opportunity in terms of a combination of search (directed effort), contingency (favourable accidents), and prior knowledge (sagacity). For example, a well-known serendipitous finding is Fleming's discovery of penicillin in 1928. "First, Fleming was actively searching for a discovery when he found penicillin. Second, the fortunate accident was that Fleming was cleaning up his laboratory when he noticed how penicillin mold had contaminated one of his old experiments — a completely unanticipated contingency. Third, sagacity enters the story because Fleming had been experimenting with the antibacterial properties of common substances for many years, and therefore had enough prior knowledge about molds to find that particular petri dish anomalous, and immediately begin to discern its potential implications" (Dew, 2009, p. 736). Serendipity is more central to the entrepreneurial process than has been credited. Serendipitous events are neither residual nor a statistical error as asserted by the deterministic laws of the entrepreneurial process. Instead, these events, though unpredictable by nature, may be worth understanding as part of entrepreneurship.

Synchronicity

Carl Jung (1960) presented the idea of synchronicity to strip off the fantasy, magic, superstition surrounding unpredictable, startling and impressive events that seem to be connected. Jung defined synchronicity as “a coincidence in time of two or more causally unrelated events which have the same or a similar meaning” (Jung, 1960, p. 34).

According to Jung (1960), two or more events constitute synchronicity when a meaningful connection or a meaningful association can be made between the events. Importantly, meaningfulness is the connecting principle between the events with no causal connections. Moreover, synchronistic events are not simply coincidences resulting from chance because they are defined by their meaningfulness.

Synchronicity emphasizes the paradox of time, and thus of change: it is both continuous and discontinuous and may play a part in meaningful change (Durant, 2002).

Synchronicity consists of two factors: a) an unconscious image comes into consciousness either directly (i.e., literally) or indirectly (symbolized or suggested) in the form of a dream, idea, or premonition. b) An objective situation coincides with the previous situation (Jung, 1960).

Black Swan Events

“Black swan” is a term made famous by Nassim Nicholas Taleb in his book “The Black Swan: The Impact of the Highly Improbable”. In it, Taleb, (2007) defines a Black Swan event as a highly improbable incident with three characteristics: a) It is totally unpredictable. b) Its impact is massive; c) It is amenable to explanation, after the fact, so that in retrospect it appears predictable, not random. As examples, he points to the creation of the Internet and the terrorist attacks of 9/11.

The concept “black swan” originally comes from the beliefs that, for centuries and before the discovery of Australia, all swans were white. An assumption based on the fact that no one in the West had ever seen a black swan. Taleb (2007) believes that human beings choose to disregard black swan events because they are more comfortable believing that the world is structured, understandable and therefore predictable.

Taleb (2007) defends that Black Swans have major influence on person's lives and in the development of organizations; indeed, they shape the very course of history. However, because of their distinctive characteristics (as "rare events"), they are outside the comprehension of formal mathematical processes (Sniedovich, 2012). Indeed, as Black Swan events are unpredictable from probabilistic or statistical considerations, strategies to cope with their consequences are of pivotal importance for managers and all stakeholders (Nafday, 2009).

This research will explore the nature of these chance events and the ways in which they may play a part in meaningful change.

RESEARCH QUESTION AND AIMS

This research intends to go to the heart of the entrepreneurial process. Our first research objective is to investigate the phenomenon of chance in the development of an entrepreneurial opportunity. Our second research objective is to find patterns of action and commonalities among entrepreneurs when grasping with chance happenings, namely serendipity, synchronicity and black swan events.

Indeed, our research question is: What leads a person to wake up one morning and decide to start a new business? And how do they go about it?

Additionally: 1) What are the patterns of action, structure of mind, traits of personality, skills and behaviours when struck by chance? 2) What are the paradigmatic changes and consequences resulting from acausal events? Specifically, what are the changes of conditions, either internal or external, to the process of developing an entrepreneurial opportunity? 3) Are experienced and expert entrepreneurs more predisposed to harness opportunities or overcome setbacks arising from chance, that is, is it path dependent? Moreover, is it context dependent?

METHODOLOGY

Social science research is complex and diverse. Researchers have their own different worldviews about the nature of knowledge and truth (Cohen, Manion, & Morrison, 2011). The choice of an appropriate research methodology involves considerations regarding the research problem, which often indicate a specific research methodology to be used; the researcher's own experiences, training, and worldview (Creswell, 2013).

Post positivists observe the patterns of social reality (Neuman, 2009) that can influence outcomes, combining deductive logic with empirical observations of the objective truth that exists "out there" in the world (Creswell, 2013). This reality is external to the researcher and must be investigated (Gray, 2014). Yet, there is some degree of uncertainty. These researchers defend that knowledge is often socially conditioned and can be subject to reinterpretations. There are mechanisms governing social behaviour that may not be observable (Porta, & Keating, 2008).

Most empirical studies in management seek to identify empirical regularities (Miller, & Tsang, 2010). This research is to be held from a post-positivist lens. This paradigm acknowledges that theories are social products, but provides insights for discovering patterns and communalities. It confronts the complexity of social phenomena by supporting explanations in terms of mechanisms that generalize and prescribe.

However, within their own ontological and epistemological believes, individual researchers should be free to identify the most effective mean for answering their research question(s). Without this freedom, there will be no growth for new and innovative research techniques (Symonds, & Gorard, 2010).

Qualitative methodology is essentially directed to understanding the complex and the elusive in a systemic perspective. Truth is more than the sum of its parts and one must account for synergetic effects (Gummesson, 2005). Hence, this research intent to use one or a combination of the following research methods:

1. Case study research provides with an input of real world data from which concepts can be formed and propositions and theory can be tried. For the development and proper validation, the steps proposed by Gummesson (1999) will be followed;
2. Grounded theory. Inductive research allows reality tell its story on its own terms and not of the extant theory. Grounded theory tries to be realistic and valid; hence researchers need to train themselves to listen without predetermined ideas. There is divergence in the academia on the methodological approach to literature review before data collection. Although being a constructivists believe, we stand with Strauss and Corbin (2015) which defends that literature review before data collection will not necessarily hinder the theory emergence. Indeed, the authors do not recommend dissociating from the literature, but rather to engage with it and use it in all phases of the research since this could further foster the process by helping the researcher to identify what is important to the developing theory. That is, as long as the researcher sustains an attitude of scepticism (Corbin & Strauss, 2015), by not allowing it to impose itself on the theory, and use appropriate research methods. For the development and proper validation, the steps proposed by (Glaser & Strauss, 1967) will be followed;

3. Narrative research. Narratives are stories about experiences and not only they can be chronological but also be a web of events around several themes or concepts: story-telling. By presenting research as a story, researchers avoid the fragmentation that is expected when one split networks of events into abstract concepts and categories (Gummesson, 2005). For the development and proper validation, the steps proposed by Riessman (2007) will be followed.

Regarding the sample, it is important to choose individuals that operate in the same economic activity so that one can fairly compare. Therefore, this research will be held in the service context of Technology-based entrepreneurship. Technology-based entrepreneurship is based on the research of new opportunities where breakthrough innovation plays a key role. In this situation universities are of pivotal importance in the incubation of new firms in order to nurture new technology-based firms (Rothaermel, Agung, & Jiang, 2007). Technology-based entrepreneurship normally evolves in fast moving environments and contingent strategies may be initiated to take advantage of small windows of opportunity. In such an environment, opportunistic strategies bring more value than systematic ones (Crick & Spence, 2005).

CONCLUSION

Entrepreneurship plays a key role in economic development and is an ever-present aspect of human activity. New venture creation involves a series of decisions centred on opportunity recognition, evaluation and exploitation. Regardless of whether opportunities exist in the environment or emerge as a creative act, individuals need to identify and exploit them, engaging in a process of opportunity development.

Entrepreneurial action can often be reasoned, but it cannot be universally assumed so. Limiting entrepreneurship research and frameworks to the realm of the intended-rational is highly restrictive and not consistent with the diversity of human behaviour in almost all domains of human activity, including entrepreneurship.

Acausal, meaningful coincidences have the potential to transform peoples' lives, and therefore to guide the passage of change. Although people have no control over the emergence of chance events, does not deny that they take deliberate intentional action. Nor are their explanations necessarily restricted to passive approaches such as "do nothing" or "do anything." Rather, recognizing the importance of randomness can be a crucial first step for meaningful change. This understanding will become more important, as people continue to face the challenge of an uncertain and changing life. Proactive efforts must be made to cultivate personal attributes that enable people to make the most of opportunities that arise unexpectedly from time to time.

In chance is the joy of the strange moment. But this does not make chance a residual after the deterministic laws of the entrepreneurial process have run their course. Instead, chance events—though by their nature individually unpredictable—may be worth understanding as a significant, recurring feature of entrepreneurship.

REFERENCES

Acs, Z. (2006). How Is Entrepreneurship Good for Economic Growth? *Innovations: Technology, Governance, Globalization*, *1*(1), 97–107. doi:10.1162/itgg.2006.1.1.97

Acs, Z., Audretsch, D. B., Braunerhjelm, P., & Carlsson, B. (2012). Growth and entrepreneurship. *Small Business Economics*, *39*(2), 289–300. doi:10.100711187-010-9307-2

Acs, Z., Audretsch, D. B., & Lehmann, E. E. (2013). The knowledge spillover theory of entrepreneurship. *Small Business Economics*, *41*(4), 757–774. doi:10.100711187-013-9505-9

Acs, Z., & Sanders, M. W. J. L. (2013). Knowledge spillover entrepreneurship in an endogenous growth model. *Small Business Economics*, *41*(4), 775–795. doi:10.100711187-013-9506-8

Agarwal, R., Echambadi, R., Franco, A. M., & Sarkar, M. (2004). Knowledge transfer through inheritance: Spin- out generation, development, and survival. *Academy of Management Journal*, *47*(4), 501–522. doi:10.2307/20159599

Alvarez, S. A., & Barney, J. B. (2007). Discovery and creation: Alternative theories of entrepreneurial action. *Strategic Entrepreneurship Journal*, *1*(1-2), 11–26. doi:10.1002ej.4

Alvarez, S. A., & Barney, J. B. (2014). Entrepreneurial Opportunities and Poverty Alleviation. *Entrepreneurship Theory and Practice*, *38*(1), 159–184. doi:10.1111/etap.12078

Alvarez, S. A., Barney, J. B., & Young, S. L. (2010). Debates in Entrepreneurship: Opportunity Formation and Implications for the Field of Entrepreneurship. In Z. J. Acs & D. B. Audretsch (Eds.), *Handbook of Entrepreneurship Research - An Interdisciplinary Survey and Introduction* (2nd ed.; pp. 23–46). Springer-Verlag New York; doi:10.1007/978-1-4419-1191-9_2

Audretsch, D. B. (2012). Entrepreneurship research. *Management Decision*, *50*(5), 755–764. doi:10.1108/00251741211227384

Bandura, A. (1998). Exploration of Fortuitous Determinants of Life Paths. *Psychological Inquiry*, *9*(2), 95–99. doi:10.120715327965pli0902_2

Bjørnskov, C., & Foss, N. J. (2008). Economic freedom and entrepreneurial activity: Some cross-country evidence. *Public Choice*, *134*(3–4), 307–328. doi:10.100711127-007-9229-y

Bright, J. E. H., Pryor, R. G. L., & Harpham, L. (2005). The role of chance events in career decision making. *Journal of Vocational Behavior*, *66*(3), 561–578. doi:10.1016/j.jvb.2004.05.001

Carlsson, B., Braunerhjelm, P., McKelvey, M., Olofsson, C., Persson, L., & Ylinenpää, H. (2013). The evolving domain of entrepreneurship research. *Small Business Economics*, *41*(4), 913–930. doi:10.100711187-013-9503-y

Carree, M. A., & Thurik, A. R. (2010). The impact of entrepreneurship on economic growth. In Z. J. Acs & D. B. Audretsch (Eds.), *Handbook of entrepreneurship research: An interdisciplinary survey and introduction* (2nd ed.; pp. 557–594). Springer-Verlag New York. doi:10.1007/978-1-4419-1191-9_20

Cohen, L., Manion, L., & Morrison, K. (2011). *Research Methods in Education* (7th ed.). Routledge.

Corbin, J., & Strauss, A. (2015). *Basics of Qualitative Research Techniques and Procedures for Developing Grounded Theory* (4th ed.). SAGE Publications, Inc.

Creswell, J. W. (2013). *Research Design: Qualitative, Quantitative, and Mixed Methods Approaches* (4th ed.). SAGE Publications, Inc.

Crick, D., & Spence, M. (2005). The internationalisation of "high performing" UK high-tech SMEs: A study of planned and unplanned strategies. *International Business Review*, *14*(2), 167–185. doi:10.1016/j.ibusrev.2004.04.007

de Rond, M. (2014). The structure of serendipity. *Culture and Organization*, *20*(5), 342–358. doi:10.1080/14759551.2014.967451

della Porta, D., & Keating, M. (Eds.). (2008). *Approaches and Methodologies in the Social Sciences - A Pluralist Perspective*. Cambridge, UK: Cambridge University Press. doi:10.1017/CBO9780511801938

Dew, N. (2009). Serendipity in Entrepreneurship. *Organization Studies*, *30*(7), 735–753. doi:10.1177/0170840609104815

Dimov, D. (2007). Beyond the Single-Person, Single-Insight Atribution in Understanding Entrepreneurial Opportunities. *Entrepreneurship Theory & Practice*, (860), 713–732.

Durant, R. (2002). Synchronicity: A post-structuralist guide to creativity and change. *Journal of Organizational Change Management*, *15*(5), 490–501. doi:10.1108/09534810210440351

França, A., Vilares, A., Frankenbach, S., Vereb, V., & Moreira, A. C. (2017). The Challenging Dynamics of Nascent Entrepreneurship. In A. Moreira, J. Dantas, & F. Valente (Eds.), *Nascent Entrepreneurship and Successful New Venture Creation*. IGI Global. doi:10.4018/978-1-5225-2936-1

Gabriel, Y., Muhr, S. L., & Linstead, S. (2014). Luck of the draw? Serendipity, accident, chance and misfortune in organization and design. *Culture and Organization*, *20*(5), 334–341. doi:10.1080/14759551.2014.967452

Glaser, B. G., & Strauss, A. L. (1967). *The discovery of grounded theory*. AldineTransaction, A Division of Transaction Publishers.

Graham, C. (2005). Insights on development from the economics of happiness. *The World Bank Research Observer*, *20*(2), 201–231. doi:10.1093/wbro/lki010

Gray, D. E. (2014). *Doing Research in the Real World* (3rd ed.). SAGE Publications Ltd.

Gummesson, E. (1999). *Qualitative Methods in Management Research* (2nd ed.). SAGE Publications, Inc.

Gummesson, E. (2005). Qualitative research in marketing: Road-map for a wilderness of complexity and unpredictability. *European Journal of Marketing*, *39*(3/4), 309–327. doi:10.1108/03090560510581791

Hoskisson, R. E., Covin, J., Volberda, H. W., & Johnson, R. (2011). Revitalizing Entrepreneurship: The Search for New Research Opportunities. *Journal of Management Studies*, *48*(6), 1141–1168. doi:10.1111/j.1467-6486.2010.00997.x

Jung, C. G. (1960). *Synchronicity: An Acausal Connecting Principle. The Collected Works of C.G. Jung* (Vol. 8). Princeton University Press.

Lennerfors, T. T., & Rehn, A. (2014). Chance interventions – on bricolage and the state as an entrepreneur in a declining industry. *Culture and Organization*, *20*(5), 377–391. doi:10.1080/14759551.2014.950660

Luke, B., Verreymme, M.-L., & Kearins, K. (2007). *Measuring the benefits of entrepreneurship at different levels of analysis*. Academic Press.

McMullen, J. S., & Shepherd, D. A. (2006). Entrepreneurial action and the role of uncertainty in the theory of the entrepreneur. *Academy of Management Review*, *31*(1), 132–152. doi:10.5465/amr.2006.19379628

Merrilees, B., Miller, D., & Tiessen, J. (1998). Serendipity, Leverage And The Process Of Entrepreneurial Internationalization. *Small Enterprise Research*, *6*(2), 3–11. doi:10.5172er.6.2.3

Miller, K. D., & Tsang, E. W. K. (2010). Testing management theories: Critical realist philosophy and research methods. *Strategic Management Journal*, *158*(32), 139–158. doi:10.1002mj

Mueller, P. (2007). Exploiting entrepreneurial opportunities: The impact of entrepreneurship on growth. *Small Business Economics*, *28*(4), 355–362. doi:10.100711187-006-9035-9

Nafday, A. M. (2009). Strategies for Managing the Consequences of Black Swan Events. *Leadership and Management in Engineering*, *9*(4), 191–197. doi:10.1061/(ASCE)LM.1943-5630.0000036

Neuman, W. L. (2009). *Social Research Methods: Qualitative and Quantitative Approaches* (7th ed.). Pearson.

Qian, H., Acs, Z., & Stough, R. R. (2013). Regional systems of entrepreneurship: The nexus of human capital, knowledge and new firm formation. *Journal of Economic Geography*, *13*(4), 559–587. doi:10.1093/jeg/lbs009

Rice, A. (2014). Incorporation of Chance Into Career Development Theory and Research. *Journal of Career Development*, *41*(5), 445–463. doi:10.1177/0894845313507750

Riessman, C. K. (2007). *Narrative Methods for the Human Sciences*. SAGE Publications, Inc.

Rothaermel, F. T., Agung, S. D., & Jiang, L. (2007). University entrepreneurship: A taxonomy of the literature. *Industrial and Corporate Change*, *16*(4), 691–791. doi:10.1093/icc/dtm023

Sarasvathy, S. D., Dew, N., Velamuri, S. R., & Venkataraman, S. (2010). Three Views of Entrepreneurial Opportunity. In Z. J. Acs & D. B. Audretsch (Eds.), *Handbook of Entrepreneurship Research - An Interdisciplinary Survey and Introduction* (2nd ed.; pp. 77–98). Springer-Verlag New York; doi:10.1007/978-1-4419-1191-9_4

Schumpeter, J. A. (1934). *The Theory of Economic Development*. Transaction Publishers.

Shanahan, M. J., & Porfeli, E. J. (2006). Chance Events in the Life Course. *Advances in Life Course Research*, *11*(6), 97–119. doi:10.1016/S1040-2608(06)11004-7

Shane, S. A. (2003). *A General Theory of Entrepreneurship: The Individual-opportunity Nexus*. Edward Elgar Publishing, Limited. doi:10.4337/9781781007990

Sirmon, D. G., Hitt, M., Ireland, R. D., & Gilbert, B. (2010). Resource Orchestration to Create Competitive Advantage: Breadth, Depth, and Life Cycle Effects. *Journal of Management*, *37*(5), 1390–1412. doi:10.1177/0149206310385695

Sniedovich, M. (2012). Black Swans, New Nostradamuses, Voodoo decision theories, and the science of decision making in the face of severe uncertainty. *International Transactions in Operational Research*, *19*(1–2), 253–281. doi:10.1111/j.1475-3995.2011.00790.x

Symonds, J. E., & Gorard, S. (2010). The Death of Mixed Methods : Research Labels and their Casualties. In *British Educational Research Annual Conference*. Edinburgh, UK: Heriot Watt University.

Taleb, N. N. (2007). *The black swan : the impact of the highly improbable*. Penguin Books Ltd; doi:10.5465/AMP.2011.61020810

Toma, S.-G., Grigore, A.-M., & Marinescu, P. (2014). Economic Development and Entrepreneurship. *Procedia Economics and Finance*, *8*(14), 436–443. doi:10.1016/S2212-5671(14)00111-7

Turkina, E., & Thai, M. T. T. (2013). Socio-psychological determinants of opportunity entrepreneurship. *The International Entrepreneurship and Management Journal*, *11*(1), 213–238. doi:10.100711365-013-0288-x

Wennekers, S., & Thurik, R. (1999). Linking entrepreneurship and economic growth. *Small Business Economics*, *13*(1), 27–55. doi:10.1023/A:1008063200484

Wood, M. S., McKelvie, A., & Haynie, J. M. (2014). Making it personal: Opportunity individuation and the shaping of opportunity beliefs. *Journal of Business Venturing*, *29*(2), 252–272. doi:10.1016/j.jbusvent.2013.02.001

ADDITIONAL READING

de Rond, M. (2014). The Structure of Serendipity. *Culture and Organization*, *20*(5), 342–358. doi:10.1080/14759551.2014.967451

Eidinow, E. (2011). *Luck, Fate, and Fortune: Antiquity and its Legacy*. Oxford: Oxford University Press.

Grey, C. (2003). The Fetish of Change. *Tamara: Journal of Critical Postmodern Organization Science*, *2*(2), 1–19.

Jalan, I., Sinha, S., & Ulus, E. (2014). Narratives of Fate and Misfortune in Organizational Life: Stories of Success and Failure. *Culture and Organization*, *20*(5), 410–429. doi:10.1080/14759551.2014.964239

Merton, R. K., & Barber, E. G. (2004). *The Travels and Adventures of Serendipity: A Study in Historical Semantics and the Sociology of Science*. Princeton, NJ: Princeton University Press.

Pollitt, J. J. (1994). An Obsession with Fortune. *Yale University Art Gallery Bulletin*, *27*(34), 12–17.

Roberts, R. M. (1989). *Serendipity: Accidental Discoveries in Science. Hokoken*. Wiley.

Sarasvathy, S. D., Dew, N., Read, S., & Wiltbank, R. (2008). Designing Organizations that Design Environments: Lessons from Entrepreneurial Expertise. *Organization Studies*, *29*(3), 331–350. doi:10.1177/0170840607088017

KEY TERMS AND DEFINITIONS

Black Swan Events: Black Swan event as a highly improbable incident with three characteristics: 1) it is totally unpredictable; 2) its impact is massive; 3) it is amenable to explanation, after the fact, so that in retrospect it appears predictable, not random.

Entrepreneurial Behavior: The ability to recognize an opportunity or even to create an opportunity and the exploitation or commercialization of the opportunity.

Entrepreneurial Opportunities: Consists of a set of ideas, beliefs, and actions that enable the creation of future goods and services in the absence of current markets for them.

Entrepreneurship: Creative human process, which implies person's will of taking on responsibilities and the mental ability of identifying opportunities where others find only chaos, contradictions, or confusion.

Opportunity: Opportunities exist when there are competitive imperfections in factor or product markets. Entrepreneurs exploit these competitive imperfections to generate economic profits.

Serendipity: Is more than luck and it can lead to surprising opportunities, serendipity addresses uncertainty rather than risk and it is in these contexts that lays the greatest potential for economic profit.

Synchronicity: Stripped off the fantasy, magic, superstition surrounding unpredictable, startling, and impressive events that seem to be connected.

Chapter 7
Contributions of Entrepreneurial Orientation to Competitive Advantage:
The Portuguese Experience of the Textile SMEs

Orlando Martins Marques Rua
Polytechnic of Porto, Portugal

ABSTRACT

The main objective of this chapter is to analyze the relationship between entrepreneurial orientation and competitive advantage on Portuguese exporting textiles small and medium enterprises (SMEs). Therefore, a quantitative methodological approach was used, conducting a descriptive, exploratory, and transversal empirical study, having applied a questionnaire to a sample of Portuguese SMEs, associated of the Portuguese textile association (ATP). The structural equations model was used for this purpose, using the partial least squares (PLS). Based on survey data from 247 firms, the empirical results indicate that 1) innovation have a positive and significant impact on differentiation, 2) proactivity and risk-taking does not have a positive and significant impact on differentiation, and 3) innovation, proactivity, and risk-taking does not have a positive and significant impact on cost leadership. This study shows that Portuguese textile SMEs seek to support and stimulate new ideas, experimentation, and creativity that surely result in new products, services, and processes.

DOI: 10.4018/978-1-5225-6942-8.ch007

INTRODUCTION

Developments in this global economy have changed the traditional balance between customer and supplier. New communications and computing technology, and the reasonably open global trading systems, mean that customers have more choices and supply alternatives are more transparent. Firms need therefore to be more customer-centric, especially since technology provide low cost information and customer solutions, and constantly re-evaluate their value propositions (Teece, 2010).

Firm survival is lowest when firms are small; thus, the development of effective strategies is critical for the continuity of business (Thornhill, & Amit, 2003). According to the extant literature, increasing business competitive position, particularly SMEs, is of pivotal importance for the development and renewal of national economies (O'Cass, & Sok, 2014). At present, although SMEs are recognised as important contributors to modern economies, our understanding of how they thrive in an increasingly competitive environment and achieve growth is limited (Anderson, & Eshima, 2013). Thus, it is urgent to understand the drivers of SME performance.

Miller (1983) argues that entrepreneurial strategies are likely to be more successful when addressing customers that value innovation and unique services. This is consistent with a dynamic environment. In these environments, where demand is unpredictable, firms that are oriented to pursue new markets, opportunities are abundant and performance is higher because they have a good fit between their strategic orientation and the environment. In other words, we would expect the alignment between Entrepreneurial Orientation (EO) and a dynamic environment to have positive performance implications (Wiklund, & Shepherd, 2005).

Our study is responsive to the call of Sousa, Martínez-López and Coelho (2008) which suggests that, in the context of international markets, firms' survival and expansion, and consequent economic growth of many countries, is strongly dependent on a better understanding of the determinants that influence export performance. In fact, the factors that set off SME growth (including exporting) are still in need of research (Stouraitis el al., 2017). So, the purpose of this paper is to broad the boundaries of entrepreneurship and strategic management literature and test the following hypotheses —— *Does entrepreneurial orientation positively influence small business competitive advantage?*

THEORETICAL FRAMEWORK

Entrepreneurial Orientation

First conceived by Miller (1983), and later extended by Covin and Slevin (1989, 1991), EO is a firm's behavioural tendency, managerial philosophy or decision-making practice that is characterized by innovativeness, proactiveness and a willingness to take risks. The focus is not on the person but in the process of undertake (Wiklund, 1999).

Contemporary studies in small business and entrepreneurship have often placed firm growth at the centre of their inquiry (Blackburn, Hart, & Wainwright, 2013). The EO–performance literature is extensive. While Wiklund and Shepherd (2011) findings indicate a positive relationship between EO and failure, there is some scholarly tendency to assume that firms with more EO have superior performance (Wiklund, & Shepherd, 2005). Several empirical studies indicate a positive correlation between entrepreneurial orientation and organizational growth (e.g. Covin, & Slevin, 1991; Davis, Bell, Payne, & Kreiser, 2010; Frank, Kessler, & Fink, 2010; Lumpkin, & Dess, 1996; Miller, 1983). Similarly, other studies also confirm that entrepreneurial orientation has a positive correlation with export's performance, enhancing business growth (e.g. Okpara, 2009; Zahra, & Garvis, 2000). Clearly, this link seems to be one of the few "universal" ones in management research. The strength of this positive association, however, varies considerably across national contexts (Semrau, Ambos, & Kraus, 2016).

Entrepreneurial orientation has been characterized by certain constructs that represent organization's behaviour. Starting from Miller's (1983) definition, three dimensions were identified: innovativeness, proactiveness and risk-taking. Innovativeness is the predisposition to engage in creativity and experimentation through the introduction of new products/services as well as technological leadership in new processes. Risk taking involves taking bold actions by venturing into the unknown and/or committing significant resources to ventures in uncertain environments. Proactiveness is an opportunity-seeking, forward-looking perspective characterized by the introduction of new products and services ahead of the competition and acting in anticipation of future demand (Rauch, & Wiklund, 2009). Collectively, these dimensions can enhance firm's ability to recognize and exploit international market opportunities well ahead of its competitors (Gil-Pechuan, Exposito-Langa, & Tomas-Miquel, 2013).

EO influences firm performance when firms strategically acquire, develop and leverage resources for opportunity exploitation in order to gain competitive advantage. Therefore, EO should be associated to the concept of competitive strategy (Lechner, & Gudmundsson, 2014).

Competitive Advantage

The different way managers interpret the same external environment leads to distinct policies formulation and differentiated actions, which, together, is reflected in organizational performance (e.g. Lumpkin, & Dess, 1996; Zahra, 1993).

The increased intensity of business competition has forced firms to adopt a non-traditional management techniques and tools. Maintaining competitive advantage is a dynamic and infinite activity (Hung, Yang, & Lien, 2010).

How firms achieve and sustain competitive advantage? This is the fundamental question in the field of strategic management (Teece et al., 1997). Porter (1985) considers simply a matter of creating value for customers and doing it better than competition.

Porter's model to classify firm strategies remains the most commonly supported and acknowledged framework in strategic management literature (Allen et al., 2006). Porter proposed four competitive strategies: broad cost leadership, broad differentiation, cost focus and differentiation focus. While cost leadership or differentiation is defined as dominant competitive strategies, focus is not a standalone strategy and "is not sufficient for above-average performance' (Porter, 1985, p. 15). Consequently, there is a tendency in the literature to recognise two main sources of competitive advantage: a) cost leadership – reaching lower costs than competitors and b) differentiation – creating more value for customers than the average firm (Lechner, & Gudmundsson, 2014). Furthermore, and according to Porter, the two logics of differentiation and cost leadership are incompatible.

Hence, we can reduce the study of competitive strategy to differentiation and cost leadership, especially if the competitive strategy is related to other strategic elements of firm's behaviour. Differentiation means to fulfil customers' needs in a unique way, based on speed, customer service and flexibility, which is consistent with innovative approaches and characteristics of entrepreneurial firms. Cost leadership requires substantial financial resources (to invest in tangible assets), is based on process innovation, learning curve benefits, economies of scale and standardization, and seems to be less appropriate for small firms, given the resource constraints (Lechner, & Gudmundsson, 2014).

Sustainable competitive advantage represents firm's competitive maintenance on the long run, whose performance is above average, resisting the dynamic evolution of competition, consumers and industry (e.g. Amit, & Schoemaker, 1993; Peteraf, 1993; Porter, 1985).

Hypotheses Derivation

Zahra and Garvis (2000) argues that operating successfully in the global market requires creativity, ingenuity and risk taking. In the process of international expansion, firms need to learn and use different skills from those used in their domestic markets, and this requires experimentation and risk taking. Thus, when firm intend to internationalize, EO can be a competitive advantage, either in existing or new markets (e.g. Miller, 1983; Zahra, & Covin, 1995).

It has been suggested that competitive strategy mediates the EO–performance relationship. Therefore, the relationship between EO and competitive strategy is key to understanding small firm performance (Lumpkin, & Dess, 1996). Since usually differentiation and cost leadership are described as opposing logics (Porter, 1985), it is unreasonable to assume that EO has an impact on the two types of competitive advantage in a similar manner (Lechner, & Gudmundsson, 2014).

H1a: Innovativeness is positively associated with cost leadership.
H1b: Innovativeness is positively associated with differentiation.
H2a: Proactiveness is positively associated with cost leadership.
H2b: Proactiveness is positively associated with differentiation.
H3a: Risk-taking is positively associated with differentiation.
H3b: Risk-taking is positively associated with cost leadership.

METHODOLOGY

Sample and Data Collection

The population of this empirical study has been drawn from Portuguese textile industry firms. Questionnaires were used as primary data sources and were carried out over the period of February 16 to April 30, 2016. The identification of companies was done through the Portugal's Textile Association (Associação Têxtil de Portugal) (ATP, 2014) database. So, in this study we use a non-probabilistic and convenient sampling.

A total of 247 complete and validated questionnaires accounting for 25% per cent of the population were obtained. This response rate is considered quite satisfactory, given that the average of top management survey response rates are in the range of 15%-20% (Menon, & Bharadwaj, 1999).

Statistical Analysis

We used PLS-SEM path modelling to test our hypothesis, specifically the software SmartPLS 3.0 (Hair el al., 2013; Sarstedt et al., 2014). We believe that the PLS-SEM path modelling is best suited to estimate our research model since: 1) this study focuses on prediction and explanation of contructs variance (in our case 2, with 5 dimensions); 2) our research model has a complex structure; 3) the relationship between entrepreneurial orientation and competitive advantage (via cost or differentiation); 4) this study uses first and second-order reflective constructs; and 5) the sample (n=247) is somewhat small.

Measures

This study uses well-validated scales from previous studies to operationalize the key constructs and adapted them to the particular context of our empirical setting.

- **Independent Variables:** To assess EO we adopted Covin and Slevin's (1989) measurements for the three dimensions of innovativeness (INNOV), proactiveness (PROAT) and risk-taking (RISKA).
- **Dependent Variable:** Competitive strategy was measured through two dimensions: differentiation (DIF); and cost leadership (COST), using Morgan et al.'s (2004) scale.

RESULTS

The structural equation model is a multiple regression analysis, with reflective indicators that are presented as an image of the unobserved theoretical construct, representing observed variables or measures, with the objective of strengthening the relationship of influence between the constructs (Marôco, 2010). The simple correlation between these indicators with their construct must have a value equal to or higher than 0.707 so that the shared variance between the construct and their indicators is higher than the error variance (Carmines, & Zeller, 1979).

Partial Least Squares (PLS) is a technique that best fits predictive applications (exploratory analysis) and theory development when it is not soundly established (Cepeda, & Roldán, 2004). This technique, on one hand, maximize the explained variance of the dependent variables (latent or observed, or both) and estimate structural models with small samples (Chin, & Newsted, 1999; Reinartz, Haenlein, & Henseler, 2009). On the other hand, it estimates reflective and formative measurement models without identification problems (Chin, 2010). PLS appear to be a preferable option for researchers with samples below 250 observations (247 in this study) (Reinartz et al., 2009).

In order to verify the reliability of overall variables we estimated the stability and internal consistency through Cronbach's alpha (α). Generally, an instrument or test is classified with appropriate reliability when α is higher or equal to 0.70 (Nunally, 1978; Chin, 2010). The result of 0.861 achieved for all variables is considered excellent, confirming the sample's internal consistency (Pestana, & Gageiro, 2000). Table 1 show all constructs largely achieved the required level.

We also use the composite reliability coefficient to assess construct validity (Chin, 1998). This coefficient reflects construct adequacy for a level higher than 0.6 using confirmatory factor analysis (Gefen, & Straub, 2005), as in our case. Table 2 illustrates that the studied constructs (all multidimensional) highly exceeded the minimum required for a good fit.

For validity assessment, two subtypes are usually examined: convergent and discriminant validity. Convergent validity implies that a set of indicators represents one and the same underlying construct (Henseler et al., 2009). Fornell and Larcker (1981) suggest using the *Average Variance Extracted* (AVE) criterion and that

Table 1. Cronbach's alpha of multidimensional variables

Dimensions	Cronbach's Alpha	*p* values
COST	0.900	0.000
DIF	0.940	0.000
INNOV	0.827	0.000
PROAT	0.853	0.000
RISKA	0.822	0.000

Source: Own.

Table 2. Composite reliability coefficient of multidimensional variables

Dimensions	Composite reliability	*p* values
COST	0.930	0.000
DIF	0.950	0.000
INNOV	0.896	0.000
PROAT	0.906	0.000
RISKA	0.004	0.987

Source: Own.

an AVE value of at least 0.5 indicates sufficient convergent validity. Next table demonstrates that only entrepreneurial orientation is below the minimum required.

Discriminant validity is the degree to which any single construct is different from the other constructs in the model. To have discriminant validity a construct must exhibit weak correlations with other latent variables that measure different phenomena. There are two measures of discriminant validity in PLS. The Fornell–Larcker criterion (1981) recommends that the AVE should be greater than the variance between a given construct and the other with which it shares the model. The second criterion suggests that the loading of each indicator is expected to be greater than all of its cross-loadings (Henseler et al., 2009).

We can observe the explanatory power of each variable in the model. EO is the only purely explanatory variable and reputational resources and absorptive capacity of knowledge exploitation the explained variables. Chin (1998) distinguishes the explanatory power from moderate to substantial. Table 4 expresses the good results in terms of discriminant validity of the research model, confirming that constructs do differ significantly.

Table 3. Convergent validity

Dimensions	AVE	*p* values
COST	0.770	0.000
DIF	0.706	0.000
INNOV	0.742	0.000
PROAT	0.764	0.000
RISKA	0.142	0.468

Source: Own.

Table 4. Discriminant validity

Fornell-Larcker Criterion	COST	DIF	INNOV	PROAT	RISKA
COST	0.877				
DIF	0.295	0.840			
INNOV	0.164	0.435	0.861		
PROAT	0.136	0.143	0.272	0.874	
RISKA	0.065	-0.253	0.001	-0.195	0.377

Source: Own.

In order to determine the significance of the studied relationships and the confidence intervals of the path coefficients, we used bootstrapping technique. The weighted coefficients indicate the relative strength of each exogenous construct. According to Hair et al. (2013), relationships between constructs, with structural coefficients higher than 0.2, are considered robust. From table 5, we thus conclude that the original model does not present non-significant paths.

Figure 1 presents the final research structural model with the effects and explained variance of latent variables.

Table 5. Model's path coefficients

Hypotheses	Original Sample (O)	Sample Mean (M)	Standard Deviation (STDEV)	T Statistics (|O/STDEV|)	P Values	2.5%	97.5%
INNOV -> COST	0.132	0.113	0.116	1.132	0.258	-0.138	0.291
INNOV -> DIF	0.442	0.440	0.055	8.038	0.000	0.334	0.536
PROAT -> COST	0.117	0.147	0.140	0.835	0.404	-0.183	0.408
PROAT -> DIF	-0.028	0.005	0.083	0.336	0.737	-0.174	0.148
RISKA -> COST	0.087	-0.048	0.150	0.581	0.561	-0.316	0.220
RISKA -> DIF	-0.258	0.002	0.209	1.234	0.218	-0.322	0.338

Source: Own.

Figure 1. Research structural model
Source: Own.

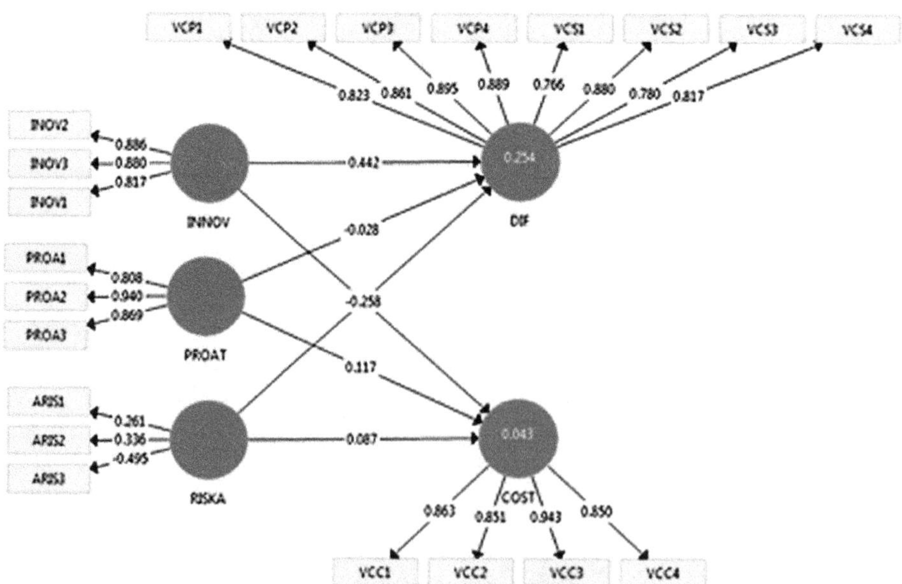

Results from Table 5 indicate that only innovation influence significantly and positively competitive advantage. Specifically, DIF, which supports H1b (β=0,442). Hence, innovative firms achieve superior competitive advantage. All the others hypotheses are not supported.

DISCUSSION AND CONCLUSION

This paper seeks to contribute to the development of the literature on factors that influence small firms export performance through a robust empirical study. The central context of this research is on SMEs, which constitute the vast majority of firms in Portugal, as in most word economies. Understanding the effects of decisions made by management in selecting strategic orientations is crucial and highly relevant to both theory and practice. Moreover, our intent is also to contribute to the ongoing scholarly conversation on the value of intangibles as strategic resources to SMEs.

Hence, this study allowed us to conclude that particularly innovation has a positive and significant impact on differentiation (H1b supported), validating previous research (e.g. Miller, 1983, Zahra and Covin, 1995). The fact that the dimensions of entrepreneurial orientation does not have a positive or significant impact on cost leadership (H1a, H2a, H2b, H3a and H3b not supported), is a sign that Portuguese textile SMEs seek to support and stimulate new ideas, experimentation and creativity that surely result in new products, services and processes. Indeed, technological innovation encompasses research and engineering efforts focused on developing new products and processes. Product innovation includes market research, design and investment on advertising and promotion. Administrative innovation is related to the development of management systems, control techniques and organizational structure. Thus, embracing innovation can generate competitive advantage and promote superior source of growth (Dess, & Lumpkin, 2005).

These results can be explained by the particular characteristics of the textile sector. In this sense, each season firms have to launch new collections (product innovations) and try to differentiate themselves from the competition (market innovations).

Theoretical and Practical Implications

Our study is responsive to the call of Sousa et al. (2008) which suggests that, in international market context, firms' survival and expansion, and consequent economic growth of many countries, is strongly dependent on a better understanding of the strategic determinants that influence competitive advantage.

Addicionally, our findings provide guidance to business practitioners, since they indicate that entrepreneurial orientation is predictor of competitive strategies. So, for small firm managers, competitive strategy does matters and the development of one type of competitive advantage.

Research Limitations

While this research provides valuable insights into SMEs in the textile industry, the study is not without its limitations. First, the state of the economy might have affected our results. The low scores of willingness to take risks might be influenced by the current context of economic crisis. In fact, in a turbulent market, risk-taking is negatively associated to SME performance (Kraus et al., 2012) and is in fact related to firm failure (Lechner, & Gudmundsson, 2014). Second, it would have been interesting to control our analysis. The fact that the research does not consider the effect of control variables such as age, location and target market of the respondents can be seen as a limitation. Third we used an online study to collect our data. While electronic data collection methods are becoming more common, strategies to encourage a greater response rate are lacking compared to other survey implementation methods. Finally, the fact that the sampling is non probabilistic and convenience is a limitation. Therefore we advise prudence in the generalization of results.

FUTURE LINES OF RESEARCH

Firstly, this study has been based on a mature sector, as is the textile sector in Portugal. The results obtained should be understood in this context. For this reason, new research could be done in more modern industries to test again the proposed relations. Second, given the irregular nature of business growth, a snapshot survey may not be able to capture strategy and performance variations over long periods of time. As such, further studies with a longitudinal perspective would be of added value to investigate why these differences persist. In other words, to find how and why some small exporters become highly successful while others, in the same industry, struggle to raise their export strengths.

REFERENCES

Allen, R. S., Helms, M. M., Takeda, M. B., White, C. S., & White, C. (2006). A Comparison of Competitive Strategies in Japan and the United States. *S.A.M. Advanced Management Journal, 71*(1), 24–34.

Amit, R., & Schoemaker, P. (1993). Strategic assets and organizational rent. *Strategic Management Journal, 14*(1), 33–46. doi:10.1002mj.4250140105

Anderson, B. S., & Eshima, Y. (2013). The influence of firm age and intangible resources on the relationship between entrepreneurial orientation and firm growth among Japanese SMEs. *Journal of Business Venturing, 28*(3), 413–429. doi:10.1016/j.jbusvent.2011.10.001

ATP. (2014). *Plano Estratégico Têxtil 2020 – Projetar o Desenvolvimento da Fileira Têxtil e Vestuário até 2020*. ATP.

Barreto, I. (2010). Dynamic Capabilities: A Review of Past Research and an Agenda for the Future. *Journal of Management, 36*(1), 256–280. doi:10.1177/0149206309350776

Blackburn, R. A., Hart, M., & Wainwright, T. (2013). Small business performance: Business, strategy and owner-manager characteristics. *Journal of Small Business and Enterprise Development, 20*(1), 8–11. doi:10.1108/14626001311298394

Carmines, E. G., & Zeller, R. A. (1979). *Reliability and Validity Assessment*. Newbury Park, CA: Sage Publications. doi:10.4135/9781412985642

Cepeda, C. G., & Roldán, S. J. L. (2004). Aplicando la Técnica PLS en la Administración de Empresas. Conocimiento y Competitividad. Congreso ACEDE, 14, 74-78.

Chin, W. W. (1998). The Partial Least Squares Approach to Structural Equation Modeling. Lawrence Erlbaum Associates.

Chin, W. W. (2010). How to write up and report PLS analyses. In V. Esposito Vinzi, W. W. Chin, J. Henseler, & H. Wang (Eds.), *Handbook of partial least squares: Concepts, methods and applications* (pp. 655–690). Berlin, Germany: Springer-Verlag. doi:10.1007/978-3-540-32827-8_29

Chin, W. W., & Newsted, P. R. (1999). Structural Equation Modeling Analysis with Small Samples Using Partial Least Squares. In R. Hoyle (Ed.), *Statistical Strategies for Small Sample Research* (pp. 307–341). Thousand Oaks, CA: Sage Publications.

Covin, J., & Slevin, D. (1989). Strategic management of small firms in hostile and benign environments. *Strategic Management Journal*, *10*(1), 75–87. doi:10.1002mj.4250100107

Covin, J., & Slevin, D. (1991). A conceptual model of entrepreneurship as firm behavior. *Entrepreneurship Theory and Practice*, *16*(1), 7–25. doi:10.1177/104225879101600102

Davis, J. L., Bell, R. G., Payne, G. T., & Kreiser, P. M. (2010). Entrepreneurial Orientation and Firm Performance: The Moderating Role of Managerial Power. *American Journal of Business*, *25*(2), 41–54. doi:10.1108/19355181201000009

Dess, G., & Lumpkin, G. (2005). The role of entrepreneurial orientation in stimulating effective corporate entrepreneurship. *The Academy of Management Executive*, *19*(1), 147–156.

Fornell, C., & Larcker, D. F. (1981). Evaluating structural equation models with unobservable variables and measurement error. *JMR, Journal of Marketing Research*, *18*(1), 39–50. doi:10.2307/3151312

Frank, H., Kessler, A., & Fink, M. (2010, April). Entrepreneurial orientation and business performance-a replication study. *Schmalenbach Business Review*, 175–199.

Gefen, D., & Straub, D. (2005). A Practical Guide To Factorial Validity Using PLS-Graph: Tutorial And Annotated Example. *Communications of the Association for Information Systems*, *16*, 91–109.

Gil-Pechuan, I., Exposito-Langa, M., & Tomas-Miquel, J. V. (2013). International entrepreneurship in SMEs: A study of influencing factors in the textile industry. *The International Entrepreneurship and Management Journal*, *9*(1), 45–57. doi:10.100711365-012-0242-3

Hair, J., Hult, G. T. M., Ringle, C. M., & Sarstedt, M. (2013). *A primer on Partial least Squares Structural Equation Modeling (PLS-SEM)*. SAGE Publications, Inc.

Henseler, J., Ringle, C. M., & Sinkovics, R. R. (2009). The use of Partial Lesat Squares Path Modeling in international marketing. In R. R. Sinkovics & P. N. Ghauri (Eds.), New Challenges to International Marketing (Advances in International Marketing). Emerald Group Publishing Limited.

Hung, R., Yang, B., Lien, B., McLean, G. N., & Kuo, Y.-M. (2010). Dynamic capability: Impact of process alignment and organizational learning culture on performance. *Journal of World Business*, *45*(3), 285–294. doi:10.1016/j.jwb.2009.09.003

Kraus, S., Rigtering, J. P. C., Hughes, M., & Hosman, V. (2012). Entrepreneurial orientation and the business performance of SMEs: A quantitative study from the Netherlands. *Review of Managerial Science*, *6*(2), 161–182. doi:10.100711846-011-0062-9

Lechner, C., & Gudmundsson, S. V. (2014). Entrepreneurial orientation, firm strategy and small firm performance. *International Small Business Journal*, *32*(1), 36–60. doi:10.1177/0266242612455034

Lumpkin, G., & Dess, G. (1996). Clarifying the entrepreneurial orientation construct and linking it to performance. *Academy of Management Review*, *21*(1), 135–172. doi:10.5465/amr.1996.9602161568

Marôco, J. (2011). *Análise estatística com o SPSS Statistics* (P. Pinheiro, Ed.). ReportNumber, Lda.

Menon, A., Bharadwaj, S., Adidam, P. T., & Edison, S. W. (1999). Antecedents and consequences of marketing strategy making: A model and a test. *Journal of Marketing*, *63*(April), 18–40. doi:10.2307/1251943

Miller, D. (1983). The correlates of entrepreneurship in three types of firms. *Management Science*, *29*(7), 770–791. doi:10.1287/mnsc.29.7.770

Morgan, N., Kaleka, A., & Katsikeas, C. S. (2004). Antecedents of Export Venture Performance : A Theoretical Model. *Journal of Marketing*, *68*(1), 90–108. doi:10.1509/jmkg.68.1.90.24028

O'Cass, A., & Sok, P. (2014). The role of intellectual resources, product innovation capability, reputational resources and marketing capability combinations in firm growth. *International Small Business Journal*, *32*(8), 996–1018. doi:10.1177/0266242613480225

Okpara, J. (2009). Entrepreneurial orientation and export performance: Evidence from an emerging economy. *Int. Rev. Bus. Res. Papers*, *5*(6), 195–211.

Pestana, M. H., & Gageiro, J. N. (2008) Análise de Dados para Ciências Sociais - A complementaridade do SPSS (5th ed.). Lisboa: Edições Silabo.

Peteraf, M. (1993). The cornerstones of competitive advantage: A resource-based view. *Strategic Management Journal, 14*(3), 179–191. doi:10.1002mj.4250140303

Porter, M. (1985). *The Competitive Advantage: Creating and Sustaining Superior Performance*. New York: Free Press.

Porter, M. (1991). Towards a dynamic theory of strategy. *Strategic Management Journal, 12*(S2), 95–117. doi:10.1002mj.4250121008

Rauch, A., & Wiklund, J. (2009). Entrepreneurial orientation and business performance: An assessment of past research and suggestions for the future. *Entrepreneurship Theory and Practice*, 1–54.

Reinartz, W., Haenlein, M., & Henseler, J. (2009). An empirical comparison of the efficacy of covariance-based and variance-based SEM. *International Journal of Research in Marketing, 26*(4), 332–344. doi:10.1016/j.ijresmar.2009.08.001

Sarstedt, M., Ringle, C. M., Smith, D., Reams, R., & Hair, J. F. Jr. (2014). Partial least squares structural equation modeling (PLS-SEM): A useful tool for family business researchers. *Journal of Family Business Strategy, 5*(1), 105–115. doi:10.1016/j.jfbs.2014.01.002

Semrau, T., Ambos, T., & Kraus, S. (2016). Entrepreneurial orientation and SME performance across societal cultures: An international study. *Journal of Business Research, 69*(5), 1928–1932. doi:10.1016/j.jbusres.2015.10.082

Sousa, C. M. P., Martínez-López, F. J., & Coelho, F. (2008). The determinants of export performance: A review of the research in the literature between 1998 and 2005. *International Journal of Management Reviews, 10*(4), 343–374. doi:10.1111/j.1468-2370.2008.00232.x

Stouraitis, V., Harris, M., Harun, M., & Kyritsis, M. (2017). Motivators of SME initial export choice and the European Union regional effect in manufacturing. *International Journal of Entrepreneurial Behaviour & Research, 23*(1), 35–55. doi:10.1108/IJEBR-05-2015-0120

Teece, D. J. (2007). Explicating dynamic capabilities : The nature and microfoundations of (sustainable) enterprise performance. *Strategic Management Journal, 1350*(13), 1319–1350. doi:10.1002mj.640

Teece, D. J. (2010). Business Models, Business Strategy and Innovation. *Long Range Planning*, *43*(2–3), 172–194. doi:10.1016/j.lrp.2009.07.003

Thornhill, S., & Amit, R. (2003). Learning about failure: Bankruptcy, firm age, and the Resource-Based View. *Organization Science*, *14*(5), 497–509. doi:10.1287/orsc.14.5.497.16761

Wiklund, J. (1999). The sustainability of the entrepreneurial orientation performance relationship. *Entrepreneurship Theory and Practice*, *24*(1), 39–50. doi:10.1177/104225879902400103

Wiklund, J., & Shepherd, D. (2005). Entrepreneurial orientation and small business performance: A configurational approach. *Journal of Business Venturing*, *20*(1), 71–91. doi:10.1016/j.jbusvent.2004.01.001

Zahra, S. (1993). A conceptual model of entrepreneurship as firm behavior: A critique and extension. *Entrepreneurship Theory and Practice*, *17*(1), 5–21. doi:10.1177/104225879301700401

Zahra, S., & Covin, J. G. (1995). Contextual influences on the corporate entrepreneurship-performance relationship: A longitudinal analysis. *Journal of Business Venturing*, *10*(1), 43–58. doi:10.1016/0883-9026(94)00004-E

ADDITIONAL READING

Allen, R. S., Helms, M. M., Takeda, M. B., White, C. S., & White, C. (2006). A Comparison of Competitive Strategies in Japan and the United States. *S.A.M. Advanced Management Journal*, *71*(1), 24–34.

Brouthers, L. E., Nakos, G., Hadjimarcou, J., & Brouthers, K. D. (2009). Key Factors for Successful Export Performance for Small Firms. *Journal of International Marketing*, *17*(3), 21–38. doi:10.1509/jimk.17.3.21

Evangelista, F., & Mac, L. (2016). The influence of experience and deliberate learning on SME export performance. *International Journal of Entrepreneurial Behaviour & Research*, *22*(6), 860–879. doi:10.1108/IJEBR-12-2015-0300

Monteiro, A., Soares, A. M., & Rua, O. L. (2017). Entrepreneurial orientation and export performance: The mediating effect of organisational resources and dynamic capabilities. *Journal of International Business and Entrepreneurship Development, 10*(1), 3–20. doi:10.1504/JIBED.2017.082749

Musso, F., & Francioni, B. (2014). International strategy for SMEs: Criteria for foreign markets and entry modes selection. *Journal of Small Business and Enterprise Development, 21*(2), 301–312. doi:10.1108/JSBED-10-2013-0149

Nag, R., Hambrick, D., & Chen, M. (2007). What is strategic management, really? Inductive derivation of a consensus definition of the field. *Strategic Management Journal, 955*(October 2006), 935–955.

Piercy, N., Kaleka, A., & Katsikeas, C. (1998). Sources of competitive advantage in high performing exporting companies. *Journal of World Business, 33*(4), 378–393. doi:10.1016/S1090-9516(99)80081-9

Schumpeter, J. A. (1934). *The Theory of Economic Development*. New Brunswick (U.S.A) and London (U.K.): Transaction Publishers.

Stoll, E. E., & Ha-Brookshire, J. E. (2012). Motivations for Success: Case of U.S. Textile and Apparel Small- and Medium-Sized Enterprises. *Clothing & Textiles Research Journal, 30*(2), 149–163. doi:10.1177/0887302X11429740

Wiklund, J., & Shepherd, D. A. (2011). Where to from here? EO-as-experimentation, failure, and distribution of outcomes. *Entrepreneurship Theory and Practice, 35*(5), 925–946. doi:10.1111/j.1540-6520.2011.00454.x

KEY TERMS AND DEFINITIONS

Competitive Advantage: Creating value for customers and doing it better than competition.

Competitive Strategies: 1) Broad cost leadership, 2) broad differentiation, 3) cost focus, and 4) differentiation focus.

Cost Leadership: Reaching lower costs than competitors.

Differentiation: Creating more value for customers than the average firm.

Entrepreneurial Orientation: Is a firm's behavioral tendency, managerial philosophy, or decision-making practice that is characterized by innovativeness, proactiveness, and a willingness to take risks; the focus is not on the person but in the process of undertake.

Innovation: Is the predisposition to engage in creativity and experimentation through the introduction of new products/services as well as technological leadership in new processes.

Proactivity: Is an opportunity-seeking, forward-looking perspective characterized by the introduction of new products and services ahead of the competition and acting in anticipation of future demand.

Risk-Taking: Involves taking bold actions by venturing into the unknown and/or committing significant resources to ventures in uncertain environments.

Chapter 8
Assessing Social Entrepreneurs' Personal Network for Resource Acquisition:
A Preliminary Study

Susana Bernardino
Politécnico do Porto, Portugal

José Freitas Santos
Politécnico do Porto, Portugal

ABSTRACT

Social entrepreneurial activity is characterized by the innovative search for resource acquisition, combination, and management to pursue opportunities aiming at fulfilling the organization's mission. The network approach to entrepreneurship assumes that entrepreneurs use their personal network to acquire resources and manage the assets of the organization. This chapter intends to analyze whether social entrepreneurs use their personal network to acquire different resources. The investigation uses a quantitative approach, based on an online survey of individuals involved in the management of Portuguese social organizations. The results attained reveal that social entrepreneurs are usually involved in strong and diversified networks. Their personal networks shape the way human, financial, and informational resources are obtained and managed. The major influence is made by social entrepreneurs' indirect contacts (weak ties) and the benefits they perceive these networks are able to provide.

DOI: 10.4018/978-1-5225-6942-8.ch008

INTRODUCTION

The perpetuation of many of the most pressing social problems led the civil society to develop new approaches to the social area. Social entrepreneurship is a new field in the entrepreneurship domain, since it blends an entrepreneurial behaviour with a social mission that is at the heart of these initiatives. The main purpose is to leverage the organization's ability to produce value for the society and to improve the viability of the social entrepreneurs' activities.

A selection of some of the most prominent definitions of social entrepreneur emphasises the role of acquiring resources and the outcomes generated to the society as a main entrepreneurial task. A popular concept defines social entrepreneurs as people who play the role of change agents in the social sector by: i) adopting a mission to create and sustain social value; ii) recognizing and relentlessly pursuing new opportunities to serve that mission; iii) engaging in the process of continuous innovation, adaptation and learning; iv) acting boldly without being limited by resources currently in hand; and v) exhibiting heightened accountability to the constituencies served and for the outcomes created (Dees, 2001; Cho, 2006). Further, the entrepreneur possesses entrepreneurial skills, ambition, and capacity to communicate the mission and inspire the staff, users and partners (Leadbeater, 1997). Schuyler (1998, p. 1) adds to the term "a vision for social change", "financial resources", "skills" and "a powerful desire to social change".

Another definition stresses the efficiency in the management of resources (people, facilities, equipment), the mission (satisfy unmet social needs), and the innovation in the way of delivering welfare services (Leadbeater, 1997). According to Thompson, Alvy and Lees (2000), social entrepreneurs are people who realize where there is an opportunity to satisfy some unmet needs that the state's welfare system will not or cannot meet, and they gather the necessary resources (generally people, often volunteers, money and premises) and use them to make a difference. One of the key features of the definitions of social entrepreneurship stated above lies in the search for resource acquisition to pursue opportunities to fulfil the organisation's mission and/or practices that yield and sustain social value (Mair & Noboa, 2006).

The intervention of social entrepreneurs at the community level is most closely associated with restricted access to resources, and emerged as a response to social problems in those communities (Obschonka, Silbereisen & Schmitt-Rodermund, 2010; Paulsen & McDonald, 2010; Seelos, Mair, Battilana & Dacin, 2011; Constanzo, Vurro, Foster, Servato & Perrini, 2014; Gordon, 2014; Lan, Zhu, Ness, Xing & Schneider, 2014). The challenge of procuring resources for the venture can become so all-consuming for the social entrepreneur that it can become a primary focus of the organisation's activities (Urban, 2010). Also, resource limitations push the social entrepreneur into finding innovative ways of obtaining new resources to generate social outcomes. In the case of social entrepreneurs, there is a distinctive nature of the resource constraints as most of the social entrepreneurs act in markets characterised by a paucity of resources (Di Domenico, Haugh & Tracey, 2010). However, acquiring resources is only a part of the equation, because the wide range of resources needs to be effectively and efficiently managed, in order to attain and pursue the mission of the social organization (Leadbeater, 1997; Schuyler, 1998; Dees, 1998, 2001; Di Domenico *et al.*, 2010).

The studies of entrepreneur's network and resource acquisition have been made basically through qualitative research in the entrepreneurship and social entrepreneurship literature (Martens, Jennings & Jennings, 2007; Miglietta, Romenti & Sartore, 2015; Roundy, 2014). This inductive approach suggests the limited amount of studies that have examined the research topic. Beyond this, a few studies in recent years have attempted to investigate the extent to which the social entrepreneur interacts with the networks during the process of capturing a different type of resource to the social organisation.

In this study, we analyse the role of social entrepreneurs' personal network on the acquisition of resources for the social organisation. The link between the social entrepreneurs' personal network and resource acquisition has received scarce attention in the social entrepreneurship empirical literature. Examining the role of social entrepreneur's personal network on the acquisition of resources will allow us to learn more about the influence of personal relationships on the acquisition of the different type of resources.

This chapter is divided into 5 sections. The first presents the relational approach to social entrepreneurship. The subsequent section reviews the literature on the relationship between the entrepreneurs' personal network and the process of resource acquisition. The methodology used in the study is described in the following section. Next, the results are presented with some preliminary analysis. Finally, the implications for social entrepreneurship are drawn, along with some future research directions.

BACKGROUND

A Network Approach to Social Entrepreneurship

A network consists of single nodes (e.g. persons, organisations) linked by a set of relationships (e.g. friendship, transfer of funds, overlapping membership), which as a whole form the structure of the network (Hoang & Antoncic, 2003). This concept was derived from social psychology, sociology and inter-organisational theory to describe the social relationships among individuals (Tichy, Tushman & Fombrun, 1979; Granovetter, 1983; 1985). In the context of entrepreneurship, there is a long tradition of studying entrepreneurial networks and their effect on a start-up's success (Birley 1985; Aldrich & Zimmer 1986; Johannisson, 1988; Birley & MacMillan, 1997; Hoang & Antoncic, 2003; Greve & Salaff, 2003; Witt, 2004). Following the network approach to entrepreneurship, we can assume the hypothesis that entrepreneurs "use their personal network of private and business contacts to acquire resources and information that they would not (or not as cheaply) be able to acquire on markets" (Witt, 2004, p. 392). Consequently, the nature of the relationships established between different parties will influence the resource exchange among its different members (donors, sponsors, friends and family) (Axelsson & Easton, 1992).

In the context of the entrepreneurial process, networks act both as a support to initial entrepreneurial activity (raising money), as well as a source of information about improvements in the operational efficiency of the business (technical advice and management of human, physical and financial resources) (Stuart & Sorenson, 2005). At an individual level, an entrepreneur that creates or develops a new venture creates formal and informal networks which include family and friends contacts, and institutional relations (Birley, 1985; Aldrich & Zimmer, 1986).

A three circles' framework has been pointed out by Granovetter (1985) and Aldrich, Elam and Reese (1997) to organise the different types of relationships. The inner circle represents a business owner's advisor circle and includes a fairly small set of strong tie relationships, usually of long duration, more reliable, based on implicit reciprocity and involving trust and emotional closeness. In this type of relationships, individuals tend to make heavy investments, requiring fairly frequent contact. The middle circle, involves weak tie relationships, usually of much shorter duration, less reliable, more ambiguous and uncertain. This type of relationships requires lower investment and frequency of contact. The third circle represents those relationships that entered for pragmatic purposes and may be best described as 'contacts' rather than as ties. This type of relationships usually occurs with strangers, or individuals with whom no prior ties have existed and are typically fleeting in duration and require little or no emotional involvement.

Social networks can be characterised according to their density and strength. The density is referred as the depth of ties and is ascertained through the potential number of contacts that are embedded into a given network (Dowla, 2011). The strength of a social network, in turn, derives from the amount of time, emotional intensity, intimacy and reciprocity that exist between its members (Zhang, Sog & Wong, 2010).

Distinct benefits have been assigned to different types of networks. Strong ties involve a closer relationship among members and have as advantages the rapid share of resources, as well as the increased trust that encourages the commitment to a sharing behaviour and reduce the likelihood of unethical procedures (Ge, Hisrich & Dong, 2009).

Bigger networks, in turn, have the advantage of providing access to a larger number of contacts that could facilitate the access to a higher potential diversity of resources, as well as early information (Burt, 1993). According to Ge *et al.* (2009, p. 225) "since range means the variety and number of connections, the broader the external network is, the easier it is to have access to resources". Likewise, as claimed by Burt (1993, p. 64) "bigger is better", since keeping everything else constant, a large and diverse network has a higher potential. For this reason, Ge *et al.* (2009) consider that the amount of resources provided by closer networks is higher than the supplied by the sparser ones. The same authors also found a positive association between networks' intensity and the resources acquisition capability, as well as resources acquisition outcome. Finally, the empirical work of Ge *et al.* (2009) supports the idea that holding broader contacts helps the resource acquisition and the outcomes that organisations can obtain.

However, as warned by Burt (1993, p. 64), "increasing network size without considering diversity can cripple the network". In fact, if the network has a large number of redundant contacts, the network leads to the same people and provides the same benefits, although having reduced reciprocity and trust between its members due to the greater extension of the network.

Similar to economic entrepreneurs, social entrepreneurs also need to maintain different networks of relationships for resource acquisition and the management of the assets of the social organization. Based on the nature of the ties and the adaptation for social entrepreneurship of the framework developed by Santos (1998), we can classify the relationships that make up the network into three different categories. The first type is the personal network that includes the set of social relationships that are established by the social entrepreneurs with family members, friends, and other entrepreneurs (social or economic) (Santos, 1998; Witt, 2004). These informal relations are grounded on common interests, personal friendship, familiar ties or demographic, social or cultural preferences. These sorts of relations are more or less frequent, and develop and strengthen the trust between the individuals.

The second type of network, called entrepreneurial network, includes certain formal and informal contacts that are established between various business partners, such as contact persons at a different level of social and private organisations (suppliers, sponsors, among others) (Santos, 1998). It should be said that this network allows relations that can be started alongside the entrepreneurial process and the acquisition, transfer and management of resources between the social organization and its business partners located in one or various regions. Although trust may not be a common attitude among all the agents involved, information can be disseminated among all of them.

Finally, the institutional network is made up of contact persons at national public institutions (governmental agencies, universities) and regional as well (local and regional organisations, such as Town Hall) that might develop efforts to stimulate social entrepreneurship at local, regional or national level. Therefore, the institutional network includes the set of relations established by the social entrepreneur with governmental agencies that support social ventures (Santos, 1998). To give a general list of the Portuguese institutions that deal with social issues, it is worth mentioning the case of the Ministry of Social Security at national level, the case of Comissão de Coordenação e Desenvolvimento Regional do Norte (CCDRN) (agency that manages and supports social programs sponsored by the European Union) at regional level and the municipality that support social organizations at the local level (payment of occasional expenses).

Dynamic interaction between the social entrepreneur and the different types of networks (personal, entrepreneurial and institutional) is expected and derives from the process of information and resource exchange. These networks can mediate the relations at all geographical levels of intervention by collecting and spreading information among the social entrepreneurs regarding management practices, technological support, legal advice, among other types of information. Also, exchange and transfer of resources may occur between the social entrepreneur and the personal, entrepreneurial and institutional networks. The personal network could be used to acquire financial resources from family, friends and acquaintances and to access donors and other sponsors. The entrepreneurial network could help the management of the social venture to be more effective and efficient by allocating workers or volunteers to other social organisations or provide help to the beneficiaries in different time periods. Also, exchange of resources may occur between the institutional network and the social entrepreneur in the form of frequency of training courses, concession of financial resources or goods and services (Birley, 1985, Aldrich & Zimmer, 1986; Johannisson, 1988; Santos, 1998; Hoang & Antoncic, 2003; Witt, 2004).

In the section that follows we examined in more detail the role of the social entrepreneurs' personal network on the acquisition of resources.

Social Entrepreneurs' Personal Network and Resource Acquisition

The relationship between the personal network of entrepreneurs and the influence on the process of resource acquisition has been explicitly recognized by Witt (2004). According to this author "founders can gain access to resources more cheaply by using their network contacts than by using market transactions, and that they can acquire resources from the network that would not be available via market transactions at all" (Witt, 2004, p. 394). Further, the "opportunity to procure resources (…) arises due to friendship or kinship ties to network partners" that "offer the entrepreneur specific resources at no charge or below the market price simply to do them a favour or to return a favour that they received earlier" (Witt, 2004, p. 394). To Aldrich and Zimmer (1986), entrepreneurship is facilitated by links between aspiring entrepreneurs, resources and opportunities that can be used to source advice, business information and help with the problems of the society. Research also demonstrates that social capital can be acquired through efficient networks in which the system helps the entrepreneur to gather the information and advice needed, independently of the time of the entrepreneur's network entrance (Birley, 1985). According to Nahapiet and Ghoshal (1998, p. 243), the social capital is "the sum of the actual and potential resources embedded within, available through, and derived from the network of relationships possessed by an individual or social unit". Therefore, entrepreneurs, through relationships, can acquire knowledge, skills and capabilities to act differently (develop human capital) and increase intellectual capital (Nahapiet & Ghoshal, 1998). A study of Krebs and Holley (2006) advocates that the networks of individual social enterprise enable social enterprise network organisations to design and implement effective strategies to link other unconnected social enterprises and increase the delivery of business support to other social enterprises.

After a review of the literature on social entrepreneurship and social networks, Dangmei (2016) concludes that social networks are useful vehicles enabling the social entrepreneurs to achieve access to important resources. Jenssen (2001) through an empirical research carried out in Norway confirms that social networks are important as channels for resources. Using the same data, Jenssen and Koenig (2002) reinforce the idea that social networks affect entrepreneurship through the resources they give access to. For Stuart and Sorensen (2005) social networks play an important role in facilitating resource mobilisation, as well as influencing the quality and the amount of resources acquired (Ge *et al.*, 2009). According to these authors, social networks are so critical for resource mobilisation and social organization's overall performance that they are considered social capital as one of the main resources of a firm. As Ge *et al.* (2009, p. 225) state "using networks allow firms to locate valuable resources and improve acquisition capability".

A resource is a productive input or competitive asset that is owned or controlled by a firm (Thompson, Peteraf, Gamble & Strickland III, 2016, p.84). Barney and Hesterly (2015, p. 86) classified the resources into four broad categories: financial resources, physical resources, individual resources, and organisational resources. These resources according to Hitt, Ireland and Hoskisson (2017) could be tangible and intangible. The resources are tangible if they can be "observed and quantified", and intangible if they are "rooted deeply in the firm's history, accumulate over time, and are relatively difficult for competitors to analyse and imitate" (Hitt *et al.*, 2017, p. 84). This categorization seems to cover all range of resources discussed in the literature but the resources that will be investigated are the financial, human and information resources. The financial resources, include money from different kinds of sources (public institutions, private firms, individual donors, etc.), and are generally considered the most important, since they can be used to obtain other resources. Human resources encompass persons that possess skills or knowledge that can be acquired by recruiting or convincing people to join the social venture. Information resources are relevant to overcome the liabilities of newness, solve problems and make management decisions more knowledgeable.

Financial Resources

The competition for government funding and the increased demand of social disadvantageous groups have been challenging the capacity of social entrepreneurs to acquire and manage the resources of the organization (Obschonka *et al.*, 2010; Paulsen & McDonald, 2010; Constanzo *et al.*, 2014; Gordon, 2014; Lan *et al.*, 2014). Therefore, social entrepreneurs need to manage a wide range of internal and external resources to attain and pursue the mission of the social organisation (Leadbeater, 1997; Schuyler, 1998; Dees, 1998, 2001; Di Domenico *et al.*, 2010). Research regarding the benefits of mobilising social networks for the entrepreneurial process recognizes that social entrepreneur networks ties represent primary sources of funding (Zhang, 2010). Indeed, network ties appear to be more effective in increasing the chances of raise capital from friends and family, acquaintances, donors, sponsors than the market methods, such as banks and investors (Zhang *et al.*, 2010). Jenssen and Koenig (2002) in a study of Norwegian entrepreneurs found that weak ties (acquaintances) give access to funding. For Stuart and Sorensen (2005) social networks influence the entrepreneurial process and trace the ties through which financial capital flows. Based on a literature review, Zhang *et al.* (2010) show that social networks have been widely recognized for successful funding, especially strong ties and particularly for initial funding acquisition. Matcht (2016) findings highlight the relevance of social networks for entrepreneurial financing, especially in larger funding operations. In addition, the positive impact of social networks on fundraising has been found within different financial sources, such as crowdfunding (Kuppuswamy & Bayus, 2014; Lehner, 2014; Skirnevskiy, Bending & Brettel, 2017; Kang, Jiang & Tan, 2017) or donations (Galaskiewicz, Bielefeld & Dowell, 2006; Herzog & Yang, 2017).

Human Resources

Social ventures depend on human resources -more or less qualified- to accomplish their mission. Compared to business firms, social ventures have more disadvantages in their quest for human resources in a dynamic and competitive labour market. Therefore, an entrepreneur's personal network becomes critical in the process of identifying and recruiting workers for the social venture (Stuart & Sorensen, 2005).

According to Zhang *et al.* (2010, p. 513), networks, especially indirect ties, "provide entrepreneurs with a channel that transmit private information pertinent to the founding teams". Based on a literature review in the profit sector, Galaskiewicz *et al.* (2006) show that social networks are useful for recruiting new people, even though they can increase employees' turnover, since individuals could use their ties to find new jobs. In the social entrepreneurship domain, a qualitative research reveals that social networks are critical for the mobilization of resources by social organisations (Bernardino, Freitas Santos & Fagundes, 2017). According to the same research, some of the human resources used to pursue the organisation's social mission are provided under the cooperation established between the social entrepreneur and his/her network. The use of networks for human resources' acquisition occurs mainly in the provision of specialised employees, that otherwise the organisation could not afford to have, and also broadens and favours the recruitment of both employees and volunteers (Bernardino, Freitas Santos & Fagundes, 2017).

Informational Resources

The access to information can be obtained through multiple pathways and the data processing mechanisms are critical for the social venture, as informational resources may lead to knowledge creation that contributes to solve a problem or expand the managerial knowledge base (Smith-Doerr & Powell, 2005). According to Burt (1993), the benefits of social networks on information acquisition can derive from: (i) access to better information quality; (ii) the time the information is provided; and (iii) the number of referrals each individual could have access to.

In the United States, many investors interviewed by Shane and Cable (2002) provided qualitative evidence that prior relationships enable them to learn about the entrepreneurs' integrity, intellect, educational and work experiences and thus reduce the perceived uncertainty of the new venture. Similar to social entrepreneurship, social networks enable entrepreneurs to transfer information about their capabilities, integrity and the perspective of their social venture to potential donors. This provides the donors with a better understanding of and greater confidence in the new social venture. If social entrepreneurs have a prior relationship with donors, the prior interaction provides donors with private information about the quality of social entrepreneurs' talents. The private information transferred through direct ties can help to build up the knowledge-based trust of the donors in the social entrepreneurs and thus facilitate the resource acquisition. Also, prior relationships enhance the trust of donors as well in the social entrepreneurs' integrity (Shane & Cable, 2002). An empirical study of entrepreneurs in Norway indicates that strong ties (close friends) are important channels for information (Jenssen & Koenig, 2002). For Stuart and Sorensen (2005) social networks shape information flows that provide the ideas, knowledge and connections required to form new organisations. Also, as claimed by Zhang *et al.* (2010, p. 512) "social network ties provide an efficient means to facilitate information transfer and reduce the problem of information asymmetry between parts in an exchange". Besides speeding up the transfer of knowledge and technology, networks also favour the reduction of the uncertainty of innovation (Ge *et al.*, 2009) and foster the identification of the venture's business opportunities, since they constrain the entrepreneurs' perception of how resources can be used (Zhang *et al.*, 2010). Consequently, social network positively impacts the entrepreneurs' ability to discover business opportunities (Zhang *et al.*, 2010). Also, the knowledge shared between the network members facilitates learning and collaboration (Zhang *et al.*, 2010), helping organisations to procure information and construct a network of knowledge (Galaskiewicz *et al.*, 2006). Through the information provided by social networks, organisations could cope with the environmental uncertainty more accurately and define their strategy more efficiently (Galaskiewicz *et al.*, 2006).

Beyond information received from the network members, the informational benefits also comprise the information that the organisation can widespread through the same network (Burt, 1993). In fact, networks enable the entrepreneur to inform stakeholders about the organisation and help to shape the reputation of the organization, since it signals the social status of the actors and could influence the stakeholders' decisions and support to the organization (Galaskiewicz *et al.*, 2006).

METHODOLOGY

Based on the network approach, this research aims to analyse whether social entrepreneurs' networks influence the way different resources are acquired. A quantitative study based on an online questionnaire was developed to collect primary data. The questionnaire comprised three groups. The first part of the questionnaire included information to characterise the respondent and the social organisation. A screening question was included to ensure that the respondents were involved in the social organisation's management. Hence, the sample for the study only included people who were involved in the organisational decision-making and well-informed about the resources acquisition processes develop in the social organisation. The second group of questions was related to the social entrepreneur's network and was based on the scale developed by Fornoni *et al.* (2012). A five-point Likert scale was used, ranging from 1 (totally disagree) to 5 (totally agree) to assess the respondents' perception of their network. In addition, the third group of questions was included to assess the importance attached by the respondents to the acquisition of different resources and to understand the relevance of different resources to the organisation. The questionnaire has been designed to give priority to the use of interval scales and, as much as possible, the five-point Likert type of scale. The questions were based on the research conducted by the National Survey of Third Setor (2008), Light (2008) and Lehner (2011). Ten experts on the field pretested the questionnaire. The final version of the questionnaire reflected a few modifications suggested by those participants.

The sample was composed of 99 of the 151 Non-governmental organisations (NGOs) listed in the directory of the Portuguese Institute for Development Assistance (IPAD – Instituto Português de Apoio ao Desenvolvimento) and the projects listed on the Portuguese Social Stock Exchange (PSSE).

Data were collected between September 9th, 2012 and January 3rd, 2013, through an open source online survey platform (Lime Survey). After multiple follow-up emails and phone calls, 68 useable responses were received on 44 NGOs and 24 PSSE projects, resulting in an overall online response rate of 53.1% (44.4% on NGO and 82.8% on PSSE). Of these, 62 responses were provided by individuals involved in the social organisation management process.

The primary data were analysed in the statistical software SPSS, version 20. For data analysis, some statistical tools were used, such as mean, variability, frequency distribution and correlations analysis.

RESULTS

Social Entrepreneurs' Personal Networks

Table 1 summarises the results related to social entrepreneurs' relationships. The analysis of the table suggests that social entrepreneurs are endowed with a considerable number of personal relationships. We observe that social entrepreneurs consider that they have a large number of acquaintances and the contacts are very often, since about 64.5% agree or strongly agree with this assertion. Furthermore, the average value attained was 3.8, on a scale ranging from 1 to 5. Only a quarter of the respondents (25 percentile) did not assign a response in the positive pole of the scale. Respondents also consider that their main contacts are people with a larger number of contacts (average of 3.9). An even greater proportion of respondents (72.6%) reported to agree or strongly agree with this statement, which suggests the relevance of establishing ties for social entrepreneurship.

When asked about the perceived benefits of networks, the respondents considered that they could be instrumental on access to information (average of 4.3), to financing (average of 4.1) and human resources (average of 3.8). In fact, the vast majority of the respondents consider that networks are important to access information (88,70%), financing (79.10%) or human resources (69.4%).

The analysis of the correlations (table 2) between the different statements about the importance of networks shows that some of the items have a strong positive correlation. Firstly, we observe that persons that have a more significant number of contacts (Ntw1) tend to relate to people with a large number of contacts ($r_{Ntw1, Ntw2}$= 0.554, α=0.01). Therefore, individuals who are best ranked on strong ties also have considerable weak ties, suggesting that both dimensions of the networks (strong and weak ties) are closely linked and that networks are uneven distributed between social entrepreneurs.

Overall, the benefits perceived on information and funding or human resources access are strongly correlated ($R_{Ntw3,Ntw4}$= 0.794, α=0.01; $R_{Ntw4,Ntw5}$= 0.292, α=0.05), suggesting that networks could strengthen the capacity of the entrepreneur to acquire different resources. The advantages of using personal networking for accessing human resources seems to be higher when social entrepreneurs have a higher number of contacts ($R_{Ntw1,Ntw5}$=0.510, α=0.01). Curiously, the benefits perceived by the use of the networks for accessing funding or other resources do not seem to be associated with the number of contacts of a social entrepreneur ($R_{Ntw1,Ntw3}$=0.042; $R_{Ntw1,Ntw4}$=0.143).

Otherwise, as the respondents consider that they have access to a wider range of contacts (through the contacts of their own contacts) the perception of the benefits is higher, both on financing ($R_{Ntw2,Ntw3}$=0.259, α=0.05), information ($R_{Ntw2,Ntw4}$=0.306, α=0.05) and especially on human resources access ($R_{Ntw2,Ntw5}$=0.645, α=0.01). Thus, typically, the higher the number of contacts at an individual level, the more he/she recognises their importance to access financial and human resources or even information. Interestingly, a more intense association between the use of networks to access resources and information is observed concerning weak ties (distant contacts) rather than strong ties (close contacts) (Table 2).

Resources Acquisition

Human Resources

Table 3 shows that respondents gave relevance either to the recruitment and retention of employees (average of 4.0), volunteers, and managers and leaders (average of 4.2). As the percentile analysis indicates, about three-quarters of the respondents classify these items at least as important. The opinion of the respondents on employees' recruitment and retention is less uniform than on another kind of human resources, as suggested by data variability. Half of the respondents refer that they attach very high importance to the topic, and 11.3% of them, in turn, gave very low importance. Only for about 3% of the respondents the recruitment and retention of volunteers or managers are considered of very low relevance.

On average, social organisations work with around 20 paid employees and 150 volunteers (Table 4). However, high variability is observed between the responses received, as revealed by the standard deviation analysis. At one extreme, one organisation reported working with a team composed of just three elements while another, at the other extreme, indicated to have a workforce of around 6 412 elements. The analysis of the quartiles confirms that the majority of the organisations work with a small number of paid employees and volunteers. In particular, a quarter of the organisations work with less than two paid employees and half of them with less than seven employees (25 and 50 percentiles, respectively). The number of volunteers is substantially higher, since a quarter of the organisations reported to work with six or fewer volunteers and a half of them with 14 or fewer volunteers. The weight of volunteering in social organisations is high, since, on average, volunteers represent 57.8% of the organisations' workforce. The upper percentile indicates that a quarter of the organisations work with a volunteer ratio of over 96.2%.

Financial Resources

Table 5 shows that social entrepreneurs value financial resources acquisition significantly, as observed by the average value obtained in each variable (greater than 4, on a 5-point scale). The highest rated questions were the ability to generate sufficient funds for the organisation in the day-to-day activities (average of 4.4) and the ability to attract donations (average of 4.3). Besides of that, the aspects that received more attention by the respondents were the existence of suitable funding sources and the organisation's ability to generate revenues (both having an average of 4.2).

Table 6 summarises the weight of external resources on social organisations' total funding. The analysis of the table shows that social entrepreneurs are not able to finance the activities of the social organisation just based on their own financial resources. To complement their financial needs, the social organisations have to appeal to external resources, such as donations or grants. A five-point scale was used, ranging from 1 (where external resources represent less than a quarter of the organisations funding sources) to 5 (where the organisation relies entirely on external resources), to assess the weight of external resources on the social organisation. The respondents revealed that fundraising external financial resources are one of the most important financing sources to face cash difficulties. Only 29% of the organisations reported addressing their financial needs mostly through revenues generated by the activities performed by the organisation (own revenues). Only about a one-fifth of the organisations (21.0%) declared to act solely recurring to external resources.

Informational Resources

Regarding how social entrepreneurs sought to obtain information (table 7), we observe that the involvement of the target-audience (average of 4.3) and the community (average of 4.1), as well as the collaboration with other organisations are perceived as quite important by the respondents. Additionally, social entrepreneurs attached considerable attention to the relationships with external stakeholders (average of 3.9), the knowledge of what stakeholders think about the social organisation (average of 3.8) and, ultimately, the implementation of changes according to stakeholders' suggestions (average of 3.7).

Social Entrepreneurs' Personal Network and Resources Acquisition

After describing the organisational practices regarding the acquisition of resources, we assess the extent to which these organisational behaviours are (or not) constrained by social entrepreneurs' network endowments.

Social Entrepreneurs' Personal Network and Human Resources Acquisition

Based on the Pearson correlation coefficient, we observe that respondents with a broader network (mainly due to weak ties) tend to use volunteers more intensively, as the volunteers' weight on the social organisation work groups tends to be higher ($r= 0.283$, $\alpha=0.05$). Social entrepreneurs' direct contacts (extension of the strong ties), in turn, are not associated significantly with different human resources acquisition practices. Further, no relevant differences are found in the number of employees or volunteers by social entrepreneurs' direct or indirect contacts.

As table 8 reveals, there is no correlation between the number of contacts of the social entrepreneur and the importance he/she attached to the recruitment and retention of different kinds of human resources. Differently, individuals who perceive the benefits of networking as higher on the access to funding, tend also to attach increased attention to the recruitment and retention of paid employees ($R_{HR1, Nwt3}= 0.491$, $\alpha=0.01$). Also, respondents who consider that personal networks help them more to access to better information are also those who focus more on recruiting and retaining employees ($R_{HR1, Nwt4}= 0.337$, $\alpha=0.05$) and managers or leaders ($R_{HR3, Nwt4}= 0.299$, $\alpha=0.05$). The importance given to volunteers' recruitment and retention is influenced neither by social entrepreneurs' perception of the benefits of networking nor the use they have of networks to access resources. Curiously, no statistically significant differences were found between the benefits perceived of networking on access to human resources and the relevance attached to different human resources practices.

Social Entrepreneurs' Personal Network and Financial Resources Acquisition

Concerning the financial resources (table 9), we observe that social entrepreneurs who consider that networks play a role in accessing financial resources also attach a major relevance to the existence of suitable funding sources ($R_{NTW3,FR1}= 0.367$, $\alpha=0.01$). Notwithstanding, no significant association was found between this perception and the importance given to the ability to generate their own revenues or donations, as well as to the weight of external resources on the fundraising strategy.

Individuals who perceive that networks play an essential role on the collection of quality information, in turn, seem to use less external resources in their financing strategy ($R_{NTW4, FR6}= -0.257$, $\alpha= 0.05$) and an increased capacity to generate their own revenues.

We do not observe any other differences in the financing structure used (weigh of external resources) in accordance with the respondents' perception about the benefits of social networks. Curiously the social entrepreneur's network endowments (strong and weak ties) are not associated significantly with different practices on financial resources acquisition. Also, it is observed that the relevance attached by social entrepreneurs to their ability to attract donations is not constrained by his/her social network endowments or the benefits perceived by the use of networks. Either, no significant association is observed between the social network variables in analysis and the importance given to financing ordinary activities or expansion investments.

Social Entrepreneurs' Personal Network and Information Acquisition

The correlation between social entrepreneurs' network and information acquisition practices are summarised in table 10. Once again, we observe that the constitution of the social entrepreneurial network (number of contacts - strong ties - and number of contacts of their colleagues and acquaintances - weak ties) is not associated, in a significant way, with different practices to acquire information. Otherwise, some differences are found when we analyse the benefits perceived by social entrepreneurs of networking. In fact, individuals who consider that networks have a more positive impact (either in finance or information access) tend to emphasise more the implementation of changes in accordance to the stakeholders' suggestions or opinions about the social organisation. No statistically significant correlations are found between information practices and the benefits that social entrepreneurs perceive on the use of networking to acquire human resources.

SOLUTIONS AND RECOMMENDATIONS

In this section we intend to discuss the main results attained. The research aimed to analyse the extent to which social entrepreneurs' personal network influence, or not, the way different resources are acquired to social organisations.

The empirical work pursued indicates that social entrepreneurs are surrounded by a considerable network of contacts, some closer to the social entrepreneur and others more distant (contacts of contacts). The benefits perceived by social entrepreneurs on networking with other persons are perceived as high and useful to access the resources they need to the social organisation. This finding is consistent with previous empirical evidence that emphasises the relevance of networking for resources and information acquisition (e.g. Aldrich & Zimmer, 1986; Jenssen & Koening, 2002; Stuart & Sorensen, 2005; Zhang *et al.*, 2010; Witt, 2004), and for Ge *et al.* (2009) that consider a critical asset to the social entrepreneurs. As argued by Axelsson and Easton (1992), we observe that the nature of the relationships established constrains the resources exchange. A strong positive correlation exists between the number of direct and indirect contacts of each respondent, suggesting that social entrepreneurs who have a more substantial number of close contacts are also those who are embedded in denser weak ties. However, although the individuals that rated highly on strong ties are also the ones ranking higher on the weak ties dimensions, we observe that weak ties have a higher potential impact on the mobilisation of resources for social entrepreneurship.

Indeed, the perceived benefits of using networks to access resources and information are higher in individuals that have a more extensive range of indirect contacts, provided by their own contacts. This fact could be explained by the diversity of contacts that weak ties hold and that comprise people with very different backgrounds, some of them that the social entrepreneur is not so attached. The particular impact of middle circle networks, according to Aldrich *et al.* (1997) classification, is consistent with the position of Burt (1993) and Ge *et al.* (2009) who claim that the diversity and extension of the networks are beneficial for resources acquisition. Apparently, the trust and commitment of its members are not negatively affected by the network size, as pointed by Burt (1993). Notwithstanding, the results attained could be constrained by the nature of the social sector where the cooperation established by the network members is expected to be higher.

The relevance of more distant contacts on resources and information acquisition also supports the idea that it is important to complement the resource acquisition strategy to some assets that the organisation needs and have less information. In addition, social entrepreneurs could intend to explore their networks, as extent as possible, due to the scarcity of resources they usually face that requires to be especially inventive in the resource and information procurement (Dees, 2001; Di Domenico *et al.*, 2010; Leadbeater, 1997) and to access resources that recurrently are not provided through market transactions (Witt, 2004). In this context, social entrepreneurs' personal network could significantly leverage the organizations' capabilities.

After describing social entrepreneurs' personal network, we have analysed the practices of resource and information acquisition pursued.

Concerning human resources acquisition, we observe that some social organisations have a higher entrepreneurial orientation on human resources attraction and management than others. While some organisations recognise the critical relevance of attracting and retaining paid employees with long-term working contracts, others tend to focus their attention primarily on attract and retain volunteers, as most of the social organisations work with small teams and are very dependent on volunteering.

The research shows that the social entrepreneur's number of contacts does not influence the dimension of the team used. However, social entrepreneurs having a more extensive network (mainly due to indirect contacts) usually have a higher ratio of volunteers in the organisation. The results suggest that social entrepreneurs do not have major difficulties to fulfil their needs of volunteers, since individuals who have access to more contacts do not have larger teams, either of paid employees or volunteers. However, when they have access to a vast number of contacts, and therefore to a higher number of people potentially interested in collaborating with the social organisations tend to rely more on volunteers (Bernardino, Freitas Santos & Fagundes, 2017; Galaskiewicz *et al.*, 2006; Zhang *et al.*, 2010). This practice could be explained by the significantly lower costs that volunteering involves. Thus, due to the increased capacity to attract volunteers, social organisations do not feel they need to spend money on resources that they can access on a free basis to pursue their social mission. This perspective, although less costly, could expose the social organisation to the uncertainties of the labour market. Nevertheless, social entrepreneurs with a more extensive personal network will probably feel more confident about how to deal with the problem, possibly because they perceive that it will be easier to replace any volunteers.

It should be highlighted that the "volunteer orientation" is only observed when we consider the number of indirect contacts. A similar correlation would also be expected about direct contacts. However, strong ties (direct contacts), when considered in isolation, are probably not able to enlarge and diversify enough the number of volunteers available to collaborate with the organisation, as previously stressed by Burt (1993) as one of the major limitations of strong ties.

Curiously, we observe that the respondents attach a similar relevance to the recruitment and retention either of paid employees, volunteers or managers, regardless of the number of contacts they have (the number of their own contacts or the number of contacts of their contacts). Initially, we could suppose that individuals with a smaller number of contacts could be more aware of the need to pay attention to the recruitment and retention of different types of human resources. On the contrary, the analysis of the data reveals that both groups of organisations (having or not a more significant number of contacts) consider these practices of great importance for the social organisations.

The data also shows that the benefits that social entrepreneurs perceive about the use of networks could influence their human resources practices. When the organisations consider the benefits of belonging to a network as higher (either on fundraising or information acquisition), they tend to attach a great relevance to paid employees' retention and recruitment and also to managers' attraction. Thus, the entrepreneurs who think their contacts could help the organisation are usually the ones that pursue more entrepreneurial human resources practices. Another explanation could be provided by the reinforcement of the financial structure of the organisation, due to the higher support is given by the network members that enable them to develop a human resources policy more oriented towards the retention of employers.

When analysing the relevance attached by the organisation to financial resources acquisition, some financial vulnerability is suggested, since they tend to attach particular importance to the day-to-day financing activities and also to donations acquisition. Data analysis also indicates an intense use of external resources to finance the social organizations' activities, as opposed to obtaining their own revenues.

Comparing the financial resources acquisition practices with the social entrepreneur's network endowment, we observe that no significant differences were found. In fact, the composition and dimension of the social entrepreneurs' personal network do not seem to influence the adoption of different financial resources practices or funding sources. This finding is contradictory with our initial expectations, since the current empirical literature has highlighted the relevance of social networks to fundraising (e.g. Kuppuswamy & Bayus, 2014; Lehner, 2014; Match, 2016; Stuart & Sorensen 2005; Zhang *et al.*, 2010). Nevertheless, the results attained do not corroborate or decline the thesis that networks extension is critical for fundraising. Indeed, if strong and weak networks could have a positive impact on both donations acquisition (Galaskiewicz *et al.*, 2006; Herzog & Yang, 2017) and other more entrepreneurial income sources (Kuppuswamy & Bayus, 2014; Lehner, 2014; Skirnevskiy *et al.*, 2017; Kang *et al.*, 2017), the percentage of external resources on the financial strategy of the organization will remain the same, regardless of the amount of the social entrepreneurs' contacts. A deeper understanding of this puzzle requires further research, in order to include the analysis of the impact of other mediating variables, such as the number of redundant contacts and other qualitative issues related with the members involved in each network (Burt, 1993).

By contrast to network endowments, the individuals' perceptions of the personal network shape the way social entrepreneurs access financial resources. We observe that individuals who consider that networks could generate higher benefits to financing also claim for the need of existing suitable funding sources. No association was found concerning different funding sources (such as donations or own revenues). This finding could possibly be explained by the fact that individuals who have a more positive perception on networking benefits consider that they could rely on fundraising mechanisms, regardless the financing nature, as long as the financing system is composed of instruments appropriate for the sector. Curiously, respondents who consider that networking has a crucial informational role (facilitating the access to better information), typically rely less on external resources and have a higher capacity to obtain external revenues. This result could be the consequence of the social entrepreneurs' contribution to enhance the ability to identify and exploit opportunities, even in the financing area, to conceive more suitable income generation strategies and to obtain an increased adherence of the stakeholders to the organisation fundraising activities.

Finally, about the acquisition of information, we observe that most of the social organisations value significantly the processes that facilitate the collection of information from their primary stakeholders. When we contrast the information acquisition practices with the respondents' network, the data indicates that a set of variables have a strong impact on the practices adopted (perceptions of the benefits of social networks). The social organisations which believe that entrepreneurs' personal network could play a more positive role in resources (financial and human) and information acquisition, tend to have greater involvement with the stakeholders. Therefore, individuals' perceptions about the benefits of networks seem to constrain their attitudes towards the outside, leading the social organisation to adopt more decentralised management and participatory decision-making processes. So, when social entrepreneurs perceive these benefits as higher, they foster a more intense contact with the outside world redesigning the ventures' strategy accordingly to the new information input. These practices are consistent with empirical evidence claiming that social networks are a privileged source for information acquisition (e.g. Burt, 1993; Galaskiewicz *et al.*, 2006; Zhang *et al.*, 2010).

Neither the number of contacts (either direct or indirect) nor the effective use of networking to access resources is associated with different information collection practices. Nevertheless, we could still admit that social entrepreneurs' personal network influences the acquisition of information.

Table 1. Social entrepreneurs' personal network

	(1)	(2)	(3)	(4)	(5)	Average	Standard Deviation	25 Percentile	50 Percentile	75 Percentile
Ntw1- I consider I have a large number of contacts and acquaintances.	3.2%	1.6%	30.6%	37.1%	27.4%	3.8	0.96	3.0	4.0	5.0
Ntw2- I consider that my main contacts are people with a large number of contacts.	1.6%	3.2%	22.6%	48.4%	24.2%	3.9	0.86	3.0	4.0	4.3
Ntw3- I believe that my contacts (network) facilitate the access to financing.	6.5%	3.2%	11.3%	33.9%	45.2%	4.1	1.14	4.0	4.0	5.0
Ntw4- I believe that my contacts (network) facilitate the access to better information.	3.2%	1.6%	6.5%	43.5%	45.2%	4.3	0.90	4.0	4.0	5.0
Ntw5- I believe that my contacts (network) facilitate the access human resources.	1.6%	8.1%	21.0%	46.8%	22.6%	3.8	0.94	3.0	4.0	4.0

Source: Authors' own elaboration

(1) I strongly disagree; (2) I disagree; (3) I neither agree nor disagree; (4) I agree; (5) I strongly agree;

Table 2. Correlation between social entrepreneurs' network questions

	Ntw1	Ntw2	Ntw3	Ntw4	Ntw5
Ntw1	1				
Ntw2	0.554**	1			
Ntw3	0.042	0.259*	1		
Ntw4	0.143	0.306*	0.794**	1	
Ntw5	0.510**	0.645**	0.184	0.292*	1

Source: Authors' own elaboration

Ntw1- I consider I have a large number of contacts and acquaintances; Ntw2- I consider that my main contacts are people with a large number of contacts; Ntw3- I believe that my contacts (network) facilitate the access to financing; Ntw4- I believe that my contacts (network) facilitate the access to better information; Ntw5- I believe that my contacts (network) facilitate the access to human resources.

* The correlation is statistically significant for $\alpha = 0.05$;

** The correlation is statistically significant for $\alpha=0.01$;

Table 3. Importance attached by social entrepreneurs to the acquisition of different human resources

	(1)	(2)	(3)	(4)	(5)	Average	Standard Deviation	25 Percentile	50 Percentile	75 Percentile
HR1- Recruitment and retention of employees	11.3%	3.2%	6.5%	29.0%	50.0%	4.0	1.32	4.0	4.5	5.0
HR2- Recruitment and retention of volunteers	3.2%	1.6%	12.9%	38.7%	43.5%	4.2	0.95	4.0	4.0	5.0
HR3- Recruitment and retention of managers and leaders	3.2%	1.6%	8.1%	41.9%	45.2%	4.2	0.92	4.0	4.0	5.0

Source: Authors' own elaboration

(1) Very low importance; (2) Low importance; (3) Null importance; (4); High importance; (5) Very high importance.

FUTURE RESEARCH DIRECTIONS

This research has implications for the theory since it allowed to produce further knowledge in a topic that, although critical, is largely underexploited in the social entrepreneurship field. Despite of the advance produced, the research suffers from some limitations. First of all, it consists of a preliminary study that is supported by a small sample that recommends some caution on generalising the conclusions attained for other geographical contexts. Further, the research is based on a survey that questions the perceptions of social entrepreneurs about the personal network of contacts.

Table 4. Overall characterisation of the social organisations work teams

	HR4- Number of Employees	HR5- Number of Volunteers	HR7- Overall Size of Work Teams	HR8- Percentage of Volunteers
Average	20.3	149.3	170.0	57.8%
Standard deviation	35.1	826.0	825.6	35.4%
Minimum	0	0	3	0.0%
Maximum	184	6 400	6 412	100.0%
25 Percentile	2.0	6.0	13.5	23.6%
50 Percentile	7.0	14.0	29.5	54.3%
75 Percentile	20.3	30.0	64.3	96.2%

Source: Authors' own elaboration

Table 5. Importance attached by social entrepreneurs to financial resources acquisition

	(1)	(2)	(3)	(4)	(5)	Average	Standard Deviation	25 Percentile	50 Percentile	75 Percentile
FR1- The existence of suitable funding sources	3.2%	1.6%	9.7%	38.7%	46.8%	4.2	0.94	4.0	4.0	5.0
FR2- The organization's ability to generate revenues	1.6%	1.6%	16.1%	35.5%	45.2%	4.2	0.89	4.0	4.0	5.0
FR3- The organization's ability to attract donations	1.6%	8.1%	11.3%	19.4%	59.7%	4.3	1.06	4.0	5.0	5.0
FR4- The organization's ability to generate sufficient funds for the organization day-to-day activities	1.6%	1.6%	8.1%	32.3%	56.5%	4.4	0.84	4.0	5.0	5.0
FR5- The organization's ability to generate funds for expansion investments	4.8%	3.2%	6.5%	46.8%	38.7%	4.1	1.01	4.0	4.0	5.0

Source: Authors' own elaboration

(1) Very low importance; (2) Low importance; (3) Null importance; (4); High importance; (5) Very high importance

Table 6. External resources weight of the social organisation funding

	< 25%	25-50%	50-75%	> 75%	100%	Average	Standard Deviation	25 Percentile	50 Percentile	75 Percentile
FR6- % of external resources	14.5%	14.5%	16.1%	33.9%	21.0%	3.03	1.60	2.00	3.50	4.00

Source: Authors' own elaboration

Table 7. Importance attached by social entrepreneurs to different information sources

	(1)	(2)	(3)	(4)	(5)	Average	Standard Deviation	25 Percentile	50 Percentile	75 Percentile
IR1- The implementation of changes, according to the suggestions of stakeholders	6.5%	4.8%	25.8%	38.7%	24.2%	3.7	1.10	3.0	4.0	4.3
IR2- The knowledge of the associations that the stakeholders have about the organization	6.5%	3.2%	19.4%	46.8%	24.2%	3.8	1.06	3.0	4.0	4.3
IR3- The involvement of the target audience in the organization	0.0%	1.6%	17.7%	33.9%	46.8%	4.3	0.81	4.0	4.0	5.0
IR4- The involvement of the community in the organization	0.0%	1.6%	25.8%	32.3%	40.3%	4.1	0.85	3.0	4.0	5.0
IR5- The relationship with external stakeholders	3.2%	4.8%	19.4%	43.5%	29.0%	3.9	0.99	3.0	4.0	5.0
IR6- The collaboration with other organizations	0.0%	1.6%	14.5%	37.1%	46.8%	4.3	0.78	4.0	4.0	5.0

Source: Authors' own elaboration

(1) Very low importance; (2) Low importance; (3) Null importance; (4); High importance; (5) Very high importance

Table 8. Correlation between social entrepreneurs' network and human resources acquisition practices

Item	Ntw1	Ntw2	Ntw3	Ntw4	Ntw5
HR1- Recruitment and retention of employees	-0.125	-0.069	0.491**	0.337**	-0.021
HR2- Recruitment and retention of volunteers	0.140	0.121	0.078	0.060	0.039
HR3- Recruitment and retention of managers and leaders	-0.104	-0.115	0.186	0.299*	0.017
HR4- Number of employees	-0.085	-0.167	0.034	0.031	0.066
HR5- Number of volunteers	-0.108	0.195	-0.017	-0.040	0.038
HR6- Dimension of work groups	-0.111	0.188	-0.015	-0.038	0.040
HR7- Percentage of volunteers	0.102	0.283*	-0.110	-0.091	-0.008

Source: Authors' own elaboration

Ntw1- I consider I have a large number of contacts and acquaintances; Ntw2- I consider that my main contacts are people with a large number of contacts; Ntw3- I believe that my contacts (network) facilitate the access to financing; Ntw4- I believe that my contacts (network) facilitate the access to better information; Ntw5- I believe that my contacts (network) facilitate the access to human resources.

* The correlation is statistically significant for $\alpha = 0.05$;

** The correlation is statistically significant for α=0.01;

Table 9. Correlation between social entrepreneurs' network and financial resources acquisition practices

Item	Ntw1	Ntw2	Ntw3	Ntw4	Ntw5
FR1- The existence of suitable funding sources	-0.193	-0.011	0.367**	0.158	-0.133
FR2- The organization's ability to generate revenues	0.002	0.006	0.145	0.197	0.207
FR3- The organization's ability to attract donations	0.157	0.012	0.186	0.028	0.170
FR4- The organization's ability to generate sufficient funds for the organization day-to-day activities	-0.142	0.032	0.086	0.055	0.101
FR5- The organization's ability to generate funds for expansion investments	-0.048	0.107	0.135	0.057	0.127
FR6- Percentage of external resources	0.116	-0.127	-0.113	-0.257*	-0.247

Source: Authors' own elaboration

Ntw1- I consider I have a large number of contacts and acquaintances; Ntw2- I consider that my main contacts are people with a large number of contacts; Ntw3- I believe that my contacts (network) facilitate the access to financing; Ntw4- I believe that my contacts (network) facilitate the access to better information; Ntw5- I believe that my contacts (network) facilitate the access to human resources.

* The correlation is statistically significant for $\alpha = 0.05$;

** The correlation is statistically significant for α=0.01;

Table 10. Correlation between social entrepreneurs' network and information practices

Item	Ntw1	Ntw2	Ntw3	Ntw4	Ntw5
IR1- The implementation of changes, according to the suggestions of stakeholders	-0.094	-0.032	0.310*	0.346**	-0.043
IR2- The knowledge of the associations that the stakeholders have about the organisation	-0.018	-0.202	0.274*	0.366**	-0.108
IR3- The involvement of the target audience in the organization	-0.030	-0.034	0.084	0.177	-0.020
IR4- The involvement of the community in the organization	0.043	0.015	-0.027	0.025	0.089
IR5- The relationship with external stakeholders	-0.086	-0.011	0.344**	0.341**	-0.109
IR6- The collaboration with other organizations	0.152	0.116	0.140	0.172	-0.034

Source: Authors' own elaboration

Ntw1- I consider I have a large number of contacts and acquaintances; Ntw2- I consider that my main contacts are people with a large number of contacts; Ntw3- I believe that my contacts (network) facilitate the access to financing; Ntw4- I believe that my contacts (network) facilitate the access to better information; Ntw5- I believe that my contacts (network) facilitate the access to human resources.

* The correlation is statistically significant for $\alpha = 0.05$;

** The correlation is statistically significant for $\alpha=0.01$;

In other studies, it would be interesting to assess on a more factual basis the number and quality of the contacts hold, and to understand if some contacts are qualitatively more prosperous than others to acquire the resources needed by the social organization.

This chapter was focused on the analysis of the social entrepreneurs' personal network. In future works, it will be valuable to explore the way entrepreneurial and institutional networks influence (or not) the resources acquisition process of the social organization. Future researches could either study the way resources are shared between different (social) organisations and the way the relationships of trust and complementarity between network members could be maximized and optimised.

In-depth qualitative methods could also be useful in future researches, in order to understand how networks are effectively used to access human, financial and informational resources. Focus groups with social entrepreneurs and different resources providers would help to get a more detailed knowledge of the subject, difficult to obtain in a preliminary quantitative study. It would also be interesting to explore the impact of these networks on social impact generation and the social organisations' sustainability.

CONCLUSION

Resource acquisition is described in the academic literature as one of the most important, but also difficult tasks of the social entrepreneurs (e.g. Dees, 2001; Cho, 2006; Leadbeater, 1997; Schuyler, 1998, among others). To pursue a social mission and address complex social problems, social entrepreneurs need to collect and mobilise a set of critical resources. However, the social organisations are usually embedded in an environment of resource scarcity (DiDomenico *et al.*, 2010) and resource restriction (Obschonaka *et al.*, 2010; Seelos *et al.*, 2011; Constanzo *et al.*, 2014). Solving this dilemma requires from the social entrepreneurs an innovative approach in the way how they acquire resources (Mair & Noboa, 2006) and effective in the way the resources are collected and managed (DiDomenico *et al.*, 2010; Dees, 1998; Dees, 2001; Leadbetarer, 1997).

Based on a quantitative approach, this research aimed to analyse the role that social entrepreneurs' personal network play on its capacity to mobilise resources and to understand the way social networks constraints or assists the process of capturing different types of resources to the social organisation.

The research reveals that social entrepreneurs are typically involved in an extensive and diversified network of contacts, composed of both strong and weak ties. These relationships tend to influence the way resources are acquired by the social organization.

The benefits perceived by the social entrepreneurs from belonging to a network are higher for individuals who have more distant contacts (weak ties) than strong ties, regardless of the density of the relationships. The extension and diversity of social entrepreneurs' network can influence human resources acquisition, the dependence the organisation is willing to take on external support and even in the social organisations' cost structure. The research further reveals that the main influence is made by social entrepreneurs' indirect contacts (the contacts of their own contacts).

Furthermore, the benefits social entrepreneurs perceive that could be provided by the network influence more the resources acquisition practices than the number of personal contacts they really have. Indeed, the perceived benefits of networking shape the relevance social entrepreneurs give to paid employees, wherein individuals who consider the advantages of networking as higher also have higher entrepreneurial orientation on the human resources management. An increased perception of the network benefits also has a short impact on fundraising strategy, based on a lower dependency on external resources. Social entrepreneurs that consider social networks a benefit for the social venture also use participatory processes in which they could collect information from their primary stakeholders and take advantage of this relationship for the social organisation. Therefore, public policy can promote programs and forums to stimulate networking between different actors in society, in order to foster the diversity of contacts between social entrepreneurs. From managerial implications, the research emphasises the relevance of social organization managers to develop an extensive network of contacts, composed of very diverse actors that could have a critical role for resources and information acquisition.

REFERENCES

Aldrich, H. E., Elam, A. B., & Reese, P. R. (1997). Strong ties, weak ties, and strangers: do women owners differ from men in their use of networking to obtain assistance? Academic Press. doi:10.4324/9780203435168.ch1

Aldrich, H. E., & Zimmer, C. (1986). Entrepreneurship through networks. In D. Sexton & R. W. Smilor (Eds.), *Art and Science of Entrepreneurship* (pp. 3–23). Cambridge, MA: Ballinger Publishing Company.

Axelsson, B., & Easton, G. (Eds.). (1992). *Industrial networks: A new view of reality*. London: Routledge.

Barney, J. B., & Hesterly, W. S. (2015). *Strategic management & competitive advantage: concepts and cases* (5th ed.). Essex, UK: Pearson Education Limited.

Bernardino, S., Freitas Santos, J., & Fagundes, S. (2017). Papel do capital social no desenvolvimento de iniciativas sociais. *European Journal of Applied Business and Management*, 91-108.

Birley, S. (1985). The role of networks in the entrepreneurial process. *Journal of Business Venturing*, *1*(1), 107–117. doi:10.1016/0883-9026(85)90010-2

Birley, S., & Mac Millan, I. C. (Eds.). (1997). *Entrepreneurship in a global context*. London: Routledge. doi:10.4324/9780203435168

Burt, R. S. (1993). The social structure of competition. In N. Nohria & R. G. Eccles (Eds.), Networks and Organizations (pp. 57-91). Cambridge, MA: Harvard Business School Press.

Cho, A. H. (2006). Politics, values and social entrepreneurship: a critical appraisal. In J. Mair, J. Robinson, & K. Kockerts (Eds.), *Social entrepreneurship* (pp. 34–56). New York: Palgrave Macmillan. doi:10.1057/9780230625655_4

Constanzo, L., Vurro, C., Foster, D., Servato, F., & Perrini, F. (2014). Dual-Mission Management in Social Entrepreneurship: Qualitative Evidence from Social Firms in the United Kingdom. *Journal of Small Business Management, 52*(4), 655–677. doi:10.1111/jsbm.12128

Dangmei, J. (2016). Social entrepreneurship and social networks for sustainable rural development in India. *Paripex – Indian Journal of Research, 5*(10), 622-624.

Dees, J. (1998). Enterprising nonprofits: What do you do when traditional sources of funding fall short? *Harvard Business Review, 76*(1), 55–67. PMID:10176919

Dees, J. G. (2001). *The meaning of "social entrepreneurship." Center for the advancement of Social Entrepreneurship*. Durham, NC: Fuqua School of Business, Duke University. Retrieved from http://www.fuqua.duke.edu/centers/case/documents/dees_SE.pdf

Di Domenico, M., Haugh, H., & Tracey, P. (2010). Social bricolage: Theorizing social value creation in social enterprises. *Entrepreneurship Theory and Practice, 34*(4), 681–703. doi:10.1111/j.1540-6520.2010.00370.x

Dowla, A. U. (2011). *How Entrepreneurs use Social Networks in their Business* (Master's thesis). Swedish University of Agricultural Sciences.

Fornoni, M., Arribas, I., & Vila, J. (2012). An entrepreneur's social capital and performance: The role of access to information in the Argentinean case. *Journal of Organizational Change Management, 25*(5), 682–698. doi:10.1108/09534811211254572

Galaskiewicz, J., Bielefeld, W., & Dowell, M. (2006). Networks and organizational growth: A study of community based nonprofits. *Administrative Science Quarterly, 51*(3), 337–380. doi:10.2189/asqu.51.3.337

Ge, B., Hisrich, R., & Dong, B. (2009). Networking, resource acquisition, and the performance of small and medium-sized enterprises; An empirical study of three major cities in China. *Managing Global Transitions, 7*(3), 221–239.

Gordon, J. (2014). A stage model of venture philanthropy. *Venture Capital: An International Journal of Entrepreneurial Finance, 16*(2), 85–107. doi:10.1080/13691066.2014.897014

Granovetter, M. (1983). The strength of weak ties: A network theory revisited. *Sociological Theory, 1*, 201–233. doi:10.2307/202051

Granovetter, M. (1985). The strength of weak ties. *American Journal of Sociology, 78*(6), 1360–1380. doi:10.1086/225469

Greve, A., & Salaff, J. W. (2003). Social networks and entrepreneurship. *Entrepreneurship Theory and Practice*, *28*(1), 1–22. doi:10.1111/1540-8520.00029

Herzog, P., & Yang, S. (2017). *Social networks and charitable giving: Trusting, doing, asking, and alter primacy*. Nonprofit and Voluntary Sector Quartely; doi:10.1177/0899764017746021

Hitt, M. A., Ireland, R. D., & Hoskisson, R. E. (2017). *Strategic management: competitiveness & globalization, concepts and cases* (12th ed.). Boston: Cengage Learning.

Hoang, H., & Antoncic, B. (2003). Network-based research in entrepreneurship: A critical review. *Journal of Business Venturing*, *18*(2), 165–187. doi:10.1016/S0883-9026(02)00081-2

Jenssen, J. I. (2001). Social networks, resources and entrepreneurship. *International Journal of Entrepreneurship and Innovation*, *2*(2), 103–109. doi:10.5367/000000001101298846

Jenssen, J. I., & Koenig, H. F. (2002). The effect of social networks on resource access and business start-ups. *European Planning Studies*, *10*(8).

Johannisson, B. (1988). Business formation - a network approach. *Scandinavian Journal of Management*, *4*(3), 83–99.

Kang, L., Jiang, Q., & Tan, C. (2017). Remarkable advocates: An investigation of geographic distance and social capital for crowdfunding. *Information & Management*, *54*(3), 336–348. doi:10.1016/j.im.2016.09.001

Krebs, V., & Holley, J. (2006). *Building smart communities through network weaving*. Appalachian Center for Economic Networks. Retrieved from: https://www.networkweaver.com/wp-content/uploads/2011/12/BuildingNetworks.pdf

Kuppuswamy, V., & Bayus, B. L. (2014). *Crowdfunding creative ideas: The dynamics of project backers in Kickstarter.* SSRN Working Paper, No. 2234765, Retrieved from ssrn.com/abstract52234765

Lan, H., Zhu, Y., Ness, D., Xing, K., & Schneider, K. (2014). The role and characteristics of social entrepreneurs in contemporary rural cooperative development in China: Case studies of rural social entrepreneurship. *Asia Pacific Business Review*, *20*(3), 379–400. doi:10.1080/13602381.2014.929300

Leadbeater, C. (1997). *The rise of the social entrepreneur*. London: Demos.

Lehner, O. (2011). The phenomenon of social enterprise in Austria: A triangulated descriptive study. *Journal of Social Entrepreneurship*, *2*(1), 53–78. doi:10.1080/19420676.2011.555775

Lehner, O. M. (2014). The formation and interplay of social capital in crowdfunded social ventures. *Entrepreneurship and Regional Development*, *26*(5-6), 478–499. doi:10.1080/08985626.2014.922623

Light, P. (2008). *The search for social entrepreneurship*. Washington, DC: Brookings Institution Press.

Mair, J., & Noboa, E. (2006). Social entrepreneurship: how intentions to create a social venture are formed. In J. Mair, J. Robinson, & K. Kockerts (Eds.), *Social entrepreneurship* (pp. 121–135). New York: Palgrave Macmillan. doi:10.1057/9780230625655_8

Martens, M. L., Jennings, J. E., & Jennings, P. D. (2007). Do the stories they tell get them the money they need? The role of entrepreneurial narratives in resource acquisition. *Academy of Management Journal*, *50*(5), 1107–1132. doi:10.5465/amj.2007.27169488

Matcht, S. (2016). Putting "entrepreneurial finance education" on the map: Including social capital in the entrepreneurial finance curriculum. *Education + Training*, *58*(9), 984–1002. doi:10.1108/ET-08-2015-0068

Miglietta, A., Romenti, S., & Sartore, A. (2015). Entrepreneurial narratives for resource acquisition in the Italian creative industries: A qualitative study. *Sinergie.*, *33*(98), 213–231.

Nahapiet, J., & Ghoshal, S. (1998). Social capital, intellectual capital, and the organizational advantage. *Academy of Management Review*, *23*(2), 242–266. doi:10.5465/amr.1998.533225

National Survey of Third Sector Organisations. (2008). *National Survey of Third Sector Organisations*. Cabinet Office of the Third Sector. Accessed on November 10, 2018, from http://www.communityplanningtoolkit.org/sites/default/files/OutcomesR4.pdf

Obschonka, M., Silbereisen, R., & Schmitt-Rodermund, E. (2010). Entrepreneurial intention as developmental outcome. *Journal of Vocational Behavior*, *77*(1), 63–72. doi:10.1016/j.jvb.2010.02.008

Paulsen, N., & McDonald, A. (2010). Doing social enterprise: A reflection and view from the field. *Third Sector Review*, *16*(2), 109–126.

Roundy, P. T. (2014). The stories of social entrepreneurship: Narrative discourse and social enterprise resource acquisition. *Journal of Research in Marketing and Entrepreneurship, 16*(2), 200–218. doi:10.1108/JRME-06-2014-0009

Santos, J. F. (1998). Location of foreign firms in Portugal: A network approach. *38th Congress of the European Regional Science Association: "Europe Quo Vadis? - Regional Questions at the Turn of the Century"*. Available: http://hdl.handle.net/10419/113413

Schuyler, G. (1998). Social entrepreneurship: Profit as a means, not an end. *CELCEE Digest, 30*, 98-7. Retrieved from http://www.eric.ed.gov/PDFS/ED434219.pdf

Seelos, C., Mair, J., Battilana, J., & Dacin, M. (2011). The embeddedness of social entrepreneurship: Understanding variation across local communities. In C. Marquis, M. Lounsbury, & R. Greenwood (Eds.), *Communities and Organizations* (pp. 333–363). Bingley, UK: Emerald Group Publishing Limited. doi:10.1108/S0733-558X(2011)0000033013

Shane, S., & Cable, D. (2002). Network ties, reputation, and the financing of new ventures. *Journal of Management Science, 48*(3), 364–381. doi:10.1287/mnsc.48.3.364.7731

Skirnevskiy, V., Bending, D., & Brettel, M. (2017). The influence of internal social capital on serial creators' success in crowdfunding. *Entrepreneurship Theory and Practice, 41*(2), 209–236. doi:10.1111/etap.12272

Smith-Doerr, L., & Powell, W. W. (2005). Networks and economic life. In N. J. Smelser & R. Swedberg (Eds.), *The handbook of economic sociology* (pp. 379–402). New York: Russel Sage Foundation.

Stuart, T. E., & Sorenson, O. (2005). Social networks and entrepreneurship. In S. Alvarez, R. Agarwal, & O. Sorensen (Eds.), *Handbook of entrepreneurship research: interdisciplinary perspectives* (pp. 233–251). New York: Springer. doi:10.1007/0-387-23622-8_11

Thompson, A. A., Peteraf, M. A., Gamble, J. E., & Strickland, A. J., III. (2016). Crafting and executing strategy: the quest for competitive advantage, concepts and cases (20th ed.). New York: McGraw-Hill Education.

Thompson, J., Alvy, G., & Lees, A. (2000). Social entrepreneurship: A new look at the people and the potential. *Management Decision, 38*(5), 328–338. doi:10.1108/00251740010340517

Tichy, N. M., Tushman, M. I., & Fombrun, C. (1979). Social networks analysis for organizations. *Academy of Management Review, 4*(4), 507–519. doi:10.5465/amr.1979.4498309

Urban, B. (2010). Creating value and innovation through social entrepreneurship. In Frontiers in Entrepreneurship. Springer. doi:10.1007/978-3-642-04502-8_5

Witt, P. (2004). Entrepreneurs' networks and the success of start-ups. *Entrepreneurship and Regional Development*, *16*(5), 391–412. doi:10.1080/0898562042000188423

Zhang, J. (2010). The problems of using social networks in entrepreneurial resource acquisition. *International Small Business Journal*, *28*(4), 338–361. doi:10.1177/0266242610363524

Zhang, J., Soh, P., & Wong, P. (2010). Entrepreneurial resource acquisition through indirect ties: Compensatory effects of prior knowledge. *Journal of Management*, *36*(2), 511–536. doi:10.1177/0149206308329963

ADDITIONAL READING

Baker, E., Onyx, J., & Edwards, M. (2011). Emergence, Social Capital And Entrepreneurship: Understanding Networks From The Inside. *Emergence*, *13*(3), 21–38.

Bidart, C., Degenne, A., & Grossetti, C. (2018). Personal networks typologies: A structural approach. *Social Networks*, *54*, 1–11. doi:10.1016/j.socnet.2017.11.003

Dubos, R. (2001). *Social Capital: Theory and Research*. New York: Routledge.

Hlady-Rispal, M., & Servantie, V. (2018). Deconstructing the Way in which Value Is Created in the Context of Social Entrepreneurship. *International Journal of Management Reviews*, *20*(1), 62–80. doi:10.1111/ijmr.12113

Oprica, R. (2013). Social Networking for Social Entrepreneurship. *Procedia - Social And Behavioral Sciences*, 92(Logos Universality Mentality Education Novelty (LUMEN 2013), Iasi, Romania, 10-13 April 2013), 664-667. doi:10.1016/j.sbspro.2013.08.735

Polzin, F., Toxopeus, H., & Stam, E. (2018). The wisdom of the crowd in funding: Information heterogeneity and social networks of crowdfunders. *Small Business Economics*, *50*(2), 251–273. doi:10.100711187-016-9829-3

Westlund, H., & Gawell, M. (2012). Building social capital for social entrepreneurship. *Annals of Public and Cooperative Economics*, *83*(1), 101–116. doi:10.1111/j.1467-8292.2011.00456.x

KEY TERMS AND DEFINITIONS

Networks: Single nodes linked by a set of relationships, which form the structure of the network.

Networks Density: Depth of the network resulting from the number of contacts that are embedded into a given network.

Resources: Set of assets, tangible or intangible, that are necessary to develop the activities of an organization.

Social Entrepreneurs: Individuals inspired by a desire for social change who focus their efforts on designing, conceiving and developing a social venture whose main purpose is to reduce the negative consequences of social problems.

Social Entrepreneurship: Field of activity dedicated to identifying and capturing social value-creating opportunities. This field employs innovative models and entrepreneurial practices to create social value in a sustainable and lasting way.

Social Venture: Organizational unit in which an entrepreneurial approach is pursued in order to produce social value in a sustainable way.

Chapter 9
Firm Growth:
Access to Venture Capital Finance

Bernard Owens Imarhiagbe
Kingston University, UK

George Saridakis
University of Kent, UK

David Smallbone
Kingston University, UK

ABSTRACT

Venture capital (VC) is an alternative means of access to finance for innovative SMEs to sustain their innovation, growth, and survival. Although VC firms are well established in the UK and USA, they are not well-known worldwide and many SMEs are unaware of their potential. This is a review of research literature on VC, its conceptualization, and synthesis over four decades. VC is gaining increased and varied significance worldwide as a way for innovative SMEs to access funds. Globalization has provided entrepreneurs the opportunity to seek VC globally as reputable VC firms are able to fund innovative projects across countries and continents. As the legal and regulatory regime improve, VC finance opportunities increase with impact on the demand and supply of VC. Innovative SMEs are encouraged to take advantage of globalization and competition among VC firms in their search for VC. Recently, VC firms have become more risk averse regardless of their traditional competence in screening and monitoring.

DOI: 10.4018/978-1-5225-6942-8.ch009

INTRODUCTION

Access to finance is important for small and medium-sized enterprises (SMEs) to start-up, innovate, grow and survive (Faria & Barbosa, 2014; Hasan et al., 2018; Jackson et al., 2012; Megginson, 2004). SMEs use different methods of raising funds for their businesses (Saridakis et al., 2008). Venture capital (VC) is an 'alternative' (Denis, 2004, p. 301) or 'substitute' (Maier & Walker, 1987, p. 207) method of raising finance for business ventures because VC funding can be used instead of debt finance. According to Maier and Walker (1987, p. 207), VC is a 'substitute, but not a perfect substitute' for funding entrepreneurial ventures following the different approach to access VC funding and debt finance. VC or private equity is one way that innovative SMEs use to raise money for their start-up and growth (Hasan et al., 2018; Meglio et al., 2017; Cumming et al., 2016; Cumming & MacIntosh, 2003; Jackson et al., 2012). Utterback and Abernathy (1975) described innovation in firms in terms of their innovative capacity, competitive strategy and production resources. However, in the business environment, there is no clear definition of best innovation because there is no universal standard of measurement for innovation from one business environment to another (Downs Jr & Mohr, 1976). Therefore, the reliance of VC firms (VCF) on innovation in their entrepreneurial funding decision varies across the VC industry; and they employ their funding criteria in making investment decisions. VCF often target their funding towards innovative SMEs as they have the potential for high growth and job creation (OECD, 2002; Smallbone et al., 1995). New growth SMEs are most likely to pursue external funding and they are more susceptible to rejections (Riding et al., 2012).

Although VC is useful for raising finance for business ventures, they are not widely available worldwide (Cumming & MacIntosh, 2003; Megginson, 2004). For example, Pistor et al. (2000) disclosed the legal and regulatory bottlenecks in transitional economies which are having negative effect on finance contracts. On the other hand, Megginson (2004) discussed the value of a strong legal and regulatory framework to protect the VC investment environment and participants alike. The level of the quality of the legal and regulatory environment can lead to the success or failure of VCF investments (Tykvová, 2018). The financial crisis of 2007 caused a reduction in the availability of VC in Israel (Avnimelech & Harel, 2012), the UK (BIS, 2012; Fraser, 2008) and other parts of the world. For example, there was a 31% decrease in VC for UK SMEs in 2010 (BIS, 2012). VCF in the UK, USA, Netherlands and France identified strategic involvement as their key role in their investment (Meglio et al., 2017; Sapienza et al., 1996). In the USA, VCF and their investments tend to be concentrated within some geographical areas (Chen et al., 2010). According to Revest and Sapio (2012), UK VCF helped the European VCF to catch up with their USA counterparts in their funding provisions. The USA and

Europe VCF have similar prospect of initial public offering (IPO) exit (Axelson & Martinovic, 2013). There is competition among VCF and these increases funding prospects and provisions for entrepreneurs (Elitsur & Gavious, 2011; Sapienza et al., 1996). Also, there is competition for VC among SMEs and some of them do not receive their desired fund. However, VC was largely unknown and clouded in secrecy about four decades ago (Bean et al., 1975).

MAIN FOCUS OF THE CHAPTER

This chapter aims to answer the following research questions associated with SMEs and their access to VC finance: (a) To what extent do innovative SMEs in the UK access VC finance? (b) Is there supply and demand equilibrium in access to VC finance in the UK? (c) Does globalisation and competition play a role in the supply of and demand for VC? (d) How has legal and regulatory regime supported VC expansion? (e) How could entrepreneurs and innovative SMEs benefit more from VC finance? These questions are very important in further understanding of the VC terrain in the UK and beyond. In a research of 21 European countries, Popov and Roosenboom (2013) found that VCF are actively involved in funding new businesses. According to Guo and Jiang (2013), VC-backed businesses in China outperform their non-VC-backed firms considerably and VC-backed firms encounter astronomical growth after their IPO exits. Although Cornelius (2005) identified risk aversion in VCF, numerous research (e.g. Lee, 2017; Meglio et al., 2017; Chen et al., 2010; Guo & Jiang, 2013; Jackson et al., 2012; Megginson, 2004; Popov & Roosenboom, 2013) show that VCF have the capacity to fund innovative entrepreneurial projects.

There is a plethora of information about formal VCF in the research and theoretical literature. Although research (Jackson et al., 2012; King, 2008) shows that formal VCF constitute a great source of access to finance, many entrepreneurs and business people are not fully aware and informed of the potentials of VCF and their investment behaviour. This is particularly apparent in the popularity of VCF in the UK and USA but less so in developing countries in Asia and Africa (Lingelbach, 2012). Different VC research literatures tend to explore minor areas at a time and it is difficult to find a single research literature resource containing enormous information relevant for key aspects of VC and VCF behaviour. The absence of such a literature resource is a research gap. This research will fill the gap in providing a concise, critical and relevant historical information resource about formal VCF, encompassing the evolutionary trend, for researchers, graduate students, business owners, entrepreneurs and policymakers. This inquiry conceptualises, synthesises and integrates the historical perspectives and evolutionary trend of VCF over a period spanning four decades to inform, including in times of economic uncertainty. This chapter explores a range of published research literature over four decades with the aim to provide research perspectives on VCF and their relationship to entrepreneurial funding activities relevant to developed and developing countries, advanced and emerging economies. Research literature will provide a more realistic account of VCF, their behaviour and investment environment. This research mostly differs from Wright and Robbie (1998) that adopted a combination of industry and firm level analytical techniques to review and synthesise the concept of VCF and private equity. Similar to their work, this research differentiate VCF as distinct from other sources of business finance but used key themes derived from different research literature to explain the behaviour of VCF and their investment environment over many decades.

The remainder of this chapter is divided into sections made up of key themes. Conceptualisation of venture capital examines the VC concept and private equity including the expansion and exposure of VCF worldwide, how debt financing differ from equity financing; Competitive business environment provides a discussion of the competitive business terrain involving the VCF and entrepreneurs as well as their investment geography; Government and the law explores the government and legal aspects of VC with reference to the legal and regulatory framework and government intervention to support VCF and participants; Behaviour of VCF reviews the behaviour of VCF including exit strategy, investment decision, the valuation of entrepreneurial project for VC purpose and the involvement of VCF in their VC-backed investment; and further discussions provide solutions and recommendations, future research directions and conclusions.

BACKGROUND AND CONCEPTUALISATION OF VENTURE CAPITAL

Formal and informal VCF are two different concepts in business, management and finance research. Harrison and Mason (2000) identified formal and informal VCF as lacking adequate research and, generally, wider research (Cumming & MacIntosh, 2003; Megginson, 2004) shows that VCF were not available worldwide until about two decades ago. Thus, as VCF were not available, their popularity was restricted to few countries such as the UK, Canada and USA. Formal VCF are the VC companies or fund managers (Mason & Stark, 2004) while informal VCF are business angels (van Osnabrugge, 2000). In discussing the difference between formal and informal VCF, researchers (e.g. Harrison & Mason, 2000; van Osnabrugge, 2000) described informal VCF as 'business angels'. The behaviour of business angels and VCF in the society tends to be similar in some ways but they are different (van Osnabrugge, 2000). Business angels may invest in VCF and vice versa, hence, there is a complex disparity between VCF and business angels in modern times. However, formal and informal VCF have some complementing features such as 'co-investing in deals; sequential investing in ventures; business angels as investors in venture capital funds; and deal referring' (Harrison & Mason, 2000, p. 223). As a major difference between formal and informal VCF, van Osnabrugge (2000) shows that they adopt a different approach in resolving agency risks associated with their investments. According to Mason and Stark (2004), business angels are more attentive to the entrepreneur than formal VCF in the process of making funding decision. To this end, it can be argued that formal VCF and business angels have some similar characteristics but they exhibit different investment behaviour, especially in the currently complex business environment characterised by globalisation and a global financial crisis. Consequently, this chapter focuses on formal VCF only.

What Is Venture Capital and Private Equity?

Venture capital and private equity finance have some similarities and differences. The following definitions and descriptions provide more clarity between both phenomena:

Private equity is medium to long-term finance provided in return for an equity stake in potentially high growth unquoted companies. Some commentators use the term "private equity" to refer only to the buy-out and buy-in investment sector. Some others, in Europe but not the USA, use the term "venture capital" to cover all stages, i.e. synonymous with "private equity". In the USA "venture capital" refers only to investments in early-stage and expanding companies (BVCA, 2010).

Venture capital firms are professional investors who dedicate 100% of their time to investing and building innovative companies on behalf of third party investors or their limited partners... Venture capital is a subset of the larger private equity asset class. The private equity asset class includes venture capital, buyouts, and mezzanine investment activity. Venture capital focuses on investing in private, young, fast growing companies (NVCA, 2013).

[Venture capital]...this is when private equity is invested into young, entrepreneur-led, high-potential companies that are typically driven by technological innovation (EVCA, 2012).

VC is defined as an 'independent, professionally managed, dedicated pools of capital that focus on equity or equity-linked investments in privately held, high growth companies' (Gompers & Lerner, 2001, p. 146). The definitions of venture capital and private equity attributed to BVCA (2010), ECVA (2012) and NVCA (2013) indicate little differences in the meaning of VC from one country to another. However, for the reason of simplicity, this research will adopt VC as a professionally managed fund focussed on equity investments in private and high growth unquoted business.

Figure 1 shows venture capital and private equity in the context of the flow of money from investors to investees. Limited partners fund is illiquid and exist for up to ten years to allow funds to be utilized for funding innovative businesses via VCF (EVCA, 2012). Although investors are able to invest directly in any investee or portfolio companies of their choice, they are also at liberty to invest in VC and private equity fund. Private equity and VCF are general partners in their fund management role. Therefore, venture capital is a subset of private equity.

The concepts of technology and biomed venture capital are extensions of the VC dynamics worldwide. According to NVCA (2013), the VCF in USA invest in different innovative SMEs which include, but not limited to, clean technology, healthcare and information technology. There is also the dynamics of seed, earliest-stage, early-stage, mixed stage and later-stage financing in VCF (Elango et al., 1995). However, regardless of the financing stage of a VCF, the basic principle of pursuing high returns and risk mitigation remains apparent in their character.

Clustering in the VC industry involves VCF investments. VCF that are concentrated in terms of their geographical location or co-location with their investment or similarity in the type of business tend to be described accordingly. For example, Rosiello and Parris (2009, p. 185) described the co-location of VC investments in dedicated biotech firms in Scotland and Cambridge as 'bio-clusters'. As VC start-up co-evolution and technology advancement started and grew in Israel, Avnimelech and Teubal (2004, p. 33) referred to the phenomenon as 'high tech cluster'. The VC investment

Figure 1. Venture capital and private equity funding

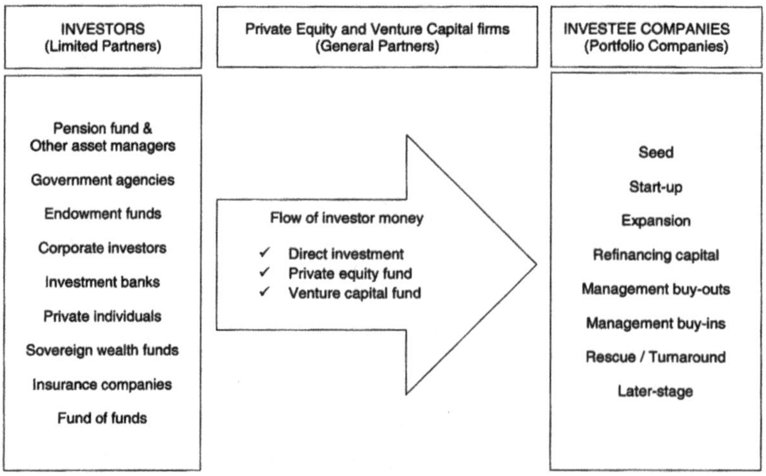

in clean environmental technology in USA has seen a drastic increase (beside biotechnology and computing) and majority of VCF in the USA are concentrated in the region of California, New York and New England as a result of the presence of other financial institutions as well as co-investment and syndication opportunities (Florida & Kenney, 1988). They described this regional concentration as regional cluster made up of reputable VC networks and investments. This research will now explore the differences between equity financing and debt financing.

Comparison Between Debt Financing and Equity Financing

There are similarities and differences between debt financing and equity financing in access to finance for SMEs (Winton & Yerramilli, 2008). Entrepreneurships in the high growth sector tend to embrace equity funding as a result of the potential size of their funding requirement, the inherent high risk and their desire for strategic support from VCF (Gompers, 1995; Greene et al., 2001; Hellmann & Puri, 2002). Amongst the many tasks of VCF in new start-up ventures, they help to 'review business plans and design contracts' (Gompers, 1995, p. 1461). VCF engage in high innovative start-up firms such as technology firms in Silicon Valley in USA to exploit their potential high returns (Meglio et al., 2017; Hellmann & Puri, 2002). This may explain why VCF are very selective in determining their entrepreneurial venture funding (Maier & Walker, 1987; Tyebjee & Bruno, 1984). Debt finance sources provide overdraft or loan facilities to entrepreneurs for their business after credit assessment of the owner has been made, and they tend to support less risky projects as well as businesses with track records (Saridakis et al., 2008). Generally, businesses with track records attract more funding opportunities from investors (Gompers et al., 2006). According to BVCA (2010), creditors have legal right to contractual interest and repayment of capital for their debt finance, whether the debtor profits or not. However, equity funding is an investment in exchange for a stake or part ownership of the funded business with the proviso to share in the risks and returns.

According to Winton and Yerramilli (2008), whilst debt finance sources are associated with less intensive monitoring, VCF engage in more intensive monitoring of the entrepreneurial venture to protect their investment. Researchers (De Bettignies & Brander, 2007; Hellmann, 1998; Kanniainen & Keuschnigg, 2004; Megginson, 2004; Pruthi et al., 2003; Sapienza et al., 1996) explored the monitoring character of VCF worldwide and it can be argued that the monitoring of VC-backed investments is associated with information asymmetry inherent in existing businesses as well as new start-up ventures. The major reason for the existence of VCF is their ability to resolve information asymmetry (Amit et al., 1998) and this is quite unlike debt finance sources. VCF have a competitive edge over debt finance sources in resolving issues of information asymmetry as they are able to use investment monitoring and selection techniques in an efficient manner (Amit et al., 1998). Thus, while traditional debt finance institutions (e.g. banks) do not monitor borrower businesses, VCF have the traditional competence in screening and monitoring of their investments.

Debt finance takes the form of overdraft or loans from banks while VC or equity funding is in the form of convertible debt (Winton & Yerramilli, 2008). A debt owed to a bank is in the form of a loan which is expected to be paid back with interest but the VCF acquires or purchases shares in the entrepreneurial venture as an investment (Cumming & MacIntosh, 2003). According to them, the number of shares purchased or acquired by the VC in relation to the total shares of the business will determine its percentage ownership and control of the business. VCF use more equity features to ensure business continuity in the most difficult and risky situation (Winton & Yerramilli, 2008). According to Gatchev et al. (2009), firms with high potential for agency cost problems and high asymmetric information are most likely to seek equity financing. However, they found that firms with high asymmetric information pursue debt financing for fixed assets.

In relation to debt finance, De Bettignies and Brander (2007, p. 808) disclosed that 'the entrepreneur keeps full control of the firm and has efficient incentives to exert effort.' However, with equity finance, De Bettignies and Brander (2007, p. 808) further revealed that 'there is a two-sided moral hazard problem' because both parties in the transaction provides 'unverifiable effort'. Entrepreneurs tend to perform better where they possess high value stake in the business and they reduce their incentive to provide effort where VCF have greater value stake (Amit et al., 1998). There is a potential to favour VC finance over debt finance because VCF contribute high productivity even with less entrepreneurial effort (De Bettignies & Brander, 2007). Also, VCF are more active in supporting their VC-backed companies while debt financiers are 'captive' because they are not involved in the running of their funded business (Bottazzi et al., 2008, p. 488). On the other hand, VCF are described as active investors because they actively participate in the affairs of their VC-backed businesses and hence, they create value (Megginson, 2004). The expansion and exposure of VCF are not the same as debt finance institutions because they have different funding behaviour.

Expansion and Exposure of Venture Capitalists

VCF started in the USA and expanded throughout the developed world including the UK, Canada and Israel (Hege et al., 2009). VCF expansion and exposure in entrepreneurial business finance tend to vary from country to country and from locality to locality (Jackson et al., 2012; Megginson, 2004; Cumming & MacIntosh, 2003). These variations in VCF existence means that exit behaviour, risks, returns and strategy are different (Cumming & MacIntosh, 2003). It has been revealed that VCF involvements in their portfolio of VC-backed investments can be affected if the VCF over-commit its available but limited resources (Jackson et al., 2012).

In 1975, 'very little' was known about VC and the government of USA could not formulate a policy to support VC because it was largely unfamiliar and the available VC information was not in the public domain (Bean et al., 1975). According to their study, whilst many VCF were looking for investment opportunities, potential entrepreneurs were looking for investors. The lack of adequate information about technological innovation and sources of funding meant that VCF were largely unidentified, unfamiliar and wrapped in confidentiality (Bean et al., 1975). However, the expansion of VCF has continued for two and a half decades (Megginson, 2004).

The international expansion of VCF has given a good funding alternative to innovative entrepreneurs to support their businesses (Sapienza et al., 1996). Hege et al. (2009, p. 1) stated that VC is an 'American invention'. The USA has 'about two-thirds of the world's total private equity fund-raising and investment'; VCF are part of 'American practices' and other countries are following the same idea to experience growth in their private equity market (Megginson, 2004, p. 89). The expansion and growth of VCF in the USA has been widely researched and Hege et al. (2009) show that the growth of VCF in the USA is continuing at a higher rate in comparison with other parts of the world. VCF are the 'primary and unique source of funding for small firms' because these small firms have limited access to the capital market, hence, they are very restricted in seeking traditional ways of accessing fund for their business innovation, growth and survival (Maier & Walker, 1987, p. 207). VCF fund 'high-risk, potentially high-reward projects' regardless of the high level of uncertainty associated with the business ventures (Gompers & Lerner, 2001, p. 145).

Alsos et al. (2006) assert that the VC industry is underdeveloped in many countries except the UK and USA. Although VCF are expanding worldwide, from developed to developing countries and from advanced to emerging economies, the expansion and exposure of VCF originated in the USA (Riding et al., 2012; Sapienza et al., 1996). According to Sapienza et al. (1996) and Hege et al. (2009), it can be argued that VCF in the USA is continuously expanding and other countries are following the pace already set by VCF in the USA. VCF in the UK and USA generated the most value in comparison with other countries (Sapienza et al., 1996). However, Hege et al. (2009) disclosed that USA VCF generate the highest value in comparison to their European counterparts. While the global VC activity is currently 80 per cent in USA, it is 13 per cent in Europe (Mason & Landström, 2012). Revest and Sapio (2012) discussed the wide expansion of UK VCF and their support for European counterparts to increase their value to reach the USA. A more recent research (Axelson & Martinovic, 2013) show that VCF in Europe and the USA have similar

IPO exit but Europe underperforms in trade sales compared to the USA. Thus, the expansion and exposure of VCF may not be as important as their business funding potential. However, it can be argued that the expansion and exposure of the VCF should be measured based on their VC-backed investment in their locality and global reach. Thus, the expansion and exposure of VCF across borders encouraged greater competition between VCF and entrepreneurs locally, nationally and internationally.

COMPETITIVE BUSINESS ENVIRONMENT

Competition Among Entrepreneurs

It is widely recognised in research that VCF provide funding for entrepreneurial ventures but there is competition for VC among entrepreneurs (Bowden, 1994; De Bettignies & Brander, 2007; Elitzur & Gavious, 2011; Gifford, 1997). Therefore, in keeping with simple economic principles, the competition among entrepreneurs for VC can affect the supply of VC available for innovative SMEs. Chen et al. (2010) and Cumming and Dai (2010) discussed the impact of localising VC-backed investments in the same location as their VCF. The major impact of localising VC-backed investments in the same location as their VCF is the competition for VC finance (Chen et al., 2010). Local bias is more prevalent if the VCF is the only investor in the area (Cumming & Dai, 2010). Although it can be argued that entrepreneurs seeking finance within the locality of VCF may be more advantageous than their counterpart outside the zone, the full assessment of a viable investment opportunity is often conducted by the VCF prior to any investment decision. Thus, the competition for funding among entrepreneurs may become more and more unfavourable the further away they are from the VCF but Megginson (2004) show that the principle of globalisation can make a positive difference to help entrepreneurial ventures. This indicates that globalisation can alter the demand and supply of VC as entrepreneurs will be able to exploit the funding opportunities available in the global VC environment. Cumming and Dai (2010) supports Megginson (2004) in that globalisation can make a difference in reducing local biases. Cumming and Dai (2010) stated that reputable VCF exhibit lesser local bias as they have the tendency to expand their reach far beyond their locality. This suggests that VCF that exhibit local, regional or sector bias are susceptible to be outperformed in the global community. However, high competition for VC finance suggests that some entrepreneurs may face timewasting in a futile pursuit resulting from a lack of VC.

Elitzur and Gavious (2011) revealed the stiff competition for VC finance among entrepreneurs but VCF are able to provide funds for proven entrepreneurial ventures. The huge effort exerted by entrepreneurs in the VC finance seeking process means that valuable entrepreneurial time are wasted in the event of funding rejection (Elitzur & Gavious, 2011). According to Cornelius (2005, p. 599), 'Competition for ever increasing pools of capital, combined with an increasingly homogenized experiential background for venture capitalists world-wide, has resulted in increased risk aversion and a preference for later stage investments'. Whilst some VCF prefer later stage investments to reduce risk, some others provide fund for early-stage investment with value-added services to mitigate the risks (Gompers & Lerner, 2001; Jackson et al., 2012; Winton & Yerramilli, 2008).

In discussing the BVCA members' funding engagements, BVCA (2013) revealed that the UK has the greatest number of companies funded as well as the greatest amount invested during 2010, 2011 and 2012. Apart from the UK, they show that BVCA members invest more in Europe than the USA and Rest of the World put together. During 2010, 2011 and 2012, BVCA members' VC-backed investments in the UK increased but declined in other parts of the world. Although the number of VC-backed companies and amount of funds invested were greater in the UK, the extended funding in the USA, Europe and Rest of the World indicate a globalisation effect and supports the globalisation phenomenon as shown in Cumming and Dai (2010) and Megginson (2004). Therefore, the increasing availability of VC through globalisation impacts positively on the entrepreneurs and SMEs seeking VC opportunity to start-up, innovate and grow their businesses.

BVCA (2013) shows the distribution of global investments of BVCA members from 2005 to 2012. Although the distribution shows an increase in the amount invested from 2005 (£11,676m) to 2007 (£31,634m), the amount fell drastically in 2008 (£20,025m) and the decline continued to 2012 (£12,288m). The initial decline in 2007 could be attributed to the financial crisis (Saridakis et al., 2008) and the UK government (BIS, 2012) also confirmed the decline in VC associated with the recessionary times. The decline in the amount invested reduced the number of VC-backed companies that could have been funded in the intervening period. As much as there is competition among entrepreneurs for VC, the competition among VCF is also strong as VCF seek good investment opportunities in their habit of screening entrepreneurial ventures.

Competition Among Venture Capital Firms

The expansion of VCF has enabled increasing competition in the industry and opened different funding choices such as better funding terms for entrepreneurs (Greene et al., 2001; Hochberg, 2010). VCF competition is on the increase (Gupta & Sapienza, 1992; Hochberg, 2010). According to Gupta and Sapienza (1992), the number of VCF increased in USA by 300% from 1980 to 1989. Thus, the expansion of VCF is a great opportunity for business formation as entrepreneurial competition for funds will become less fierce as more VCF begin to compete for entrepreneurial project funding. As VCF increase locally and globally, their competition will increase with greater supply of VC to satisfy the demand among innovative SMEs.

The international expansion of VC has enabled more entrepreneurs to benefit from business funding from VCF (Sapienza et al., 1996). Their study shows that the international expansion of VCF will encourage globalisation to create a larger market to support entrepreneurs in their start-up, innovation and growth. According to Megginson (2004, p. 89), 'a global market for venture capital and private equity is emerging'. They added that VCF in Western Europe and North America are experiencing similarly high levels of funding provision, funding patterns and rate of return. Hence, as the number of VCF increase from national territories to the international stage, their competition will also increase at an alarming rate. That indicates the impact of globalisation on VCF and how innovative SMEs will benefit from the competition.

Tian (2011) suggested that some VCF engage in staged financing of entrepreneurial ventures towards a positive investment outcome. Staged financing can compel the management of entrepreneurial ventures to deliver better returns as a pre-condition for further VC finance. VCF with reputation contribute to better investment performance (Nahata, 2008). They revealed that the reputation of VCF is largely built on their cumulative performance in IPO exits. This suggests that VCF with reputation have competitive advantage over their counterparts and entrepreneurs seeking finance for their ventures are most likely to approach them. It also shows that VCF with reputation have a higher success rate in achieving their funding objective, improved firm growth and contribute to better economic growth. There is competition between one VCF and another (Elitsur & Gavious, 2011). Therefore, as competition is rife between VCF, it creates better funding opportunities for innovative SMEs as they access funds for their businesses. Competition in VCF and among entrepreneurs is not restricted by geographical location and globalisation has played a major enabling role to determine the demand and supply of VC.

Geographical Situation

There is an advantage in concentrating VC investments in the immediate locality of the VCF (Chen et al., 2010). Denis (2004) is also in support of the localisation of VC investments. Hence, localisation of VC funding opportunity has the capacity to increase local supply of funds in the immediate vicinity of the VC firm. This shows that the geographical location of the VC can impact the supply of VC if the VCF has locality bias and vice versa. VCF and their investment in the USA were concentrated in San Francisco, Boston and New York (Chen et al., 2010). They also reported that the concentration of the VCF and their associated investment-backed companies in certain geographical locations impacts funding outcomes. VCF consider geographical location for their investment as a result of monitoring requirement because the VCF may not be able to adequately resource the monitoring of distant VC-backed firms (Denis, 2004). It will be better for government to encourage the establishment of new VCF rather than subsidise existing VCF (Chen et al., 2010). Therefore, the establishment of new VCF could improve the existence of more VC-backed investments and promote competition among VCF to the advantage of entrepreneurs and, eventually, the economy.

The cost of monitoring the proposed VC-backed firm in its geographical location is a key determining factor for VCF investment (Denis, 2004). Consequently, if the perceived monitoring cost cannot be justified for the geographical location, there could be a decision to decline VC for the business. This shows that the cost of monitoring can impact VCF decision to invest causing a possible fall in supply of VC where the monitoring cost is high. Although Chen et al. (2010) show the benefit for VCF in engaging in localised investment, the decision to invest or not in any business is part of the pre-screening assessment of any VCF. Hence, Denis (2004) agreed that the geographical location is very important in reaching that decision. However, Tian (2011) argued that localisation may not be necessary as staged financing can mitigate the high cost of monitoring distant VCF investments.

The use of distant geographical location to determine rejection of VC can be disadvantageous in a competitive market (Hochberg, 2010; Megginson, 2004). VCFs that invest in distant entrepreneurial ventures use staging as a strategic solution to ensure better outcome (Tian, 2011). Staging is a strategic tool for resolving high monitoring cost and Ahlstrom and Bruton (2006) argue that VCF in developed economies have a tendency for rich features in their VC provisions to support their funded businesses. Hence, the strategic staging mechanism for resolving high monitoring costs may not be present in developing, emerging and transitional economies.

VCF in the UK make up 60% of VCF in Europe (BVCA, 2010). This suggests that VCF in the UK are greater in size and reach than VCF in other European countries. According to BVCA (2013), the percentage of VC invested by BVCA members in the UK and Overseas in 2012 was 47% in the UK, USA 12%, Europe 38% and Rest of the world 3%. They revealed that whilst seed capital and total expansion funds have fallen in recent times, other financing stages such as management buy-out / management buy-in had increased VC finance. According to them, although the demand for seed capital VC has increased recently, many VCF have concentrated their investment on later-stage, management buy-out and buy-in thereby increasing the supply of the associated VC.

GOVERNMENT AND THE LAW IN VENTURE CAPITAL FUNDING

Legal and Regulatory Framework

Different countries have different rules and regulations guiding their VCF to protect the market and participants (Tykvová, 2018; Cumming et al., 2010; Cumming & MacIntosh, 2003). Tykvová (2018), Cumming and MacIntosh (2003) and La Porta et al. (1998) identified the impact of the legal and regulatory regime in VCF across different countries. VCF in mature economies like the UK and USA are more advanced and feature-filled to support business funding engagement (Ahlstrom & Bruton, 2006). The quality of the legal and regulatory framework can determine the success of VC investments (Tykvová, 2018). According to Cumming et al. (2010, p. 54), 'better laws facilitate faster deal screening and deal origination, a higher probability of syndication and a lower probability of potentially harmful co-investment'. The emerging economies are undergoing the processes of economic changes and institutional transformation to attain maturity (Ahlstrom & Bruton, 2006). Consequently, it can be argued that the main contributory factor to the maturity of VCF in the UK and USA is the advanced legal and regulatory systems protecting all participants through valid contractual engagements. Thus, VCF in emerging and transitional economies could still have some teething problems associated with underdeveloped legal and regulatory systems. VCF are more inclined to fund SMEs where there are valid legal protection for their fund with impact on the demand or supply of VC (Ahlstrom & Bruton, 2006; Cumming et al., 2010).

Developing economies are characterised by high agency fees of monitoring associated with asymmetric information, difficulty in contract enforcement and weak regulatory framework (Dutz et al., 2000). Amidst developed legal framework in law books, there are still constraints on financial markets because the documented legal framework in transition economies (e.g. Bulgaria, Romania, Poland and Uzbekistan) is not adequately exercised by the legal institutions in those countries (Pistor et al., 2000). Therefore, the quality of the legal and regulatory framework documented in the national law books should be implemented to make it relevant in financial transactions for the protection and benefit of all participants. Developing economies are characterised by underdeveloped financial and legal systems (Beck et al., 2005) and these put huge financial constraints on SMEs as VCF are discouraged from investing.

Government policies can exert a remarkable influence on regulating and galvanising financial operations (Jeng & Wells, 2000). Efficient and effective legal and regulatory regime has the potential to create better financial relationships (Cumming et al., 2006). There are difficulties in initiating VC system through policy formulation in India as the Indian macroeconomic environment is characterised by lack of stability and history of government ownership (Dossani & Kenney, 2002). Thus, the benefit of sound government policies cannot be overemphasised because a reliable and relevant government policy will result in an efficient and effective legal framework to support and protect the VC investment environment and participants. Megginson (2004) and Cumming et al. (2006) discussed the usefulness of a relevant legal regime to protect the investment environment and their participants. Research shows that 'countries with English common law codes offer greater protection to investors' and apart from USA, the 'European Union has had little success in establishing community-wide commercial laws, taxation regimes, or corporate governance policies (Megginson, 2004, p. 89). Each of the countries in the European Union have a 'segmented national markets, and investment also tends to be largely localized' (Megginson, 2004, p. 89). They further argued that the Asian markets are even more fragmented than the European Union markets because VC market is underdeveloped in Japan and China as they lack the requisite basic legal infrastructure to support VCF. Although the introduction of VCF in China can be traced back to the 1980s, substantial development did not start until recently with the support of VCF in major economies like USA (Lu & Tan, 2012). Indeed, the majority of the countries in Asia are either developing or emerging economies, hence the VC industry is still not advanced and this will have effect on the available legal and regulatory framework.

La Porta et al. (1998, 2000) and Cumming et al. (2006) discussed the usefulness of a reliable legal system to support VC relationship with their VC-backed companies. According to Cumming et al. (2006, p. 214), 'Legality is a central mechanism which mitigates agency problems between outside shareholders and entrepreneurs, thereby fostering the mutual development of IPO markets and venture capital markets.' Although the relevance of a good regulatory regime is well established, research shows that countries have varying levels of soundness in their framework (La Porta et al., 1998, 2000). According to Cumming et al. (2006, p. 214), 'the quality of a country's legal system is much more directly connected to facilitating VC-backed IPO exits than the size of a country's stock market.' Therefore, in the absence of a solid legal and regulatory regime, there could be less VCF and the agency cost will be high. However, staged financing may reduce the high agency cost (Dutz et al., 2000) associated with SMEs in emerging and developing economies but this is largely unproven. Consequently, the demand and supply of VC relies on the quality of the legal framework in operation and where the legal provision supports investors as well as investees, there will be favourable VC funding opportunities.

Government Intervention

Governments now recognise the value of VCF in economic development (Megginson, 2004; Cornelius, 2005; Chen et al., 2010). Chen et al. (2010) recommends the establishment of new VCF rather than subsidising existing VCF because new VCF will be able to support new portfolio of VC-backed companies. The government should carefully target support for VC initiatives that can support portfolio companies to boost economic gains (Cornelius, 2005). The governments should direct their effort to support VCF by 'eliminating regulatory road-blocks, lowering taxes, and providing a favourable investor climate' (Megginson, 2004, p. 89). VCF with reputation contribute to greater entrepreneurial venture success (Nahata, 2008). Accordingly, as VCF with reputation fulfil their objective of delivering excellent result for SMEs, there will be a positive impact on economic development. Therefore, the government can encourage VCF to forge an excellent reputation, and thereby provide indirect support for entrepreneurial ventures.

The government of any nation has the responsibility to ensure laws and their enforcements are effective and efficient at all times to support VCF and other financial deals, especially to protect investors and uphold positive corporate governance (La Porta et al., 1998, 2000). Cumming et al. (2006) also argued for the relevance and value of legality in VCF and entrepreneurial venture funding with particular reference to exit strategy. Israeli VC environment was facilitated by the involvement of the Israeli government using targeted programmes at different groups including start-ups, university spin-offs and incubators (Avnimelech & Harel, 2012). The support of businesses with high growth potential and VCF is an encouragement for better economic growth (Lerner, 2010). Therefore, as well as innovative businesses, VCF require government support in policy formulation to contribute to greater economic development.

BEHAVIOUR OF VENTURE CAPITAL FIRMS

Exit Strategy

The exit strategies of VCF vary between countries (Black & Gibson, 1998; Cumming & MacIntosh, 2003). Exit strategies also vary between VCF (Hasan et al., 2018). Cumming and MacIntosh (2003) disclosed two levels of VCF exits including full and partial exits. These two levels of VCF exits can be subdivided into 'full acquisition..., partial acquisition…, write-off… and partial write-off' (Cumming & MacIntosh, 2003, p. 514). There are two exit strategies associated with VCF in the USA including rapid exit from portfolio investment and exit through an IPO (Black

& Gibson, 1998). Partial exits could be a tax efficient way to limit tax burden on exit thereby eradicating or reducing tax liability at a later date (Cumming & MacIntosh, 2003). Partial exit strategy in VCF ownership shows a signal of quality (Cumming & MacIntosh, 2003). In measuring IPO success, experienced VCF and entrepreneurs contribute to a better exit factor (Axelson & Martinovic, 2013). However, it can be argued that the reason for partial exit could be a ploy to limit losses and make the business appear attractive to potential investors or it could be an attempt to share the huge losses of the business with other potential investors. So, a partial exit signal should not be used to determine VCF investment decision or measure potential returns on investment.

The VCF is unable to exactly time its exit from the market (Ball et al., 2011). Consequently, the entry and exit of VCF from the market is a valid business decision, however, the timing of entry and exit can be impacted by normal market forces, the activities of other participants and economic downturn. To this end, economic downturn such as the financial crisis of 2007 can impact negatively on IPO exit. Axelson and Martinovic (2013) disclosed the use of trade sales as an exit strategy. They believe that Europe VCF have 8% lower probability of achieving trade sales compared to USA. The experience of the entrepreneur and VCF can determine the level of success in their exit (Axelson & Martinovic, 2013). However, VCF exit strategy associated with trade sales could be impacted by economic conditions such as the financial crisis of 2007.

Investment Decision

The decision to invest or not in an entrepreneurial venture is the sole responsibility of the VCF considering its investment criteria (Lahr & Mina, 2016; Chen et al., 2010; Denis, 2004; Hisrich & Jankowicz, 1990). Investment decisions take huge management time and depend on the portfolio composition of the VCF (Petty & Gruber, 2011). The role of 'intuition' in the VCF investment decision process is very important and entrepreneurs seeking VC should adopt different approaches to meet the requirements of different VCF (Hisrich & Jankowicz, 1990, p. 49). Although some VCF may adopt intuition in their funding decision (Hisrich & Jankowicz, 1990), the same approach may not be relevant to other VCF because Elitsur and Gavious (2011) show that high competition exist among VCF for entrepreneurial funding opportunities. VCF pursue patent signals in their desire to invest in commercially viable businesses (Lahr & Mina, 2016). Peer network of VCF may encourage joint deal financing and can lead to greater impact in VC funding provision (Lee, 2017). VCF which has board member representation in a firm can develop enhanced knowledge and visibility towards a better investment decision (Hasan et al., 2018). Cleantech VCF is different from a typical VCF because of the inherently high capital-intensive investment required, high technology risk and uncertainty in investment returns (Cumming et al., 2016). International VCF has lower emotional and social attachment to their investment when compared with local VCF (Devigne et al., 2018). Ewens et al. (2018) introduced the concept of 'spray and pray' investment strategy which enables the VCF to provide little funding with little governance to potentially viable start-up firms. According to Pierrakis and Saridakis (2017), private VCFs have stronger impact on patent creation than public VCFs. As there are diverse VCF, entrepreneurs seeking VC finance should widen their approach to different VCF (Hisrich & Jankowicz, 1990). There are different types of VCF and they adopt different approaches to their funding decisions (Elango et al., 1995). Therefore, whilst some VCF engage in early or late stage of project funding, others are more flexible in pursuing a mixed investment agenda. However, recent research shows that there is concentration of VC funding opportunities in the later-stages and management buy-out/buy-in because VCF have become more risk averse (Cornelius, 2005). Hence, entrepreneurs can expand their funding search as wide as possible to attract potential VCF.

Franke et al. (2006, p. 803) acknowledged 'similarity biases' associated with the evaluation of VCF investment. There are VCF that concentrate their investment on entrepreneurial ventures similar to themselves in their investment decision (Franke et al., 2006). They confirmed that VCF with experience of new business formation or large companies tend to give priority to the entrepreneurs exhibiting such contextual traits. Also, 'VCF who themselves have an engineering and managerial education tend to rate teams in which both competencies are present' (Franke et al., 2006, p. 803). According to them, other similarity biases identified are age and educational attainment.

The unwillingness to take risk is dominating the world of VC (Cornelius, 2005); hence, the rejection of funding based on the over riskiness of the entrepreneurial project could become the norm. However, there is overwhelming research which supports the propensity of VCF to take risk both at the early-stage and later-stage of entrepreneurial venture formation and growth (Gompers & Lerner, 2001; Jackson et al., 2012; Winton & Yerramilli, 2008). According to Tyebjee and Bruno (1984), VCF are able to assess the riskiness of projects prior to funding decision in accordance with their criteria. However, VCF have the potential to over-commit themselves in their VC finance decision (Jackson et al., 2012). Also, some VCF have 'prior business experience' to support their investment decision (Bottazzi et al., 2008, p. 488). Cumming and Dai (2010) argued that some VCF developed a rule whereby their VC-backed firm must be within twenty minutes travel from their office location. To this end, different VCF adopt different approaches to funding projects and whilst some VCF engage in traditional funding approaches, others are more flexible. As a result, the rejection decision of one VCF may not affect the acceptance decision of another.

VCF tend to use excessive control rights as a contract tool in their entrepreneurial venture funding (Hellmann, 1998) but Black and Gibson (1998) show that some VCF give good entrepreneurs the opportunity to retake their rights to control their business through an exit IPO. Hence, at the time of contract, VCF ensure they have control rights over the VC-backed companies so that they can adequately protect their interest in the entrepreneurial venture. There can be tension between VCF and the entrepreneur in determining their rights during their relationship as a result of conflicting interests (Black & Gibson, 1998). According to Hellmann (1998, p. 57), the excessive control rights of the VCF can include 'the right to fire entrepreneurs.' The use of control rights enables the VCF to remove the strong hold-up of the entrepreneur from the leadership of the business venture to allow more 'superior management team' (Hellmann, 1998, p. 57). However, entrepreneurs could interpret the excessive control rights of VCF as meddling with the potential to heighten tension and conflict. Meanwhile, Florin (2005) show that entrepreneurs who do not wish to relinquish business control may not seek VC because Hellmann (1998) suggest that VCF are known to exert control rights over their investment at the possible detriment of the entrepreneur.

Risks and Returns

Indeed, to exit or not is a strategic business decision that must be taken to ensure optimal performance of the VCF and the associated portfolio of VC-backed companies. The decision to invest is marred by complexity and difficulty with serious risks of adverse selection (Fried & Hisrich, 1994). VCF have limited resources to invest and they engage in protectionist activities (such as screening, monitoring and controlling) aimed at reducing their investment risks and maximising returns (Jackson et al., 2012). Hence, VCF activism can improve investment performance to a limited extent unless it is optimally resourced. The growth of the portfolio size tends to over-extend the available scarce resources of the VCF with reduction in returns (Jackson et al., 2012). Kanniainen and Keuschnigg (2004, p. 1935) revealed the existence of 'optimal VC portfolio size with a trade-off between the number of companies and the value of managerial advice.' Using the simple principle of economics, whilst the portfolio size growth of VCF investment increases to an optimum level, there will be increasing returns but at the stage where the VCF investment increases beyond the optimum level, there will be diminishing returns resulting from lesser performance associated with scarce human and financial resources.

The monitoring of VC-backed companies may become reduced with the increase in the portfolio of VC-backed companies (Jackson et al., 2012). VCF increase the monitoring of their investment in response to the inherent agency risks involved (Sapienza et al., 1996). VCF increase monitoring at the early-stage ventures following the intrinsic uncertainty involved (Sapienza et al., 1996). Kanniainen and Keuschnigg (2004) also argued that VCF strictly monitor entrepreneurial start-up investments. VCF has the potential to reduce their risk if they have board member representation in a firm as that can enhance their knowledge of investing in the firm (Hasan et al., 2018). There can be a perceived reduction in cleantech VCF investment following the avoidance of uncertainty associated with high technology risks and capital-intensive need with no clear returns (Cumming et al., 2016). Risk is a key reason for VCF monitoring (Gompers, 1995). Many VCF opt for later-stage investments to limit their risk and increase returns (Cornelius, 2005). Thus, the reduced monitoring of high risk VC-backed companies could lead to business failure of the associated investment and financial losses for the VCF.

Pruthi et al. (2003) discussed the investment monitoring behaviour of foreign and local VCF to determine similarities and differences. In India, Pruthi et al. (2003, p. 175) disclosed that foreign VCF were more involved at 'strategic level' while domestic VCF were more involved at 'operational level'. According to Pruthi et al. (2003), to limit risks, foreign VCF engage in limiting their VC-backed companies from further borrowing commitments. Thus, the restriction on further borrowing could be a form of staged financing, which is a strategic tool to raise the performance of the VC-backed firm and reduce potential losses.

The VCF financing of projects associated with serial entrepreneurs tend to produce huge success for the VCF investors (Gompers et al., 2006). Entrepreneurs with previous record of accomplishment in their business are more likely to progress than new entrepreneurs without experience (Gompers et al., 2006). Researchers (e.g. Cumming & Dai, 2011; Jackson et al., 2012; Kanniainen & Keuschnigg, 2004; Sapienza et al., 1996) corroborate the usefulness of experience in entrepreneurial capability in business performance. According to Gompers et al. (2006), the success of a previous business venture is a signal of the capability and quality of the entrepreneurs thereby increasing their chance of getting more funding for further business ventures.

Whilst Beckham et al. (2007) revealed that the composition of the management team of the entrepreneurial venture being VC-backed can determine success or failure of the investment, King (2008) disclosed that the use of funding rounds will ensure the management team perform better with clear milestones. According to Beckham et al. (2007), the presence of rich diversity in the team demography of the management team improves broad access to information about the firm performance and helps to support the VC-backed business. The top management team show huge improvement because of a diversity of prior affiliations and extensive experiences with functional diversity in the management team (Beckham et al., 2007). They revealed the value of a diversity of management skills, experience and affiliations in limiting the risk of failure in VC-backed companies. There were better positive outcomes recorded for VCF investment in entrepreneurial businesses with excellent top management team and returns were impacted positively (Beckham et al., 2007). The VCF may introduce the concept of funding rounds to release funding in stages to meet certain critical milestone (King, 2008). Tian (2011) also supported the use of funding rounds as a staged funding arrangement that can lead to positive outcomes. Hence, unless the entrepreneurial venture can fulfil the expected milestone, the next funding round could be delayed or cancelled. The release of funds in stages puts the management team of the VC-backed business in check and improves the success of the business or reduces the loss associated with possible business failure (King, 2008; Tian, 2011). VC-backed entrepreneurial ventures in distant places get funding through the process of staged funding rounds and leads to positive entrepreneurial outcomes as the funded business is able to progress to IPO in a short time (Tian, 2011).

The arrival of a new generation of industry participants has changed the original character of VCF from being inclined to take risk to more risk aversion (Cornelius, 2005). This suggests that there is increased risk aversion over time among VCF as they reduce their investment concentration in start-up businesses. Although VCF may reduce their funding for seed and early stage entrepreneurial projects, they could increase funding for other financing stages like management buy-out or buy-in (BVCA, 2013). Thus, investing in management buy-out or buy-in is a risk reduction strategy. Megginson (2004) and Chen et al. (2011) show that VCF have tolerance for high risk depending on the business venture and King (2008) provided a strategic safeguard against risk using staged financing in different rounds with milestone review. Whilst some VCF specialise in early-stage funding, another type of VCF engage more in later-stage (Gompers & Lerner, 2001; Jackson et al., 2012; Winton & Yerramilli, 2008). However, the early-stage funders in high technology innovative SMEs with high risk have the potential for huge returns. Therefore, VCF may fund a business after successful risk assessment but the real test is the marketplace where the product is expected to outperform its rivals to produce high returns.

Valuation of Entrepreneurial Ventures

The valuation of entrepreneurial ventures during the initiation of VC finance is a controversial issue and subject to intense negotiations (Cumming & Dai, 2011). VCF aims to maximise their returns on their investment as much as possible (Jackson et al., 2012). Networked VCF can restrict market entrants and determine the valuation of entrepreneurial projects as they force a decrease in actual market valuation to benefit themselves (Hochberg et al., 2010). They found extremely lower market valuations recorded for densely networked markets. Thus, there is a great need for equitable project valuation to ensure fairness during the negotiation stages of the VC finance arrangement. Apart from public company valuation, private company valuations are subject to negotiations between the entrepreneur and the VCF (Cumming & Dai, 2011). Unlike public company valuation, Cumming and Dai (2011) revealed that there are no established guidelines for private company valuation. Hence, networked VCF can limit new entrants with a restricted market in their favour and lead to undervaluing of proposed VC-backed businesses (Hochberg et al., 2010). According to Cumming and Dai (2011, p. 2), 'firm valuations are positively correlated to measures of limited attention.' Thus, the greater the value of the firm on valuation and the greater the VC ownership, the more attention the VC firm will show to the investment and vice versa. The VCF increases its power of negotiation where there is a proportionate increase in the value of its ownership of the VC-backed company (Cumming & Dai, 2011).

Bowden (1994, p. 307) identified the concept of 'cooperative bargaining' as an encounter between the VCF and the entrepreneur in the process of arranging VC finance. It is cooperative bargaining that determines the terms of the funding arrangement between the VCF and the entrepreneur to create mutually beneficial arrangement (Bowden, 1994). A networked VCF environment (Hochberg et al., 2010) could artificially determine the deal between the VCF and the entrepreneur thereby removing cooperative bargaining. Thus, whilst the VC and entrepreneur will cooperatively reach a mutually beneficial arrangement in the funding transaction in a non-networked VCF domain, there could be no mutually beneficial bargain in a networked VC environment. The findings of Hochberg et al. (2010) about networked VCF suggests that market forces of demand and supply could be altered artificially in favour of networked VCF in the valuation of entrepreneurial ventures.

VC Involvement

VCF in the UK and USA are more involved in their VC-backed investments than their counterpart in other parts of the world (Sapienza et al., 1996). The involvement of VCF in their portfolio companies is an attempt to reduce information asymmetry and show their desire to protect their investment towards attaining better return while reducing risk considerably (Hasan et al., 2018; Amit et al., 1998). However, Jackson et al. (2012) show that the involvement of VCF in their VC-backed companies can become overstretched to the point of overextending their limited resources. They further argued that financial and human resources are limited to the extent that when they become depleted, the capacity of the VCF to fulfil further investment opportunities becomes reduced or non-existent. Therefore, VCF cannot overextend their scarce resources and continually attain success in their VC-backed investments. Also, the support and mentoring of VC-backed business in a syndicated arrangement can be problematic (Cumming et al., 2010) but some VCF are involved in co-investment and syndication (Hasan et al., 2018; Lee, 2017; Florida and Kenney, 1988) to support their risk exposure.

Sapienza et al. (1996, p. 439) identified 'strategic involvement' as one of the key role of VCF in their investment. VCF provide strategic role in supporting new ventures through scouting and coaching with the result of dynamic growth (Meglio et al., 2017). VCF provide 'financial and business advice and functioning as a sounding board' (Sapienza et al., 1996, p. 439). Keuschnigg and Nielsen (2003) echoed the significance of good business advice to aid the survival of businesses. According to Brocken (2015), sustainable VCFs breed sustainable businesses because they provide business advice and networking support. Interpersonal and networking roles are other valuable functions of VCF for their portfolio companies (Sapienza et al., 1996). They described interpersonal roles of the VCF to include mentoring and confidant of the executive officers of the VC-backed business. According to them, the networking role of VCF is characterised by the maintaining of valuable professional contacts to support their VC-backed companies. The presence of a board member representation in the VC-backed firm is an advantage for the VCF (Hasan et al., 2018).

Timmons and Bygrave (1986) discussed the involvement of VCF in their VC-backed companies as an opportunity of adding value to the entrepreneurial venture. Timmons and Bygrave (1986) stated that intelligent entrepreneurs who seek VC finance tend to approach VCF with reputation, recognition and experience as a way of adding value to the entrepreneurial venture rather than funding alone. Nahata (2008) also identified the relevance of a reputable VCF in entrepreneurial search for fund because such VCF can support their VC-backed investment for a quicker IPO with better asset value. Therefore, knowledgeable entrepreneurs seek funding and value-added involvement from VCF. This shows that apart from VCF verification and validation of entrepreneurial venture suitability for funding, intelligent entrepreneurs also perform checks on their VCF for funding suitability. VCF who are able to play a highly productive role in new and evolving firms will attract better quality ventures (Timmons & Bygrave, 1986). Hence, a highly constructive role for VCF will encompass strategic, interpersonal and networking involvement in their VC-backed companies.

VCF are actively involved in their VC-backed companies to ensure success (Gifford, 1997). The partial ownership of the funded business venture dilutes the incentive of the entrepreneur to provide effort (De Bettignies & Brander, 2007). There is a preference of VC finance over debt finance where the productivity of VCF is higher relative to lower entrepreneurial productivity (De Bettignies & Brander, 2007). The VCF pursues an efficient allocation of attention because it considers the opportunity cost of giving attention to all its VC-backed companies (Gifford, 1997). The VCF allocates its attention optimally to provide for its existing portfolio of VC-backed companies as well as the assessment of potential projects for funding (Gifford, 1997; Shepherd et al., 2005). The selecting and monitoring of investments is a major function of VCF in protecting their business interest (Amit et al., 1998).

SOLUTIONS AND RECOMMENDATIONS

As was already discussed in literature earlier, innovative SMEs in the UK and outside the UK have access to VC finance. However, there are limitations in the supply of VC depending on the entrepreneurial project viability and its level of innovativeness. As there is no clear universally accepted definition of best innovation, VCF make investment decisions on the basis of their criteria. As a result, different VCF make their investment decisions using their selection strategy. There is no supply and demand equilibrium in access to VC finance in the UK and beyond because there is no uniform supply of and demand for VC finance. Recently, VCF have targeted their investment on later-stage, management buy-out and buy-in to limit their risks and increase returns. In their risk aversion, VCF have become more stringent in their entrepreneurial project selection and monitoring with reduced funding of seed and early stage of projects. As UK VC funders are involved in global VC finance, their risk aversion has spread abroad. UK VCF invests more in the UK than other countries and this may reflect a localisation bias. However, localisation bias also applies to the USA because VCF are concentrated in some localities (such as San Francisco, New York and Boston) and the total investment of USA VCF in their locality exceeds their investments outside the USA. Therefore, innovative SMEs should first exploit their immediate locality for VC finance.

Globalisation has positively impacted the demand and supply of VC; and innovative SMEs and entrepreneurial projects are at an advantage. The expansion of VCF from the USA, the source of VC civilisation, to outermost part of the world opens a massive potential market for innovative SME access to VC finance. As competition for VC increases among entrepreneurs, competition for entrepreneurial venture funding also increase among VCF following national and international expansion thereby creating a balanced and competitive environment to support businesses from both sides of entrepreneurs and VCF. Hence, globalisation has provided entrepreneurs with the opportunity to seek funding beyond immediate locality as reputable VCF are now global and able to fund innovative SME projects at a distance across countries and continents.

The major contributor to the highly developed VC environment in the UK is the provision of a good legal and regulatory regime. This has allowed a greater chance of VCF expansion, hence, making the UK and USA the pioneers in VC expansion. The level of maturity of the legal and institutional framework impacts positively on the expansion of VCF and their capacity to support VC-backed investment. It is well known that a good legal and regulatory framework provides protection for financial contracts to help VCF and SMEs. The government of other countries should intervene to ensure adequate and valid regulatory framework to support VC provisions and participants to boost new business formation, business growth and improve job creation towards better economic development. This research could stimulate discussion around existing legal and regulatory regimes around the world as policymakers can refocus their existing policies to support a better VC environment for SMEs, investors and investees. The government and policymakers in emerging, transitional and developing economies can now emulate VC developments in advanced countries like the USA and the UK. However, the UK and other developed economies should promote a stable economic and financial sector development to support the continued existence, growth and advancement of VC. While there are underdeveloped financial and legal systems, there is no encouragement for VCF to invest, expand and flourish.

Entrepreneurs and SMEs are encouraged to use this research as their VC knowledge base to help them make appropriate decision when seeking VC for their innovative business venture. In seeking access to VC finance, knowledgeable entrepreneurs and innovative SMEs could target experienced and reputable VCF suited to the project domain and relevant to the funding stage. Globalisation is a force for good to support entrepreneurs in VC finance-seeking worldwide. Therefore, growth oriented entrepreneurs should be able to channel their funding application widely to a suitable VCF for their innovative project locally, nationally or internationally.

VC-backed firms grow astronomically and outperform their non-VC-backed firms by a wide margin in growth and performance. VCF target high growth companies and innovative SMEs because such businesses exhibit high potential for job creation, high growth and innovative behaviour with consequent positive effect on returns and the economy. As a result, non-innovative SMEs may not be successful in their quest for VC regardless of their firm size. Although VCF have different areas of specialism, they target innovative SMEs at various stages of their formation and existence to take advantage of their innovative characteristics with the potential for higher than average returns.

FUTURE RESEARCH DIRECTIONS

Further research is required to advance VC provisions and knowledge base to support innovative SMEs in the UK and worldwide. Specifically, VCF are increasing in popularity but declining in their funding provision and it is not clear why this is the case. VCF have gained increasing popularity since their introduction in the USA during the last four decades; however, VCF have become more risk averse even in a globalised business environment amidst their financial risk management, screening and monitoring capabilities. This is not traditionally compatible with their huge appetite for high risk and high returns. Therefore, this is an area requiring further research.

CONCLUSIONS

Formal VCF and their funding behaviour have increased in popularity, reach and significance because globalisation has enabled the expansion and exposure of VCF worldwide, though at a varied pace from one country to another. Debt finance and equity funding satisfies the financial needs of businesses. Whilst debt finance is used for less risky entrepreneurial projects, VCF fund more risky projects with monitoring and screening as mitigation against risks. Although VCF are selective in their funding, they represent an alternative funding source for entrepreneurial ventures such as high-risk but potentially profitable projects. VCF understand that if high-risk projects are strategically managed, they have the potential to become profitable and VCF exert control rights over their VC-backed investments for their benefit. In recent recessionary times, risk aversion has been introduced to VCF investment decision-making process with the result that less start-up firms are funded, except for management buy-outs and buy-ins. However, there are differences between VCF depending on their specialisation including seed, early-stage, later-stage and mixed group. Different types of VCF make different types of VC-backed funding decisions to support innovative SMEs and entrepreneurs.

REFERENCES

Ahlstrom, D., & Bruton, G. D. (2006). Venture capital in emerging economies: Networks and institutional change. *Entrepreneurship Theory and Practice*, *30*(2), 299–320. doi:10.1111/j.1540-6520.2006.00122.x

Alsos, G. A., Isaksen, E. J., & Ljunggren, E. (2006). New venture financing and subsequent business growth in men - and women-led businesses. *Entrepreneurship Theory and Practice*, *30*(5), 667–686. doi:10.1111/j.1540-6520.2006.00141.x

Amit, R., Brander, J., & Zott, C. (1998). Why do venture capital firms exist? Theory and Canadian experience. *Journal of Business Venturing*, *13*(6), 441–466. doi:10.1016/S0883-9026(97)00061-X

Avnimelech, G., & Harel, S. (2012). Global venture capital 'hotspots': Israel. In Handbook of Research on Venture Capital: Volume 2: A Globalizing Industry (pp. 209-226). Cheltenham, UK: Edward Elgar Publishing.

Avnimelech, G., & Teubal, M. (2004). Venture capital start-up co-evolution and the emergence & development of Israel's new high tech cluster. *Economics of Innovation and New Technology*, *13*(1), 33–60. doi:10.1080/1043859042000156020

Axelson, U., & Martinovic, M. (2013). *European venture capital: Myths and facts.* Retrieved October 6, 2014, from http://www.bvca.co.uk/Portals/0/library/Files/News/2013/European_MandF_Report_21Jan13.pdf

Ball, E., Chiu, H. H., & Smith, R. (2011). Can the VCF time the market? An analysis of exit choice for venture-backed firms. *Review of Financial Studies*, *24*(9), 3105–3138. doi:10.1093/rfs/hhr042

Bean, A. S., Schiffel, D. D., & Mogee, M. E. (1975). The venture capital market and technological innovation. *Research Policy*, *4*(4), 380–408. doi:10.1016/0048-7333(75)90003-7

Beck, T., Demirguc-Kunt, A., & Maksimovic, V. (2005). Financial and legal constraints to growth: Does firm size matter? *The Journal of Finance*, *LX*(1), 137–177. doi:10.1111/j.1540-6261.2005.00727.x

Beckham, C. M., Burton, M. D., & O'Reilly, C. (2007). Early teams: The impact of team demography on VC financing and going public. *Journal of Business Venturing*, *22*(2), 147–173. doi:10.1016/j.jbusvent.2006.02.001

BIS. (2012) *SME access to external finance*. BIS Economics Paper Number 16, Department for Business, Innovation & Skills. Retrieved July 17, 2014, from https://www.gov.uk/government/uploads/system/uploads/attachment_data/file/32263/12-539-sme-access-external-finance.pdf

Black, B. S., & Gibson, R. J. (1998). Venture capital and the structure of capital markets: Banks versus stock markets. *Journal of Financial Economics*, *47*(3), 243–277. doi:10.1016/S0304-405X(97)00045-7

Bocken, N. M. P. (2015). Sustainable venture capital – catalyst for sustainable start-up success? *Journal of Cleaner Production, 108*(A), 647-658.

Bottazzi, L., Da Rin, M., & Hellmann, T. (2008). Who are the active investors?: Evidence from venture capital. *Journal of Financial Economics, 89*(3), 488–512. doi:10.1016/j.jfineco.2007.09.003

Bowden, R. J. (1994). Bargaining, size, and return in venture capital funds. *Journal of Business Venturing, 9*(4), 307–330. doi:10.1016/0883-9026(94)90010-8

BVCA. (2010). *A guide to private equity*. Retrieved March 27, 2014, from http://www.bvca.co.uk/researchpublications/bvcaguidetoprivateequity.aspx

BVCA. (2013). *BVCA private equity and venture capital report on investment activity 2012*. Retrieved March 27, 2014, from http://www.bvca.co.uk/Portals/0/library/Files/News/2013/RIA_2012.pdf

Chen, H., Gompers, P., Kovner, A., & Lerner, J. (2010). Buy local? The geography of venture capital. *Journal of Urban Economics, 67*(1), 90–102. doi:10.1016/j.jue.2009.09.013

Cornelius, B. (2005). The institutionalisation of venture capital. *Technovation, 25*(6), 599–608. doi:10.1016/j.technovation.2003.12.001

Cumming, D., & Dai, N. (2010). Local bias in venture capital investments. *Journal of Empirical Finance, 17*(3), 362–380. doi:10.1016/j.jempfin.2009.11.001

Cumming, D., & Dai, N. (2011). Fund size, limited attention and valuation of venture capital backed firms. *Journal of Empirical Finance, 18*(1), 2–15. doi:10.1016/j.jempfin.2010.09.002

Cumming, D., Fleming, G., & Schwienbacher, A. (2006). Legality and venture capital exits. *Journal of Corporate Finance, 12*(2), 214–245. doi:10.1016/j.jcorpfin.2004.12.004

Cumming, D., Henriques, I., & Sadorsky, P. (2016). 'Cleantech' venture capital around the world. *International Review of Financial Analysis, 44*, 86–97. doi:10.1016/j.irfa.2016.01.015

Cumming, D., Schmidt, D., & Walz, U. (2010). Legality and venture capital governance around the world. *Journal of Business Venturing, 25*(1), 54–72. doi:10.1016/j.jbusvent.2008.07.001

Cumming, D. J., & MacIntosh, J. G. (2003). A cross-country comparison of full and partial venture capital exits. *Journal of Banking & Finance*, *27*(3), 511–548. doi:10.1016/S0378-4266(02)00389-8

De Bettignies, J., & Brander, J. A. (2007). Financing entrepreneurship: Bank finance versus venture capital. *Journal of Business Venturing*, *22*(6), 808–832. doi:10.1016/j.jbusvent.2006.07.005

Denis, D. J. (2004). Entrepreneurial finance: An overview of the issues and evidence. *Journal of Corporate Finance*, *10*(2), 301–326. doi:10.1016/S0929-1199(03)00059-2

Devigne, D., Manigart, S., & Wright, M. (2016). Escalation of commitment in venture capital decision making: Differentiating between domestic and international investors. *Journal of Business Venturing*, *31*(3), 253–271. doi:10.1016/j.jbusvent.2016.01.001

Dossani, R., & Kenney, M. (2002). Creating an environment for venture capital in India. *World Development*, *30*(2), 227–253. doi:10.1016/S0305-750X(01)00110-3

Downs, G. W. Jr, & Mohr, L. B. (1976). Conceptual issues in the study of innovation. *Administrative Science Quarterly*, *21*(4), 700–714. doi:10.2307/2391725

Dutz, M. A., Ordover, J. A., & Willig, R. D. (2000). Entrepreneurship, access policy and economic development: Lessons from industrial organization. *European Economic Review*, *44*(4-6), 739–747. doi:10.1016/S0014-2921(00)00030-1

Elango, B., Fried, V. H., Hisrich, R. D., & Polonchek, A. (1995). How venture capital firms differ. *Journal of Business Venturing*, *10*(2), 157–179. doi:10.1016/0883-9026(94)00019-Q

Elitzur, R., & Gavious, A. (2011). Selection of entrepreneurs in the venture capital industry: An asymptotic analysis. *European Journal of Operational Research*, *215*(3), 705–712. doi:10.1016/j.ejor.2011.06.029

EVCA. (2012). *The little book of private equity*. Retrieved March 27, 2014, from https://www.evca.eu/media/19732/Little-book-of-Private-Equity.pdf

Ewens, M., Nanda, R., & Rhodes-Kropf, M. (2018). Cost of experimentation and the evolution of venture capital. *Journal of Financial Economics*, *128*(3), 422–442. doi:10.1016/j.jfineco.2018.03.001

Faria, A. P., & Barbosa, N. (2014). Does venture capital really foster innovation? *Economics Letters*, *122*(2), 129–131. doi:10.1016/j.econlet.2013.11.014

Florida, R. L., & Kenney, M. (1988). Venture capital, high technology and regional development. *Regional Studies*, *22*(1), 33–48. doi:10.1080/00343408812331344750

Florin, J. (2005). Is venture capital worth it? Effects on firm performance and founder returns. *Journal of Business Venturing, 20*(1), 113–135. doi:10.1016/j.jbusvent.2003.12.006

Franke, N., Gruber, M., Harhoff, D., & Henkel, J. (2006). What you are is what you like – similarity biases in venture capitalists' evaluations of start-up teams. *Journal of Business Venturing, 21*(6), 802–826. doi:10.1016/j.jbusvent.2005.07.001

Fraser, S. (2008). *Small firms in the credit crisis: Evidence from the UK survey of SME finances*. Warwick, UK: The University of Warwick.

Fried, V. H., & Hisrich, R. D. (1994). Toward a model of venture capital investment decision making. *Financial Management, 23*(3), 28–37. doi:10.2307/3665619

Gatchev, V. A., Spindt, P. A., & Tarhan, V. (2009). How do firms finance their investments?: The relative importance of equity issuance and debt contracting costs. *Journal of Corporate Finance, 15*(2), 179–195. doi:10.1016/j.jcorpfin.2008.11.001

Gifford, S. (1997). Limited attention and the role of the venture capitalist. *Journal of Business Venturing, 12*(6), 459–482. doi:10.1016/S0883-9026(96)00130-9

Gompers, P. A. (1995). Optimal investment, monitoring, and the staging of venture capital. *The Journal of Finance, 50*(5), 1461–1489. doi:10.1111/j.1540-6261.1995.tb05185.x

Gompers, P. A., Kovner, A., Lerner, J., & Scharfstein, D. S. (2006). Skill vs. luck in entrepreneurship and venture capital: Evidence from serial entrepreneurs. *Social Science Research Network –NBER Working Paper Series, 12592*, 1–28.

Gompers, P. A., & Lerner, J. (2001). The venture capital revolution. *The Journal of Economic Perspectives, 15*(2), 145–168. doi:10.1257/jep.15.2.145

Greene, P. G., Brush, C. G., Hart, M. M., & Saparito, P. (2001). Patterns of venture capital funding: Is gender a factor? *Venture Capital: An International Journal of Entrepreneurial Finance., 3*(1), 63–83. doi:10.1080/13691060118175

Guo, D., & Jiang, K. (2013). Venture capital investment and the performance of entrepreneurial firms: Evidence from China. *Journal of Corporate Finance, 22*, 375–395. doi:10.1016/j.jcorpfin.2013.07.001

Gupta, A. K., & Sapienza, H. J. (1992). Determinants of venture capital firms' preferences regarding the industry diversity and geographic scope of their investments. *Journal of Business Venturing, 7*(2), 347–362. doi:10.1016/0883-9026(92)90012-G

Harrison, R. T., & Mason, C. M. (2000). Venture capital market complementarities: The links between business angels and venture capital funds in the United Kingdom. *Venture Capital: An International Journal of Entrepreneurial Finance.*, *2*(3), 223–242. doi:10.1080/13691060050135091

Hasan, I., Khurshed, A., Mohamed, A., & Wang, F. (2018). Do venture capital firms benefit from a presence on boards of directors of mature public companies? *Journal of Corporate Finance*, *49*, 125–140. doi:10.1016/j.jcorpfin.2017.04.018

Hege, U., Palomino, F., & Schwienbacher, A. (2009). Venture Capital Performance: The disparity between Europe and the United States. *Finance.*, *30*(1), 1–39.

Hellmann, T. (1998). The allocation of control rights in venture capital contracts. *The Rand Journal of Economics*, *29*(1), 57–76. doi:10.2307/2555816

Hellmann, T., & Puri, M. (2002). Venture capital and the professionalization of start-up firms: Empirical evidence. *The Journal of Finance*, *57*(1), 169–197. doi:10.1111/1540-6261.00419

Hisrich, R. D., & Jankowicz, A. D. (1990). Intuition in venture capital decisions: An exploratory study using a new technique. *Journal of Business Venturing*, *5*(1), 49–62. doi:10.1016/0883-9026(90)90026-P

Hochberg, Y. V., Ljungqvist, A., & Lu, Y. (2010). Networking as a barrier to entry and the competitive supply of venture capital. *The Journal of Finance*, *65*(3), 829–859. doi:10.1111/j.1540-6261.2010.01554.x

Jackson, W. E. III, Bates, T., & Bradford, W. D. (2012). Does venture capitalist activism improve investment performance? *Journal of Business Venturing*, *27*(3), 342–354. doi:10.1016/j.jbusvent.2011.02.003

Jeng, L. A., & Wells, P. C. (2000). The determinants of venture capital funding: Evidence across countries. *Journal of Corporate Finance*, *6*(3), 241–289. doi:10.1016/S0929-1199(00)00003-1

Kanniainen, V., & Keuschnigg, C. (2004). Start-up investment with scarce venture capital support. *Journal of Banking & Finance*, *28*(8), 1935–1959. doi:10.1016/j.jbankfin.2003.07.005

Keuschnigg, C., & Nielsen, S. B. (2003). Tax policy, venture capital, and entrepreneurship. *Journal of Public Economics*, *87*(1), 175–203. doi:10.1016/S0047-2727(01)00170-0

King, B. L. (2008). Strategizing at leading venture capital firms: Of planning, opportunism and deliberate emergence. *Long Range Planning*, *41*(3), 345–366. doi:10.1016/j.lrp.2008.03.006

La Porta, R., Lopez-de-Silanes, F., Shleifer, A., & Vishny, R. (2000). Investor protection and corporate governance. *Journal of Financial Economics*, *58*(1-2), 3–27. doi:10.1016/S0304-405X(00)00065-9

La Porta, R., Lopez-de-Silanes, F., Shleifer, A., & Vishny, R. W. (1998). Law and finance. *Journal of Political Economy*, *106*(6), 1113–1155. doi:10.1086/250042

Lahr, H., & Mina, A. (2016). Venture capital investments and the technological performance of portfolio firms. *Research Policy*, *45*(1), 303–318. doi:10.1016/j.respol.2015.10.001

Lee, H. S. (2017). Peer networks in venture capital. *Journal of Empirical Finance*, *41*, 19–30. doi:10.1016/j.jempfin.2016.12.006

Lerner, J. (2010). The future of public efforts to boost entrepreneurship and venture capital. *Small Business Economics*, *35*(3), 255–264. doi:10.100711187-010-9298-z

Lingelbach, D. (2012). Global venture capital 'hotspots': developing countries. In Handbook of Research on Venture Capital: Volume 2: A Globalizing Industry (pp. 251-282). Edward Elgar Publishing. doi:10.4337/9781781009116.00020

Lu, H., & Tan, Y. (2012). Global venture capital 'hotspots': China. In Handbook of Research on Venture Capital: Volume 2: A Globalizing Industry (pp. 227-250). Edward Elgar Publishing.

Maier, J. B. II, & Walker, D. A. (1987). The role of venture capital in financing small business. *Journal of Business Venturing*, *2*(3), 207–214. doi:10.1016/0883-9026(87)90009-7

Mason, C., & Landström, H. (2012). Introduction. In Handbook of Research on Venture Capital: Volume 2: A Globalizing Industry (pp. 3-16). Edward Elgar Publishing.

Mason, C., & Stark, M. (2004). What do investors look for in a business plan? A comparison of the investment criteria of bankers, venture capitalists and business angels. *International Small Business Journal*, *22*(3), 227–248. doi:10.1177/0266242604042377

Megginson, W. L. (2004). Toward a global model of venture capital? *Journal of Applied Corporate Finance*, *16*(1), 89–107. doi:10.1111/j.1745-6622.2004.tb00599.x

Meglio, O., Li Destri, A. M., & Capasso, A. (2017). Fostering dynamic growth in new ventures through venture capital: Conceptualizing venture capital capabilities. *Long Range Planning*, *50*(4), 518–530. doi:10.1016/j.lrp.2016.09.003

Nahata, R. (2008). Venture capital reputation and investment performance. *Journal of Financial Economics*, *90*(2), 127–151. doi:10.1016/j.jfineco.2007.11.008

NVCA. (2013). *National Venture Capital Association FAQ*. Retrieved January 20, 2014, from http://www.nvca.org/

OECD. (2002). *High-growth SMEs and employment*. Paris: OECD.

Petty, J. S., & Gruber, M. (2011). "In pursuit of the real deal" A longitudinal of VC decision making. *Journal of Business Venturing*, *26*(2), 172–188. doi:10.1016/j.jbusvent.2009.07.002

Pierrakis, Y., & Saridakis, G. (2017). Do publicly backed venture capital investments promote innovation? Differences between privately and publicly backed funds in the UK venture capital market. *Journal of Business Venturing Insights*, *7*, 55–64. doi:10.1016/j.jbvi.2017.02.002

Pistor, K., Raiser, M., & Gelfer, S. (2000). Law and finance in transition economies. *Economics of Transition*, *8*(2), 325–368. doi:10.1111/1468-0351.00047

Popov, A., & Roosenboom, P. (2013). Venture capital and new business creation. *Journal of Banking & Finance*, *37*(12), 4695–4710. doi:10.1016/j.jbankfin.2013.08.010

Pruthi, S., Wright, M., & Lockett, A. (2003). Do foreign and domestic venture capital firms differ in their monitoring of investees? *Asia Pacific Journal of Management*, *20*(2), 175–204. doi:10.1023/A:1023840432241

Revest, V., & Sapio, A. (2012). Financing technology-based small firms in Europe: What do we know? *Small Business Economics*, *39*(1), 179–205. doi:10.100711187-010-9291-6

Riding, A., Orser, B., Spence, M., & Belanger, B. (2012). Financing new venture exporters. *Small Business Economics*, *38*(2), 147–163. doi:10.100711187-009-9259-6

Rosiello, A., & Parris, S. (2009). The patterns of venture capital investment in the UK bio-healthcare sector: The role of proximity, cumulative learning and specialisation. *Venture Capital: An International Journal of Entrepreneurial Finance.*, *11*(3), 185–211. doi:10.1080/13691060902973016

Sapienza, H. J., Manigart, S., & Vermeir, W. (1996). Venture capitalist governance and value added in four countries. *Journal of Business Venturing*, *11*(6), 439–469. doi:10.1016/S0883-9026(96)00052-3

Saridakis, G., Mole, K., & Storey, D. J. (2008). New small firm survival in England. *Empirica*, *35*(1), 25–39. doi:10.100710663-007-9049-9

Shepherd, D. A., Armstrong, M. J., & Levesque, M. (2005). Allocation of attention within venture capital firms. *European Journal of Operational Research*, *163*(2), 545–564. doi:10.1016/j.ejor.2003.11.006

Smallbone, D., Leig, R., & North, D. (1995). The characteristics and strategies of high growth SMEs. *International Journal of Entrepreneurial Behaviour & Research*, *1*(3), 44–62. doi:10.1108/13552559510100657

Tian, X. (2011). The causes and consequences of venture capital stage financing. *Journal of Financial Economics*, *101*(1), 132–159. doi:10.1016/j.jfineco.2011.02.011

Timmons, J. A., & Bygrave, W. D. (1986). Venture capital's role in financing innovation for economic growth. *Journal of Business Venturing*, *1*(2), 161–176. doi:10.1016/0883-9026(86)90012-1

Tyebjee, T. T., & Bruno, A. V. (1984). Venture capital: Investor and investee perspectives. *Technovation*, *2*(3), 185–208. doi:10.1016/0166-4972(84)90003-8

Tykvová, T. (2018). Legal framework quality and success of (different types of) venture capital investments. *Journal of Banking & Finance*, *87*, 333–350. doi:10.1016/j.jbankfin.2017.10.015

Utterback, J. M., & Abernathy, W. J. (1975). A dynamic model of process and product innovation. *Omega*, *3*(6), 639–656. doi:10.1016/0305-0483(75)90068-7

Van Osnabrugge, M. (2000). A comparison of business angel and venture capitalist investment procedures: An agency theory-based analysis. *Venture Capital: An International Journal of Entrepreneurial Finance.*, *2*(2), 91–109. doi:10.1080/136910600295729

Winton, A., & Yerramilli, V. (2008). Entrepreneurial finance: Banks versus venture capital. *Journal of Financial Economics*, *88*(1), 51–79. doi:10.1016/j.jfineco.2007.05.004

Wright, M., & Robbie, K. (1998). Venture capital and private equity: A review and synthesis. *Journal of Business Finance & Accounting*, *25*(5-6), 521–570. doi:10.1111/1468-5957.00201

KEY TERMS AND DEFINITIONS

Cluster: Venture capital firms that are concentrated in terms of their geographical location or co-location with their investment.

Entrepreneur: A person who establishes a business and assumes responsibility for risks and returns.

Globalization: A process whereby a business operates across countries and continents.

Innovative: Applying new idea.

Monitoring: Actively check the performance of a venture capital-backed investment.

Private Equity: An asset class of medium to long-term finance invested in the equity share of potentially high growth and private unquoted companies.

Risk Averse: Unwilling to take risk.

Screening: Verify for venture capital funding suitability.

Venture Capital: A professionally managed fund focused on equity investments in private and potentially high-growth unquoted companies.

Chapter 10
Entrepreneurship Development in the Urban Metropolitan Guadalajara:
Growth Startups and Precursor of Innovation and Economic Development

José G. G. Vargas-Hernández
University of Guadalajara, Mexico

Justyna Zdunek-Wielgołaska
Warsaw University of Technology, Poland

ABSTRACT

This chapter analyzes startups from the perspective of the theory of entrepreneurship. Based on a literature review, the historical context of entrepreneurship in the metropolitan area of Guadalajara (MAG) is explored, evaluating the variables that are important to successful entrepreneurship. The authors conclude that Mexico from their national policies and the state of Jalisco from its development plan created the conditions to promote the entrepreneurial ecosystem; however, there are key indicators that slow the growth of startups based on technology and innovation.

DOI: 10.4018/978-1-5225-6942-8.ch010

INTRODUCTION

Entrepreneurship is an activity that has developed over hundreds of years. However, the treatment study of entrepreneurship has had different approaches over time and has sometimes been confused and mixed definitions. Entrepreneurship awarded the creation of new businesses. However, how such a concept has several implications across different studies and related disciplines, sometimes often confused with theories of administration and management.

Over the years and due to the dynamism of markets, globalization and other external factors is that the characteristics of the firms have modified and adapted. It is no exception in the stage of starting a business. For them is that new models have emerged some models of companies because of its specific features is that do not fall into the traditional categories of the firm. Therefore, the study of these is very vague. However, in recent years these enterprises, which later will call as start-ups is starting to become more important in the economic and business context. It is likely to start and consider them as the birth of a new type of firm. Perhaps it is ambitious, granting this category to these new emerging firms. However, the international context starts showing that the start-ups are a model of companies that begin to take a strong role in the global context.

Following this new trend in business dynamics that also involves issues such as technological development, innovation, scalability, internationalization among other transcendental concepts, it is necessary to understand the position assumed by the country and the region to this phenomenon. This in order to avoid business and economic backwardness, which sometimes translate into knowledge and intellectual backwardness and detonate in slowing economic development.

BACKGROUND OF THE PROBLEM

Entrepreneurship is an activity that has taken place for hundreds of years. However, the treatment study of entrepreneurship has had different approaches over time and has sometimes been confused and mixed definitions. In the text, the authors Griesa & Naude cite David Hart entrepreneurship defined as the process if begin, and continue the expansion of new businesses (Hart, 2003, p 5). Because of this, entrepreneurship credited as the creation of new businesses. However, as such the concept of entrepreneurship has several implications across different studies and related disciplines.

One could understand the theoretical historical development of entrepreneurship as follows, based on the theoretical review in the book "Entrepreneurship in Theory and History". The history of entrepreneurship dates back to 300 years ago, according Pepelasis (2005) which shows a summary of the main theoretical contributions of entrepreneurship and its historical development since the beginning of the term venture. Casis (2005) summarizes the contribution of Richard Cantillon as follows: The entrepreneur is the specialist in risk taking. The entrepreneur assumes the risks caused by price fluctuations in consumer markets. Unlike employees who receive a 'safe' salary in the short run, the entrepreneurs are willing to take the risk of economic transactions (Pepelasē & Cassis 2005).

Moreover, according to Pepelasē & Cassis (2005) the author Frank Knigth redefined the contribution of Cantillon, distinguishing between the concept of risk and uncertainty. By separating these two concepts, assume that the risk can be "insured" and by blunted, however, the uncertainty is no assured.

Given that, the risk refers to the relative frequency based on experience of a phenomenon. Uncertainty refers to the unique events and that the probability of occurrence is under an assumption. On the other hand, it claims that the gain or business profits are the reward for assuming uninsurable risks and uncertainty, is the reward of the pure entrepreneur. With the freedom of entry into the industry, profits in one industry may exceed profits in other industry in the long term, only if the uncertainties are greater in the most profitable industry, in other words, if demands on entrepreneurship are higher in that industry (Pepelasē & Cassis 2005).

Years later Joseph Schumpeter (1934), Austrian economist awarded the most basic notions of entrepreneurship who gives a heroic vision of entrepreneurs. He tells that entrepreneur generates dynamism, after creating new industries, which makes it a precursor of structural changes in the economy. Among the characteristics of the entrepreneur, Schumpeter mentions that innovates through new or existing elements, so, it can be understood that is not pure inventive and sometimes turn to adapting existing inventions. Also he mentions that the entrepreneur is not the owner of capital, since in most cases are funded by external entities, which is another characteristic of entrepreneurs, the constant search for resources, but they are the ones who make the crucial decision to take the risk.

Schumpeter (1934) developed his work Theory of Economic Development; in this theory rejected two great courses. The first is that economic change develops exogenously, and the second is that business activity is a response to exogenous forces. In refuting these assumptions, he built endogenous growth theory. In this theory, he defines the entrepreneur as the precursor source of all dynamic change in the economy. Schumpeter attributed the adjective "creative rebels" to entrepreneurs. They are responsible for generating the necessary imbalance generated by the dynamism of the economic system; therefore, they play a key role in economic development, breaking with routine processes and systems through innovations and value creation.

Israel Kirzner (1973) cited by Pepelasē & Cassis, (2005), another Austrian economist, entrepreneurs are largely precursors of economic activity since for them one of the main motivators is the pursuit of high economic performance. For Kizner they seek for their benefit in buying low and selling high. Another characteristic attributable to entrepreneurs is that they possess the quality of a clearer judgment to improvise decisions when faced with a discrepancy. Coining to Kizner that through their studies embedded in the Stream of Neo- Austrian School is emerging concepts such as the "entrepreneurial spirit; which already formally defined as alertness to profit opportunities. Under this assumption of constant alert to opportunities, the entrepreneur is a balancing force between the opportunities and the economic environment.

Finally, according to Mark Casson (1990) entrepreneurs are very important figures in the capitalist economy and society. They are decision makers in complex cases appealed to his trial, for example, when resources are scarce or there is a situation of uncertainty.

After detailed explanation of the historical development of entrepreneurship, it is understandable that it is possible to undertake it within traditional structures of the firm. However, the emergence of dynamic conditions and global demands are emerging new structures outside the canons of traditional firms.

URBAN DEVELOPMENT AND ENTREPRENEURIAL DEVELOPMENT

There is a lag in the urban development process and entrepreneurial development in the operation as a public service despite that local governments have greater autonomy despite that they remain subject to policies and resources.

Local governments received the mandate to establish an entrepreneurial urban planning, to negotiate and operate investments (Pacione, 2011: 172) and contribute to entrepreneurial development. The modernist urban planning approach was prevalent after the Second World War characterized by low density suburban development. Market-liberalism is a version of liberal-individualism influencing urban planning in the 80s rejecting the concept of public interest changing the role of planner from public regulator to policy entrepreneur (Campbell and Marshall, 2002:173–4). In the last three decades, urban planning has been abandoned by the state in favor of the market models.

Substantive theories of planning are related to the nature of specific problems, social processes, public policy sectors, etc., such as urban development, etc. Urban development planning needs a conceptual and regulatory framework and changes from a top-down to bottom-up scheme. A holistic approach to urban development integrates sustainability through urban planning. Urban planning links spaces, processes and resources to benefit the city as a whole through the enhancement of resources, public urban assets, public health, etc., setting the foundations for urban development. Urban planning need an integrated approach to cover urban policy, governance and sustainable urban development. A sustainable urban development can be achieved through an urban planning process UN (2009) that "responds to the requirements of sustainable urban development is needed for the sake of sustainable cities. Left to themselves, market forces cannot deliver an adequate and sustainable living environment" (Amado, Santos, Moura, and Silva, 2009).

The urban strategic planning process promote the actions of leaders and stakeholders working together to ensure sustainable governance planning and decision making. Also, it supports local governments in consultation with stake holders to develop urban development plans. Sustainable urban planning is a governance tool to achieve sustainable urban development. Urban planning is a core component of an urban governance model to promote democracy, inclusion, participation, transparency and accountability aimed to ensure sustainable urban development. Urban planning is linked to budgeting in terms of investments in infrastructure and services to balance economic growth, social equity and environmental challenges.

Governing institutions design urban development policies which are shaped by urban land use planners (Van Stigt, Driessen and Spit, 2013). Urban land use planners must consider short-term economic issues and co-operation with other stakeholders when making decisions. To tackle the increasing development challenges such as climate change and socio-economic problems in urban settlements, it is required to incorporate urban spatial planning in sustainable development under the term sustainable urban development. Urban planning considers land use planning as plot ratios, roads, building forms, percentage of open space and other mechanisms for urban development.

The framework methodology of urban development planning is based on participation of interest groups and their assumed commitments in the planning processes (Ortegón, Pacheco, and Prieto, 2005; Team Technologies, Middleburg, Virginia 2005, and European Integration Office 2011). Urban Planning and Management Framework (UPMF) is an inclusive and action-oriented planning approach advocating strategic urban development plans by participatory process.

Sustainable strategic urban development planning focuses in developing a common vision, mission, goals, strategies and policies, as the result of stakeholder´s risk sharing. The urban stakeholder's analysis identifies the stakeholders for engagement in urban development plan and maximize their opportunities and interests they have in urban planning and co-funding urban improvements. As part of the integral urban spatial plan, some sustainable development planning objectives should be attached to contemporary urban development trends. This notion has permeated urban spatial planning systems and other terms such as urban development and planning (Welbank, 1996; Girardet, 1999), urban land use policy (Owens, 1992), urban infrastructure development (Ostrom *et al.*, 1993), etc.

Sustainable urban planning is a methodological framework as a toolkit to transform a vision into reality using urban spaces as resources to engage stakeholders for achieving urban development. Planning legislation and open dialogue with stakeholder groups are important factors for the urban development of green urban areas, sustainable urban development and urban containment and densification. The urban development planner must sustain his behavior in ethical grounds and moral philosophy framed by a neomodernist sustainable urban planning ethos.

Urban development planning based on a rational systemic approach arouse during the 1950s, 1960s and 1970s in the context of a centralized planning in a mixed economy (Faludi, 1973; Allmendinger, 2002). Urban planning was supported by the scientific method. In 1976 in Mexico, the General Law on Human Settlements (Diario Oficial de la Federación, 1976) begins to concern on urban development planning which regulated land use. In 1976 comprehensive urban planning and development was regulated with the constitutional reforms to Article 27 on land ownership, Article 115 on States and Municipalities, and the General Law on Human Settlements.

Urban development planning is formalized as a public service with the establishment of the National Planning System for Urban Development. In 1983, the Ministry of Urban Development and Ecology integrated urban development planning and environmental protection. In the 1990s, state functions on urban planning and control were transferred to an administrative unit responsible for urban planning in the municipalities Thus; urban development planning was conducted by decentralized public units with designed urban development policies, plans and programs. The Ministry of Social Development was created in 1992 integrating the functions of urban development planning and social development. Among the functions of urban development is planning and projecting the population distribution and land regulation under sustainable development criteria in cities and metropolitan areas (SEDATU, 2015).

Territorial and urban planning has been neglected in Mexico to the extent that until 2012 it was still in forced the 2000-2006 National Urban Development Programme (UN-HABITAT, 2013). The National Programme for Urban Development and Territorial Ordering (NPUDTO) focuses on urban mobility management and strengthen the urban planning mechanisms. Strategic urban planning as a tool for sectoral integration is conducted through multi-stakeholder involvement. Some outputs produced by the municipal institutes of planning are the urban development plans, comprehensive Land Use Plan, neighborhood and community planning, sector plans (Peña 2012) among others. In some cases, the recommendations of urban planning institutes were undermined by local governments to control and manage urban development and growth (Fuentes and Cervera, 2004; Fuentes, 2009)

CONDITIONS TO GENERATE AN ENTREPRENEURIAL ECOSYSTEM

Sustainable entrepreneurial ecosystem is defined how interconnected groups and networks of actors in a community are committed to the development and creation of new companies (Cohen, 2006). This is a very general definition for it to achieve to be more specific, is that a detailed list of these networks and specific groups that must exist in order to affirm that the conditions is given to generate venture in a city. Then the author Cohen (2006) presents a list of the seven main elements of the necessary conditions to generate venture.

1. Informal networks
2. Formal networks
3. Universities
4. Government
5. Professionals and support services
6. Capital services
7. Reserve and talent generation

Given the specific characteristics of a start-up and the context of the ecosystem of entrepreneurship, both in Mexico and in the Metropolitan Area of Guadalajara (MAG), it needs to define whether there are appropriate conditions to encourage the creation of start-ups and the variables of the entrepreneurial ecosystem models in which to take action.

START-UPS OPERATING IN A SMART CITIES SEGMENT

There are two ways to analyze the impact that startups can have on a city. The first one directly points to the area of new solutions' application, which remains the focus of new businesses' interest and research, while the second shows how physically - in the morphological, functional, aesthetic and social dimensions - the city changes where the new businesses' creators have settled.

With its all complexity and intricacy of processes that shape it, a city is undoubtedly a wide field for seeking improvements in its various manifestations. The target group of urban life improvements is potentially more than half the world's population, because such a percentage lives in cities. What's more, the process of urbanization is still progressing and most likely will remain at least on the same level in the near future. We also know that urban life consumes natural resources to an extent that should definitely be under greater control. Cities account for ca. ¾ of the world's consumption of resources (Angelidou, 2014). It is not without reason that many countries undertake efforts for change in this respect, first of all to reduce the city's servicing costs, but also to reduce its negative environmental impact. Although some politicians, especially in less developed countries, consider being "eco" as another whim of the rich, when confronted with hard data they only reveal their own irresponsibility and hypocrisy, because continuation of such policy reduces the chances for a better future for future generations, which underlies the contemporary thinking about the world in the spirit of sustainable development. Therefore, the division into "good" and "bad" cities, depending on their openness to eco or smart solutions' implementation, clearly begins to rule the political language of the global investment map (Nam & Pardo, 2011).

What's more, what has been the sustainable development paradigm cornerstone today seems obvious and unquestionable, and the challenge of tomorrow has become the search for "smart" city development model. The civilization development and the momentum of changes, especially in the sphere of computerization of many processes, have forced the emergence of a new category of cities. In the 21st century, the trend in urban strategies has shifted from a model focused on sustainable development to "smart" development, as shown by studies of Ahvenniemi, Hannele Huovila, Aapo Pinto-Seppä, Isabel Airaksinen, and Miimu, who used 958 indicators to demonstrate this regularity (Ahvenniemi, Huovila, Pinto-Seppä, & Airaksinen, 2017), so changes should be expected also in the search for tools to implement these strategies, where smartups that will explore these opportunities can play an important role. These researchers have rightly noticed mutual deficiencies in the applied smart and sustainable city frameworks, assuming that the most complete, when it comes to the future challenges, will be a model combining elements of both directions in the form of "smart sustainable city". Consequently, the implementation of a vision of a green, sustainable, technologically advanced and information-accessible city will generate new businesses and possible capital accumulation (Harvey, 1989).

Startups' main task will be to support cities in reducing their energy demand, i.e. energy consumption, and controlling the use of natural resources by optimizing their management processes and supporting solutions that increase users' mobility in such a way that they do not generate additional transportation problems, but they relieve the existing infrastructure. A field for exploration of the new ideas will be urbanization in many dimensions, including urban industry, transport and communication in general.

Development of the startups operating in the smart cities segment will be particularly dynamic. With regard to cities, it is this sphere that will answer the questions of the future and will take up the challenge of predicting the most likely scenarios of changes that will occur in the broadly-meant urban life or even dictate new trends. Already today we observe qualitative changes in this area. Thanks to new ideas, our daily life becomes easier, for example paying with a card or phone for parking, or the ideas of car sharing or renting for minutes, which relieves the transport infrastructure. Some cities have already taken up the challenge of replacing urban lighting with more economical one, just to mention the LED lighting in entire Barcelona or DELP Domestic Efficient Lighting Program in India. The environment's improvement largely depends on the quality of its monitoring systems (air quality testing sensors have become the norm). There is a great chance to increase the efficiency of monitoring changes in cities, especially those involving smart solutions. Since the state of the art technologies are involved in the implemented new solutions anyway, an increase should be expected also in the demand for measurable outcome assessment. Technologically advanced, they require more and more complex algorithms to guarantee more precise results.

Increasingly, cities use computer systems, sensors, data and artificial intelligence to make them more friendly to their residents. Technological progress shall be widely available and should include users' participation in a certain range of its control. This calls for tools in the form of, for example, affordable and understandable applications. One would be tempted to set the basic areas of urban life where immediate qualitative changes are needed and bring them to: reducing traffic jams, saving valuable raw materials and natural resources, including the most important one, that is water, increasing our safety, and rubbish disposal but the list does not end there. Generally, these activities aim at creating the ideal of a technologically advanced city, efficiently and accessibly managed, green, and socially inclusive.

The new technology friendly cities change the reality from the level of management. In order to make changes at this level, political will is therefore necessary. Governments and local self-governments of less developed countries, often technologically backward, are quite unlikely to take on smart challenges, let alone those that are not fully tested and involve the risk of failure. In such cases, there is a kind of bottom-up pressure from the society, which, mainly due to quick access and flow of information and increasing mobility, demands action, for example in the case of increasing air pollution in urban areas. Also, despite the authorities' inactivity in water and energy consumption control, solutions are implemented at the level of individual homes. These are individual projects, mainly due to the need to rationalize the costs of managing the home budget, from heating control to garden watering systems related to weather monitoring. This industry is in focus of startups' interest, and they look for new solutions for its large market. In the perspective of our reality's high saturation with electronics and our society's willingness to absorb technological innovations, it can be assumed that a qualitative change may also be driven bottom up, though it is largely associated with fashion, promoted lifestyle and requires social education. Previous solutions show how inefficiently we manage our cities. However, regardless of whether these are city or resident level solutions, it is important to explore new opportunities and approach still unsolved problems in an innovative way. If city has not actually adopted a development strategy open to smart solutions, the will and money to welcome such solutions can be hardly expected.

Large agglomerations, such as Guadalajara, will play a major role in setting new trends in the future development of cities. The scale of these urbanization forms with more than a few million inhabitants, often called megacities, multiplies many problems in their area. Therefore, qualitative changes in them will have significant impact on a large scale. It is not surprising, then, that more and more activities are being undertaken to attract new businesses to their areas, which will change the image of the mother cities themselves, but above all, with their discoveries will improve the quality of life in global terms. Opening up to startups means measurable and qualitative changes in the future, which is why many cities compete in the rankings for the best places to set up new businesses. It turns out that the implementation of a "smart" development strategy pays off, and what's more, as development model called "disciplined" city (Vanolo, 2014) it allows mitigation of conflicts and more effective control of its development. Although it may seem that the largest cities compete with each other on this ground, there is also a sphere of information and practice exchange in this area. Among other things, the success of many initiatives lies in creative use of the relevant available knowledge and use of opportunities resulting from the synergy effect. This subject is lively and up-to-date and promotes cooperation between different units at different levels of city management, thanks to which the network of city alliances is growing and gaining importance. Because this issue concerns a number of interdisciplinary problems, it engages scientists, practitioners and city governments in the discourse. Visionary strategies are drawn out, even if certain solutions are obviously Utopian.

Such an accumulation of creative potential in one area brings about changes in the city landscape and the way it functions. Cities can greatly benefit from these businesses what helps to develop business ecosystems and develop local economics. If urban policy aims to create conditions conducive to the development of this type of business, like the Silicon Valley, it attracts young people to settle within it, which has an impact on the age and education statistics of the users living in a given area. If the development of a modern district or a smart city is assumed, then they must be attractive to founders of startups. Although the nature of work has changed and we work often without leaving home, this does not mean that we do not want to be in the center of events. Therefore, quasi cities are built, smart principle based and bristling with technology districts which constitute a kind of science laboratory. Furnished with sensors, cameras and other tracking technologies, they cannot only collect information, but immediately process it with appropriate programs into decisions in space. The city offer is to attract talented, young, engineers to start businesses, but also to relate their private lives to the workplace. In order to attract such activities effectively, governments and local self-governments must first and foremost ensure a transparent and accessible law, as well as financial incentives. Also important is the proximity of universities, general standard of living, also translated into urban infrastructure, which guarantees mobility, international transport links, well-established network of organizations, events and incubators, cultural and entertainment offer. Such a city should be easily accessible in all dimensions and offer attractive real estate prices. And although it is believed that a successful startup can get started up anywhere, no one can challenge the potential arising from intellectual capital in the San Francisco Bay Area.

Research Question

Are there adequate conditions for generating start- ups for the ZMG?

Justification

It is Important to assess the context of entrepreneurship in the local area, since many adjectives are being Attributed to Jalisco as the "Mexican Silicon Valley" or "Jalisco Capital of innovation" Doing this analysis will allow to understand this situation.

The analysis on this matter is justified in few studies on the dynamics of start-ups in Mexico and much less to specific ecosystems like the MAG. There are some agencies and studies already evaluating entrepreneurship in various dimensions from the current conditions of the country to promote entrepreneurship to more specific indicators related to innovation and technology, but without taking into account the specific context that require start-ups.

Moreover, to study the dynamics of Startups as a new business structure is as important as this phenomenon is showing up increasingly and is emerging more strongly. There are hubs, innovation, and entrepreneurship ecosystems, which created the atmosphere and the conditions for growth start-up, such as the city of Victoria in Canada, Silicon Valley in California and Tel Aviv in Israel.

Given the specific characteristics of a start-up and context of the ecosystem of entrepreneurship, both in Mexico and in the MAG, it is a need to define whether there are appropriate conditions to encourage the creation of start-ups and what are the variables if the entrepreneurial ecosystem models in which action is taken.

CONCEPTUAL-THEORETICAL FRAMEWORK

Entrepreneurship

The process of initiating and continuing the expansion of new Businesses (Hart, 2003, p.5) to entrepreneurship is credited the creation of new businesses. However, such a concept has diverse implications across the distinct studies and related disciplines.

Startups

A start-up is a technology-based business, high growth potential and a high degree of scalability. Startups research has focused on analyzing how new companies have the ability to develop new products and services and reach a large number of customers in a shorter period (Rasmussen, E. S., & Tanev, S, 2015). About the growth of start-ups is reaching more customers in a shorter period known as scalability, which can be one of the main features of a start-up.

According to Steve Blank, a startup is a temporary organization in search of a business model scalable and replicable (Blank, 2010). Temporal refers to having a lifetime to stop being start- up and become a consolidated, or fail and evolve to another detected business opportunity. The word search refers to the market in which it is involved, unlike traditional businesses operating in mature markets, start- ups seeking new business models in order to create, modify or have existing markets (Blank 2010).

Characteristics of Startups

A scalable start-up usually requires a population of over 100 million people. If your country does not have that, the start-up needs to be born world (Blank, 2010). Trimi and Berbegal-Mirabent (2012) have discussed new trends in the design of the business model, focusing on open innovation, customer development, agile development, and methodologies "lean". That conclusion they reach is that the design of business models based on innovation should seek quick iterations and the adoption of a philosophy of trial and error to validate the assumptions of the business model and the specific characteristics of goods or services.

According to Stavnsager and Tanev (2015) the authors make a comparison between startups and global firms must be born yet we only we will focus on the features that the authors listed about start-ups.

1. **Type of Company:** Start-up technology.
2. **Market:** New market niches.
3. **Marketing Strategy Product:** Model cycle technology adoption / cross into new market niches.
4. **Product Development:** New product development / prototyping / testing / Dynamic Development.
5. **Business Model:** dynamic model / pop business.
6. **Focus Entrepreneurship:** entrepreneurship directed hypothetically.
7. **Outlook Key Attributes of Business:** Ex ante.

Importance of Startups

According to the Mexican Institute for Competitiveness, the dynamics of startups has come to challenge much of the theoretical structures have on the theories of the firm, business management and economic behavior. For example, some technology startups in less than 5 years have achieved greater value assessed to all listed companies belonging to a conglomerate. Given to this dynamism has made that capital investment in technology issues have a growing five times greater than the rest of the economy.

INNOVATION IN MEXICO

According to the World Intellectual Property Organization (WIPO), Mexico improved 16 places in the Global Innovation Index 2013 over the previous year. In 2012, it was in the 79th position and managed to move to position 63. This puts it in a position slightly above the average of the 142 countries assessed. However, its position remains less competitive than other Latin American countries like Costa Rica (39), Argentina (56) and Colombia (60)

There is another report issued by the World Economic Forum, Global Technology Report 2014 puts Mexico at the site 79 of 148 countries surveyed, down 16 positions from the previous year. Although the report can recognize similar to those highlighted by WIPO strengths, it indicates that the innovation ecosystem in Mexico needs to be strengthened and, in general, Mexican companies have a low capacity to innovate, resulting in low economic impacts and population which focuses heavily on low-productivity activities, and few jobs that are considered knowledge-intensive (Gallegos, 2015).

Quantitative Investment Analysis Innovation

According to the World Intellectual Property Organization (WIPO) investment in research and development, according to the World Bank, in 2012, Mexico spent the equivalent of 0.37 Per cent of GDP, while Russia, for example, spent 1.0 Per cent, Brazil 1.1 Per cent, China 1.4 Per cent and South Korea 3.2Per cent.

One of the policies of the federal government has decided to attack with the aim of gradually increasing investment category at least the equivalent of 1 Per cent of GDP. International experience shows that the most successful entrepreneurship based on innovation, cases are those articulated under models "triple helix": that is, innovation does not arise in isolation, but thrives on networks that bring together entrepreneurs, research centers and support from government agencies.

In Mexico, by 2010 according to the SEP used in the report of the World Intellectual Property Organization (WIPO), 25 Per cent of Mexican companies that conducted research and development, it was in connection with a research center. According to this report, a key incentive is to have a robust and effective system of protection of intellectual property rights, and intangible to be a tool for entrepreneurs.

According to WIPO, Mexico local produce 0.7 patents per 10,000 inhabitants. Brazil produces twice, Russia 20 times and China 40 times. In the Federal District 36.3 patent applications filed per million inhabitants in 2012. In Oaxaca there were only two. Similarly, the Federal District has 14.9 researchers per 10,000 inhabitants, while Oaxaca has only one. In the innovation landscape in Mexico, there are cases of innovative regional clusters of remarkable success. The generation of new clusters of entrepreneurship and innovation requires an integrated strategy that responds to local vocations (Gallegos, 2015).

MEXICO AND ENTREPRENEURSHIP

Public Policies in Mexico

In matters of importance to the government in entrepreneurship theory, for the promotion of appropriate conditions for the development of fruitful economic activities and enterprise creation conditions, an issue tops the public agenda and is evident in the country's development Plan. As a general goal, the National Development Plan 2013- 2018 locates the entrepreneurship and innovation within the national goal of "Achieving a prosperous Mexico" leads to the strategy to develop the strategic sectors of the country" and a specific action line is "to encourage entrepreneurs and strengthen micro, small and medium enterprises.

About to encourage entrepreneurs and strengthen micro, small and medium enterprises, the following specific action lines are as follows:

1. Support the successful integration of micro, small and medium enterprises to the value chains of more dynamic strategic sectors, with more potential for growth and job creation, in agreement with the state governments of the country.
2. To promote entrepreneurship through the creation of an educational environment, finance, legal protection and adequate competition.
3. Design and implement an information system, monitoring, evaluation and dissemination of the impact of entrepreneurs and micro, small and medium enterprises.
4. Promote intensive programs to develop skills in information and communications technology, and innovation to promote the creation of high added value of micro, small and medium enterprises ecosystems.
5. Improving technical advisory services to build an entrepreneurial culture.
6. Facilitate access to financing and capital to entrepreneurs and micro, small and medium enterprises.
7. Create entrepreneurial vocation from an early age to increase the critical mass of entrepreneurs.
8. Support the business escalation of micro, small and medium-sized Mexican companies.
9. Increase the participation of micro, small and medium enterprises in production chains, as well as its export capacity.
10. To promote social projects, green entrepreneurs and high impact.
11. To promote the creation of jobs through the development of entrepreneurial projects.
12. Encourage the creation and sustainability of formal small businesses.

Within these 12 lines of strategic action, it can highlight specific actions such as the creation of the National Fund of the entrepreneur. A fund aims to encourage national, regional and sectorial economic growth by fostering productivity and innovation in micro, small and medium enterprises in strategic sectors. That promotes the orderly strengthening, planned and systematic entrepreneurship and business development throughout the national territory and the consolidation of an innovative, dynamic and competitive economy.

Table 1.

Entrepreneur Ecosystem Assessment (GEM)	Entrepreneurship, Innovation and Technology Ecosystem Assessment (IMCO)
GEM: Global Entrepreneur Monitor	IMCO: Mexican Institute of Competitiveness
1. Finance	1. Innovation
2. Government Policies: Entrepreneurship as a priority and support for business.	2. Environment for doing business
3. Governmental programs	3. Support infrastructure
4. Education and entrepreneurial training	4. Human capital
5. Technology transfer	5.Financing
6. Commercial infrastructure	6.Demand profile
7. Internal market: Dynamics	7. Industrial integration
8. Physical infrastructure	8. Entrepreneurial culture
9. Social and cultural norms	9. Governmental policies

Entrepreneur Ecosystem Assessments

In order to evaluate the factors influencing entrepreneurial activity and entrepreneurial activity related to innovation and technology are taken two tests that are performed in these contexts in particular. Firstly, the GEM (Global Entrepreneur Monitor) Analyzes environmental conditions to undertake and IMCO (Mexican Institute for Competitiveness) analyzes the environmental conditions to undertake but from a more specific vision of entrepreneurship in areas of technology, and innovation (Table 1).

Knowing the context of entrepreneurship is evaluated it is valuable because it allows to limit what are the determining variables. However, more importantly is to evaluate and assign a weighting to understand in clear and quantitative terms. Where does it meet? What is doing well? In addition, what can be improved? (Table 2).

Results of that evaluation by IMCO (Table 3) in terms of technological entrepreneurship and innovation in terms of a comparison sheds alarming results that might make look like a laggard country. A recent study found that only teachers and students at Stanford University have created 40,000 companies and generated 5.4 million jobs since 1930. These businesses generated an added value of 2.7 trillion dollars that is more than the size of the Mexican economy. According to the Financial Report Stanford University 1995, the federal government accounted for 40 Per cent of funding for the institution in the field (Gallegos, 2015). (Table 3).

Table 2.

Entrepreneur Ecosystem Assessment GEM Mexico 2014 GEM: Global Entrepreneur Monitor	
1. **Finance**	As for funding by 2014 the outlook is bleak, the element with the worst result indicates that there is not enough equity of entrepreneurs in Mexico to finance new and growing businesses.
2. **Government Policies: entrepreneurship as a priority and support**	Compared to 2013, the year 2014 assesses negatively in all factors, concluding that the general perception is that support for new and growing businesses is not a priority the policy of the federal government.
3. **Governmental programs**	There is a perception that science parks and incubators provide effective support for new and growing companies.
4. **Education and entrepreneurial training**	There is not a good perception of entrepreneurial education offering, but has improved compared to 2010.
5. **Technology transference**	Technology transference perceives that science and technology developed in Mexico allow the creation of technology-based companies in the global level.
1. **Commercial infrastructure**	In 2014, there was a negative perception in commercial and professional infrastructure, which leads to lack of adequate for the development of entrepreneurial ecosystem conditions.
2. **Internal market: dynamics**	Perceives that new and growing companies cannot easily enter new markets, or assume the cost of entry this implies.
3. **Physical infrastructure:**	Although there are generally positive assessments regarding physical infrastructure, the results is lower in comparison to 2013.
4. **Social and cultural norms**	Norms presented a decrease in earnings during 2014. The worst evaluated element was no stimulation to taking entrepreneurial risk.

JALISCO IN ENTREPRENEURSHIP

In Table 4 it is shown the objectives and strategies of the National Development Plan 2013-2016 Jalisco.

Conclusions State Enterprise Development Plan

This National Development Plan proposes as a priority objective foster a business climate that facilitates access to financing and encouraging the creation, innovation and expansion of companies, but with a special emphasis on the consolidation of MSMEs.

To assess the impact of entrepreneurship in the case of Jalisco four indicators are relevant: the number of registered companies, their operating capacity, retention of businesses and financing volume: Using this summary, are analyzed the challenges of these four indicators.

Table 3.

Factor	Evaluation
1. Innovation	This is the most backward factor according to IMCO. This is due to low investment in research and development compared with other countries. In Mexico 30 Per cent of investment in R & D comes from the private sector, in other countries like South Korea, this represents 80 Per cent. In addition, there is a perception that there are no institutional links between academia and industry; therefore, companies do not resort to the academy for innovation.
2. Environment for doing business	This is the third worst evaluated factor and it is not surprising as it coincides with other studies indicating the high cost and difficulty in performing procedures in Mexico, including paying taxes. The gap for the growth of corruption is huge and therefore perceives as a constraint to doing business in Mexico.
1. Support infrastructure	10 years ago, pushes the creation of incubators in Mexico resulting in nearly 500 institutions throughout the country by 2012, its results have not been the expected. Only one in seven incubators has some type of a tracking system of their companies. This explains why 70 Per cent of entrepreneurs who have obtained financing on the market do not come from any incubator.
2. Human capital	The main problems have to do with the lack of English proficiency. Because of the one-dimensional model of undergraduate education in Mexico, systems engineers, even though they have a technical soundness lack business elements. Similarly, business students lack the technical skills to carry out an ICT business.
3. Financing	Financing is considered one of the laggard's factors. In Mexico invests 0.06 Per cent of GDP in that market while in Colombia and Chile twice reversed in relative terms. On the other hand, the credit market companies are limited. In 2010, the percentage of credit to companies accounted for 21 Per cent of GDP while the Latin American average was 36 Per cent .5 As a result; entrepreneurs tend to finance their projects with family and personal funds. Mexican businesspersons prefer to invest in traditional sectors, new markets, which have inhibited the creation of angel investors.
4. Demand profile	This factor refers to the ability of a country to adopt and promote the use of technological developments. Its relevance is because those small businesses are the fastest growing permanently using ICTs to interact with their customers, according to a recent study by BCG. However, e-commerce in Brazil is three times that of Mexico in relation to GDP due to

Table 4.

Sectorial objective	
OD8O1	Expand and improve the supply of financing on appropriate terms for productive projects.
OD8O1E1	Strengthen specialized funds guarantees
OD8O1E2	Encourage financial institutions and bodies of state financial support to generate operating rules and guarantees according to the possibilities of MSMEs
OD8O1E3	Promote a state system of financing that consolidate and coordinate programs appropriate to the type and size of companies.
OD8O1E4	Enhance competition in lending to entrepreneurs to reduce interest rates
OD8O1E5	Boosting the financing companies of international migrants return
OD8O2	Sectorial objective: Strengthen the capacities of MSMEs operation
OD8O2E2	Strengthen educational programs and higher education in corporate financial education
OD8O2E3	Improve systems incubation, acceleration and entrepreneurship of universities and business organizations that promote, support and follow up on formal businesses with high added value and innovation
OD8O2E5	Generate incentives in coordination with the federal government and municipal governments to install new formal businesses seize the economic vocation and regional potential.
OD8O2E6	Strengthen the network of actors that make up the system entrepreneurs.
OD8O2E7	Generate comprehensive programs that allow potentiate the initiatives of entrepreneurs and creating high-impact companies.
OD8O2E8	Generate comprehensive programs that help expand niche markets MSMEs

One of the main areas of opportunity to boost funding and entrepreneurship is within the structure of the State System of Entrepreneurship. In Jalisco there are 45 Incubators registered with the INADEM, there Jalisco Enterprise Development Fund (FOJAL) supports entrepreneurs through training and / or accompaniment

Jalisco in Innovation

Jalisco faces several problems with competitiveness and economic growth. In 2012 Jalisco was located at position 13 Competitiveness Index nationwide calculates the Mexican Institute for Competitiveness (IMCO) see Table 5.

Table 5.

OD13O1E1	Encourage the formation of high level human capital
OD13O1E2	Develop a dual model of higher education to strengthen the link between universities and industries and to encourage innovation and entrepreneurship with the vision to produce value added.
OD13O1E3	Develop marketing networks technology to the productive sector
OD13O1E4	Encourage the creation of a network of information and technology transfer to give added value to all productive sectors of identity.
OD13O1E5	Seek or venture capital fund for scientific and technological projects, academy-industry
OD13O1E6	Increase investment in innovation, science and technology as a percentage of state GDP, to form in the next few years an investment at least equal to the national average investment.
OD13O1E7	Motivate through a program the interest of industry research
OD13O1E8	Harnessing local research groups recognized in different areas to create specific poles of scientific development (e.g. biotechnology)
OD13O1E9	Promote a triple helix model linking the academy, industry and government to the generation of scientific development and innovation.
OD1302. SECTOR OBJECTIVE: To promote innovation and entrepreneurship for scientific and technological development.	
OD13O2E1	Create specialized technology platforms to support high-tech entrepreneurs that allow incubation, integration into clusters. Accelerating and innovation (i.e digital creative city and centers of innovation and business acceleration)
OD13O2E2	Promote the development of the information society and knowledge through a statewide system of Entrepreneurship and a state innovation system, including sectoral strategic information.

Conclusions of the State Development Plan Innovation and Technology

Scientific research, technology development and innovation are three important elements, as has been demonstrated in various latitudes that these components of development have a direct impact on business competitiveness index. According to the ranking of Science, Technology Mexico and Innovation in 2011, conducted by the Scientific and Technological Consultative Forum (FCCyT), Jalisco is located in fourth place nationally in terms of quantity and quality of resources in Science, Technology and Innovation (CTI). Only surpassed by the Federal District, Nuevo Leon and Morelos (General Secretariat of Government of the State of Jalisco, 2013).

However, this position not reflects an impact to increase business competitiveness of the state, because, on the level of business competitiveness, Jalisco ranks in tenth position by 2012. Some of the causes of why the state Jalisco is located in this position are that there is poor linkage between academia and industry for the generation of research and technological development. As it has been reviewing over the text in a nutshell, companies do not go to universities to generate innovation (General Secretariat of Government of the State of Jalisco, 2013).

According to the State Development Plan of Jalisco 2013- 2033, the results of the position of Jalisco also due to a low level of enrollment in undergraduate and graduate programs are related to the development of science and technology. In Jalisco, only 28.4 Per cent of undergraduate enrollment is located in engineering and technology programs, while nationally the proportion is 33.4 Per cent.

Another of the limitations that exist in the state for generating innovation, science and technology, is the number of researchers who are in state so that researchers who are attached to the SNI (National Research System) are taken into account. By 2011, in Jalisco, for every 10 thousand members of the EAP (Economically Active Population), there are 2.8 researchers from the SNI, with respect to this stated, Jalisco is located at number 12 in the country. (General Secretariat of Government of the State of Jalisco, 2013).

One of the main constraints to generate own business innovation is that this must be done by each and investment of own funds according to indicators of companies investing in innovation. Eighty-seven Per cent of its total investment comes from own resources, although in the case of microenterprises this proportion rises to 92 Per cent. In addition, the nature of investment banking in Mexico and the likelihood that funding granted for innovation issues is very low. Regarding public funds are equivalent to only 2 Per cent and international funds less than 1Per cent. (General Secretariat of Government of the State of Jalisco, 2013)

In conclusion, the State Development Plan summarizes these two problems: First, there are no adequate financing mechanisms for high-tech entrepreneurs. In addition, there are no real mechanisms to support specialized entrepreneurs in high-tech incubators. It is also remarkable the digital divide that prevents the exploitation and use of Information Technology and Communication (ICT) for development of the state. Smaller and more companies to survive problems tend to use less resources and take advantage of ICT (General Secretariat of Government of the State of Jalisco, 2013)

RESEARCH METHOD

In this research, it is used the qualitative method based on literature review of studies in Mexico and investigations in other countries. Also, there are analyzed statistics presented by national and international institutional bodies and public and private bodies are used in order to explain and describe the phenomenon that is the object of study.

ANALYSIS OF RESULTS

If it should be analyzed the conditions of the state of Jalisco that promote entrepreneurship and innovation, and with them the generation start-ups, it can be concluded that are aligned to the policies that both the federal government and the state government has ruled in their plans development. However, results in innovation and entrepreneurship in the state mostly have negative results.

As reviewed from the national sphere the two main constraints to which start-ups face, are the lack of availability of capital and financial instruments and low incentives that have to invest in research and development. Companies are still struggling to resolve operational and financial issues leaving aside the daily budgets and resources for this type of activities that add value.

Finally, it should be emphasized that both the IMCO report as on the findings of State Development Plan, although it is established clearly as a strategic line, collaboration between industry, academia and government is called the triple helix and it is already a proven to encourage high-value activities in a city model. There are alarming figures in which it shows that companies do not resort to universities, educational centers and research to generate innovation, which is a bit absurd in terms of policies judged as the creation of a Ministry of Innovation, Science and Technology.

CONCLUSION AND RECOMMENDATIONS

There are two main reasons why it is important to study the evolution and development of Startups in the MAG. The first is because there is evidence that the creation of startups based on technology and innovation has a positive impact on the economic development of the region. The second reason is that it is important to analyze the nature of what we might call a new type of firm and that for various reasons are unable to fit into conventional corporate structures and it is that is increasing the detailed study of the characteristics, dynamics and structure of startups.

Concluding that Mexico from its national policies and the State of Jalisco from State Development Plan, has tried to promote in the MAG conditions to promote the entrepreneurial ecosystem. However, there are key indicators that slow detonation and growth of startups based on technology and innovation.

Although public policies at the State and Federal level institutions create and allocate resources to encourage entrepreneurial activity, this can grow in terms of traditional business and of little value. However, to encourage start-ups and businesses based on technology and innovation, it is necessary that public policies not only focus on increasing Numeralia of companies created or loans granted. To increase the value should pay attention to specific indicators, greater reach and more intellectual, long-term nature.

The problem of creating value is not resolved with a high volume of micro-credits or incentives for micro and small businesses. However, there must be public policy incentives to the creation of intellectual capital, to prevent leakage of knowledge and generation of instruments for more solid financing and not only seek short-term returns.

REFERENCES

Ahvenniemi, H., Huovila, A., Pinto-Seppä, I., & Airaksinen, M. (2017). What are the differences between sustainable and smart cities? *Cities (London, England)*, *60*, 234–245. doi:10.1016/j.cities.2016.09.009

Allmendinger, P. (2002). *Planning theory* (2nd ed.). Palgrave Macmillan.

Amado, M. P., Santos, C. V., Moura, E. B., & Silva, V. G. (2009). Public Participation in Sustainable Urban Planning. *World Academy of Science: Science and Engineering*, *53*, 597–603.

Angelidou, M. (2014). Smart city policies: A spatial approach. *Cities (London, England)*, *41*, S3–S11. doi:10.1016/j.cities.2014.06.007

Blank, S. (2010). *Entrepreneurship-Steve Blank*. Retrieved from Obtenido de Entrepreneurship-Steve Blank: https://steveblank.com/2010/01/25/whats-a-startup-first-principles/

Campbell, H., & Marshall, R. (2002). Utilitarianism's Bad Breath? A Re-evaluation of the Public Interest Justification for Planning. *Planning Theory*, *1*(2), 165–189. doi:10.1177/147309520200100205

Casson, M. (1990). *Enterprise and Competitiveness: A System View of Inernational Business*. Oxford University Press.

Cohen, B. (2006). Sustainable valley entrepreneurial ecosystems. *Business Strategy & The Environment, 15*(1), 1-14. doi:10.1002/bse.428

Diario Ofiial de la Federación. (1976). *Ley General de Asentamientos Humanos*. Author.

European Integration Office. (2011). *Guide to the logical framework approach*. Republic of Serbia Government European Integration Office. Available: http://www.evropa.gov.rs/Evropa/ShowDocument.aspx?Type=Home&Id=525

Faludi, A. (1973). *Planning Theory*. Pergamon.

Fuentes, C. (2009). La planeación estratégica como instrumento de un nuevo modelo de gestión del desarrollo urbano en Ciudad Juárez: Retos y oportunidades. In J. M. Ramos & I. Aguilar (Eds.), *La gestión del desarrollo local en México: Problemas y agenda*. Miguel Ángel Porrúa and El Colegio de la Frontera Norte.

Fuentes, C., & Cervera, L. (2004). La gestión del suelo urbano en Ciudad Juárez, Chihuahua: La difícil transición de la gobernabilidad autoritaria a la gobernabilidad democrática. In Gobernabilidad o ingobernabilidad en la región Paso del Norte. Ciudad Juárez, Mexico: EON, UACJ and COLEF.

Gallegos, R. (2015). *Los Emprendedores de TIC en México*. IMCO.

Girardet, H. (1999). *Creating sustainable cities*. Green Books for the Schumacher Society.

Gobierno Federal. (2013). Plan Nacional de Desarrollo.

Gries, T., & Naudé, W. (2009). Entrepreneurship and regional economic growth: Towards general theory of start-ups. Innovation. *European Journal of Soil Science, 22*(3), 309–328. doi:10.1080/13511610903354877

Hart, D. M. (2003). Entrepreneurship policy: what it is and where it came from. In D. M. Hart (Ed.), *The emergence of entrepreneurship policy: governance, start-ups and growth in the US knowledge economy* (p. 3). Cambridge, UK: Cambridge University Press. doi:10.1017/CBO9780511610134.001

Harvey, D. (1989). *The Condition of Postmodernity: An Enquiry Into the Origins of Cultural Change*. Oxford, UK: Blackwell. Retrieved from https://scholar.google.com/scholar_lookup?hl=en&publication_year=1989b&issue=1&author=D.+Harvey&title=The+Condition+of+Postmodernity

Nam, T., & Pardo, T. A. (2011). Conceptualizing smart city with dimensions of technology, people, and institutions. *Proceedings of the 12th Annual International Digital Government Research Conference on Digital Government Innovation in Challenging Times - dg.o '11*, 282. 10.1145/2037556.2037602

Ortegón, E., Pacheco, J. F., & Prieto, A. (2005). *Metodología del marco lógico para la planificación, el seguimiento y la evaluación de proyectos y programas, Serie Manuales No. 42*. Instituto Latinoamericano y del Caribe de Planificación Económica y Social (ILPES), Santiago de Chile. Available: http://www.cepal.org/es/publicaciones/5607-metodologia-del-marco-logico- para-la-planificacion-el-seguimiento-y-laevaluacion

Ostrom, E., Schroeder, L., & Wynne, S. (1993). *Institutional Incentives and Sustainable Development*. Boulder, CO: Westview Press.

Owens, S. (1992). Energy, Environmental Sustainability and Land-Use Planning. In M. Breheny (Ed.), *Sustainable Development and Urban For* (pp. 79–105). London: Pion.

Pacione, M. (2011). *Urban Geography: A Global Perspective*. Routledge.

Peña, S. (2012). Recent Trends and Practice in Spatial Planning in Mexico. The Municipal Planning and Research Institutes. *Gestión y Política Pública, 21*(2), 407-449.

Pepelasē, M. I., & Cassis, Y. (2005). Entrepreneurship in Theory and History. Houndmills, UK: Palgrave Macmillan.

Rasmussen, E. S., & Tanev, S. (2015). The Emergence of the Lean Global Startup as a New Type of Firm. *Technology Innovation Management Review*, *5*(11), 12–19. doi:10.22215/timreview/941

Schumpeter, J. (1934). *The Theory of Economic Development*. Cambridge, MA: Harvard University Press.

Secretaría General de Gobierno del Estado de Jalisco. (2013). *Plan Estatal de Desarrollo Jalisco 2013-2033*. Author.

SEDATU. (2015). Available: http://www.sedatu.gob.mx/sraweb/

Team Technologies, Middleburg, Virginia. (2005). *The Logframe Handbook, a logical framework approach to project cycle management*. The World Bank. Available: http://documents.worldbank.org/curated/en/2005/01/5846691/logframe-handbook-logical- frameworkapproach-project-cycle-management

Trimi, S., & Berbegal-Mirabent, J. (2012). Business Model Innovation in Entrepreneurship. *The International Entrepreneurship and Management Journal*, *8*(4), 449–465. doi:10.100711365-012-0234-3

UN. (2009). *Human Settlements Program; Planning Sustainable Cities: Global Report on Human Settlements 2009*. London: Earthscan.

UN-Habitat. (2013). *State of the World's Cities 2012/2013: Prosperity of Cities*. New York: Routledge.

Van Stigt, R., Driessen, P. P. J., & Spit, T. J. M. (2013). Compact City Development and the Challenge of Environmental Policy Integration: A Multi-Level Governance Perspective. *Environmental Policy and Governance*, *23*(4), 221–233. doi:10.1002/eet.1615

Vanolo, A. (2014). Smartmentality: The Smart City as Disciplinary Strategy. *Urban Studies (Edinburgh, Scotland)*, *51*(5), 883–898. doi:10.1177/0042098013494427

Welbank, M. (1996). The search for a sustainable urban form. In *Institutions and Environmental Change*. Cambridge, MA: MIT Press. doi:10.4324/9780203362372_The_Search_for_a_Sustainable_Urban

Compilation of References

Acs, Z. (2006). How Is Entrepreneurship Good for Economic Growth? *Innovations: Technology, Governance, Globalization*, *1*(1), 97–107. doi:10.1162/itgg.2006.1.1.97

Acs, Z. J., Desai, S., & Hessels, J. (2008). Entrepreneurship, economic development and institutions. *Small Business Economics*, *31*(3), 219–234. doi:10.100711187-008-9135-9

Acs, Z. J., & Szerb, L. (2007). Entrepreneurship Economic Growth and Public Policy. *Small Business Economics*, *28*(2-3), 109–122. doi:10.100711187-006-9012-3

Acs, Z., Audretsch, D. B., Braunerhjelm, P., & Carlsson, B. (2012). Growth and entrepreneurship. *Small Business Economics*, *39*(2), 289–300. doi:10.100711187-010-9307-2

Acs, Z., Audretsch, D. B., & Lehmann, E. E. (2013). The knowledge spillover theory of entrepreneurship. *Small Business Economics*, *41*(4), 757–774. doi:10.100711187-013-9505-9

Acs, Z., & Sanders, M. W. J. L. (2013). Knowledge spillover entrepreneurship in an endogenous growth model. *Small Business Economics*, *41*(4), 775–795. doi:10.100711187-013-9506-8

Agarwal, R., Echambadi, R., Franco, A. M., & Sarkar, M. (2004). Knowledge transfer through inheritance: Spin- out generation, development, and survival. *Academy of Management Journal*, *47*(4), 501–522. doi:10.2307/20159599

Ahl, H. (2006). Why research on women entrepreneurs needs new directions. *Entrepreneurship Theory and Practice*, *30*(5), 595–621. doi:10.1111/j.1540-6520.2006.00138.x

Ahlstrom, D., & Bruton, G. D. (2006). Venture capital in emerging economies: Networks and institutional change. *Entrepreneurship Theory and Practice*, *30*(2), 299–320. doi:10.1111/j.1540-6520.2006.00122.x

Ahvenniemi, H., Huovila, A., Pinto-Seppä, I., & Airaksinen, M. (2017). What are the differences between sustainable and smart cities? *Cities (London, England)*, *60*, 234–245. doi:10.1016/j.cities.2016.09.009

Akar, E., & Topcu, B. (2011). An Examination of the Factors Influencing Consumers' Attitudes Toward Social Media Marketing. *Journal of Internet Commerce*, *10*(1), 35–67. doi:10.1080/15332861.2011.558456

Alderighi, M., Bianchi, C., & Lorenzini, E. (2016). The impact of local food specialities on the decision to (re)visit a tourist destination: Market-expanding or business-stealing? *Tourism Management*, *57*, 323–333. doi:10.1016/j.tourman.2016.06.016

Aldrich, H. E., Elam, A. B., & Reese, P. R. (1997). Strong ties, weak ties, and strangers: do women owners differ from men in their use of networking to obtain assistance? Academic Press. doi:10.4324/9780203435168.ch1

Aldrich, H. E., & Zimmer, C. (1986). Entrepreneurship through networks. In D. Sexton & R. W. Smilor (Eds.), *Art and Science of Entrepreneurship* (pp. 3–23). Cambridge, MA: Ballinger Publishing Company.

Allen, E., Langowitz, N., Elam, A., & Dean, M. (2007). *The Global Entrepreneurship Monitor 2007 Report On Women and Entrepreneurship*. Academic Press.

Allen, R. S., Helms, M. M., Takeda, M. B., White, C. S., & White, C. (2006). A Comparison of Competitive Strategies in Japan and the United States. *S.A.M. Advanced Management Journal*, *71*(1), 24–34.

Allmendinger, P. (2002). *Planning theory* (2nd ed.). Palgrave Macmillan.

Alsos, G. A., Isaksen, E. J., & Ljunggren, E. (2006). New venture financing and subsequent business growth in men - and women-led businesses. *Entrepreneurship Theory and Practice*, *30*(5), 667–686. doi:10.1111/j.1540-6520.2006.00141.x

Alvarez, S. A., & Barney, J. B. (2007). Discovery and creation: Alternative theories of entrepreneurial action. *Strategic Entrepreneurship Journal*, *1*(1-2), 11–26. doi:10.1002ej.4

Alvarez, S. A., & Barney, J. B. (2014). Entrepreneurial Opportunities and Poverty Alleviation. *Entrepreneurship Theory and Practice*, *38*(1), 159–184. doi:10.1111/etap.12078

Alvarez, S. A., Barney, J. B., & Young, S. L. (2010). Debates in Entrepreneurship: Opportunity Formation and Implications for the Field of Entrepreneurship. In Z. J. Acs & D. B. Audretsch (Eds.), *Handbook of Entrepreneurship Research - An Interdisciplinary Survey and Introduction* (2nd ed.; pp. 23–46). Springer-Verlag New York; doi:10.1007/978-1-4419-1191-9_2

Amado, M. P., Santos, C. V., Moura, E. B., & Silva, V. G. (2009). Public Participation in Sustainable Urban Planning. *World Academy of Science: Science and Engineering*, *53*, 597–603.

Amit, R., Brander, J., & Zott, C. (1998). Why do venture capital firms exist? Theory and Canadian experience. *Journal of Business Venturing*, *13*(6), 441–466. doi:10.1016/S0883-9026(97)00061-X

Amit, R., & Schoemaker, P. (1993). Strategic assets and organizational rent. *Strategic Management Journal*, *14*(1), 33–46. doi:10.1002mj.4250140105

Anderson, B. S., & Eshima, Y. (2013). The influence of firm age and intangible resources on the relationship between entrepreneurial orientation and firm growth among Japanese SMEs. *Journal of Business Venturing*, *28*(3), 413–429. doi:10.1016/j.jbusvent.2011.10.001

Anderson, C. (2006). *The Long Tail: Why the Future of Business is Selling Less of More*. New York: Hyperion.

Anderson, P., & Gordon, R. (2011). Science and alcohol policy: A case study of the EU strategy on alcohol. *Addiction (Abingdon, England)*, *106*(1), 55–66. PMID:21324022

Andreoli, T. P., & Borges, W. A. (2007). Empreendedorismo Feminino: Uma Análise do Perfil Empreendedor e das Dificuldades Enfrentadas por Mulheres Detentoras de Um Pequeno Negócio. Presented paper at the XI EPEAD – Encontro Paranaense dos Estudantes de Administração, Paraná.

Angelidou, M. (2014). Smart city policies: A spatial approach. *Cities (London, England)*, *41*, S3–S11. doi:10.1016/j.cities.2014.06.007

Ansari, A., & Mela, C. F. (2003). E-customization. *JMR, Journal of Marketing Research*, *40*(2), 131–145. doi:10.1509/jmkr.40.2.131.19224

Apergis, N., & Economou, V. P. (2010). Incentives and female entrepreneurial activity: Evidence from panel firm level data. *International Advances in Economic Research, 16*(4), 371–387. doi:10.100711294-010-9277-9

APME – Associação Portuguesa de Mulheres Empresárias. (2017). *A APME e o empreendedorismo*. Lisboa: Author.

Araújo, C. A. (2006). Bibliometria: Evolução histórica e questões atuais. Em Questão, 12(1), 11–32.

ATP. (2014). *Plano Estratégico Têxtil 2020 – Projetar o Desenvolvimento da Fileira Têxtil e Vestuário até 2020*. ATP.

Audretsch, D. B. (2012). Entrepreneurship research. *Management Decision, 50*(5), 755–764. doi:10.1108/00251741211227384

Avnimelech, G., & Harel, S. (2012). Global venture capital 'hotspots': Israel. In Handbook of Research on Venture Capital: Volume 2: A Globalizing Industry (pp. 209-226). Cheltenham, UK: Edward Elgar Publishing.

Avnimelech, G., & Teubal, M. (2004). Venture capital start-up co-evolution and the emergence & development of Israel's new high tech cluster. *Economics of Innovation and New Technology, 13*(1), 33–60. doi:10.1080/1043859042000156020

Axelson, U., & Martinovic, M. (2013). *European venture capital: Myths and facts*. Retrieved October 6, 2014, from http://www.bvca.co.uk/Portals/0/library/Files/News/2013/European_MandF_Report_21Jan13.pdf

Axelsson, B., & Easton, G. (Eds.). (1992). *Industrial networks: A new view of reality*. London: Routledge.

Azeez, A. E. (2014). Revisiting the prospects of social entrepreneurship on social development: An analysis. *Quest Journal of Management & Research, 5*(1). Retrieved from https://www.researchgate.net/publication/308803998

Ball, E., Chiu, H. H., & Smith, R. (2011). Can the VCF time the market? An analysis of exit choice for venture-backed firms. *Review of Financial Studies, 24*(9), 3105–3138. doi:10.1093/rfs/hhr042

Bandura, A. (1998). Exploration of Fortuitous Determinants of Life Paths. *Psychological Inquiry, 9*(2), 95–99. doi:10.120715327965pli0902_2

Barnes, D., Clear, F., Dyerson, R., Harindranath, G., Harris, L., & Rae, A. (2012). Web 2.0 and microbusinesses: An exploratory investigation. *Journal of Small Business and Enterprise Development*, *19*(4), 687–711. doi:10.1108/14626001211277479

Barney, J. B., & Hesterly, W. S. (2015). *Strategic management & competitive advantage: concepts and cases* (5th ed.). Essex, UK: Pearson Education Limited.

Baronchelli, G., & Cassia, F. (2014). Exploring the antecedents of born-global companies' international development. *The International Entrepreneurship and Management Journal*, *10*(1), 67–79. doi:10.100711365-011-0197-9

Barreto, I. (2010). Dynamic Capabilities: A Review of Past Research and an Agenda for the Future. *Journal of Management*, *36*(1), 256–280. doi:10.1177/0149206309350776

Bartlett, D., & Dibben, P. (2002). Public Sector Innovation and Entrepreneurship: Case Studies from Local Government. *Local Government Studies*, *28*(4), 107–121. doi:10.1080/714004159

Bastian, B. L., Sidani, Y. M., & El Amine, Y. (2018). Women entrepreneurship in the Middle East and North Africa: A review of knowledge areas and research gaps. *Gender in Management*, *33*(1), 14–29. doi:10.1108/GM-07-2016-0141

Bayagan, G. (2000), Women Entrepreneurs in SMEs: realizing the benefits of globalization and the knowledge – based Economy. *OECD, Workshop 4: Improving knowledge about women's entrepreneurship.*

Bean, A. S., Schiffel, D. D., & Mogee, M. E. (1975). The venture capital market and technological innovation. *Research Policy*, *4*(4), 380–408. doi:10.1016/0048-7333(75)90003-7

Beckham, C. M., Burton, M. D., & O'Reilly, C. (2007). Early teams: The impact of team demography on VC financing and going public. *Journal of Business Venturing*, *22*(2), 147–173. doi:10.1016/j.jbusvent.2006.02.001

Beck, T., Demirguc-Kunt, A., & Maksimovic, V. (2005). Financial and legal constraints to growth: Does firm size matter? *The Journal of Finance*, *LX*(1), 137–177. doi:10.1111/j.1540-6261.2005.00727.x

Bekkers, V., & Tummers, L. (2018). Innovation in the public sector: Towards an open and collaborative approach. *International Review of Administrative Sciences*, *84*(2), 209–213. doi:10.1177/0020852318761797

Bell, J., McNaughton, R., & Young, S. (2001). Born-again global' firms: An extension to the 'born global' phenomenon. *Journal of International Management*, *7*(3), 173–189. doi:10.1016/S1075-4253(01)00043-6

Bernardino, S., Freitas Santos, J., & Fagundes, S. (2017). Papel do capital social no desenvolvimento de iniciativas sociais. *European Journal of Applied Business and Management*, 91-108.

Bernier, L., & Hafsi, T. (2007, May). The changing nature of public entrepreneurship. *Public Administration Review*.

Bilance. (1997, September). A world in balance – Bilance stands for Social Development: Policy paper. *Oegstgeest*.

Birley, S. (1985). The role of networks in the entrepreneurial process. *Journal of Business Venturing*, *1*(1), 107–117. doi:10.1016/0883-9026(85)90010-2

Birley, S., & Mac Millan, I. C. (Eds.). (1997). *Entrepreneurship in a global context*. London: Routledge. doi:10.4324/9780203435168

BIS. (2012) *SME access to external finance*. BIS Economics Paper Number 16, Department for Business, Innovation & Skills. Retrieved July 17, 2014, from https://www.gov.uk/government/uploads/system/uploads/attachment_data/file/32263/12-539-sme-access-external-finance.pdf

Bjørnskov, C., & Foss, N. J. (2008). Economic freedom and entrepreneurial activity: Some cross-country evidence. *Public Choice*, *134*(3–4), 307–328. doi:10.100711127-007-9229-y

Black, B. S., & Gibson, R. J. (1998). Venture capital and the structure of capital markets: Banks versus stock markets. *Journal of Financial Economics*, *47*(3), 243–277. doi:10.1016/S0304-405X(97)00045-7

Blackburn, R. A., Hart, M., & Wainwright, T. (2013). Small business performance: Business, strategy and owner-manager characteristics. *Journal of Small Business and Enterprise Development*, *20*(1), 8–11. doi:10.1108/14626001311298394

Blank, S. (2010). *Entrepreneurship-Steve Blank*. Retrieved from Obtenido de Entrepreneurship-Steve Blank: https://steveblank.com/2010/01/25/whats-a-startup-first-principles/

Bocken, N. M. P. (2015). Sustainable venture capital – catalyst for sustainable start-up success? *Journal of Cleaner Production*, *108*(A), 647-658.

Bose, M., & Godói-de-Sousa, E. (2012). Empreendedorismo social e desenvolvimento social: Desafios e oportunidades. In ENANPEGS, VI. São Paulo: Gestão Social, Políticas Públicas e Território.

Boszczowski, A. K., & Teixeira, R. (2012). O empreendedorismo sustentável e o processo empreendedor: em busca de oportunidades de novos negócios como solução para problemas sociais e ambientais. In *Encontro Nacional da Associação Nacional de Pós-Graduação e Pesquisa em Administração*. São Paulo: Anais.

Bottazzi, L., Da Rin, M., & Hellmann, T. (2008). Who are the active investors?: Evidence from venture capital. *Journal of Financial Economics*, *89*(3), 488–512. doi:10.1016/j.jfineco.2007.09.003

Bowden, R. J. (1994). Bargaining, size, and return in venture capital funds. *Journal of Business Venturing*, *9*(4), 307–330. doi:10.1016/0883-9026(94)90010-8

Boyne, S., & Hall, D. (2004). Place promotion through food and tourism: Rural branding and the role of websites. *Place Branding*, *1*(1), 80–92. doi:10.1057/palgrave.pb.5990007

Brady, M., Fellenz, M. R., & Brookes, R. (2008). Researching the role of information and communications technology (ICT) in contemporary marketing practices. *Journal of Business and Industrial Marketing*, *23*(2), 108–114. doi:10.1108/08858620810850227

Bright, J. E. H., Pryor, R. G. L., & Harpham, L. (2005). The role of chance events in career decision making. *Journal of Vocational Behavior*, *66*(3), 561–578. doi:10.1016/j.jvb.2004.05.001

Brush, C., Edelman, L. F., Manolova, T., & Welter, F. (2018). A gendered look at entrepreneurship ecosystems. *Small Business Economics*, 1–16. doi:10.100711187-018-9992-9

Bryla, P. (2015). The role of appeals to tradition in origin food marketing. A survey among Polish consumers. *Appetite*, *91*(1), 302–310. doi:10.1016/j.appet.2015.04.056 PMID:25916623

Bulearca, M., & Bulearca, S. (2010). Twitter: A viable marketing tool for SMEs? *Global Business & Management Research*, *2*(4), 296–309.

Burt, R. S. (1993). The social structure of competition. In N. Nohria & R. G. Eccles (Eds.), Networks and Organizations (pp. 57-91). Cambridge, MA: Harvard Business School Press.

Buttner, E. H. (2001). Examining female entrepreneur management styles: An Analysis Using a Relational Frame. *Journal of Business Ethics*, *29*(3), 253–269. doi:10.1023/A:1026460615436

BVCA. (2010). *A guide to private equity*. Retrieved March 27, 2014, from http://www.bvca.co.uk/researchpublications/bvcaguidetoprivateequity.aspx

BVCA. (2013). *BVCA private equity and venture capital report on investment activity 2012*. Retrieved March 27, 2014, from http://www.bvca.co.uk/Portals/0/library/Files/News/2013/RIA_2012.pdf

Bygrave, W. D. (1993). Theory Building in the Entrepreneurship Paradigm. *Journal of Business Venturing*, *8*(3), 255–280. doi:10.1016/0883-9026(93)90031-Y

Campbell, H., & Marshall, R. (2002). Utilitarianism's Bad Breath? A Re-evaluation of the Public Interest Justification for Planning. *Planning Theory*, *1*(2), 165–189. doi:10.1177/147309520200100205

Camps, D., Recuero, Y., Samar, M. E., & Ávila, R. (2005). Análisis bibliométrico de tesis de doctorado del área de las ciencias de la salud: Primera parte, Odontología. *Revista de la Facultad de Ciencias Medicas de la Universidad Nacional de Cordoba*, *62*, 53–56.

Carlsson, B., Braunerhjelm, P., McKelvey, M., Olofsson, C., Persson, L., & Ylinenpää, H. (2013). The evolving domain of entrepreneurship research. *Small Business Economics*, *41*(4), 913–930. doi:10.1007/s11187-013-9503-y

Carmines, E. G., & Zeller, R. A. (1979). *Reliability and Validity Assessment*. Newbury Park, CA: Sage Publications. doi:10.4135/9781412985642

Carpintério, J. N. C., & Bacic, M. J. (2001). Empreendedorismo e desenvolvimento. In *World Conference no Business Incubation, outubro*, Rio de Janeiro, Brazil.

Carree, M. A., & Thurik, A. R. (2010). The impact of entrepreneurship on economic growth. In Z. J. Acs & D. B. Audretsch (Eds.), *Handbook of entrepreneurship research: An interdisciplinary survey and introduction* (2nd ed.; pp. 557–594). Springer-Verlag New York. doi:10.1007/978-1-4419-1191-9_20

Caruana, A., Ewing, M. T., & Ramaseshan, B. (2002). Effects of some environmental challenges and centralization on the entrepreneurial orientation and performance of public sector entities. *The Service Industries Management Journal*, *22*(2), 43–58. doi:10.1080/714005076

Casero, J. C. D., Urbano, D., & Mogollón, R. H. (2005). Teoría económica institucional y creación de empresas. *Revista Investigaciones Europeas de Dirección y Economía de la Empresa*, *11*(3), 209–230.

Casson, M. (1990). *Enterprise and Competitiveness: A System View of Inernational Business*. Oxford University Press.

Cavusgil, S. T., & Knight, G. (2009). *Born global firms: A new international enterprise*. New York: Business Expert Press. doi:10.4128/9781606490136

Célestin, J.-B. (2002). *A Qualidade de Emprego. Direcção-Geral do Emprego e Formação Profissional*. Lisboa: DGEFP.

Cepeda, C. G., & Roldán, S. J. L. (2004). Aplicando la Técnica PLS en la Administración de Empresas. Conocimiento y Competitividad. Congreso ACEDE, 14, 74-78.

Cesinger, B., Danko, A., & Bouncken, R. (2012). Born globals: (almost) 20 years of research and still not 'grown up'? *International Journal of Entrepreneurship and Small Business*, *15*(2), 171–190. doi:10.1504/IJESB.2012.045203

Chaffey, D. (2015). *Digital business and E-commerce management*. Pearson Education Limited.

Chell, E. (2007). Social enterprise and entrepreneurship: Towards a convergent theory of the entrepreneurial process. *International Small Business Journal*, *25*(1), 3–19. doi:10.1177/0266242607071779

Chen, H., Gompers, P., Kovner, A., & Lerner, J. (2010). Buy local? The geography of venture capital. *Journal of Urban Economics*, *67*(1), 90–102. doi:10.1016/j.jue.2009.09.013

Chin, W. W. (1998). The Partial Least Squares Approach to Structural Equation Modeling. Lawrence Erlbaum Associates.

Chin, W. W. (2010). How to write up and report PLS analyses. In V. Esposito Vinzi, W. W. Chin, J. Henseler, & H. Wang (Eds.), *Handbook of partial least squares: Concepts, methods and applications* (pp. 655–690). Berlin, Germany: Springer-Verlag. doi:10.1007/978-3-540-32827-8_29

Chin, W. W., & Newsted, P. R. (1999). Structural Equation Modeling Analysis with Small Samples Using Partial Least Squares. In R. Hoyle (Ed.), *Statistical Strategies for Small Sample Research* (pp. 307–341). Thousand Oaks, CA: Sage Publications.

Cho, A. H. (2006). Politics, values and social entrepreneurship: a critical appraisal. In J. Mair, J. Robinson, & K. Kockerts (Eds.), *Social entrepreneurship* (pp. 34–56). New York: Palgrave Macmillan. doi:10.1057/9780230625655_4

Cloutier, L., Bernard, P., & Tremblay, D. G. (2009). Job quality and gender inequality: Key changes in Québec over the last decade. *Studies in Social Justice*, *3*(2), 191–212. doi:10.26522sj.v3i2.1015

Cohen, B. (2006). Sustainable valley entrepreneurial ecosystems. *Business Strategy & The Environment*, *15*(1), 1-14. doi:10.1002/bse.428

Cohen, B., & Winn, M. I. (2007). Market imperfections, opportunity and sustainable entrepreneurship. *Journal of Business Venturing*, *22*(1), 29–49. doi:10.1016/j.jbusvent.2004.12.001

Cohen, L., Manion, L., & Morrison, K. (2011). *Research Methods in Education* (7th ed.). Routledge.

Comini, G., Barki, E., & Aguiar, L. T. (2012). A three-pronged approach to social business: A Brazilian multi-case analysis. *Revista ADM*, *47*(3), 385–397. doi:10.5700/rausp1045

Constanzo, L., Vurro, C., Foster, D., Servato, F., & Perrini, F. (2014). Dual-Mission Management in Social Entrepreneurship: Qualitative Evidence from Social Firms in the United Kingdom. *Journal of Small Business Management*, *52*(4), 655–677. doi:10.1111/jsbm.12128

Corbin, J., & Strauss, A. (2015). *Basics of Qualitative Research Techniques and Procedures for Developing Grounded Theory* (4th ed.). SAGE Publications, Inc.

Cornelius, B. (2005). The institutionalisation of venture capital. *Technovation*, *25*(6), 599–608. doi:10.1016/j.technovation.2003.12.001

Corrall, S., Kennan, M. A., & Afzal, W. (2013). Bibliometrics and Research Data Management Services: Emerging Trends in Library Support for Research. *Library Trends*, *61*(3), 636–674. doi:10.1353/lib.2013.0005

Correia, M. J., & Rua, O. L. (2016). Innovation in the Portuguese health sector organizations: Empirical evidence from the Community Innovation Survey. *Tékhne - Review of Applied Management Studies*, *14*, 2-9.

Coviello, N. (2015). Re-thinking research on born globals. *Journal of International Business Studies*, *46*(1), 17–26. doi:10.1057/jibs.2014.59

Covin, J., & Slevin, D. (1989). Strategic management of small firms in hostile and benign environments. *Strategic Management Journal*, *10*(1), 75–87. doi:10.1002mj.4250100107

Covin, J., & Slevin, D. (1991). A conceptual model of entrepreneurship as firm behavior. *Entrepreneurship Theory and Practice*, *16*(1), 7–25. doi:10.1177/104225879101600102

CPI. (2016). *Enter the public entrepreneur: Implementing innovation in the public sector*. Briefing Bulletin. Retrieved from: https://www.centreforpublicimpact.org/public-entrepreneurship-briefing-bulletin/

Creswell, J. W. (2013). *Research Design: Qualitative, Quantitative, and Mixed Methods Approaches* (4th ed.). SAGE Publications, Inc.

Crick, D., & Spence, M. (2005). The internationalisation of "high performing" UK high-tech SMEs: A study of planned and unplanned strategies. *International Business Review*, *14*(2), 167–185. doi:10.1016/j.ibusrev.2004.04.007

Cumming, D. J., & MacIntosh, J. G. (2003). A cross-country comparison of full and partial venture capital exits. *Journal of Banking & Finance*, *27*(3), 511–548. doi:10.1016/S0378-4266(02)00389-8

Cumming, D., & Dai, N. (2010). Local bias in venture capital investments. *Journal of Empirical Finance*, *17*(3), 362–380. doi:10.1016/j.jempfin.2009.11.001

Cumming, D., & Dai, N. (2011). Fund size, limited attention and valuation of venture capital backed firms. *Journal of Empirical Finance*, *18*(1), 2–15. doi:10.1016/j.jempfin.2010.09.002

Cumming, D., Fleming, G., & Schwienbacher, A. (2006). Legality and venture capital exits. *Journal of Corporate Finance*, *12*(2), 214–245. doi:10.1016/j.jcorpfin.2004.12.004

Cumming, D., Henriques, I., & Sadorsky, P. (2016). 'Cleantech' venture capital around the world. *International Review of Financial Analysis*, *44*, 86–97. doi:10.1016/j.irfa.2016.01.015

Cumming, D., Schmidt, D., & Walz, U. (2010). Legality and venture capital governance around the world. *Journal of Business Venturing*, *25*(1), 54–72. doi:10.1016/j.jbusvent.2008.07.001

Dangmei, J. (2016). Social entrepreneurship and social networks for sustainable rural development in India. *Paripex – Indian Journal of Research*, *5*(10), 622-624.

Danik, L., & Kowalik, I. (2015). Success factors and development barriers perceived by the Polish born global companies. Empirical study results. *Journal for East European Management Studies*, *20*(3), 360–390. doi:10.5771/0949-6181-2015-3-360

Davis, J. L., Bell, R. G., Payne, G. T., & Kreiser, P. M. (2010). Entrepreneurial Orientation and Firm Performance: The Moderating Role of Managerial Power. *American Journal of Business*, *25*(2), 41–54. doi:10.1108/19355181201000009

De Bettignies, J., & Brander, J. A. (2007). Financing entrepreneurship: Bank finance versus venture capital. *Journal of Business Venturing*, *22*(6), 808–832. doi:10.1016/j.jbusvent.2006.07.005

de Rond, M. (2014). The structure of serendipity. *Culture and Organization*, *20*(5), 342–358. doi:10.1080/14759551.2014.967451

Dees, J. G. (1998). *The meaning of social entrepreneurship* (Working paper). Kauffman Center for Entrepreneurial Leadership.

Dees, J. (1998). Enterprising nonprofits: What do you do when traditional sources of funding fall short? *Harvard Business Review*, *76*(1), 55–67. PMID:10176919

Dees, J. G. (2001). *The meaning of "social entrepreneurship." Center for the advancement of Social Entrepreneurship*. Durham, NC: Fuqua School of Business, Duke University. Retrieved from http://www.fuqua.duke.edu/centers/case/documents/dees_SE.pdf

della Porta, D., & Keating, M. (Eds.). (2008). *Approaches and Methodologies in the Social Sciences - A Pluralist Perspective*. Cambridge, UK: Cambridge University Press. doi:10.1017/CBO9780511801938

Delors, J. (1996). *Educação, um tesouro a descobrir: Relatório para a UNESCO da Comissão Internacional sobre Educação para o século XXI*. São Paulo: Cortez.

Demo, P. (1995). *Metodologia Científica em Ciências Sociais*. São Paulo: Editora Atlas.

Denis, D. J. (2004). Entrepreneurial finance: An overview of the issues and evidence. *Journal of Corporate Finance*, *10*(2), 301–326. doi:10.1016/S0929-1199(03)00059-2

Dess, G., & Lumpkin, G. (2005). The role of entrepreneurial orientation in stimulating effective corporate entrepreneurship. *The Academy of Management Executive*, *19*(1), 147–156.

Devigne, D., Manigart, S., & Wright, M. (2016). Escalation of commitment in venture capital decision making: Differentiating between domestic and international investors. *Journal of Business Venturing*, *31*(3), 253–271. doi:10.1016/j.jbusvent.2016.01.001

Dew, N. (2009). Serendipity in Entrepreneurship. *Organization Studies*, *30*(7), 735–753. doi:10.1177/0170840609104815

Dhliwayo, S. (2017). *Defining public-sector entrepreneurship. A conceptual operational construct*. University of Johannesbourg. Retrieved from http://hdl.handle.net/10210/241340

Di Domenico, M., Haugh, H., & Tracey, P. (2010). Social bricolage: Theorizing social value creation in social enterprises. *Entrepreneurship Theory and Practice*, *34*(4), 681–703. doi:10.1111/j.1540-6520.2010.00370.x

Diario Ofiial de la Federación. (1976). *Ley General de Asentamientos Humanos*. Author.

Diáz-Garcia, M. C., & Jiménez-Moren, J. (2010). Entrepreneurial intention: The role of gender. *The International Entrepreneurship and Management Journal*, *6*(3), 261–283. doi:10.100711365-008-0103-2

Diefenbach, F. E. (2011). *Entrepreneurship in the Public Sector: When Middle Managers Create Public Value* (Dostoral Dissertation). Gabler Research, Gabler Verlag Wiesbaden. Retrieved from: http://www1.unisg.ch/www/edis.nsf/SysLkpByIdentifier/3883/$FILE/dis3883.pdf

Dimov, D. (2007). Beyond the Single-Person, Single-Insight Atribution in Understanding Entrepreneurial Opportunities. *Entrepreneurship Theory & Practice*, (860), 713–732.

Dossani, R., & Kenney, M. (2002). Creating an environment for venture capital in India. *World Development*, *30*(2), 227–253. doi:10.1016/S0305-750X(01)00110-3

Dowla, A. U. (2011). *How Entrepreneurs use Social Networks in their Business* (Master's thesis). Swedish University of Agricultural Sciences.

Downs, G. W. Jr, & Mohr, L. B. (1976). Conceptual issues in the study of innovation. *Administrative Science Quarterly*, *21*(4), 700–714. doi:10.2307/2391725

Drucker, P. (1998). *Desafios gerenciais para o século XXI*. São Paulo: Pioneira.

Durant, R. (2002). Synchronicity: A post-structuralist guide to creativity and change. *Journal of Organizational Change Management*, *15*(5), 490–501. doi:10.1108/09534810210440351

Durkin, M., McGowan, P., & McKeown, N. (2013). Exploring social media adoption in small to medium-sized enterprises in Ireland. *Journal of Small Business and Enterprise Development*, *20*(4), 716–734. doi:10.1108/JSBED-08-2012-0094

Dutz, M. A., Ordover, J. A., & Willig, R. D. (2000). Entrepreneurship, access policy and economic development: Lessons from industrial organization. *European Economic Review*, *44*(4-6), 739–747. doi:10.1016/S0014-2921(00)00030-1

Eagly, A. (1987). *Sex differences in behavior: A social-role interpretation*. Hillsdale, NJ: Academic Press.

Edwards, R., & Holland, J. (2013). *What is Qualitative Interviewing*? New York: Bloombury.

Edwards, C., Jones, G., Lawton, A., & Llewellyn, N. (2002). Public entrepreneurship: Rhetoric, reality, and context. *International Journal of Public Administration*, *25*(12), 1539–1554. doi:10.1081/PAD-120014260

Elango, B., Fried, V. H., Hisrich, R. D., & Polonchek, A. (1995). How venture capital firms differ. *Journal of Business Venturing*, *10*(2), 157–179. doi:10.1016/0883-9026(94)00019-Q

Elitzur, R., & Gavious, A. (2011). Selection of entrepreneurs in the venture capital industry: An asymptotic analysis. *European Journal of Operational Research*, *215*(3), 705–712. doi:10.1016/j.ejor.2011.06.029

Elkington, J., & Hartigan, P. (2008). *The power of unreasonable people: How social entrepreneurs create markets that change the world*. Boston: Harvard Business School Publishing.

European Integration Office. (2011). *Guide to the logical framework approach*. Republic of Serbia Government European Integration Office. Available: http://www.evropa.gov.rs/Evropa/ShowDocument.aspx?Type=Home&Id=525

EVCA. (2012). *The little book of private equity*. Retrieved March 27, 2014, from https://www.evca.eu/media/19732/Little-book-of-Private-Equity.pdf

Evers, N. (2011). International new ventures in "low tech" sectors: A dynamic capabilities perspective. *Journal of Small Business and Enterprise Development, 18*(3), 502–528. doi:10.1108/14626001111155682

Ewens, M., Nanda, R., & Rhodes-Kropf, M. (2018). Cost of experimentation and the evolution of venture capital. *Journal of Financial Economics, 128*(3), 422–442. doi:10.1016/j.jfineco.2018.03.001

Faludi, A. (1973). *Planning Theory*. Pergamon.

Faria, A. P., & Barbosa, N. (2014). Does venture capital really foster innovation? *Economics Letters, 122*(2), 129–131. doi:10.1016/j.econlet.2013.11.014

Faria, P. M. O., Leal, E. A., Soares, M. A., & Godoi-de-Sousa, E. (2013). Pesquisa em Contabilidade Gerencial no Brasil: um estudo bibliométrico de 2002 a 2012 nos principais periódicos nacionais. In *Congresso Brasileiro de Custos, 20, Uberlândia. Anais*. São Leopoldo: Associação Brasileira de Custos.

Florida, R. L., & Kenney, M. (1988). Venture capital, high technology and regional development. *Regional Studies, 22*(1), 33–48. doi:10.1080/00343408812331344750

Florin, J. (2005). Is venture capital worth it? Effects on firm performance and founder returns. *Journal of Business Venturing, 20*(1), 113–135. doi:10.1016/j.jbusvent.2003.12.006

Fontana, A., & Frey, J. H. (1994). Interviewing: The art of science. In N. K. Denzin & Y. S. Lincoln (Eds.), *Handbook of Qualitative Research* (pp. 361–376). Thousand Oaks, CA: Sage Publications.

Fornell, C., & Larcker, D. F. (1981). Evaluating structural equation models with unobservable variables and measurement error. *JMR, Journal of Marketing Research, 18*(1), 39–50. doi:10.2307/3151312

Fornoni, M., Arribas, I., & Vila, J. (2012). An entrepreneur's social capital and performance: The role of access to information in the Argentinean case. *Journal of Organizational Change Management*, *25*(5), 682–698. doi:10.1108/09534811211254572

Fossen, F. M. (2011). Gender differences in entrepreneurial choice and risk aversion – a decomposition based on a microeconometric model. *Applied Economics*, *44*(14), 1795–1812. doi:10.1080/00036846.2011.554377

França, A., Vilares, A., Frankenbach, S., Vereb, V., & Moreira, A. C. (2017). The Challenging Dynamics of Nascent Entrepreneurship. In A. Moreira, J. Dantas, & F. Valente (Eds.), *Nascent Entrepreneurship and Successful New Venture Creation*. IGI Global. doi:10.4018/978-1-5225-2936-1

Frank, H., Kessler, A., & Fink, M. (2010, April). Entrepreneurial orientation and business performance-a replication study. *Schmalenbach Business Review*, 175–199.

Franke, N., Gruber, M., Harhoff, D., & Henkel, J. (2006). What you are is what you like – similarity biases in venture capitalists' evaluations of start-up teams. *Journal of Business Venturing*, *21*(6), 802–826. doi:10.1016/j.jbusvent.2005.07.001

Fraser, S. (2008). *Small firms in the credit crisis: Evidence from the UK survey of SME finances*. Warwick, UK: The University of Warwick.

Freeman, S., & Cavusgil, S. T. (2007). Toward a typology of commitment states among managers of born-global firms: A study of accelerated internationalization. *Journal of International Marketing*, *15*(4), 1–40. doi:10.1509/jimk.15.4.1

Freire, D. A., Corrêa, R., & Ribeiro, H. C. (2011). *Género e empreendedorismo: um olhar sobre a pesquisa do G.E.M. – Global Entrepreneurship Monitor*. Empreendedorismo e Inovação.

Fried, V. H., & Hisrich, R. D. (1994). Toward a model of venture capital investment decision making. *Financial Management*, *23*(3), 28–37. doi:10.2307/3665619

Fuentes, C., & Cervera, L. (2004). La gestión del suelo urbano en Ciudad Juárez, Chihuahua: La difícil transición de la gobernabilidad autoritaria a la gobernabilidad democrática. In Gobernabilidad o ingobernabilidad en la región Paso del Norte. Ciudad Juárez, Mexico: EON, UACJ and COLEF.

Fuentes, C. (2009). La planeación estratégica como instrumento de un nuevo modelo de gestión del desarrollo urbano en Ciudad Juárez: Retos y oportunidades. In J. M. Ramos & I. Aguilar (Eds.), *La gestión del desarrollo local en México: Problemas y agenda*. Miguel Ángel Porrúa and El Colegio de la Frontera Norte.

Gabrielsson, M., Kirpalani, V., Dimitratos, P., Solberg, C., & Zucchella, A. (2008). Born globals: Propositions to help advance the theory. *International Business Review*, *17*(4), 385–401. doi:10.1016/j.ibusrev.2008.02.015

Gabriel, Y., Muhr, S. L., & Linstead, S. (2014). Luck of the draw? Serendipity, accident, chance and misfortune in organization and design. *Culture and Organization*, *20*(5), 334–341. doi:10.1080/14759551.2014.967452

Galaskiewicz, J., Bielefeld, W., & Dowell, M. (2006). Networks and organizational growth: A study of community based nonprofits. *Administrative Science Quarterly*, *51*(3), 337–380. doi:10.2189/asqu.51.3.337

Gallegos, R. (2015). *Los Emprendedores de TIC en México*. IMCO.

Ganitsky, J. (1989). Strategies for innate and adoptive exporters: Lessons from Israel's case. *International Marketing Review*, *6*(5), 50–65. doi:10.1108/EUM0000000001523

Garousi, V. (2015). A bibliometric analysis of the Turkish software engineering research community. *Scientometrics*, *105*(1), 23–49. doi:10.100711192-015-1663-x

Gatchev, V. A., Spindt, P. A., & Tarhan, V. (2009). How do firms finance their investments?: The relative importance of equity issuance and debt contracting costs. *Journal of Corporate Finance*, *15*(2), 179–195. doi:10.1016/j.jcorpfin.2008.11.001

Ge, B., Hisrich, R., & Dong, B. (2009). Networking, resource acquisition, and the performance of small and medium-sized enterprises; An empirical study of three major cities in China. *Managing Global Transitions*, *7*(3), 221–239.

Gefen, D., & Straub, D. (2005). A Practical Guide To Factorial Validity Using PLS-Graph: Tutorial And Annotated Example. *Communications of the Association for Information Systems*, *16*, 91–109.

GEM. (2007). *Avaliação do potencial empreendedor em Portugal*. The Global Entrepreneurship Monitor, Project GEM Portugal.

GEM. (2008). *Global Entrepreneurship Monitor (GEM)*. Executive Report.

GEM. (2012). *Um estudo sobre o Empreendedorismo*. The Global Entrepreneurship Monitor, Project GEM Portugal.

GEM. (2016). *Global Entrepreneurship Monitor (GEM)*. Executive Report.

GEM. (2017). *Global Entrepreneurship Monitor 2016/2017 – Report on Women's Entrepreneurship*.

GEM. (2018). *Global Entrepreneurship Monitor (GEM)*. Global Report 2017/18.

Gerhardt, T., & Silveira, D. (2009). *Métodos de Pesquisa*. Porto Alegre: Editora da UFRGS.

Gifford, S. (1997). Limited attention and the role of the venture capitalist. *Journal of Business Venturing*, *12*(6), 459–482. doi:10.1016/S0883-9026(96)00130-9

Gilmore, A., Carson, D., & Grant, K. (2001). SME marketing in practice. *Marketing Intelligence & Planning, Bradford*, *19*(1), 6–11. doi:10.1108/02634500110363583

Gil-Pechuan, I., Exposito-Langa, M., & Tomas-Miquel, J. V. (2013). International entrepreneurship in SMEs: A study of influencing factors in the textile industry. *The International Entrepreneurship and Management Journal*, *9*(1), 45–57. doi:10.100711365-012-0242-3

Girardet, H. (1999). *Creating sustainable cities*. Green Books for the Schumacher Society.

Glaser, B. G., & Strauss, A. L. (1967). *The discovery of grounded theory*. AldineTransaction, A Division of Transaction Publishers.

Gnyawali, D., & Fogel, D. (1994). Environments for entrepreneurship development: Key dimensions and research implications. *Entrepreneurship Theory and Practice*, *18*(4), 43–62. doi:10.1177/104225879401800403

Gobierno Federal. (2013). Plan Nacional de Desarrollo.

Gomes, A. F., Santana, W. G., Antonialli, L. M., & Correia, E. L. (2009). Trajetórias e estratégias de mulheres: Um estudo conquistense. *Revista de Gestão USP*, *16*(1), 69–87. doi:10.5700/rege359

Gompers, P. A., Kovner, A., Lerner, J., & Scharfstein, D. S. (2006). Skill vs. luck in entrepreneurship and venture capital: Evidence from serial entrepreneurs. *Social Science Research Network –NBER Working Paper Series, 12592*, 1–28.

Gompers, P. A. (1995). Optimal investment, monitoring, and the staging of venture capital. *The Journal of Finance, 50*(5), 1461–1489. doi:10.1111/j.1540-6261.1995.tb05185.x

Gompers, P. A., & Lerner, J. (2001). The venture capital revolution. *The Journal of Economic Perspectives, 15*(2), 145–168. doi:10.1257/jep.15.2.145

Goodman, D. (2003). The quality 'turn' and alternative food practices: Reflections and agenda. *Journal of Rural Studies, 19*(1), 1–7. doi:10.1016/S0743-0167(02)00043-8

Gordon, J. (2014). A stage model of venture philanthropy. *Venture Capital: An International Journal of Entrepreneurial Finance, 16*(2), 85–107. doi:10.1080/13691066.2014.897014

Gosselin, L. H., & Grisé, J. (1990). Are women owner-managers challenging our definitions of entrepreneurship? An in-depth survey. *Journal of Business Ethics, 9*(4/5), 423–433. doi:10.1007/BF00380341

Gouveia, P. (2009). *Municípios, Economia Solidária e Desenvolvimento Local: caminho possível para um "outro" desenvolvimento*. Departamento de Economia do Instituto Universitário de Lisboa, 2009. Retrieved from: https://repositorio.iscte-iul.pt/handle/10071/3718

Graham, C. (2005). Insights on development from the economics of happiness. *The World Bank Research Observer, 20*(2), 201–231. doi:10.1093/wbro/lki010

Granitz, N., & Pitt, L. (2011). Teaching about Marketing and Teaching Marketing with Innovative Technology: Introduction to the Special Edition. Journal of Marketing Education, 33(2), 127-130.

Granovetter, M. (1983). The strength of weak ties: A network theory revisited. *Sociological Theory, 1*, 201–233. doi:10.2307/202051

Granovetter, M. (1985). The strength of weak ties. *American Journal of Sociology, 78*(6), 1360–1380. doi:10.1086/225469

Gray, D. E. (2014). *Doing Research in the Real World* (3rd ed.). SAGE Publications Ltd.

Greene, P. G., Brush, C. G., & Gatewood, E. G. (2007). Perspectives on women entrepreneurs: Past findings and new directions. *Praeger Perspectives on Entrepreneurship, 1*, 181–204.

Greene, P. G., Brush, C. G., Hart, M. M., & Saparito, P. (2001). Patterns of venture capital funding: Is gender a factor? *Venture Capital: An International Journal of Entrepreneurial Finance.*, *3*(1), 63–83. doi:10.1080/13691060118175

Greve, A., & Salaff, J. W. (2003). Social networks and entrepreneurship. *Entrepreneurship Theory and Practice*, *28*(1), 1–22. doi:10.1111/1540-8520.00029

Gries, T., & Naudé, W. (2009). Entrepreneurship and regional economic growth: Towards general theory of start-ups. Innovation. *European Journal of Soil Science*, *22*(3), 309–328. doi:10.1080/13511610903354877

Gummesson, E. (1999). *Qualitative Methods in Management Research* (2nd ed.). SAGE Publications, Inc.

Gummesson, E. (2005). Qualitative research in marketing: Road-map for a wilderness of complexity and unpredictability. *European Journal of Marketing*, *39*(3/4), 309–327. doi:10.1108/03090560510581791

Guo, D., & Jiang, K. (2013). Venture capital investment and the performance of entrepreneurial firms: Evidence from China. *Journal of Corporate Finance*, *22*, 375–395. doi:10.1016/j.jcorpfin.2013.07.001

Gupta, A. K., & Sapienza, H. J. (1992). Determinants of venture capital firms' preferences regarding the industry diversity and geographic scope of their investments. *Journal of Business Venturing*, *7*(2), 347–362. doi:10.1016/0883-9026(92)90012-G

Guvenen, F., Kuruscu, B., & Ozkan, S. (2009). *Tributação de Capital Humano e Desigualdade Salarial: Uma Análise Cross-Country*. National Bureau of Economic Research Working Paper, 15526.

Haguette, T. M. F. (1997). *Metodologias qualitativas na Sociologia*. Petrópolis: Vozes.

Hair, J., Hult, G. T. M., Ringle, C. M., & Sarstedt, M. (2013). *A primer on Partial least Squares Structural Equation Modeling (PLS-SEM)*. SAGE Publications, Inc.

Harrigan, P., Schroeder, A., Qureshi, I., Yulin, F., Ibbotson, P., Ramsey, E., & Meister, D. (2010). Internet technologies, ECRM capabilities, and performance benefits for SMEs: An exploratory study. *International Journal of Electronic Commerce*, *15*(2), 7–46. doi:10.2753/JEC1086-4415150201

Harris, L., & Rae, A. (2009). Social networks: The future of marketing for small business. *The Journal of Business Strategy*, *30*(5), 24–31. doi:10.1108/02756660910987581

Harrison, R. T., & Mason, C. M. (2000). Venture capital market complementarities: The links between business angels and venture capital funds in the United Kingdom. *Venture Capital: An International Journal of Entrepreneurial Finance.*, *2*(3), 223–242. doi:10.1080/13691060050135091

Hart, D. M. (2003). Entrepreneurship policy: what it is and where it came from. In D. M. Hart (Ed.), *The emergence of entrepreneurship policy: governance, start-ups and growth in the US knowledge economy* (p. 3). Cambridge, UK: Cambridge University Press. doi:10.1017/CBO9780511610134.001

Hasan, I., Khurshed, A., Mohamed, A., & Wang, F. (2018). Do venture capital firms benefit from a presence on boards of directors of mature public companies? *Journal of Corporate Finance*, *49*, 125–140. doi:10.1016/j.jcorpfin.2017.04.018

Hege, U., Palomino, F., & Schwienbacher, A. (2009). Venture Capital Performance: The disparity between Europe and the United States. *Finance.*, *30*(1), 1–39.

Heinonen, J. (2001). *Entrepreneurship in public sector organisations*. Turku School of Economics and Business Administration, Small Business Institute, Finland. 2011. Retrieved from: http://citeseerx.ist.psu.edu/viewdoc/summary?doi=10.1.1.199.5050

Hellmann, T. (1998). The allocation of control rights in venture capital contracts. *The Rand Journal of Economics*, *29*(1), 57–76. doi:10.2307/2555816

Hellmann, T., & Puri, M. (2002). Venture capital and the professionalization of start-up firms: Empirical evidence. *The Journal of Finance*, *57*(1), 169–197. doi:10.1111/1540-6261.00419

Henseler, J., Ringle, C. M., & Sinkovics, R. R. (2009). The use of Partial Lesat Squares Path Modeling in international marketing. In R. R. Sinkovics & P. N. Ghauri (Eds.), New Challenges to International Marketing (Advances in International Marketing). Emerald Group Publishing Limited.

Herzog, P., & Yang, S. (2017). *Social networks and charitable giving: Trusting, doing, asking, and alter primacy*. Nonprofit and Voluntary Sector Quartely; doi:10.1177/0899764017746021

Hisrich, R. D., & Jankowicz, A. D. (1990). Intuition in venture capital decisions: An exploratory study using a new technique. *Journal of Business Venturing*, *5*(1), 49–62. doi:10.1016/0883-9026(90)90026-P

Hisrich, R. D., & Peters, M. P. (2004). *Empreendedorismo*. São Paulo: Bookman.

Hitt, M. A., Ireland, R. D., & Hoskisson, R. E. (2017). *Strategic management: competitiveness & globalization, concepts and cases* (12th ed.). Boston: Cengage Learning.

Hoang, H., & Antoncic, B. (2003). Network-based research in entrepreneurship: A critical review. *Journal of Business Venturing*, *18*(2), 165–187. doi:10.1016/S0883-9026(02)00081-2

Hochberg, Y. V., Ljungqvist, A., & Lu, Y. (2010). Networking as a barrier to entry and the competitive supply of venture capital. *The Journal of Finance*, *65*(3), 829–859. doi:10.1111/j.1540-6261.2010.01554.x

Hoskisson, R. E., Covin, J., Volberda, H. W., & Johnson, R. (2011). Revitalizing Entrepreneurship: The Search for New Research Opportunities. *Journal of Management Studies*, *48*(6), 1141–1168. doi:10.1111/j.1467-6486.2010.00997.x

Hung, R., Yang, B., Lien, B., McLean, G. N., & Kuo, Y.-M. (2010). Dynamic capability: Impact of process alignment and organizational learning culture on performance. *Journal of World Business*, *45*(3), 285–294. doi:10.1016/j.jwb.2009.09.003

Hwang, H., & Powell, W. (2004). Institutions and entrepreneurship. *The Handbook of Entrepreneurship*. Retrieved from: https://web.stanford.edu/group/song/papers/HwangPowell.pdf

IDC. (2016). Digital Transformation at Scale. Innovation in a changed world. *Diretions 2016*. Retrieved from http://www.idc.pt/research/reshome.jsp

INE. PORDATA. (2018). *Pequenas e médias empresas em % do total de empresas: total e por dimensão*. Retrieved from https://www.pordata.pt/Portugal/Pequenas+e+m%c3%a9dias+empresas+em+percentagem+do+total+de+empresas+total+e+por+dimens%c3%a3o-2859

Informa D&B (2016). *O empreendedorismo em Portugal* (2nd ed.). Retrieved from http://biblioteca.informadb.pt/files/files/Estudos/SE_Retrato-Empreendedorismo-Portugal.pdf

Instituto Nacional de Estatística - INE. (2013). *Censos 2011*. Lisboa: INE.

Instituto Nacional de Estatística – INE. (2013). *Destaque – Informação à comunicação social. 8 de março: Dia Internacional da Mulher*. Lisboa: INE.

Ireland, R. D., Hitt, M. A., Camp, S. M., & Sexton, D. L. (2001). Integrating entrepreneurship and strategic management actions to create firm wealth. *The Academy of Management Executive*, *15*(1), 49–63.

Isenberg, D. (2013). *The Entrepreneurship Ecosystem Strategy as a New Paradigm for Economic Policy: Principles for Cultivating Entrepreneurship*. Dublin, Ireland: Institute of International European Affairs.

Jackson, W. E. III, Bates, T., & Bradford, W. D. (2012). Does venture capitalist activism improve investment performance? *Journal of Business Venturing*, *27*(3), 342–354. doi:10.1016/j.jbusvent.2011.02.003

Jeng, L. A., & Wells, P. C. (2000). The determinants of venture capital funding: Evidence across countries. *Journal of Corporate Finance*, *6*(3), 241–289. doi:10.1016/S0929-1199(00)00003-1

Jenssen, J. I. (2001). Social networks, resources and entrepreneurship. *International Journal of Entrepreneurship and Innovation*, *2*(2), 103–109. doi:10.5367/000000001101298846

Jenssen, J. I., & Koenig, H. F. (2002). The effect of social networks on resource access and business start-ups. *European Planning Studies*, *10*(8).

Johannisson, B. (1988). Business formation - a network approach. *Scandinavian Journal of Management*, *4*(3), 83–99.

Jonathan, E. G. (2005). Mulheres empreendedoras: Medos, conquistas e qualidade de vida. *Psicologia em Estudo*, *10*(3), 373–382. doi:10.1590/S1413-73722005000300005

Jones, P., Simmons, G., Packham, G., Beynon-Davies, P., & Pickernell, D. (2014). An exploration of the attitudes and strategic responses of sole proprietor micro-enterprises in adopting information and communication technology. *International Small Business Journal*, *32*(3), 285–306. doi:10.1177/0266242612461802

Jung, C. G. (1960). *Synchronicity: An Acausal Connecting Principle. The Collected Works of C.G. Jung* (Vol. 8). Princeton University Press.

Justo, R. (2008). *La influencia del género y entorno familiar en el éxito y fracaso de las iniciativas emprendedoras* (Doctoral dissertation). Universidad Autonoma de Madrid, Spain.

Kang, L., Jiang, Q., & Tan, C. (2017). Remarkable advocates: An investigation of geographic distance and social capital for crowdfunding. *Information & Management*, *54*(3), 336–348. doi:10.1016/j.im.2016.09.001

Kanniainen, V., & Keuschnigg, C. (2004). Start-up investment with scarce venture capital support. *Journal of Banking & Finance*, *28*(8), 1935–1959. doi:10.1016/j.jbankfin.2003.07.005

Karra, N., Philips, N., & Tracey, P. (2008). Building the born global firm developing entrepreneurial capabilities for international new venture success. *Long Range Planning*, *41*(4), 440–459. doi:10.1016/j.lrp.2008.05.002

Kearney, C., Hisrich, R. D., & Roche, F. (2009). Public and private sector entrepreneurship: Similarities, differences or a combination? *Journal of Small Business and Enterprise Development*, *16*(1), 26–46. doi:10.1108/14626000910932863

Kearney, C., & Meynhardt, T. (2016). Directing Corporate Entrepreneurship Strategy in the Public Sector to Public Value: Antecedents, Components, and Outcomes. *International Public Management Journal*, *19*(4), 543–572. doi:10.1080/10967494.2016.1160013

Keuschnigg, C., & Nielsen, S. B. (2003). Tax policy, venture capital, and entrepreneurship. *Journal of Public Economics*, *87*(1), 175–203. doi:10.1016/S0047-2727(01)00170-0

Kim, H., Lee, I., & Lee, C. (2011). Building Web 2.0 enterprises: A study of small and medium enterprises in the United States. *International Small Business Journal*, *31*(2), 156–174. doi:10.1177/0266242611409785

Kim, Y. (2010). Stimulating Entrepreneurial Practices in the Public Sector: The Roles of Organizational Characteristics. *Administration & Society*, *42*(7), 780–814. doi:10.1177/0095399710377432

King, B. L. (2008). Strategizing at leading venture capital firms: Of planning, opportunism and deliberate emergence. *Long Range Planning*, *41*(3), 345–366. doi:10.1016/j.lrp.2008.03.006

Klein, P. G., Mahoney, J. T., McGahan, A. M., & Pitelis, C. N. (2010). Toward a theory of public entrepreneurship. *European Management Review*, *7*(1), 1–15. doi:10.1057/emr.2010.1

Knight, G. (2001). Entrepreneurship and strategy in the international SME. *Journal of International Management*, *7*(3), 155–171. doi:10.1016/S1075-4253(01)00042-4

Knight, G. A., & Cavusgil, S. T. (2004). Innovation, organizational capabilities, and the born-global firm. *Journal of International Business Studies*, *35*(2), 124–141. doi:10.1057/palgrave.jibs.8400071

Knight, G. A., & Liesch, P. W. (2015). Internationalization: From incremental to born global. *Journal of World Business*, *51*(1), 93–102. doi:10.1016/j.jwb.2015.08.011

Kraus, S., Rigtering, J. P. C., Hughes, M., & Hosman, V. (2012). Entrepreneurial orientation and the business performance of SMEs: A quantitative study from the Netherlands. *Review of Managerial Science*, *6*(2), 161–182. doi:10.100711846-011-0062-9

Krebs, V., & Holley, J. (2006). *Building smart communities through network weaving*. Appalachian Center for Economic Networks. Retrieved from: https://www.networkweaver.com/wp-content/uploads/2011/12/BuildingNetworks.pdf

Kuppuswamy, V., & Bayus, B. L. (2014). *Crowdfunding creative ideas: The dynamics of project backers in Kickstarter.* SSRN Working Paper, No. 2234765, Retrieved from ssrn.com/abstract52234765

La Porta, R., Lopez-de-Silanes, F., Shleifer, A., & Vishny, R. (2000). Investor protection and corporate governance. *Journal of Financial Economics*, *58*(1-2), 3–27. doi:10.1016/S0304-405X(00)00065-9

La Porta, R., Lopez-de-Silanes, F., Shleifer, A., & Vishny, R. W. (1998). Law and finance. *Journal of Political Economy*, *106*(6), 1113–1155. doi:10.1086/250042

Lahr, H., & Mina, A. (2016). Venture capital investments and the technological performance of portfolio firms. *Research Policy*, *45*(1), 303–318. doi:10.1016/j.respol.2015.10.001

Laing, A., & Royle, J. (2013). Bookselling online: An examination of consumer behaviour patterns. *Publishing Research Quarterly*, *29*(2), 110–127. doi:10.100712109-013-9318-3

Langowitz, N., & Minniti, M. (2007). The entrepreneurial propensity of women. *Entrepreneurship Theory and Practice*, *31*(3), 341–364. doi:10.1111/j.1540-6520.2007.00177.x

Lan, H., Zhu, Y., Ness, D., Xing, K., & Schneider, K. (2014). The role and characteristics of social entrepreneurs in contemporary rural cooperative development in China: Case studies of rural social entrepreneurship. *Asia Pacific Business Review*, *20*(3), 379–400. doi:10.1080/13602381.2014.929300

Leadbeater, C. (1997). *The rise of the social entrepreneur*. London: Demos.

Lechner, C., & Gudmundsson, S. V. (2014). Entrepreneurial orientation, firm strategy and small firm performance. *International Small Business Journal*, *32*(1), 36–60. doi:10.1177/0266242612455034

Leeflang, P. S., Verhoef, P. C., Dahlström, P., & Freundt, T. (2014). Challenges and solutions for marketing in a digital era. *European Management Journal*, *32*(1), 1–12. doi:10.1016/j.emj.2013.12.001

Lee, H. S. (2017). Peer networks in venture capital. *Journal of Empirical Finance*, *41*, 19–30. doi:10.1016/j.jempfin.2016.12.006

Lehner, O. (2011). The phenomenon of social enterprise in Austria: A triangulated descriptive study. *Journal of Social Entrepreneurship*, *2*(1), 53–78. doi:10.1080/19420676.2011.555775

Lehner, O. M. (2014). The formation and interplay of social capital in crowdfunded social ventures. *Entrepreneurship and Regional Development*, *26*(5-6), 478–499. doi:10.1080/08985626.2014.922623

Leitão, J., & Alves, H. (2016). *Entrepreneurial and innovative practices in Public Institutions. A quality of life approach*. Springer International Publishing. doi:10.1007/978-3-319-32091-5

Leite Filho, G. A. (2008). Padrões de produtividade de autores em periódicos e congressos na área de contabilidade no Brasil: Um estudo bibliométrico. *Revista de Administração Contemporânea, Curitiba*, *12*(2), 533–554. doi:10.1590/S1415-65552008000200011

Lennerfors, T. T., & Rehn, A. (2014). Chance interventions – on bricolage and the state as an entrepreneur in a declining industry. *Culture and Organization*, *20*(5), 377–391. doi:10.1080/14759551.2014.950660

Lerner, J. (2010). The future of public efforts to boost entrepreneurship and venture capital. *Small Business Economics*, *35*(3), 255–264. doi:10.100711187-010-9298-z

Leyden, D. P. (2016). Public-sector entrepreneurship and the creation of a sustainable innovative economy. *Small Business Economics*, *46*(4), 553–564. doi:10.100711187-016-9706-0

Leyden, D. P., & Link, A. N. (2015). *Public Sector Entrepreneurship: U.S. Technology and Innovation Policy*. New York: Oxford University Press. doi:10.1093/acprof:oso/9780199313853.001.0001

Light, P. (2008). *The search for social entrepreneurship*. Washington, DC: Brookings Institution Press.

Limal, F. S., & Santos, A. B. C. (2017). The Characteristics and Challenges of Female Entrepreneurship in the Market. *International Journal of Advances in Management and Economics*, *6*(4), 1–4.

Lindo, M. R., Cardoso, P. M., Rodrigues, M. E., & Wetzel, U. (2007). Vida pessoal e vida profissional: Os desafios de equilíbrio para mulheres empreendedoras do Rio de Janeiro. *Revista de Administração Contemporânia*, *1*(1), 1–15.

Lingelbach, D. (2012). Global venture capital 'hotspots': developing countries. In Handbook of Research on Venture Capital: Volume 2: A Globalizing Industry (pp. 251-282). Edward Elgar Publishing. doi:10.4337/9781781009116.00020

Llewellyn, N., & Jones, G. (2003). Controversies and conceptual development. Examining public entrepreneurship. *Public Management Review*, *5*(2), 245–266. doi:10.1080/1461667032000066426

López-Zafra, E., Garcia-Retamero, R., & Eagly, A. H. (2009). Congruencia del rol de género y aspiraciones de las mujeres a posiciones de liderazgo. *Revista de Psicología Social*, *24*(1), 99–108. doi:10.1174/021347409786923005

Lu, H., & Tan, Y. (2012). Global venture capital 'hotspots': China. In Handbook of Research on Venture Capital: Volume 2: A Globalizing Industry (pp. 227-250). Edward Elgar Publishing.

Luke, B., Verreymme, M.-L., & Kearins, K. (2007). *Measuring the benefits of entrepreneurship at different levels of analysis*. Academic Press.

Lumpkin, G. T., & Dess, G. G. (1996). Clarifying the Entrepreneurial Orientation Construct and Linking it to Performance. *Academy of Management Review*, *21*(1), 135–172. doi:10.5465/amr.1996.9602161568

Machado, V. H. (1999). *Tendências do comportamento gerencial da mulher empreendedora*. Paper presented at the XXIII Encontro da Associação Nacional de Pós-Graduação em Administração – ENANPAD, Foz do Iguaçu.

Machado, V. H. (2002). *Identidade empreendedora de mulheres no Paraná* (Doctoral dissertation). Universidade Federal de Santa Catarina, Florianópolis.

Machado, V. H., St-Cyr, L., Mione, A., & Alves, M.C. (2003), O Processo de criação de empresas por mulheres. *Revista de Administração Económica – RAE*, *2*(2). Doi:10.1590/S1676-56482003000200007

Madsen, T. K., & Servais, P. (1997). The internationalization of born globals: An evolutionary process? *International Business Review*, *6*(6), 561–583. doi:10.1016/S0969-5931(97)00032-2

Maier, J. B. II, & Walker, D. A. (1987). The role of venture capital in financing small business. *Journal of Business Venturing*, *2*(3), 207–214. doi:10.1016/0883-9026(87)90009-7

Mair, J., & Martí, I. (2006). Social entrepreneurship research: A source of explanation, prediction, and delight. *Journal of World Business*, *41*(1), 36–44. doi:10.1016/j.jwb.2005.09.002

Mair, J., & Noboa, E. (2006). Social entrepreneurship: how intentions to create a social venture are formed. In J. Mair, J. Robinson, & K. Kockerts (Eds.), *Social entrepreneurship* (pp. 121–135). New York: Palgrave Macmillan. doi:10.1057/9780230625655_8

Marlow, S., & Patton, D. (2005). All credit for men? Entrepreneurship, finance and gender. *Entrepreneurship Theory and Practice*, *29*(6), 717–735. doi:10.1111/j.1540-6520.2005.00105.x

Marôco, J. (2011). *Análise estatística com o SPSS Statistics* (P. Pinheiro, Ed.). ReportNumber, Lda.

Martens, M. L., Jennings, J. E., & Jennings, P. D. (2007). Do the stories they tell get them the money they need? The role of entrepreneurial narratives in resource acquisition. *Academy of Management Journal, 50*(5), 1107–1132. doi:10.5465/amj.2007.27169488

Mason, C., & Landström, H. (2012). Introduction. In Handbook of Research on Venture Capital: Volume 2: A Globalizing Industry (pp. 3-16). Edward Elgar Publishing.

Mason, C., & Brown, R. (2013). Creating good public policy to support high-growth firms. *Small Business Economics, 40*(2), 211–225. doi:10.100711187-011-9369-9

Mason, C., & Stark, M. (2004). What do investors look for in a business plan? A comparison of the investment criteria of bankers, venture capitalists and business angels. *International Small Business Journal, 22*(3), 227–248. doi:10.1177/0266242604042377

Matcht, S. (2016). Putting "entrepreneurial finance education" on the map: Including social capital in the entrepreneurial finance curriculum. *Education + Training, 58*(9), 984–1002. doi:10.1108/ET-08-2015-0068

Matthews, J. (2014). Entrepreneurship in the public sector: new possibilities? In P. Davidsson (Ed.), *Australian Centre for Entrepreneurship Research Exchange Conference 2014. Proceedings*. Sydney, NSW: Queensland University of Technology. Retrieved from http://eprints.qut.edu.au/71108/2/Matthews__Entrepreneurship_in_the_public_sector_-_ACERE.pdf

Maxwell, J. A. (1996). *Qualitative Research Design: An Interactive Approach*. London: Sage.

McAfee, A., Brynjolfsson, E., Davenport, T. H., Patil, D. J., & Barton, D. (2012). Big data: The management revolution. *Harvard Business Review, 90*(10), 60–68. PMID:23074865

Mcclelland, D. C. (1961). *The Achieving Society*. New York: Irvington Publishers. doi:10.1037/14359-000

McDougall, P. P., & Oviatt, B. M. (2000). International entrepreneurship: The intersection of two research paths. *Academy of Management Journal, 43*, 902–908.

McKay, S., Phillimore, J., & Teasdale, S. (2010). *Exploring the 'Gendered' nature of social entrepreneurship: Women's leadership, employment and participation in the third sector*. Paper presented in the 60th Political Studies association annual conference, Edinburgh, UK.

McMullen, J. S., & Shepherd, D. A. (2006). Entrepreneurial action and the role of uncertainty in the theory of the entrepreneur. *Academy of Management Review, 31*(1), 132–152. doi:10.5465/amr.2006.19379628

Megginson, W. L. (2004). Toward a global model of venture capital? *Journal of Applied Corporate Finance, 16*(1), 89–107. doi:10.1111/j.1745-6622.2004.tb00599.x

Meglio, O., Li Destri, A. M., & Capasso, A. (2017). Fostering dynamic growth in new ventures through venture capital: Conceptualizing venture capital capabilities. *Long Range Planning, 50*(4), 518–530. doi:10.1016/j.lrp.2016.09.003

Menon, A., Bharadwaj, S., Adidam, P. T., & Edison, S. W. (1999). Antecedents and consequences of marketing strategy making: A model and a test. *Journal of Marketing, 63*(April), 18–40. doi:10.2307/1251943

Merrilees, B., Miller, D., & Tiessen, J. (1998). Serendipity, Leverage And The Process Of Entrepreneurial Internationalization. *Small Enterprise Research, 6*(2), 3–11. doi:10.5172er.6.2.3

Meynhardt, T., & Diefenbach, F. (2012). What Drives Entrepreneurial Orientation in the Public Sector? Evidence from Germany's Federal Labor Agency. *Journal of Public Administration Research and Theory Advance Access*. Retrieved from: https://www.researchgate.net/publication/260100763

Miglietta, A., Romenti, S., & Sartore, A. (2015). Entrepreneurial narratives for resource acquisition in the Italian creative industries: A qualitative study. *Sinergie., 33*(98), 213–231.

Miller, D. (1983). The correlates of entrepreneurship in three types of firms. *Management Science, 29*(7), 770–791. doi:10.1287/mnsc.29.7.770

Miller, K. D., & Tsang, E. W. K. (2010). Testing management theories: Critical realist philosophy and research methods. *Strategic Management Journal, 158*(32), 139–158. doi:10.1002mj

Minniti, M., & Naude, W. (2010). What do we know about the patterns and determinants of female entrepreneurship across countries? *European Journal of Development Research, 22*(3), 277–293. doi:10.1057/ejdr.2010.17

Moon, M. J. (1999). The Pursuit of Managerial Entrepreneurship: Does Organization Matter? *Public Administration Review, 59*(1), 31–46. doi:10.2307/977477

Moore, D. P., & Buttner, E. H. (1997). *Women entrepreneurs moving beyond the glass ceiling*. London: Sage.

Moraes, R. O., Igarashi, E. T., Camacho, R. R., & Marques, K. C. M. (2013). Gestão estratégica de custos: Investigação da produção científica no período de 2008 a 2012. In Congresso Brasileiro de Custos, 20, Uberlândia. São Leopoldo: Associação Brasileira de Custos.

Morgan, N., Kaleka, A., & Katsikeas, C. S. (2004). Antecedents of Export Venture Performance : A Theoretical Model. *Journal of Marketing*, *68*(1), 90–108. doi:10.1509/jmkg.68.1.90.24028

Morris, M., & Jones, F. (1999). Entrepreneurship in established organisations: The case of the public sector. *Entrepreneurship Theory and Practice*, *24*(1), 71–91. doi:10.1177/104225879902400105

Morrow, J. F. (1988). International entrepreneurship: A new growth opportunity. *Nursing Management*, *3*, 59–61.

Mueller, P. (2007). Exploiting entrepreneurial opportunities: The impact of entrepreneurship on growth. *Small Business Economics*, *28*(4), 355–362. doi:10.100711187-006-9035-9

Mulhern, F. J. (2009). Integrated marketing communications: From media channels to digital connectivity. *Journal of Marketing Communications*, *15*(2/3), 85–101. doi:10.1080/13527260902757506

Murani, M. (2003). *As novas fronteiras da desigualdade: homens e mulheres no mercado de trabalho*. São Paulo: Senac.

Nafday, A. M. (2009). Strategies for Managing the Consequences of Black Swan Events. *Leadership and Management in Engineering*, *9*(4), 191–197. doi:10.1061/(ASCE)LM.1943-5630.0000036

Nahapiet, J., & Ghoshal, S. (1998). Social capital, intellectual capital, and the organizational advantage. *Academy of Management Review*, *23*(2), 242–266. doi:10.5465/amr.1998.533225

Nahata, R. (2008). Venture capital reputation and investment performance. *Journal of Financial Economics*, *90*(2), 127–151. doi:10.1016/j.jfineco.2007.11.008

Nam, T., & Pardo, T. A. (2011). Conceptualizing smart city with dimensions of technology, people, and institutions. *Proceedings of the 12th Annual International Digital Government Research Conference on Digital Government Innovation in Challenging Times - dg.o '11*, 282. 10.1145/2037556.2037602

National Survey of Third Sector Organisations. (2008). *National Survey of Third Sector Organisations.* Cabinet Office of the Third Sector. Accessed on November 10, 2018, from http://www.communityplanningtoolkit.org/sites/default/files/OutcomesR4.pdf

Naudé, W. (Ed.). (2013). *Entrepreneurship and economic development: Theory, evidence and policy.* New York: Palgrave Macmillan.

Neuman, W. L. (2009). *Social Research Methods: Qualitative and Quantitative Approaches* (7th ed.). Pearson.

Nolan, A. (2003). *Entrepreneurship and Local Economic Development: Policy Innovations in Industrialized Countries.* Retrieved from: http://citeseerx.ist.psu.edu/viewdoc/download?doi=10.1.1.199.4169&rep=rep1&type=pdf

NVCA. (2013). *National Venture Capital Association FAQ.* Retrieved January 20, 2014, from http://www.nvca.org/

O'Cass, A., & Sok, P. (2014). The role of intellectual resources, product innovation capability, reputational resources and marketing capability combinations in firm growth. *International Small Business Journal, 32*(8), 996–1018. doi:10.1177/0266242613480225

O'Meally, N. B. (2000). *Fostering women's entrepreneurship: education, management training and societal values.* Paper presented at the Conference on Women Entrepreneurs in SMEs: Realising the Benefits of Globalization and the Knowledge-based Economy, Paris, France.

Obschonka, M., Silbereisen, R., & Schmitt-Rodermund, E. (2010). Entrepreneurial intention as developmental outcome. *Journal of Vocational Behavior, 77*(1), 63–72. doi:10.1016/j.jvb.2010.02.008

OECD. (2002). *High-growth SMEs and employment.* Paris: OECD.

OECD. (2003). *Entrepreneurship and Local Economic Development.* Paris: OECD.

Okpara, J. (2009). Entrepreneurial orientation and export performance: Evidence from an emerging economy. *Int. Rev. Bus. Res. Papers*, *5*(6), 195–211.

Oliveira, G. B. (2002). Uma discussão sobre o conceito de desenvolvimento. *Revista da FAE, Curitiba*, *5*(2), 37–48.

Oliveira, S. C. M., Barbosa, E. S., Rezende, I. C. C., Silva, R. P. A., & Albuquerque, L. S. (2013). *Bibliometria em artigos de contabilidade aplicada ao setor público. In Congresso Brasileiro de Custos*. São Leopoldo: Associação Brasileira de Custos.

Ortegón, E., Pacheco, J. F., & Prieto, A. (2005). *Metodología del marco lógico para la planificación, el seguimiento y la evaluación de proyectos y programas, Serie Manuales No. 42*. Instituto Latinoamericano y del Caribe de Planificación Económica y Social (ILPES), Santiago de Chile. Available: http://www.cepal.org/es/publicaciones/5607-metodologia-del-marco-logico-para-la-planificacion-el-seguimiento-y-laevaluacion

Ostrom, E., Schroeder, L., & Wynne, S. (1993). *Institutional Incentives and Sustainable Development*. Boulder, CO: Westview Press.

Oviatt, B. M., & McDougall, P. P. (1994). Toward a theory of international new ventures. *Journal of International Business Studies*, *25*(1), 45–64. doi:10.1057/palgrave.jibs.8490193

Oviatt, B. M., & McDougall, P. P. (1999). A framework for understanding accelerated international entrepreneurship. In A. M. Rugman & R. W. Wright (Eds.), *Research in global strategic management: International entrepreneurship* (pp. 23–40). Stamford, CT: JAI Press. doi:10.1016/S1064-4857(99)07055-2

Owens, S. (1992). Energy, Environmental Sustainability and Land-Use Planning. In M. Breheny (Ed.), *Sustainable Development and Urban For* (pp. 79–105). London: Pion.

Pacione, M. (2011). *Urban Geography: A Global Perspective*. Routledge.

Parracho, A. R. (2017). *The Portuguese Startup Ecosystem: Key Success Factors on the Entrepreneurial Ecosystem*. Universidade Católica Portuguesa. Retrieved from: https://repositorio.ucp.pt/bitstream/10400.14/21833/1/152115100.pdf

Paulsen, N., & McDonald, A. (2010). Doing social enterprise: A reflection and view from the field. *Third Sector Review*, *16*(2), 109–126.

Payne, N. J., Campbell, C., Bal, A. S., & Piercy, N. (2011). Placing a Hand in the Fire: Assessing the Impact of a YouTube Experiential Learning Project on Viral Marketing Knowledge Acquisition. *Journal of Marketing Education*, *33*(2), 204–216. doi:10.1177/0273475311410853

Peltier, J., Zhao, Y., & Schibrowsky, J. (2012). Technology adoption by small businesses: An exploratory study of the interrelationships of owner and environmental factors. *International Small Business Journal*, *30*(4), 406–431. doi:10.1177/0266242610365512

Peña, S. (2012). Recent Trends and Practice in Spatial Planning in Mexico. The Municipal Planning and Research Institutes. *Gestión y Política Pública, 21*(2), 407-449.

Peñaloza, V., Diógenes, C. G., & Sousa, S. J. (2008). Escolha profissional no curso de administração: Tendências empreendedoras e gênero. *Revista de Administração Mackenzie*, *9*(8), 151–167. doi:10.1590/S1678-69712008000800009

Pepelasē, M. I., & Cassis, Y. (2005). Entrepreneurship in Theory and History. Houndmills, UK: Palgrave Macmillan.

Pérez-Pérez, C., & Avilés-Hernández, M. (2016). Explanatory factors of female entrepreneurship and limits elements. *Suma de Negócios*, *7*(15), 25–31. doi:10.1016/j.sumneg.2015.12.004

Pestana, M. H., & Gageiro, J. N. (2008) Análise de Dados para Ciências Sociais - A complementaridade do SPSS (5th ed.). Lisboa: Edições Silabo.

Peteraf, M. (1993). The cornerstones of competitive advantage: A resource-based view. *Strategic Management Journal*, *14*(3), 179–191. doi:10.1002mj.4250140303

Petty, J. S., & Gruber, M. (2011). "In pursuit of the real deal" A longitudinal of VC decision making. *Journal of Business Venturing*, *26*(2), 172–188. doi:10.1016/j.jbusvent.2009.07.002

Pierrakis, Y., & Saridakis, G. (2017). Do publicly backed venture capital investments promote innovation? Differences between privately and publicly backed funds in the UK venture capital market. *Journal of Business Venturing Insights*, *7*, 55–64. doi:10.1016/j.jbvi.2017.02.002

Pinchot, G. (1985). *Intrapreneuring: Why you don't have to leave the Corporation to become an entrepreneur*. New York: Harper & Row.

Pinchot, G., & Pellman, R. (2004). *Intra-empreendedorismo na prática: um guia de inovação nos negócios*. Rio de Janeiro: Elsevier.

Pistor, K., Raiser, M., & Gelfer, S. (2000). Law and finance in transition economies. *Economics of Transition*, *8*(2), 325–368. doi:10.1111/1468-0351.00047

Popov, A., & Roosenboom, P. (2013). Venture capital and new business creation. *Journal of Banking & Finance*, *37*(12), 4695–4710. doi:10.1016/j.jbankfin.2013.08.010

Portela, J., Hespanha, P., Nogueira, C., Teixeira, M. S., & Batista, A. (2008). *Microempreendedorismo em Portugal: experiências e perspetivas*. Lisboa: Instituto António Sérgio do Sector Cooperativo – INSCOOP.

Porter, M. (1985). *The Competitive Advantage: Creating and Sustaining Superior Performance*. New York: Free Press.

Porter, M. (1991). Towards a dynamic theory of strategy. *Strategic Management Journal*, *12*(S2), 95–117. doi:10.1002mj.4250121008

Pruthi, S., Wright, M., & Lockett, A. (2003). Do foreign and domestic venture capital firms differ in their monitoring of investees? *Asia Pacific Journal of Management*, *20*(2), 175–204. doi:10.1023/A:1023840432241

Qian, H., Acs, Z., & Stough, R. R. (2013). Regional systems of entrepreneurship: The nexus of human capital, knowledge and new firm formation. *Journal of Economic Geography*, *13*(4), 559–587. doi:10.1093/jeg/lbs009

Quevedo, L. M., Izar, J. M., & Romo, R. L. (2010). Factores endógenos y exógenos de mujeres y hombres empreendedores de España, Estados Unidos y México. *Investigacion y Ciencia*, *18*(46), 57–63.

Ramamurti, R. (1986). Public entrepreneurs: Who they are and how they operate. *California Management Review*, *28*(3), 142–158. doi:10.2307/41165207

Raposo, K. C. S., & Astoni, S. A. F. (2007). A mulher em dois tempos: A construção do discurso feminino nas revistas dos anos 50 e na atualidade. *Revista do Centro Universitário São Camilo*, *8*(2), 36–37.

Rasmussen, E. S., & Tanev, S. (2015). The Emergence of the Lean Global Startup as a New Type of Firm. *Technology Innovation Management Review*, *5*(11), 12–19. doi:10.22215/timreview/941

Rauch, A., & Wiklund, J. (2009). Entrepreneurial orientation and business performance: An assessment of past research and suggestions for the future. *Entrepreneurship Theory and Practice*, 1–54.

Reinartz, W., Haenlein, M., & Henseler, J. (2009). An empirical comparison of the efficacy of covariance-based and variance-based SEM. *International Journal of Research in Marketing*, *26*(4), 332–344. doi:10.1016/j.ijresmar.2009.08.001

Rennie, M. (2016). Born global. *The McKinsey Quarterly*, *4*, 45–52.

Revest, V., & Sapio, A. (2012). Financing technology-based small firms in Europe: What do we know? *Small Business Economics*, *39*(1), 179–205. doi:10.100711187-010-9291-6

Rialp, A., Rialp, J., Urbano, D., & Vaillant, J. (2005). The Born-global phenomenon: A comparative case study research. *Journal of International Entrepreneurship*, *3*(2), 133–171. doi:10.100710843-005-4202-7

Ribau, C. P., Moreira, A. C., & Raposo, M. (2015). Internationalisation of the firm theories: A shematic synthesis. *International Journal of Business and Globalisation*, *15*(4), 528–554. doi:10.1504/IJBG.2015.072535

Ribau, C. P., Moreira, A. C., & Raposo, M. (2018). SME internationalization research: Mapping the state of the art. *Canadian Journal of Administrative Sciences*, *35*(2), 280–303. doi:10.1002/cjas.1419

Rice, A. (2014). Incorporation of Chance Into Career Development Theory and Research. *Journal of Career Development*, *41*(5), 445–463. doi:10.1177/0894845313507750

Riding, A., Orser, B., Spence, M., & Belanger, B. (2012). Financing new venture exporters. *Small Business Economics*, *38*(2), 147–163. doi:10.100711187-009-9259-6

Riessman, C. K. (2007). *Narrative Methods for the Human Sciences*. SAGE Publications, Inc.

Robbins, S. P. (2001). *Administração: mudanças e perspetivas*. São Paulo: Saraiva.

Roberts, N. C. (1992). Public entrepreneurship and innovation. *Policy Studies Review*, *11*(1), 55–74. doi:10.1111/j.1541-1338.1992.tb00332.x

Rosiello, A., & Parris, S. (2009). The patterns of venture capital investment in the UK bio-healthcare sector: The role of proximity, cumulative learning and specialisation. *Venture Capital: An International Journal of Entrepreneurial Finance.*, *11*(3), 185–211. doi:10.1080/13691060902973016

Rothaermel, F. T., Agung, S. D., & Jiang, L. (2007). University entrepreneurship: A taxonomy of the literature. *Industrial and Corporate Change*, *16*(4), 691–791. doi:10.1093/icc/dtm023

Roundy, P. T. (2014). The stories of social entrepreneurship: Narrative discourse and social enterprise resource acquisition. *Journal of Research in Marketing and Entrepreneurship*, *16*(2), 200–218. doi:10.1108/JRME-06-2014-0009

Rousseau, R. (2001). Indicadores bibliométricos y econométricos en la evaluación de instituciones científicas. *Acimed*, *9*, 23–29.

Royle, J., & Laing, A. (2014). The digital marketing skills gap, International Journal of Information Management. *The Journal for Information Professionals*, *34*(2), 65-73.

Rubio-Banón, A., & Esteban-lloret, N. (2016). Cultural factors and gender role in female entrepreneurship. *Suma de Negocios*, *7*(15), 9–17. doi:10.1016/j.sumneg.2015.12.002

Sá, A. L. (2007). *Ética profissional* (8th ed.). São Paulo: Atlas.

Sadler, R. J. (2000). Corporate entrepreneurship in the public sector: The dance of the chameleon. *Australian Journal of Public Administration*, *59*(2), 25–43. doi:10.1111/1467-8500.00149

Santos, C., & Teixeira, A. C. C. (2009). The evolution of the literature on entrepreneurship. Uncovering some under researched themes. *FEP Working Papers*, *335*, 1–41.

Santos, J. F. (1998). Location of foreign firms in Portugal: A network approach. *38th Congress of the European Regional Science Association: "Europe Quo Vadis? - Regional Questions at the Turn of the Century"*. Available: http://hdl.handle.net/10419/113413

Santos, G. C. D. (2015). Análise bibliométrica dos artigos publicados como estudos bibliométricos na história do congresso Brasileiro de custos. *Pensar Contábil, 17*(62), 4–13.

Sapienza, H. J., Manigart, S., & Vermeir, W. (1996). Venture capitalist governance and value added in four countries. *Journal of Business Venturing, 11*(6), 439–469. doi:10.1016/S0883-9026(96)00052-3

Sarasvathy, S. D., Dew, N., Velamuri, S. R., & Venkataraman, S. (2010). Three Views of Entrepreneurial Opportunity. In Z. J. Acs & D. B. Audretsch (Eds.), *Handbook of Entrepreneurship Research - An Interdisciplinary Survey and Introduction* (2nd ed.; pp. 77–98). Springer-Verlag New York; doi:10.1007/978-1-4419-1191-9_4

Saridakis, G., Mole, K., & Storey, D. J. (2008). New small firm survival in England. *Empirica, 35*(1), 25–39. doi:10.100710663-007-9049-9

Sarstedt, M., Ringle, C. M., Smith, D., Reams, R., & Hair, J. F. Jr. (2014). Partial least squares structural equation modeling (PLS-SEM): A useful tool for family business researchers. *Journal of Family Business Strategy, 5*(1), 105–115. doi:10.1016/j.jfbs.2014.01.002

Schneider, M., & Teske, P. (1992). Toward a theory of the political entrepreneur: Evidence from local government. *The American Political Science Review, 86*(3), 737–747. doi:10.2307/1964135

Schnellenbach, J. (2007). Public entrepreneurship and the economics of reform. *Journal of Institutional Economics, 3*(2), 183–202. doi:10.1017/S1744137407000641

Schumpeter, J. A. (1934). *The Theory of Economic Development*. Transaction Publishers.

Schumpeter, J. A. (1988). *A teoria do desenvolvimento econômico*. São Paulo: Nova Cultural.

Schuyler, G. (1998). Social entrepreneurship: Profit as a means, not an end. *CELCEE Digest, 30*, 98-7. Retrieved from http://www.eric.ed.gov/PDFS/ED434219.pdf

Seabre. (2008). *Serviço Brasileiro de Apoio às Micro e Pequenas Empresas*. Relatório do Prêmio Mulher de Negócios 2006-2010. Brasilia.

Secchi, L. (2010). Entrepreneurship and participation in public management reforms at the local level. *Local Government Studies*, *36*(4), 511–527. doi:10.1080/03003930.2010.494103

Secretaría General de Gobierno del Estado de Jalisco. (2013). *Plan Estatal de Desarrollo Jalisco 2013-2033*. Author.

SEDATU. (2015). Available: http://www.sedatu.gob.mx/sraweb/

Seelos, C., Mair, J., Battilana, J., & Dacin, M. (2011). The embeddedness of social entrepreneurship: Understanding variation across local communities. In C. Marquis, M. Lounsbury, & R. Greenwood (Eds.), *Communities and Organizations* (pp. 333–363). Bingley, UK: Emerald Group Publishing Limited. doi:10.1108/S0733-558X(2011)0000033013

Selltiz, M., Jahoda, S. W. C., & Deutsch, M. (1987). *Métodos de pesquisa nas relações sociais*. São Paulo: EPU.

Semrau, T., Ambos, T., & Kraus, S. (2016). Entrepreneurial orientation and SME performance across societal cultures: An international study. *Journal of Business Research*, *69*(5), 1928–1932. doi:10.1016/j.jbusres.2015.10.082

Sen, A. K. (2012). *Desenvolvimento como liberdade*. São Paulo: Companhia de Bolso.

Shanahan, M. J., & Porfeli, E. J. (2006). Chance Events in the Life Course. *Advances in Life Course Research*, *11*(6), 97–119. doi:10.1016/S1040-2608(06)11004-7

Shane, S. A. (2003). *A General Theory of Entrepreneurship: The Individual-opportunity Nexus*. Edward Elgar Publishing, Limited. doi:10.4337/9781781007990

Shane, S., & Cable, D. (2002). Network ties, reputation, and the financing of new ventures. *Journal of Management Science*, *48*(3), 364–381. doi:10.1287/mnsc.48.3.364.7731

Shepherd, D. A., Armstrong, M. J., & Levesque, M. (2005). Allocation of attention within venture capital firms. *European Journal of Operational Research*, *163*(2), 545–564. doi:10.1016/j.ejor.2003.11.006

Silva, M. R. (2004). *Análise bibliométrica da produção científica docente do programa de pós-graduação em educação especial/UFSCar (Mestrado em Educação Especial)*. São Carlos, Brasil: Universidade Federal de São Carlos.

Silveira, A., & Gouvêa, A. B. (2008). Empreendedorismo Feminino: Mulheres Gerentes de Empresas. *Faces Revista de Administração*, *7*(3), 124–138.

Simmons, G., Armstrong, G., & Durkin, M. (2011). An exploration of small business website optimization: Enablers, influencers and an assessment approach. *International Small Business Journal*, *29*(5), 534–561. doi:10.1177/0266242610369945

Simply Digital Marketing. (2012). *What is Digital Marketing?* Retrieved from http://www.simplydigitalmarketing.com/what-is-digital-marketing

Sims, R. (2009). Food, place and authenticity: Local food and the sustainable tourism experience. *Journal of Sustainable Tourism*, *17*(3), 321–336. doi:10.1080/09669580802359293

Singer, J. J., Amoros, J. E., & Moska, D. (2015). *Global Entrepreneurship Monitor 2014*. Global Report.

Sirmon, D. G., Hitt, M., Ireland, R. D., & Gilbert, B. (2010). Resource Orchestration to Create Competitive Advantage: Breadth, Depth, and Life Cycle Effects. *Journal of Management*, *37*(5), 1390–1412. doi:10.1177/0149206310385695

Skirnevskiy, V., Bending, D., & Brettel, M. (2017). The influence of internal social capital on serial creators' success in crowdfunding. *Entrepreneurship Theory and Practice*, *41*(2), 209–236. doi:10.1111/etap.12272

Slaughter, S., & Leslie, L. (1997). *Academic Capitalism: Politics, Policies and the Entrepreneurial University*. Baltimore, MD: Johns Hopkins University Press.

Smallbone, D., Leig, R., & North, D. (1995). The characteristics and strategies of high growth SMEs. *International Journal of Entrepreneurial Behaviour & Research*, *1*(3), 44–62. doi:10.1108/13552559510100657

Smith-Doerr, L., & Powell, W. W. (2005). Networks and economic life. In N. J. Smelser & R. Swedberg (Eds.), *The handbook of economic sociology* (pp. 379–402). New York: Russel Sage Foundation.

Sniedovich, M. (2012). Black Swans, New Nostradamuses, Voodoo decision theories, and the science of decision making in the face of severe uncertainty. *International Transactions in Operational Research*, *19*(1–2), 253–281. doi:10.1111/j.1475-3995.2011.00790.x

Sousa, C. M. P., Martínez-López, F. J., & Coelho, F. (2008). The determinants of export performance: A review of the research in the literature between 1998 and 2005. *International Journal of Management Reviews*, *10*(4), 343–374. doi:10.1111/j.1468-2370.2008.00232.x

Stanisauskaite, V., & Kock, S. (2016). The dynamic development of international entrepreneurial networks. In H. Etemad, S. Denicolai, B. Hagen, & A. Zucchella (Eds.), *The changing global economy and its impact on international entrepreneurship* (pp. 119–135). Cheltenham, UK: Edward Elgar. doi:10.4337/9781783479849.00012

Startup Europe Partnership. (2016). Startups: ecossistema português cresce o dobro da média europeia *SEP Monitor Report*. Retrieved from https://startupeuropepartnership.eu/

Stephens, M., Partridge, D., & Faggian, A. (2013). Innovation, entrepreneurship and economic growth in lagging regions. *Journal of Regional Science*, *53*(5), 778–812. doi:10.1111/jors.12019

Stevenson, H., & Jarillo, J. C. (1990). A paradigm of entrepreneurship: Entrepreneurial management. *Strategic Management Journal, EUA*, *11*, 17–27.

Stokes, D. (2000). Putting into marketing: the process of entrepreneurial marketing. *Journal of Research in Marketing and Entrepreneurship*, *2*(1), 1-16.

Stought, R. (2016). Entrepreneurship and Regional Economic Development: Some reflections. *Investigaciones Regionales – Journal of Regional Research, 36,* 129-150.

Stouraitis, V., Harris, M., Harun, M., & Kyritsis, M. (2017). Motivators of SME initial export choice and the European Union regional effect in manufacturing. *International Journal of Entrepreneurial Behaviour & Research*, *23*(1), 35–55. doi:10.1108/IJEBR-05-2015-0120

Stuart, T. E., & Sorenson, O. (2005). Social networks and entrepreneurship. In S. Alvarez, R. Agarwal, & O. Sorensen (Eds.), *Handbook of entrepreneurship research: interdisciplinary perspectives* (pp. 233–251). New York: Springer. doi:10.1007/0-387-23622-8_11

Symonds, J. E., & Gorard, S. (2010). The Death of Mixed Methods : Research Labels and their Casualties. In *British Educational Research Annual Conference*. Edinburgh, UK: Heriot Watt University.

Taleb, N. N. (2007). *The black swan : the impact of the highly improbable*. Penguin Books Ltd; doi:10.5465/AMP.2011.61020810

Tanev, S. (2012). Global from the start: The characteristics of born-global firms in the technology sector. *Technology Innovation Management Review*, *2*(3), 5–8. doi:10.22215/timreview/532

Team Technologies, Middleburg, Virginia. (2005). *The Logframe Handbook, a logical framework approach to project cycle management*. The World Bank. Available: http://documents.worldbank.org/curated/en/2005/01/5846691/logframe-handbook-logical-frameworkapproach-project-cycle-management

Teece, D. J. (2007). Explicating dynamic capabilities : The nature and microfoundations of (sustainable) enterprise performance. *Strategic Management Journal*, *1350*(13), 1319–1350. doi:10.1002mj.640

Teece, D. J. (2010). Business Models, Business Strategy and Innovation. *Long Range Planning*, *43*(2–3), 172–194. doi:10.1016/j.lrp.2009.07.003

Teixeira, A. C., & Silva, C. (2012). A new perspective on local political entrepreneurship: Evidence from Portugal. *Local Economy*, *27*(4), 332–354. doi:10.1177/0269094212439151

Themudo, N. S. (2009). Gender and the nonprofit sector. *Nonprofit and Voluntary Sector Quarterly*, *38*(4), 663–683. doi:10.1177/0899764009333957

Thompson, A. A., Peteraf, M. A., Gamble, J. E., & Strickland, A. J., III. (2016). Crafting and executing strategy: the quest for competitive advantage, concepts and cases (20th ed.). New York: McGraw-Hill Education.

Thompson, J., Alvy, G., & Lees, A. (2000). Social entrepreneurship: A new look at the people and the potential. *Management Decision*, *38*(5), 328–338. doi:10.1108/00251740010340517

Thornhill, S., & Amit, R. (2003). Learning about failure: Bankruptcy, firm age, and the Resource-Based View. *Organization Science*, *14*(5), 497–509. doi:10.1287/orsc.14.5.497.16761

Tian, X. (2011). The causes and consequences of venture capital stage financing. *Journal of Financial Economics*, *101*(1), 132–159. doi:10.1016/j.jfineco.2011.02.011

Tichy, N. M., Tushman, M. I., & Fombrun, C. (1979). Social networks analysis for organizations. *Academy of Management Review*, *4*(4), 507–519. doi:10.5465/amr.1979.4498309

Tidd, J., Bessant, J., & Pavitt, K. (2008). Gestão da Inovação. *The Bookman*.

Timmons, J. A., & Bygrave, W. D. (1986). Venture capital's role in financing innovation for economic growth. *Journal of Business Venturing*, *1*(2), 161–176. doi:10.1016/0883-9026(86)90012-1

Toma, S.-G., Grigore, A.-M., & Marinescu, P. (2014). Economic Development and Entrepreneurship. *Procedia Economics and Finance*, *8*(14), 436–443. doi:10.1016/S2212-5671(14)00111-7

Trettin, L., & Welter, F. (2011). Challenges for spatially oriented entrepreneurship research. *Entrepreneurship and Regional Development*, *23*(7/8), 575–602. doi:10.1080/08985621003792988

Trimi, S., & Berbegal-Mirabent, J. (2012). Business Model Innovation in Entrepreneurship. *The International Entrepreneurship and Management Journal*, *8*(4), 449–465. doi:10.100711365-012-0234-3

Turkina, E., & Thai, M. T. T. (2013). Socio-psychological determinants of opportunity entrepreneurship. *The International Entrepreneurship and Management Journal*, *11*(1), 213–238. doi:10.100711365-013-0288-x

Tyebjee, T. T., & Bruno, A. V. (1984). Venture capital: Investor and investee perspectives. *Technovation*, *2*(3), 185–208. doi:10.1016/0166-4972(84)90003-8

Tykvová, T. (2018). Legal framework quality and success of (different types of) venture capital investments. *Journal of Banking & Finance*, *87*, 333–350. doi:10.1016/j.jbankfin.2017.10.015

UN. (2009). *Human Settlements Program; Planning Sustainable Cities: Global Report on Human Settlements 2009*. London: Earthscan.

UN-Habitat. (2013). *State of the World's Cities 2012/2013: Prosperity of Cities*. New York: Routledge.

Urban, B. (2010). Creating value and innovation through social entrepreneurship. In Frontiers in Entrepreneurship. Springer. doi:10.1007/978-3-642-04502-8_5

Utterback, J. M., & Abernathy, W. J. (1975). A dynamic model of process and product innovation. *Omega*, *3*(6), 639–656. doi:10.1016/0305-0483(75)90068-7

Valos, M., Ewing, M., & Powell, I. (2010). Practitioner prognostications on the future of online marketing. *Journal of Marketing Management*, *26*(3/4), 361–376. doi:10.1080/02672571003594762

Van Osnabrugge, M. (2000). A comparison of business angel and venture capitalist investment procedures: An agency theory-based analysis. *Venture Capital: An International Journal of Entrepreneurial Finance.*, 2(2), 91–109. doi:10.1080/136910600295729

Van Stigt, R., Driessen, P. P. J., & Spit, T. J. M. (2013). Compact City Development and the Challenge of Environmental Policy Integration: A Multi-Level Governance Perspective. *Environmental Policy and Governance*, *23*(4), 221–233. doi:10.1002/eet.1615

Vanolo, A. (2014). Smartmentality: The Smart City as Disciplinary Strategy. *Urban Studies (Edinburgh, Scotland)*, *51*(5), 883–898. doi:10.1177/0042098013494427

Vasconcellos, M. A., & Garcia, M. E. (1998). *Fundamentos de economia*. São Paulo: Saraiva.

Veiga, J. E. (2005). *Desenvolvimento Sustentável: O Desafio do Século XXI*. Rio de Janeiro: Garamond.

Villareal, O. (2017). Is it desirable, necessary and possible to perform research using case studies? *Cuadernos de Gestión*, *17*(1), 147–172. doi:10.5295/cdg.140516ov

Wach, K. (2015). Entrepreneurial orientation and business internationalisation process: The theoretical foundations of international entrepreneurship. *Entrepreneurial Business and Economics Review*, *3*(2), 9–24. doi:10.15678/EBER.2015.030202

Wach, K., & Wehrmann, C. (2014). Entrepreneurship in international business: International entrepreneurship as the intersection of two fields. In A. S. Gubik & K. Wach (Eds.), *International Entrepreneurship and Corporate Growth in Visegrad Countries* (pp. 9–22). Miskolc: University of Miskolc.

Weerawardena, J., Mort, G. S., Liesch, P. W., & Knight, G. (2007). Conceptualizing accelerated internationalization in the born global firm: A dynamic capabilities perspective. *Journal of World Business*, *42*(3), 294–306. doi:10.1016/j.jwb.2007.04.004

Welbank, M. (1996). The search for a sustainable urban form. In *Institutions and Environmental Change*. Cambridge, MA: MIT Press. doi:10.4324/9780203362372_The_Search_for_a_Sustainable_Urban

Wennekers, S., & Thurik, R. (1999). Linking entrepreneurship and economic growth. *Small Business Economics*, *13*(1), 27–55. doi:10.1023/A:1008063200484

Wiklund, J. (1999). The sustainability of the entrepreneurial orientation performance relationship. *Entrepreneurship Theory and Practice*, *24*(1), 39–50. doi:10.1177/104225879902400103

Wiklund, J., & Shepherd, D. (2005). Entrepreneurial orientation and small business performance: A configurational approach. *Journal of Business Venturing*, *20*(1), 71–91. doi:10.1016/j.jbusvent.2004.01.001

Wiklund, J., & Shepherd, D. A. (2011). Where to from here? EO-as-experimentation, failure, and distribution of outcomes. *Entrepreneurship Theory and Practice*, *35*(5), 925–946. doi:10.1111/j.1540-6520.2011.00454.x

Winkler, C. A., & Medeiros, J. (2011). *Mulheres empreendedoras: uma questão de género*. Paper presented at the Simpósio Género e Políticas Públicas, Londrina.

Winton, A., & Yerramilli, V. (2008). Entrepreneurial finance: Banks versus venture capital. *Journal of Financial Economics*, *88*(1), 51–79. doi:10.1016/j.jfineco.2007.05.004

Witt, P. (2004). Entrepreneurs' networks and the success of start-ups. *Entrepreneurship and Regional Development*, *16*(5), 391–412. doi:10.1080/0898562042000188423

Wood, M. S., McKelvie, A., & Haynie, J. M. (2014). Making it personal: Opportunity individuation and the shaping of opportunity beliefs. *Journal of Business Venturing*, *29*(2), 252–272. doi:10.1016/j.jbusvent.2013.02.001

Wright, M., & Robbie, K. (1998). Venture capital and private equity: A review and synthesis. *Journal of Business Finance & Accounting*, *25*(5-6), 521–570. doi:10.1111/1468-5957.00201

Wymbs, C. (2011). Digital marketing: The time for a new "academic major" has arrived. *Journal of Marketing Education*, *33*(1), 93–106. doi:10.1177/0273475310392544

Yin, R. (2014). *Case Study Research. Design and Methods*. London: Sage.

Zahra, S. (1993). A conceptual model of entrepreneurship as firm behavior: A critique and extension. *Entrepreneurship Theory and Practice*, *17*(1), 5–21. doi:10.1177/104225879301700401

Zahra, S., & Covin, J. G. (1995). Contextual influences on the corporate entrepreneurship-performance relationship: A longitudinal analysis. *Journal of Business Venturing*, *10*(1), 43–58. doi:10.1016/0883-9026(94)00004-E

Zahra, S., & Garvis, D. (2000). International corporate entrepreneurship and firm performance: The moderating effect of international environmental hostility. *Journal of Business Venturing*, *15*(5-6), 469–492. doi:10.1016/S0883-9026(99)00036-1

Zampetakis, L., & Moustakis, V. (2007). Entrepreneurial behaviour in the Greek public sector. *International Journal of Entrepreneurial Behaviour & Research*, *13*(1), 19–38. doi:10.1108/13552550710725165

Zander, I., McDougall-Covin, P., & Rose, E. (2015). Born globals and international business: Evolution of a field of research. *Journal of International Business Studies*, *46*(1), 27–35. doi:10.1057/jibs.2014.60

Zerbinatia, S., & Souitarisb, V. (2005). Entrepreneurship in the public sector: A framework of analysis in European local governments. *Entrepreneurship and Regional Development*, *17*(1), 43–64. doi:10.1080/0898562042000310723

Zhang, J. (2010). The problems of using social networks in entrepreneurial resource acquisition. *International Small Business Journal*, *28*(4), 338–361. doi:10.1177/0266242610363524

Zhang, J., Soh, P., & Wong, P. (2010). Entrepreneurial resource acquisition through indirect ties: Compensatory effects of prior knowledge. *Journal of Management*, *36*(2), 511–536. doi:10.1177/0149206308329963

Zhao, D. (2011). Bibliometrics and LIS education: How do they fit together? *Proceedings of the American Society for Information Science and Technology: ASIST*, *48*(1), 1–4.

About the Contributors

Orlando Rua is an Adjunct Professor of Management at the Porto Accounting and Business School (ISCAP) of the Polytechnic of Porto (Portugal). Researcher at Center for Organizational and Social Studies (CEOS.PP) (Polytechnic of Porto – ISCAP) and at Management Applied Research Unit (UNIAG) of the Association of Polytechnic Institutes of Northern Portugal (APNOR). He holds a PhD in Economics and Management. His major subjects are entrepreneurship, innovation and strategy. His papers have been published in several relevant international journals and scientific conferences.

* * *

Belem Barbosa is Adjunct Professor at the University of Aveiro and member of GOVCOPP, the research unit on Governance, Competitiveness and Public Policy. She received her PhD in Business and Management Studies – specialisation in Marketing and Strategy from the University of Porto, Portugal. Her research interests lie primarily in the area of internet marketing and consumer behaviour, including word-of-mouth communication, sustainability marketing, tourism and events marketing.

Susana Bernardino is Assistant Professor of Management at the Polytechnic of Porto - Institute of Accounting and Administration (ISCAP), S. Mamede de Infesta, Portugal, and researcher at CEOS.PP/ISCAP. She completed her under-graduation degree in Management at the Faculty of Economics of the University of Porto, where also obtained the curricular part of the master's course in Finance. She got her PhD in Management in 2014 from the Portucalense University. Her research interests focus on social entrepreneurship, entrepreneurship, social and solidarity economy, smart cities, urban and regional development. and crowdfunding.

Lisa Raquel de Freitas Ferraz has a bachelor's degree in Actuarial Sciences, at the University of Aveiro, Portugal. She is in the writing up stage of her dissertation in the Master in Management also at the University of Aveiro, Portugal. She specializes in co-branding strategies between luxury brands and wine brands.

Bernard Owens Imarhiagbe holds a PhD in Business and Management. He is a researcher at Kingston University Business School. He is involved in academic research, teaching, writing, publishing and empirical analysis. His research focuses on small business finance, entrepreneurship and technology innovation. He is an Associate Fellow of the Higher Education Academy. He previously worked as IT Consultant for an international IT consulting and services organisation for many years.

Diana Martins is a student and junior researcher at Católica Porto Business School. Graduated from the Faculty of Economics of University of Porto in 2017, with a BSc in Economics. Currently enrolled at a double degree programme between Católica Porto Business School, MSc in Business Economics, and Lancaster University Management School, MSc in Money, Banking and Finance.

Diogo Filipe Fontinha Martins has a bachelor's degree in Actuarial Sciences, at ESTGA, University of Aveiro, Portugal. He is in the writing up stage of his Master dissertation in Languages and Business Relationships also at the University of Aveiro, Portugal.

António C. Moreira obtained a Bachelor's degree in Electrical Engineering and a Master's degree in Management, both from the University of Porto, Portugal. He received his PhD in Management from UMIST-University of Manchester Institute of Science and Technology, England. He has a solid international background in industry leveraged working for a multinational company in Germany as well as in Portugal. He has also been involved in consultancy projects and in research activities. He is Assistant Professor at the Department of Economics, Management, Industrial Engineering, and Tourism, University of Aveiro, Portugal, where he headed the Bachelor and Master Degrees in Management for five years. He is member of GOVCOPP research unit.

Raquel Pereira graduated in Economical and Political International Relations by Minho University. Master in Business and Industrial Economy. PhD in Economics by Santiago de Compostela University. Started her professional activity at former ICEP (Investment and External Commerce of Portugal) now designated as AICEP (Portuguese Agency for Investment and External Commerce). Nowadays she is a Professor at School of Accounting and Administration of Porto. She is also the Director of the graduation programme in International Commerce.

Assunção Mariana Ramos graduated in Agronomic Engineering in 2008 from the University of Trás-os-Montes and Alto Douro, Portugal. She attended the Intensive Quality Management Program for the Supply Chain of Vegetables (IP-QMHortChains) at the University of Hannover, coordinated by the University of Wageningen, Germany. She has been professionally involved in sustainable production methods in farming. She has also been involved in consultancy activities in computer science in agrarian management. Between 2011 and 2016 he served as Regional Delegation of the Confederation of Portuguese Farmers (CAP) in the region of Trás-os-Montes, promoting the agri-food sector in the North of Portugal. Since 2017 she has been actively involved in the CAP's Centro region (Aveiro, Coimbra and Viseu) activities. She is finishing her master's degree in Management.

George Saridakis is a Professor of Small Business and Entrepreneurship at the Kent Business School, where he directs the Centre for Employment, Competitiveness and Growth.He is also an Honorary Professor at the University of the West Indies, St. Augustine, Trinidad and Tobago. He received his PhD in Economics from the Institute for Social and Economic Research (ISER) at the University of Essex in 2006.

Sandrina Francisca Teixeira is Professor at the Higher Institute of Accounting and Administration of Porto, at the Polytechnic Institute of Porto, in the area of Marketing, Digital Marketing and Digital Communication. She holds a PhD in Communication, Advertising and Public Relations from the University of Vigo. She is director of the master's degree in Digital Marketing and the degree in Business Communication. She is a Researcher at CEOS.PP (Center for Organizational and Social Studies of Porto) and CEPESE. She develops several research activities in the areas of Luxury Brands, Marketing and Digital Communication. She integrates several projects funded in the areas of management, marketing and digital communication. She is a member of the Scientific Council of indexed international scientific journals. She is a member of the Scientific Committee of several events and has several national and international scientific publications.

José G. Vargas-Hernández, M.B.A., Ph.D., Member of the National System of Researchers of Mexico, and a research professor at University Center for Economic and Managerial Sciences, University of Guadalajara. Professor Vargas-Hernández has a Ph. D. in Public Administration and a Ph.D. in Organizational Economics. He has undertaken studies in Organisational Behaviour and has a Master of Business Administration, published four books and more than 200 papers in international journals and reviews (some translated to English, French, German, Portuguese, Farsi, Chinese, etc.) and more than 300 essays in national journals and reviews. He has obtained several international Awards and recognition.

Index

G

H

I

K

L

M

N

O

P

R

S

T

V

W

www.ingramcontent.com/pod-product-compliance
Lightning Source LLC
LaVergne TN
LVHW061542290926
849162LV00004B/884